CHARLES MAIR: LITERARY NATIONALIST

Charles Mair

LITERARY NATIONALIST

NORMAN SHRIVE

University of Toronto Press

Printed in Canada
Reprinted in 2018
ISBN 978-1-4875-8063-6 (paper)

TO BARBARA

PREFACE

THIS IS THE STORY of a man whose significance in the development of Canada and of her literature is today almost unknown. Charles Mair, both famous and notorious during his own lifetime, has in fact slipped so far into oblivion that many academics who might be expected to know at least something about his reputation do not recognize even his name. Who he was and what made him notable are questions answered in the following pages. Why he has been forgotten, however, is a problem that the reader himself may have to resolve, reminded that Mair lived in a country that has never been inclined to view its nationhood with great seriousness or to remember even its major historical figures with passion.

Admittedly, some Canadian historians have remembered Mair—perhaps only too well—as a controversial figure in a controversial event: the Riel uprising of 1869–70. But their accounts, both fair and prejudiced, of the part he played in that historical episode are concerned with only a few months of a life that lasted nearly ninety years, and he has been depicted, therefore, in a very limited context. On the other hand Canadian literary scholars have ignored him altogether or have dismissed him condescendingly, preferring to name Roberts, Carman, Lampman, and Scott as their "Confederation Poets," despite the fact that none of these more famous figures was over the age of seven in 1867 or published anything until almost fifteen years after that date. But Charles Mair not only gave Canada what was regarded in 1868 as its first significant collection of verse; he also, unlike Roberts and Carman, retained faith, however dim at times, in his country's future, and, unlike Lampman, lived long enough to see that faith justified. He offers to the Canadian literary historian, in fact, an ideal illustration of the struggle of post-Confederation letters for survival and recognition.

For even when Mair is revealed as a precious fool and a bad poet he provides a singularly striking parallel to the cross-currents of aspiration and frustration, of success and failure, of even the tragedy, that marked that struggle. His life gives us a tableau of some of the most significant aspects of Canadian history—of pioneering in the Ottawa Valley, of the Canada First movement in politics, of both Riel rebellions, of the opening up of the West. His writings and the influences behind them reveal the cultural climate in which he lived—more particularly, the way in which nationalism and its judgments can intrude into literary matters, not only in the nineteenth century but also in a much later period. Because Mair and his work were so closely associated with the political and cultural development of Canada, there is little wonder that Bernard McEvoy could call him a "marvel of miscellaneousness" who had "the knack of carrying a load of versatility," or that the late Lorne Pierce could describe Mair's life as "a thrilling romance" and his work as part of "the structure of our national life." Or, perhaps, that Louis Riel could find him "a barely civilized" Upper Canadian who found amusement in "uttering follies to the world."

The almost insignificant number of published writings about Charles Mair might in itself justify this study of his life and career. But there is to be considered in addition the very limited value of those writings. John Garvin's supposedly authoritative biographical essay in the *Master-Works of Canadian Authors* edition is ludicrous in its bias and pretentiousness, its critical posturings and unscholarly inaccuracies. And the articles on Mair in newspapers and periodicals are of the "popular" type: in them he is invariably depicted as a "great singer of Canadian Literature" or as a "saviour of Canada's nationhood." The suspicions stimulated by such apotheosizing are confirmed of course when one reads those social and political histories that have included Mair in their scope; for in these works he is revealed as a quite different figure. Part of this contrast is often explainable by personal and commercial prejudices (J. J. Hargrave's *Red River*), by religious intolerance (R. E. Lamb's *Thunder in the North*), or by journalistic indulgence to popular taste and by distortion of historical evidence (Joseph Kinsey Howard's *Strange Empire*). But an unattractive Mair is also to be found in works of scholarly excellence such as W. L. Morton's *Alexander Begg's Red River Journal* and G. F. Stanley's *The Birth of Western Canada* and *Louis Riel*; as has been noted, however, all of these latter studies, objective or otherwise, present the Mair of only a particular period, and are consequently of qualified significance to anyone wishing to see him in a larger perspective. Between them and the extreme of the *Master-Works* and the newspaper articles there are only two other published commentaries on Mair, both of them recent and both by the same author, that deserve particular notice. J. P. Matthews, in *Tradition in Exile* and in his essay on Mair in Robert McDougall's latest (1965) series of *Our Living Tradition*, not only has reached several conclusions similar to my own about Mair as a literary nationalist but also, by emphasizing his significance amid a host of better-known writers, has made a comprehensive study even more desirable.

In this book I have attempted to bring together for the first time all the available material relevant to Mair's life and writings, and to interpret that material as objectively as possible. If at times Mair appears admirable it is not merely because he was a Protestant from Ontario; indeed, in that role he is often, it seems, least admirable. Nor as a student of Canadian letters am I concerned with proclaiming the genius of a native son. Many of the following pages should at least imply that we have had too much of such literary chauvinism. Instead I have proposed to present Mair from the point of view of contemporary scholarship and not from that of religious, provincial, or national bias. And since he was a human being with a human being's virtues and vices, joys and sorrows, I have tried to reflect him as such and not as either all poltroon or all patriot. Much of his attractiveness is due, indeed, to his having been at various times a great deal of both.

The theme of this study, then, is the life and career of an interesting and significant personality. More particularly it is an examination of a literary nationalist who did not confine the expression of his patriotism to pen and paper, but became closely involved in some of the important events and movements of his time. And here it should be noted that I have made no attempt to be exhaustive in my commentary on certain aspects of political, social, and literary history, aspects that, although they are of moment in any depiction of Mair, are more properly subjects of separate studies. The Canada First movement, for example, demands a more comprehensive analysis than that given to it up to the present by Canadian historians. Some of the personalities besides Mair who were part of the movement—and who were significant for other reasons as well—are by necessity of secondary importance in this work. Thirty years ago, A. H. U. Colquhoun was prevented from writing a biography of George T. Denison because Mair's daughter refused him access to pertinent documents and papers. That material is now available. Another question that should be stimulated by the following pages is that concerning the whole matter of literary taste in Canada. The reception given to Mair's writings at different times indicates not only the critical standards of those times but also the way in which the standards were changing.

To my knowledge the only research yet done on this subject is represented by a single article written over a decade ago by Dr. Claude Bissell. It is possible therefore that this book will provide starting-points as well as further stimulation to a number of additional studies.

My principal sources of material were the Mair Papers, in the Douglas Library, Queen's University, and the Denison Papers, in the Public Archives of Canada. These two collections offer the researcher what is surely an unparalleled example of the correspondence between two men who were close friends for nearly sixty years and who exchanged many hundreds of letters on matters of interest and significance in Canadian history. Many of Mair's letters and manuscripts were, unfortunately, confiscated by Riel and probably destroyed; many, also, were lost or ruined in a British Columbia flood some years later. But Mair himself would probably be surprised—and, perhaps, annoyed—if he could see some of the papers that are now at Queen's. To attempt to indicate here my debt to other material in both the Douglas Library and the Public Archives would incur the risk of committing sins of omission and tedium; let it suffice that such debt is great and that it is reflected in my bibliography.

More important was the encouragement and aid given to me by persons, many of whom I shall probably never meet, in every province west of Quebec. Professor Henry Alexander, former Head of the Department of English, Queen's University, deserves first mention because he made possible the arrangements by which I might undertake the work. Dr. Malcolm Ross, formerly James Cappon Professor of English Literature at Queen's, and now Professor of English at Trinity College, University of Toronto, has probably forgotten that 24th of May, 1954, when he not only approved the project as one suitable for graduate study but also gave me strong assurance of its importance. Since that time Dr. Ross has been a kind and exacting critic of my manuscript, and no recognition such as this can ever cancel my indebtedness to him. To H. Pearson Gundy, Librarian of Queen's University, I owe particular gratitude for his having introduced me to a personality in Canadian history and letters of whom I before had known very little. To Mr. Gundy, also, goes my sincere appreciation for his many hours of reading the manuscript and for his providing without restriction the facilities of what must be one of the pleasantest university libraries in Canada. Professor S. F. Wise of the Department of History of Queen's allowed our friendship to influence his judgment of the work in the only way we agreed that it should—by his most questioning and discriminating analysis of my interpretation of historical evidence. For the many hours he spent on my behalf I thank him once again.

The late Dr. Lorne Pierce was of great assistance in a number of ways. Through him I was granted special privileges in the use of certain manuscripts, including the Garvin Papers, then in the possession of Mr. Herbert Orr of Toronto and now at Queen's University. Dr. Pierce was also able to give me invaluable information based on his personal knowledge of Charles Mair and to direct me to sources of material I otherwise should not have considered. Above all, he gave me the constant interest and encouragement that he always gave to students of Canadian letters. Others to whom I am indebted for detailed information are Mr. Herbert Orr and Mrs. Woodburn Langmuir of Toronto, Colonel T. Gelley of the Royal Military College of Canada, Mrs. M. Willis, Mrs. W. Machan, and Mr. John Herron of Lanark, Ontario, Professor W. L. Morton of the University of Manitoba, Mr. Charles Beer of Queen's University, Mr. Richmond Mayson, Mr. I. C. Collins, and Mr. A. Agnew of the Prince Albert Historical Society, Mrs. A. F. Willet of Kelowna and Miss E. M. McCullough of Vancouver, British Columbia. These people, either in correspondence, conversation, or interview, were able to help me solve many of the sometimes fascinating, sometimes vexing problems concerning Mair's life.

I should also like to acknowledge the assistance afforded by the staffs of libraries and archives departments in various parts of Canada. Particularly helpful were Mr. W. Ormsby and his staff at the Public Archives of Canada, Miss Edith Jarvi of the Windsor Public Library, Miss Marjorie Morley, Provincial Librarian of Manitoba, Mr. Allan Turner of the Saskatchewan Archives Board, Miss Edith Gostick, Provincial Librarian of Alberta, Miss Flora Macleod of the Calgary Public Library, and Mr. W. E. Ireland, Provincial Librarian of British Columbia. Much general help was also given by the staffs of the Perth Museum, the Hamilton Public Library, the Toronto Public Library, the McMaster, Queen's, and Toronto university libraries and the Ontario Provincial Archives. The skill of Mr. A. J. Whorwood of McMaster University is reflected in the high quality he achieved in reproducing some of the very early photographs of Mair. Miss Jean Houston of the University of Toronto Press was a most perceptive critic of my manuscript.

For less specific but hardly less valuable assistance I am indebted to Professors G. C. Haddow and R. M. Wiles, and to Barbara Shrive, Ann Doyle, Marcia Beaubien, Dorothy Brown, and Irene Johnston.

The University College Grants Committee of McMaster University patiently and encouragingly provided necessary funds for travel, microfilm, and typing during the approximately four years I was collecting and organizing my material. And finally, I am pleased to acknowledge that this work has been published with the help of a grant from the Humanities Research Council of Canada using funds provided by the Canada Council, and with the assistance of the Scholarly Publications Fund of the University of Toronto Press.

NORMAN SHRIVE

McMaster University
June, 1965

CONTENTS

ILLUSTRATIONS

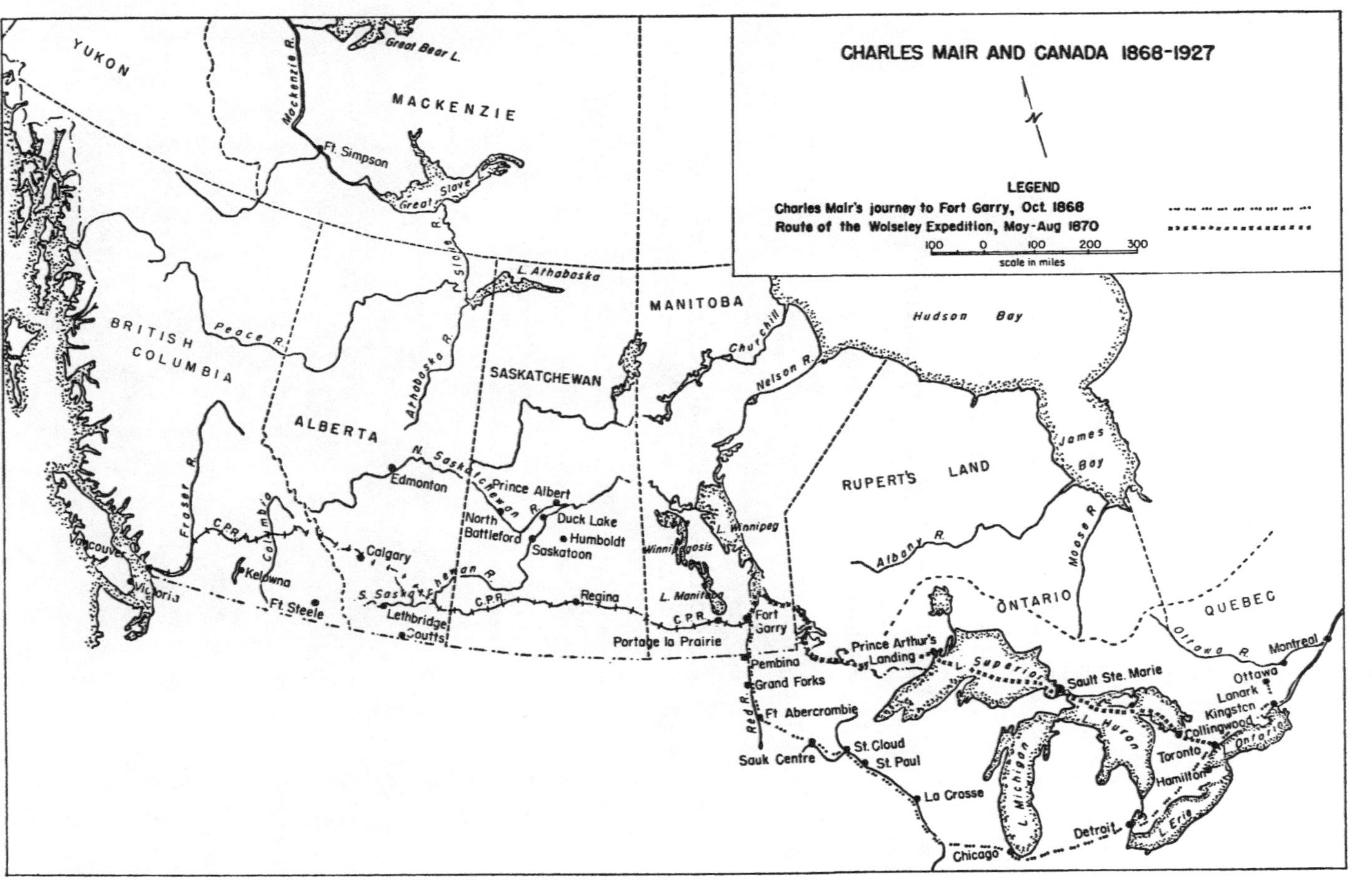
CHARLES MAIR AND CANADA 1868-1927
N
LEGEND
Charles Mair's journey to Fort Garry, Oct. 1868
Route of the Wolseley Expedition, May-Aug 1870
100 0 100 200 300
scale in miles
YUKON
MACKENZIE
Great Bear L.
Mackenzie R.
Ft. Simpson
Great Slave
Slave R.
L. Athabaska
BRITISH COLUMBIA
Peace R.
Athabaska R.
ALBERTA
SASKATCHEWAN
MANITOBA
Churchill
Nelson R.
Hudson Bay
James Bay
RUPERT'S LAND
Albany R.
Moose R.
ONTARIO
QUEBEC
Ottawa R.
Montreal
Ottawa
Lanark
Kingston
Collingwood
Toronto
Hamilton
L. Ontario
L. Erie
Detroit
L. Huron
L. Michigan
Chicago
La Crosse
Sault Ste. Marie
L. Superior
Prince Arthur's Landing
St. Cloud
St. Paul
Sauk Centre
Ft Abercrombie
Red R.
Grand Forks
Pembina
Fort Garry
Portage la Prairie
C.P.R.
L. Manitoba
Winnipegosis
L. Winnipeg
Regina
Humboldt
Duck Lake
Prince Albert
Saskatoon
North Battleford
N. Saskatchewan R.
Edmonton
Calgary
S. Saskatchewan R.
Lethbridge
Coutts
Ft. Steele
Kelowna
Columbia
Fraser R.
C.P.R.
Vancouver
Victoria

ABBREVIATIONS

DP	George T. Denison Papers, Public Archives of Canada, Ottawa
GP	Garvin Papers, Queen's University Library, Kingston
MP	Mair Papers, Queen's University Library, Kingston
PAC	Public Archives of Canada, Ottawa
PWF	Public Works Files, Ottawa

Documents and records to which only occasional reference is made are identified by their full titles: e.g., Macdonald Papers, McDougall Papers.

CHARLES MAIR: LITERARY NATIONALIST

I. New Lanark-on-the-Clyde

IN EARLY MAY, 1868, a young man left a sturdy stone house in the little village of Lanark, Ontario, a house that in this, the year following the Confederation of Canada, was already old, and after passing the ten milestones and four toll-gates separating the village from the county-town of Perth, turned north onto the highroad to Ottawa. The young man was short but robust in stature, and when he changed carriages at the crossroads he walked briskly and confidently. A year or so later, when he had become much better known than he was now, observers were to comment on the brilliant blue of his eyes, his round, ruddy face, and his mass of brown curly hair. Some of them, particularly those who disliked him, were to say that he gave an impression of cockiness; all, certainly, could agree that he did not lack self-assurance.

This was Charles Mair, aged twenty-nine, on his way to the capital with a manuscript of verse in his pocket. To see this first book through the press was the main purpose of the journey, and any excitement Mair may have felt on that particular day was probably due to the understandable pride of a young author in his first literary achievement. The trip itself he could hardly have considered an adventure. He had been to Ottawa many times before, and a youth spent in the midst of the still virtually primitive Ottawa Valley had already offered experiences much more exciting than even a villager's trip to the city.

And yet, although Charles Mair was to live to be a very old man, was not, in fact, to die before Confederation had celebrated its Diamond Jubilee in 1927, the events set in motion by that journey in 1868 were an influence the whole of his life. They were to influence other lives as well, were even, indeed, to have a significant impact upon the history of the Dominion itself.

Mair was an unusual young man. As an aspiring poet whose work had been accepted for publication he warranted some distinction at least. Until a week or so before he had also been a medical student at Queen's College in Kingston. In addition he had already proved himself a competent businessman and he had had considerable experience in the great but hazardous square-timber trade of the Ottawa Valley. Such a varied background, of course, does not necessarily make a significant figure. More important, perhaps, was the characteristic that Mair himself was most conscious of, the one that certainly had a particular relevance to his own time and place: Charles Mair was an ardent Canadian nationalist. Because he was, and at that particular time, he was to help shape Canada's political and literary history.

The almost thirty years previous to this particular spring had been preparing Charles Mair, nationalist, until time and place themselves were ready for him. And it is perhaps appropriate that from the very beginning someone who was to be a figure of controversy should present problems to the biographer. For no known account of the life of Charles Mair is completely accurate in respect of exact place and date of birth. Over thirty years after his death, the *Encyclopedia Canadiana* (1958) gave the date as 1832, thereby showing at least a refreshing independence of Henry J. Morgan's date of 1840[1], which became the incorrect authority for nearly all sketches on Mair. And in 1948, when the Historic Sites and Monuments Board of Canada, probably influenced by a photograph in John Garvin's *Master-Works* edition of Mair, was about to affix a plaque to the old stone house in Lanark that was commonly accepted as his birthplace, it was informed by a knowledgeable old-timer of the village that "Charlie" Mair had been born across the road in a house long since burned down.[2] Only,

[1]*Canadian Men and Women of the Time* (1898), p. 600. But Morgan, who was one of Mair's closest friends, had received his information from the subject himself. In a letter to Garvin (MP, Sept. 28, 1915), Mair wrote: "I was born in 1838, not in 1840, as Morgan says, and as I myself supposed until I raked up my baptismal entry some ten years ago." His Queen's College registration of 1856 lists his age as 16; yet the censuses of 1851 and 1861 give ages 13 and 23 respectively, implying that someone in the Mair household knew his actual birth date. Wilfrid Eggleston, one of the most recent commentators (*The Frontier and Canadian Letters*, p. 128), gives 1839.

[2]The plaque was placed in the town hall. Garvin, however, printed the photograph against Mair's advice. Nearly two years before the *Master-Works* appeared, Mair wrote (MP, Mair to Garvin, June 18, 1925): "Instead of calling my father's house . . . 'the house I was born in' you will call it the house '*I was brought up in*,' for I have had much research over this matter and believe now that I was 3 years

indeed, when Mair was a very old man did he himself attempt to record his early years, and then only in personal letters to close friends. One such letter gives more than merely factual information. "I was born," he writes, "on September 21st, in that ill-starred rebellion year, 1838, in the village of Lanark, Upper Canada, and was called after my father's youngest brother, Charles, who was killed in the Peninsular War at the storming of Badajos."[3] Written when he was eighty-five, these lines well reveal Mair's lifelong and somewhat romantic pride that he had been born at such a time and, perhaps, that he had been named after a youthful uncle who had died for his king in an historic battle. More significant is his further comment, "I should not be the Canadian I am if I had not been born in the Ottawa Valley in its primitive day and grown up with it." To Mair there was no question of different types of Canadians, only degrees, and the real Canadian came from a background such as his. Of this there could be no doubt, even when tragic events were to beg for the qualification of such a view.

But there also can be no question that Charles Mair came of hardy stock. The same Peninsular War that had taken his uncle had been an important factor in founding the very village in which he was born. The Napoleonic Wars generally had caused such economic and social disturbances in Great Britain that by 1820 the plight of Scottish weavers, particularly in the vicinity of Glasgow and Paisley, had reached starvation proportions, and these desperate people were forced to plead to the Government for aid. As early as 1816 large numbers of their fellow Scots had emigrated to Perth, Upper Canada; perhaps they too could begin new lives in British North America.

The story of the Bathurst District settlers has been fully told and documented by one of the area's distinguished sons[4] and is only indirectly relevant here, but the McDougalls, Caldwells, McLarens, and Frasers of contemporary Lanark can trace their family histories to at least July 4, 1820, when the *Prompt* sailed from Greenock with thirty-three families, the destitution of each being more readily appreciated, perhaps, when it is realized that the passenger list of over three

old when this house was built. I have always casually thought of it as the house I was born in but, though not quite equivalent to a birth place, it was its equivalent in value as being the house in which my earliest youth was spent." The town hall, with the plaque, was destroyed in the disastrous fire that swept Lanark on June 15, 1959, but the Mair home was not damaged. Some sketches also give Mair's home town as "Bathurst," which is not a town at all, but a "district," a term used for a territorial subdivision until 1849.

[3]MP, Mair to J. B. Allen, Nov. 23, 1923.

[4]Andrew Haydon, *Pioneer Sketches in the District of Bathurst.*

hundred names implies an average of about ten persons per family. Two months later they landed at Quebec and encouraged by a promise of one hundred acres to each family and ten pounds sterling for each person, they set out by way of Brockville for the Ottawa Valley, a virtually unknown land. "On September 30," an anonymous historian of 1880 relates,

> they were conveyed in waggons as far as the present site of Lanark village, where they found a paper nailed to a tree in the heart of the forest, through which they had cleared a roadway for the waggons where necessary; and the placard referred to contained the startling revelation, "This is Lanark," though the fundamental attributes of a village were conspicuous by their absence. . . .
>
> There was . . . one Robert Forest, who got lost in the woods, but was accidentally discovered by John Donald and Jas. Duncan, whose providential finding of the lost man in all probability was the sole cause of our not having a much more melancholy incident to chronicle in connection with the original settlement. . . .[5]

Charles Mair's grandfather, William Mair, came to New Lanark-on-the-Clyde in 1824, towards the end of this wave of emigration, and began general merchandising businesses in Lanark and Perth and lumbering, first on the Clyde and afterwards on his limits in Blythfield and the two townships on the Madawaska River. An old gravestone that once stood in Lanark cemetery recorded his death at the age of ninety in 1836, and that of his wife, Janet, in 1825, less than a year after her arrival.[6] Mair's father, James, immigrated in 1831 with his wife Margaret Holmes, his daughter Margaret, three sons, Holmes, William, and Richard, and a sister Elizabeth. Another son, James, was born in 1832, and Charles, the youngest, in 1838, as he himself commented, "after a lapse of years in child bearing."[7]

James Sr., like his father before him, engaged extensively in the square-timber trade in the Ottawa Valley; but unlike his father, he

[5] *Illustrated Atlas of the Dominion of Canada* (Lanark County Edition), p. x.

[6] Erasures and corrections on a genealogical table written by Charles Mair probably not long before he died (MP, "C. Mair and Family," *ca.* 1926) indicate that at one time he believed his grandfather had immigrated earlier—a belief supported by research in the Public Archives by an old Lanark friend, D. E. Forbes, who forwarded to him a list of the first Lanark settlers (MP, April 2, 1914). Number fifteen on the list is one James Mair, and Mair's table gives his grandfather's name as James and his date of arrival in British North America as 1820. Evidence now reveals, however, that Mair's grandfather was William, that he came out in 1824, and that a James Mair, of no known relationship, came to Lanark in 1820 with his wife and eight children and engaged in a tannery and shoemaking business.

[7] John W. Garvin, ed., *Master-Works of Canadian Authors*, XIV, p. xlix.

had apparently arrived in the new country with capital to invest, and by the mid eighteen-forties, as advertisements in the Bathurst *Courier* reveal, had flourishing general stores in both Lanark and Perth as well as his timber business along the Clyde, Mississippi, and Madawaska rivers. The beautiful old homes of Perth, some of them veritable mansions, to this day attest to the prosperity of the town when the Mairs extended their operations towards the north. The establishment of one Henry Glass, "a busy place," according to a *Courier* historian of 1906, was bought by the progressive family from Lanark, "who tore down the old frame building and erected a substantial stone edifice, the first one approaching the modern idea of a store."[8] And James's continuing prominence in Lanark is reflected by the large store and warehouse that he built beside the Mair home. The building, having become a woollen mill, stood until 1917, and Charles Mair wrote of it in the Lanark *Era* of August 15 of that year:

> I only got your account of the deeply regrettable Clyde Woollen Mills fire . . . the other day. It is a great loss to the village; it is even a great loss to myself through old associations, for the building was erected by my family. I do hope the dwelling house was spared, the fine old home in which I was brought up, and to which my earliest recollections cling like ivy. . . . Dear old Lanark, embosomed among its hills and vales, there is a poetry about it which is imperishable.

But such poetry as the young Mair found implicit and imperishable in little Lanark, with its lovely hills and its quiet Clyde winding through it, was more explicit, if less enduring, in the square-timber trade that surrounded it. In 1850 the upper Ottawa Valley was still in primitive forest—the original possessors of the land, the Algonquins, were very much in evidence—and the timber trade was the prime industry and sole dependence of the farming communities for a home market and winter employment throughout the Canadas. And to the young Mair it was obviously an occupation tinged with romance and adventure. He was even to say, just before he died three-quarters of a century later, that his last months were being made more comfortable by the thought that his nursing home was operated by the granddaughter of an old Bytown friend, the Crown Timber Agent, and "of old Mr. Ross, a wholesale grocer in Quebec, who used to supply

[8]"Mercantile Business of Seventy Years Ago," Perth *Courier*, Nov. 16, 1906. The writer of the item recalls further the kindness of the Mair's warehouse man, "who treated him to a little wine as he was going to school and caused him not a little trouble during the afternoon."

the Ottawa lumberman long ago" and whom he had known.[9] "I loved the river life," he once wrote,

> the great pineries in winter, where the timber was felled and squared, the "drive" in spring, the rafting up of timber at Calebogie, Lake Arnprior, or on the Madawaska or Mississippi, where it was formed into cribs, securely withed and chained, and united into enormous rafts which were floated to Quebec, to berth at Wolfe's cove or Cape Rouge or elsewhere. It was there sold to timber dealers, broken up and shipped to England in large fleets of sail which came for it twice or thrice a year.[10]

With all its fascination, however, the square-timber trade was full of vicissitudes, both physical and economic. Mair could recall the dangerous jams at unslided chutes where the timber piled up and volunteers would cut the "lock-sticks" to set the jam free, the unimproved rivers with their shoals, twists, and turns, the great rapids at the Carillon and the Long Sault, the sudden storms on Lake St. Peter that blew many a raft to single sticks, and the dependence, before the advent of steam tugs, upon current, sail, and oar. So, although the rivers brought wealth, their banks were dotted with the graves of many a log-driver who died in helping achieve it. Mair lived to see the adventurous trade supplanted by the saw-mill, which, through water, steam, and electric power and through the vast development of rail and highway transport, became the major supplier of overseas markets. He also lived to see the vast forests that once had echoed to the sound of men and axes, where a whole raft of timber might be laid on the frozen river by teams of horses or oxen, become a wilderness of a different type—of stumps, rubbish, and the scattered beginnings of second growth.

The great timber trade was also conducive to another type of excitement in the Ottawa Valley. As early as 1816, when settlers began arriving in significant numbers, the framework of law and order had been laid down by the establishment of quarter sessions and the appointment of sheriffs and justices of the peace. In other words, although the Ottawa Valley was characterized by a "frontier society," any lawlessness that took place did so in the presence of law and not, as in the American West, for example, in its absence. But largely because of the timber trade and the men associated with it, the Valley was more turbulent in terms of lawbreaking than any other district in Upper Canada. One of Mair's earliest recollections was of the family

[9]DP, 6456, Mair to Helen Denison, Nov. 5, 1925.
[10]MP, MS., *ca.* 1920.

homestead under siege by a gang of timber workers, outlaws called "Shiners," part of, he said, a "horde of semi-civilized savages from the wilds of western Ireland."[11] Armed with long pikes, mad with drink and threatening to destroy the house, these miscreants were held off by the Mair family under the direction of father James, "whose Scottish blood was up,"[12] and who, in fact, was the employer of many of the howling mob outside:

I think I see them still: as well, the stern bearing of my father . . . , the barricading of the doors; the loading of fire-arms by his people within; the fears of my mother and sister that the ruffians would set fire to the out-buildings—all is more vivid in my mind today than the things of yesterday. I have been in more than one tight place since, but nothing clings so tenaciously to my memory as that childish episode.[13]

The "Shiners" represent an episode of the Ottawa Valley and of the life of Mair himself that has long been forgotten. Their existence was both brief and ferocious. Admirably suited to the rough necessities of the timber "drive," these fiery men, in the space of a very few years, brought Ottawa lumbermen to a state of tame submission, and the total population on both sides of the river, particularly the French Canadians, to a state of almost abject terror. Violently resenting whatever they felt to be undue interference by their employers, the "Shiners" would often leave their assigned tasks in the forests and arrogantly forbid the owners or other workers to set foot upon the timber-rafts. Sometimes they would lie in wait in their numerous little "shebeens" along the river banks, board the rafts as they floated by, and toss their crews into the water or forcibly run them ashore. But it was at Bytown, after the rafts had reached the Ottawa, or the Grand, as it was then called, that the outrages began in earnest: "To burn down a house, to tar and feather men and women, to smash furniture, to break up a funeral, to interrupt divine service, to waylay and maltreat innocent passersby—these and the like enormities entered into their programme, and as each of them provoked reprisals, there was little lull in the race conflict which made the Ottawa Valley the

[11]*Ibid.*

[12]C. Mair, "The Ottawa Shiners," Toronto *Week*, Aug. 18, 1893, p. 895. The term "Shiner" has at least two possible etymologies. The most likely is that it was originally "Moonshiner," analogous to "Moonlighter" – also a term used in the Ottawa Valley (but with meaning different from that of the contemporary American term!). The other is that a horse named "Shiner" was cropped and mutilated by these outlaws and thus gave his name to them.

[13]*Ibid.*

scene of many a bloody struggle."[14] At Quebec, supported by the numerous Irish there, these men celebrated the trip's conclusion by a great debauch, making the Lower Town "a hell until their means were spent, after which they borrowed from their rueful employers and returned with soddened frames to the wilderness."[15]

Because of their seeming hatred for the French-Canadian raftsmen, the "Shiners" were believed by some to be ardent Orangemen, but these latter were victims of "Shiner" attacks to the same extent as the *habitant.* It was, in fact, a particular abuse to a prominent Orangeman that finally convinced the outlaws that the law of the strong by which they lived could bring their own undoing. One Jimmie Johnstone, M.P., was pitched over Sappers' Bridge by a number of them with the result that a force of Orangemen marched down from Richmond on a day afterwards remembered as "Stony Monday" and in a pitched battle on a Bytown street put the "Shiners" to ignominious flight.[16] But the "Shiners" were not altogether fools; otherwise the timber trade of the Ottawa would not have been as great as it was. In the woods their axes worked strongly and the timber reached Quebec even if "they did as they pleased and ended the winter's work religiously on St. Patrick's Day."[17]

The "Shiners" represent the more elemental aspects of the social and environmental forces that were preparing a young Charles Mair for trials to come. But there were other, more civilized aspects of Ottawa Valley life that tended to balance such primitiveness. There were, for example, what a modern, sophisticated society likes to call "the pioneer virtues." In 1925, when he was eighty-seven and over two thousand miles away, Mair replied to an invitation to attend Old Home Week celebrations in Perth:

I can imagine the enthusiasm evoked when you all meet! The clasped hands, the warm hearts, the grateful reverence for the past, for the stern, almost incredible stories of [your] fathers' lives. But though these pioneer days were days of sternest toil, of man's endurance and woman's devotion at their best, of perplexing privations, [they] had their redeeming features and their sunny side—the simple and innocent pleasures—the tree, the

[14]J. M. Oxley, "A Habitan Hercules," *The Lake,* I (Sept., 1892), 90.

[15]Mair, "The Ottawa Shiners," p. 896. See also A. R. M. Lower, *Canadians in the Making,* p. 195.

[16]MP, John Munro, Kincardine, to Mr. Martin, Dec. 12, 1892. Munro, an old-timer formerly of Ottawa, states in this letter that the horse referred to in n. 12, *supra,* belonged to Jimmie Johnstone, and ended its days driving a brick machine in Renfrew, "where he was long a curiosity with his cut ears and bare tail."

[17]Mair, "The Ottawa Shiners," p. 896.

dance, the canoeing, the sports, and the romantic adventures when young people fell in love. . . . All these I have beheld or enjoyed in my time.[18]

These comments are conventional, platitudinous, sentimental, uncritical. But perhaps, it may be said, explainable by a nostalgic old man's looking back romantically on days and places he will never actually see again. In Mair's case such is true to only a limited degree, for here again there is essentially the same attitude as is expressed by the previously noted "I should not be the Canadian I am . . . ," an attitude that did not evolve only in old age but characterized his whole life. It is an attitude that implies that the life in his little Upper-Canadian community is an ideal one, at least the best one; indeed, Mair later states in the same letter that the members of that community were unquestionably "governed by the highest traits in human nature, when duty and faith went hand in hand." And "duty and faith" were just as surely concomitant with "British loyalty and freedom." All were part of a sacred inheritance that was given to some and not to others. Even if Mair's retrospective vision of old Lanark was tinted by the years and by a vivid imagination, his pride in this inheritance and his loyalty towards Queen and country were unchanging. Any attempt, indeed, to explain later events of personal and of national significance in Ottawa and the North-West must take such attitudes into account.

The young Charles Mair was proud, therefore, that the people of Lanark and Perth were prepared, in their own backwoods way, to fight for their beliefs—more specifically, to fight the encroaching menace of the disloyal country to the south. So "Training Day" was an exciting military observance, calling out all the male inhabitants above a prescribed age to be drilled by one of the many Napoleonic War veterans—he probably being the only man in uniform:

The men were of all conditions, and in every variety of garb or comparative lack of it, in bare feet, or shoe-packs, or with straw ropes for belts, and indescribable hats. It was a comical crowd. Drawn into long lines on the field for drill it was grotesque in some of its features, but the men were thoroughly in earnest. They were no poltroons, but hard workers and toilers, who loved the flag and would have died for it.[19]

However nuclear-age cynicism may view loving a flag and dying for it, "Training Day" certainly seems to have been an inspiring one to Mair and his friends as they emulated their elders by marching, armed

[18]MP, Mair to C. L. Stone, June 20, 1925.
[19]*Master-Works*, p. lii.
[20]*Ibid.*

with painted laths, up and down the village street; "Woe to the Yankee boy," he said, "had he appeared among us then."[20] And since enthusiasm was extreme, and whiskey only a shilling a gallon, what was more fitting than that the day should end "in a glorious carouse"?

The lure of the woods and rivers, the excitements of outlawry, and the threat of Yankee invasion were strong formative influences on Charles Mair. But there were others at least as strong. One of the major concerns of the "Societies" that formed around Glasgow and Paisley for the purposes of beginning a new life in Lanark, Upper Canada, was the education of not only those children who were emigrating but also those who would be born in the new country. Among the first settlers, therefore, was Robert Mason, dominie, of Paisley, a man who seems more at home in a Scott novel than in the Ottawa Valley, but whose name is still familiar to the villagers of Lanark. "For nearly thirty years," the Reverend Joshua Fraser, one of his former pupils, recorded, "he taught and thrashed" in first the log, then the stone, schoolhouse of the village:

> He was a tall, gaunt, rawboned, beetle-browed Scotchman, an elder in the Kirk, and a true-blue Presbyterian of the hardest and sternest cast. . . . He seldom smiled, and when he did, it was as if under protest from his grim and iron nature. He was withal, an exceedingly irascible old man; and from his long tenure of office, without hindrance of interference from anyone—for there was no board of trustees in those days, nor did anyone dare to counsel or censure—he had become despotic and severe to the last degree. He was just as absolute, and upon occasions tyrannical, in his way, as any aristocrat of the Middle Ages.[21]

Mair recalled Robbie Mason as a "portentous figure when armed with his weapon, the taws, cut from heavy sole leather, or his birch rod—the terror of the school."[22] Fraser records that his "castigations and punishments were simply horrible, yea fiendish," that Mason had

> an honest, conscientious conviction in his soul that the beginning and end of all sound and effective imparting of knowledge lay in the tips of the taws. . . . With this awful weapon in his hand he would go to work as a man chopped down a tree. I have seen as many as a dozen pupils ranged before him, each waiting in gloomy silence his turn to undergo chastisement. If it was in warm weather each one as he came forward had to lay his hand down on the cold stove . . . and then after a long, deliberate wipe of his forehead, shaggy eyebrows, nose, mouth and chin,

[21]Joshua Fraser, *Shanty, Forest, and River Life in the Backwoods of Canada*, pp. 286–7.

[22]*Master-Works*, p. xlix.

with his left hand he would bring down the taws upon the hand of the luckless culprit with a mighty pegh! just as you hear a man give with every swing of the axe into the tree before him. After each one had received his dozen or more allotted "licks" the old man would be somewhat exhausted, but I believe it was a pleasant kind of exhaustion to him, and kept him in good humor for hours afterwards.[23]

In a building twenty feet square, packed with boys and girls of all ages, it was perhaps inevitable that dominie Mason would occasionally encounter rebellion. Some of the boys were in fact young men in their early twenties, still at school only by the insistence of stern Scots parents; and often unable to contain further his smouldering resentment towards Mason and his weapon, a stalwart youth might suddenly turn up his coat sleeves, spit on his hands, and call out, "Maister, I'll fecht you." According to legend and historic record, the outcome was always the same: Mason holding the rebel to the floor and calling for his taws. As Mair reflected, "No other class of teacher could have controlled the country schools of the time; and . . . he had the respect not only of the old, but of the young whom he belaboured so heartily."[24] And Mason undoubtedly taught thoroughly, if only fundamentally. "Reading, spelling, writing and 'countin' made up the sum total of his instruction," Fraser records,[25] and Mair ascribed little of his own poetic talent to the stern Scots master. "He seemed to like Pope," he recalled, "for Pope entered largely into our advanced 'readers' in those days, and he knew his Burns of course. But he never quoted poetry in class, or dealt with it unless in connection with prosody. . . ."[26]

According to the testimony of those who knew him, Charles Mair was neither well-behaved in class nor devoted to his studies. Mrs. Woodburn Langmuir of Toronto, grand-niece of Mair,[27] commented to the writer that "Uncle Charles was considered an unruly boy," and Mair's own schoolmate, Joshua Fraser, has left an indicative, if somewhat romantically exaggerated memoir of his days under dominie Mason:

. . . of all the boys who at that time were afflicted with the visitation of the rod, perhaps Chas. M— had to undergo the severest ordeal. Charlie's besetting sin was truant-playing; he hated the school with a perfect and undying hatred, and it was only under the direst compulsion that he was

[23]*Shanty, Forest, and River Life*, pp. 289–90. [24]*Master-Works*, p. 1.
[25]*Shanty, Forest, and River Life*, p. 287. [26]*Master-Works*, p. 1.
[27]Mrs. Langmuir's father, Col. G. T. Denison, married Helen Mair, daughter of Mair's brother James.

there at all; and I can safely aver that all the mental and scholastic attainments that he gained during that period were absolutely *nil*.[28]

To the young Mair the fascination of the outdoors was far greater than that of Robbie Mason and his disciplinary and academic fundamentals. "There is not a hill, valley or creek, not a mile of wood or river that I fished or shot over in my youth but is still familiar to me in my mind's eye," he later wrote.[29] His correspondence reveals that he once had "a narrow escape when caught in a brush fire near Lanark,"[30] and that on another occasion he "fell from a bridge near Lanark when a boy and was nearly drowned."[31] But such risks were evidently not so certain as those incurred by truancy. Fraser relates that as soon as young Charles's absence was discovered, a pupil would be despatched to seek him out. If he were not at home two of the more stalwart boys, "whose faithfulness or cowardly obsequiousness could be relied upon," would be sent to scour the banks of the Clyde or the trails of the woods and to bring the truant in, by force if necessary. Mair's father was evidently quite in sympathy with such action and with the penalty that invariably followed: "It was quite a common thing to see him appear at the schoolhouse door, leading Charlie by the hand, and stalking up to the desk with stern aldermanic dignity, he would say: 'There, Maister, tak' him, and thresh the deevil out of him.'" And yet Fraser, himself a teacher before he led a kirk in 1883, could say of his refractory former school-mate, "a brighter genius never attended a Canadian village school than Chas. M–, which has been abundantly shown by his career since."[32]

This high praise referred to Charles Mair, poet; and poets, bright geniuses or otherwise, invariably have some direction, some introduction at least, to the models that their own first efforts imitate. Dominie Mason's use of Pope and Burns was obviously uninspiring; Mair's work shows no obligation to either. And there was little, as Wilfrid Eggleston has noted, in the social and cultural life of Lanark village favourable to "the moulding of a literary figure."[33] Even by the time of Mair's youth, three decades after the first settlers had arrived at the valley of the new Clyde, the hardworking Scots were still beset by the problems of making a living, and had little time for the refine-

[28]*Shanty, Forest, and River Life*, pp. 294–95.
[29]MP, Mair to T. B. Caldwell, August 30, 1920.
[30]MP, Mrs. James McCrae to Mair, June 8, 1927.
[31]MP, Mair to M. O. Hammond, April 3, 1927.
[32]*Shanty, Forest, and River Life*, pp. 295, 296.
[33]*The Frontier and Canadian Letters*, p. 128.

ments of a more stable society. Indeed, such refinements, if attempted, would probably have been considered highly suspect. A visitor from Glasgow found even one of the pillars of Scots communal life, the kirk, on a shaky foundation: "I met with one on Sabbath day," he related. "Is this the Sabbath? he exclaimed, and acknowledged he had forgotten it. He said it was not at all like a Sabbath with them, for they came in with their waggons full, and transact all their business on the Lord's day."[34] The church eventually became strong in Lanark; but nowhere can the researcher find records of literary or "cultural" societies.

Charles Mair was in some respects fortunate, however, in being the youngest and consequently, perhaps, the indulged son of affluent parents. And he supplies evidence, as Eggleston remarks, "of the value in the early days of effective parental links with the larger literary world overseas."[35] James Mair envisioned for his son a calling other than that of the forests or of the general store. It was decided that he should study medicine at Queen's College in Kingston, and to this end the elder Mair, supported by dominie Mason, insisted that his son attend the local school. Despite this intention, however, the father evidently too often gave in to the boy's wishes and allowed him for days on end to live with the timber men in their "chantiers" and to ride with them on their "drives" down the tributaries of the Ottawa, even down to Quebec itself. And so it was to his mother, who, like Susanna Moodie, was never really happy in her Canadian surroundings, that Mair owed his first acquaintanceship with a wider range of British literature than Mason was inclined to reveal.

Mrs. James Mair appears now as the most significant single influence in her son's life. He himself said he inherited from her his love of books and his poetical talent: "My father was a highly intelligent man of affairs . . . , had a well-chosen library, took *Blackwood's*, the Quarterlies, and *Punch*, also our own *Literary Garland*"; but "my mother was very fond of poetry and well read in it";[36] "she was a great reader, loved poetry, and had an inborn instinct for good literature."[37] Throughout his life Mair often referred to his mother and to her influence upon him, but made scant reference to his father. When he was preparing to write his autobiography he seemed satisfied that "the [Mair] breed is limited and the original family came from

[34]John McDonald, *Narrative of a Voyage to Quebec and Journey from thence to New Lanark in Upper Canada*, p. 28.

[35]*The Frontier and Canadian Letters*, pp. 127–28.

[36]*Master-Works*, p. lv.

[37]*Ibid.*, p. xlix.

France . . . to Scotland centuries ago";[38] but his correspondence reveals that he made persistent efforts to trace his mother's lineage. Her grandfather, Richard Holmes, was "of a landed family whose seat was not far from Newcastle-upon-Tyne,"[39] and had served with an English regiment in Scotland during the Stuart uprising of 1745. While there, Captain Holmes had married a Miss Paterson, becoming "estranged from his family by marrying the daughter of a reputed Jacobite."[40] He had died in early middle age, leaving an only son, also Richard by name, the father of Margaret Holmes Mair, and like his daughter after him, a bequeather of the love of reading. "Mr. Holmes enjoyed good literature," his grandson Charles recorded, "particularly the novels of 'The Great Unknown' as they came out, and his daughter, my mother, devoured them."[41] Perhaps even more noteworthy here than Mair's particular attachment to his mother is his general pride in her family's background, in its social and cultural heritage. A maternal great-grandfather who came from "a landed family" with a country "seat" and who helped to suppress a rebellion against the Crown is given an added dash of romantic characterization by marrying a daughter of the enemy and consequently "estranging" himself from his estate. This, surely, is plot-material worthy of Scott, "The Great Unknown," himself.

One of Mair's friends once stated that Mrs. Mair "loved her children with the love of a panther," and that particularly upon Charles did she bestow the benefits of her "most discriminating and penetrating mind."[42] Mair himself has recorded that

After the fairy tales of childhood, she gave me Spenser's *Fairy Queen* in Charles Knight's excellent edition for a boy, in which the finest stanzas were connected by descriptive prose, and never wearied me. Other books followed: *Robinson Crusoe*, of course, *Gulliver's Travels, Pilgrim's Progress*. . . . When old enough I read . . . Chaucer's *Canterbury Tales*, Malory's . . . *Morte d'Arthur*, Chapman's *Odyssey*, and a good many of Shakespeare's dramas. . . . I always thought *Tom Jones* our greatest novel, *Rob Roy* the next, and *Jacob Faithful* one of the best.[43]

Scott and Marryat he considered the "consummate delineators of clean and manly British life." Also, significantly, he enjoyed "an

[38]DP, 5595, Mair to Denison, May 6, 1909.

[39]MP, Mair to Registrar of Births, Deaths and Marriages, Peterhead, Scotland, May 3, 1915.

[40]*Master-Works*, p. xlviii.

[41]*Ibid.*, p. xlix.

[42]H. R. Morgan, "Dr. Charles Mair," *Willisons Monthly*, II (Aug., 1926), 110. H. R. Morgan was the son of H. J. Morgan.

[43]*Master-Works*, p. lv.

admirably edited newspaper, The New York *Albion*, delightfully British; but the Yankees would not allow it to live."[44]

Comment on this selection of reading may seem superfluous. That the "Yankees would not allow" a "delightfully British" paper to live in New York State is understandable, but many years later Mair is still resentful. The poetry and novels are from the "greats," the "classics," of British literature and one can only agree with Mair that he was fortunate in his semi-primitive environment to be able to obtain them. There is to be noticed, however, an emphasis upon moralistic works—Spenser, Defoe, Bunyan, and, above all, Scott. "The Great Unknown" (and *this* is surely romantic) was enormously popular when Mair was a youth, but Mair had a life-long reverence for his works. No probings into character, but generous melodramatic tinsel, duty and faith rewarded, and above all, the delineation of "clean and manly British life." But no Blake, no Austen, no philosophically critical or satirical writings except *Gulliver's Travels*, the inclusion of which in this list implies that it was probably read as an adventure story.

Margaret Holmes Mair and dominie Robbie Mason did their best, and by 1851 Charles Mair was attending the high school in Perth, one step closer to Queen's and a medical career. And again he might have given in to his fondness for the outdoor life if he had not at this time come under the close supervision of his sister's husband, the principal of the school. John Macintyre was a man of varied talents. He left teaching, probably during Mair's time at the school, and became a banker in Perth; but he was a graduate of Queen's and an accomplished scholar whose knowledge of literature was comprehensive and whose quiet authority was a new experience for his young brother-in-law. So Mair now went to live in Perth, either with one of his brothers or with the Macintyres, rather than make the twenty-mile journey from and to Lanark every day, and this change of residence, perhaps to the home of the principal himself, eventually led him in 1856 to Kingston and Queen's College.

This stay at Queen's was brief—only for the 1856–57 session—but an eighteen-year-old Mair found much there that impressed itself upon his memory. When Lorne Pierce informed him in 1923 that his former University had decided to award him an honorary LL.D., he wrote in reply: "I have very warm remembrances of old Queen's—memories of 'Tis Sixty year since', or nearer seventy, and I doubt if there are many survivors of my time. There may be some who were

[44]*Ibid.*, p. liv.

fellow students . . . and I should dearly love to meet them. We were a merry lot in those good old days, and I am sure they are none the worse for it."[45] Joshua Fraser, his old friend from Lanark, was there, preparing for the ministry. Also there, from Amherstburg, Ontario, and after two years at Oberlin College, Ohio, was a certain John Christian Schultz, like Mair a medical student, but a young man destined to play an important part in his life.

In his enthusiastic introduction to the *Master-Works* edition of Mair's works, Robert Norwood says (p. xv) that Mair "gave up the Arts Course to assist in his father's fascinating business. It is evident that the lure of the woods distracted the student, and made him lonely for the river and the pineries." The statement contains half-truths: while at Queen's, Mair probably often missed the exciting life of the Ottawa Valley, but he just as probably would have remained at Queen's if he had not been drawn away by an influence more demanding than "the lure of the woods." He returned to Lanark, not so much "to assist" in his father's business as to help save it from calamity. Norwood also is obviously referring to the elder Mair's timber trade, but it was to the hardly "fascinating" general merchandise business in Lanark and Perth that young Charles was called, in order, probably, to allow his hard-pressed father and brothers to devote more effort to their timber interests. Apparently the commercial depression of 1857 in general, and the failure of a Liverpool trading house and of the Bank of England in Hull, the great consigning point of square timber, in particular, placed their affairs in jeopardy, and to meet the reverse the Mairs, in the late 'fifties and early 'sixties, used several combinations of family manpower to extricate themselves. Advertisements in the Lanark *Observer* and the Perth *Courier* reveal that "James Mair & Sons" became "H. &. J. Mair" (Holmes and James Jr.); then "J. Mair" (Jr.); then, in 1861, "J. & C. Mair." The year 1861 must have been particularly depressing for the Mairs, because in that year the elder Mair died, leaving his sons to carry on alone. Richard apparently never did take part in the family business and had died in Toronto when Charles was very young. Holmes is listed by the 1861 census as "out of business," perhaps because he was afield in the timber trade. And William, who was helping to manage the Perth store, disappeared about 1863, never to be heard of again.[46] In early 1866, the firm of J. & C. Mair closed out in Lanark and centralized its operations in Perth, but later

[45]MP, Nov., 1923.

[46]In MP, the genealogical table, "C. Mair & Family," gives the cryptic comment after William's name: "Killed in the Battle of the Wilderness, Am^{n} Civil War."

in the same year Holmes Mair opened a new store in Lanark "on his own account, and in the Turner Property next door to the Town Hall."[47] Finally, in October, 1866, the Mairs of Perth "entirely wind up their store business,"[48] James Jr. devoting himself exclusively to the timber trade, and Charles presenting his share of the business to Holmes, who became the sole Mair engaged in general merchandising.

To state simply that Charles Mair, now nearly thirty and after ten years behind the various Mair store counters, returned to Queen's to resume his medical studies would be to imply that the period was merely an interruption in the programme his parents had long before intended for him. By now, however, other factors were involved. That business life was hateful to him he has left some indication. In a letter to Henry J. Morgan in 1866 he wrote:

> Lord! What a lovely day and I not in the woods. Odds creeks and pools! I wouldn't give one day in the woods for all the ghastly pleasures of society in Christendom. Think of the rustling leaves; think of the owls hooting at midnight and the lynx's frantic scream. It drives me mad. I have been summoned as a juryman at the assizes. Think of me as a juryman! Tents and triggers, I shall condemn them root and branch. Why should the liberties of the subject be invaded thus? And this beautiful October weather to be tainted with musty records![49]

These lines constitute a rather amusing piece of conventional pretension, but they probably reflect Mair's real distaste for the confinements of business. And business did not take all of Mair's time. Besides taking refuge in the woods and in an occasional "drive" down the Ottawa he continued his reading. He also began to write, first of all, evidently, for the sheer pleasure of expressing himself, then for the newspapers and periodicals. His contributions, in both prose and verse, consisted of book reviews, articles on nature, and fugitive pieces that were published, often anonymously, in papers such as the Montreal *Transcript* and the Kingston *Daily News* and in the short-lived periodical, the *British American Magazine*. Most of them are virtually impossible to trace—those in the newspapers, for example—but the one or two that can be found provide rewarding evidence of Mair's early interests and abilities.

Two descriptive poems, "The Pines" and "Summer," were read in 1862 before the Botanical Society of Canada at Kingston and brought to Mair honorary membership in the Society as well as high

[47]Perth *Courier*, May 18, 1866. [48]*Ibid*., Oct. 19, 1866.

[49]Quoted by Morgan's son, H. R. Morgan, in the Perth *Courier*, June 18, 1926, but not to be found in PAC, Morgan Papers.

tribute from the Reverend Principal Leitch of Queen's: " 'The Pines,' " he said, "is a truly Canadian production, inspired by an acquaintance with and love of the forest, while 'Summer' has more of the old world stamp shewing by the impress a style of its literature. Canada ought to be proud of Mr. Mair's poems."[50] Two sonnets, "To a Humming Bird" and "To a Sleeping Child," appeared in the *British American* (October, 1863, and March, 1864, respectively) and, although creditable, even commendable, in some lines, as first efforts, they give ample evidence of "the old world stamp"—particularly of Shelley and Keats:

> It comes!—this strange bird, from a distant clime
> Has fled with arrowy speed on flutt'ring wing,
> From the sweet south, all sick of revelling;
>
> . . . .
>
> Go, gentle flutterer, my blessing take:—
> Less like a bird thou hast appeared to me
> Than some sweet fancy in old poesie.

And in "Sleeping Child" the poet is made to weep,

> To think how Care and Age may come and flood
> Thine eyes with tears—rough-visaged pards which creep
> Into men's hearts and steal their vigorous blood.

The latter poem also gives pointed example of the almost grotesque indelicacy that was to characterize even some of Mair's best work. Of the watching mother he writes:

> Now bends she o'er thee and recalls the kiss
> And throes which gave thee being and time,
> And made thee doubly dear!

Also in the *British American* (November, 1863) was an early prose piece, "Frogs and Their Kin," a sometimes witty but consistently well-written *tour de force* of vocabulary and learning. Quotations from Milton, Wordsworth, and Dante as well as from the Greek and Roman classics illuminate, not an article on natural history, but a light, familiar essay on the analogy of the "*genus rana*" and their kin, humanity. Most significant, as a modern critic has well noted,[51] is the essay's statement regarding the proper subject-matter for Canadian poetry. What poet of his own time, asks Mair, would dream of inditing a sonnet to a frog?

[50]Henry J. Morgan, *Bibliotheca Canadensis*, p. 246.

[51]R. L. McDougall, "A Study of Canadian Periodical Literature of the Nineteenth Century" (unpublished Ph.D. thesis), p. 236.

And yet within the domain of its habits and associations are to be found the materials of real poetry; not the maudlin, washed-out stuff of the boarding schools, but the genuine poetry of nature, which when written, is part of nature's self, plus artistic expression, and like her is imperishable. It is to be hoped that some poet will yet arise with a mind not too loftily poised to sing of the frogs.

Archibald Lampman, born just before Mair's essay appeared, was a generation later to fulfil this hope with a sonnet-sequence to "The Frogs." But "Frogs and Their Kin" points to Mair's fascination with nature, almost, at this time, to the exclusion of everything else. A letter from Henry Y. Hind, the naturalist and explorer, begins with scientific seriousness: "My dear Sir, your bird just received in rather a damp condition is the American Coot. (*Sulica American*, Bonap-[arte] or *Sulica Atra*, Wilson—or Cinereous Coot of Nutt)."[52] One can only infer that Mair the enthusiast had sent the bird to be identified and stuffed.

Hind is significant here in another respect. He was the editor of the *British American*, and in the same letter he gives indirectly at least a further insight into Mair's interests. Thanking Mair for stimulating support of his periodical in Lanark and district, he urges his young friend to do everything in his power "to get an additional number of subscribers"; otherwise the magazine will fail. There is no record of how successful Mair was, but the fact of his support of a Tory-conservative, anti-American magazine is important. As R. L. McDougall has noted, in the *British American* there are "to be heard some of the theme-preludes to Confederation, and it is clear that Canadian nationalist sentiment has by this time made substantial gains both in definition and in strength."[53] Part of this nationalist sentiment expressed itself in terms of the North-West: under the editorship of Hind, by commentary and article, the *British American* reflected and emphasized a growing interest in that virtually unknown land, a land that the magazine and its contributors took for granted would have to be part of any unified Dominion. Charles Mair was in harmony with that interest: "I was one of the few Canadians," he said, "who at that early date had read many of the considerable number of books which constituted even then a literature of the North-West." It was characteristic that he should add: "Though strictly true they also contained that fine flavour of romance, inseparable from the wilderness."[54]

52MP, Oct. 31, 1863.
53Abstract of "Canadian Periodical Literature of the Nineteenth Century."
54MP, MS., "Article for *Free Press*," *ca.* 1905.

With most of these factors Mair's return to Kingston in 1867 and his registration in Queen's College Medical School have connection—that is, if one further element is considered. John Christian Schultz had been a contemporary of Mair during his previous brief sojourn at the College. There is no record that they were acquaintances, although since enrolment was small, they probably were. Schultz stayed until 1860, went on to Victoria College, Cobourg, perhaps received his medical degree there,[55] and soon afterwards began to practise in the infant Red River Settlement of Rupert's Land. Stimulated by his own increasing absorption with the North-West, Mair, about 1863, began corresponding with Schultz, and before long he had decided that as soon as he could escape the trammels of business he would return to Queen's, graduate in medicine as Schultz had done, and then join his friend at Red River.

This was the plan, and by the spring of 1868, a first year of medical studies completed, Mair seemed to be working towards its evolution. Family finances, aided, probably, by the selling out of the interests in Perth and the consolidation under Holmes Mair in Lanark, as well as by the recovery of the timber trade, were sound enough to permit him to continue his studies. They even provided for the expense of bringing out a little volume of verse—a first book that Dawsons' of Montreal had undertaken to publish and that was to go through the Desbarats printing house in Ottawa while its author was vacationing from Queen's.

So the young man who stepped down from his hackney cab in front of Ottawa's Russell House on the May afternoon of 1868 was a personality well able to make his imprint upon time and place. Even the signature he made in the hotel register reflected at least part of him. Written boldly and with obvious flourish, it indicated self-confidence, even, perhaps, the propensity towards unruliness that had characterized his school days. And yet, the firm, clear letters, the straight underlining stroke, could just as aptly have testified to the stern discipline of a Scots father and a country dominie, to the scholarly exactitude of a high school principal in Perth. There were other aspects of character and inclination, however, not so apparent in a signature. It might reflect a quality of initiative inherited from

[55]The doubt is suggested by the lack of any official record at Victoria College that Schultz acquired a medical degree there. Such a degree, however, could be purchased from any one of a number of twilight or "quack" organizations then operating in Ontario, although it seems highly likely that a man with as many enemies as Schultz was to have would have been exposed in this respect.

Scots and English pioneers and sharpened by confronting the hazards of the river and forest. But probably not the sense of superiority instilled by a devoted mother, proud of her upper middle-class lineage. And certainly not the sentimentality that found expression in derivative verse often incongruously, even grotesquely, revelatory of the less refined features of a backwoods environment. Nor the pro-British, anti-American nationalism that was romantically and increasingly coloured by an interest in the North-West and by a vision of a great, unified country.

Because of his background, his personality, his ideals, young Charles Mair was an "Upper-Canadian" nationalist. The influences upon him were British colonial, and more particularly, through his mother, English colonial. He fits admirably, indeed, into a pattern well delineated by A. R. M. Lower in his appropriately entitled *Canadians in the Making*. The "historical climate" of the nineteenth century, especially the middle third of it, says Professor Lower, "was marked by warm emotions, by passionate concern, sentiment descending to sentimentality, by causes, movements, crusades." Such a climate influenced Mair in lower- and middle-class Lanark. Complicating these forces in his case were others, those that probably came principally through his mother—the conservative, proud attitudes of the once privileged English family. By Margaret Holmes Mair, Charles had been encouraged in a romantic idealization of places and times far distant. But in the years immediately surrounding Confederation Mair had also been stimulated by "another kind of romanticism,"

> easily understood by those who caught a gleam of hope, as every colonist had, one that might be called the romanticism of accomplishment. It was equally under the spell of the mystery of life, if not the mystery of medieval life, and equally convinced that things are bigger than they seem. It was logical for persons with this kind of dream to turn to the giant task of creating a "brave new world."[56]

Mair's earlier, formative years were behind, the traditions of loyalty to the Crown and to his own inheritance had been firmly established. Optimism and idealism were seeking expression. But in 1868 he was still naïvely unaware of the strength of forces that neither man or nation can control completely. He might versify about the encroachments of "Care" and "Age," the "rough-visaged pards," but he could not yet say, as he eventually did with considerable authority, "There is no such thing as free will; destiny rules!"

[56]*Canadians in the Making*, pp. 214–15.

II. Canada First

TWO GREAT WARS and the possibility of another have made the twentieth century wary of nationalism. Even the word itself is now commonly used in a derogatory sense, carrying, it is felt, implications of excessive zeal for national welfare and aggrandizement over other states and countries. Modern history has only too clearly revealed that when a state is dominated by a group that has nationalistic ideals, strong efforts are made to compel alien groups within the country concerned and even other nations to surrender their identity, their language and culture, to that of the aspiring group. It has also revealed that human survival itself may now depend upon values largely opposed to those held by the nationalist—at least the more extreme nationalist. But in the second half of the nineteenth century, when nationalism was considered to be of positive value, a force that liberated and created whole countries and states, before it had utilized the potentiality of massed millions of armed men and of modern technology, it was a *zeitgeist* of tremendous inspiration. And to a new nation like Canada it seemed to be the only means by which identity could be achieved and maintained. To Charles Mair and others it was, indeed, the spiritual cohesive that would bind a country until then united on only a paper document.

In the spring of 1868 when the young Mair arrived in Ottawa the federal union of the British North American provinces was preparing to celebrate its first anniversary. But the political achievement of the previous year, although great, had been only a beginning, and the implementation of the national programme set forth at that time was still very much in the future. Physically, the new nation did not even approach the realization of the dream of extending *a mari usque ad mare*. The union consisted of only the two provinces now known as Ontario and Quebec, and two maritime provinces, Nova Scotia and New Brunswick. Not only were Prince Edward Island and Newfoundland beyond its boundaries, but so also was that great area stretching west and north beyond Ontario to the Pacific and Arctic oceans—a vast land of which even much of the geography was unknown. Politically, young Canada's problems seemed to be growing in number and complexity. Internal questions of Dominion-provincial relations, of the material development of the great empty spaces, were more than matched by those of external significance. What was to be Canada's position in the British Empire? Would independence be better, or would not independence have "as its inescapable corollary"[1] annexation to the United States? What about tariffs? What about British Columbia, still undecided on joining the federation; and if she did come in, how could she be connected more closely with eastern Canada, two thousand miles away? These were only some of the questions that faced the young nation after July 1, 1867, questions that revolved around the larger issue of Canada's destiny and in the sphere, it was hoped, of her true interests.

But what were the new country's "true interests"? Most men who thought about it at all could agree with one young patriot that "Canada was now a country with immense resources and great possibilities" calling forth "visions of a great and powerful country stretching from ocean to ocean and destined to be one of the dominant powers of the world."[2] But they could not agree on how such visions could be made a reality, how Canada could fulfil this great destiny. And the answers, it was obvious, would have to be forthcoming in the light of two very significant factors. In 1867 loyalty to the Crown had been at its highest, and yet, as Donald Creighton remarks, "when the debate on the British North America Act was on, the English Parliament could scarcely conceal its excruciating boredom; and when the ordeal was over, it turned with great relief to a really national problem—the English dog tax."[3] John A. Macdonald himself complained that the English viewed Confederation "as if the B.N.A. Act were a private Bill uniting two or three English parishes."[4] This indifference, how-

[1]W. R. Graham, "Liberal Nationalism in the Eighteen-Seventies," *Report of the Canadian Historical Association* (1946), p. 101.

[2]G. T. Denison, *The Struggle for Imperial Unity*, p. 9.

[3]*Dominion of the North*, pp. 312–13.

[4]J. Pope, *Correspondence of Sir John Macdonald*, p. 451.

ever, was contrasted with an American attitude not only of awareness but also of suspicion, even of hostility. The end of the Civil War, the purchase of Alaska, the *Alabama* claims, American expansion in the West, were all factors that influenced a steadily growing agitation in the United States that Canada should be annexed "within the magic circle of the American Union."[5] Both of these attitudes were of extreme importance to the embryo Canadian nation. British indifference might lead to independence, but independence, in the minds of many, had that "inescapable corollary." The Canadian Militia could handle incursions such as the Fenian raid on Fort Erie in 1866, but in the face of organized aggression by a well-armed power, its need for assistance from the mother country would be vital.

Such factors helped to create the sense of urgency felt by responsible Canadians of the time. The necessity of translating the "vision" into governmental policy was obvious; but to many the promptitude and directness with which this might be done were also of great importance. The two political parties responsible for turning opinion and theory into policy were already opposed over its formulation, and dissension and discouragement were beginning to appear as the sad sequel to the real accomplishment of Confederation. The young Canadian nation was in danger before it had opportunity to gain strength. To save it, to nurture it, became the self-appointed task of Charles Mair and the four other young men he was to meet in Ottawa that spring of 1868.

Very soon after his arrival in the capital Mair went to the Revere Hotel and called upon his close friend, Henry J. Morgan. Morgan was a civil servant, a clerk in the office of the Secretary of State, and, at the age of twenty-six, already a man of some achievement. He had entered the governmental service at eleven, been page, sessional clerk, and private secretary to Isaac Buchanan, and in 1868 was about to be placed in charge of the records of the state department. His first book, an account of the tour of the Prince of Wales through Canada and the United States, was published in 1860, when Morgan was only eighteen. This was followed by *Sketches of Celebrated Canadians* in 1862, by *Bibliotheca Canadensis*—a still valuable "manual" of Canadian literature—in 1867, and by editions of the speeches and writings of D'Arcy McGee and of Isaac Buchanan. His production in later years was to be even greater.

[5]W. H. Seward, quoted by Creighton, *op.cit.*, p. 313.

Mair had met Morgan in Quebec in 1864[6] and had frequently corresponded with him since. Their friendship perhaps explains the glowing tribute that Morgan pays to Mair in the *Bibliotheca*, where, on the basis of the few slight pieces referred to in chapter I, he extols the young poet's "superior talents and education, his extensive and varied knowledge, and his refined taste and judgment."[7] Morgan and Mair were later to have differences that almost severed their friendship, but in 1868 they were ambitious young men with common interests, and within a few days after Mair's arrival, the genial and gregarious Morgan had introduced his friend to three other kindred spirits also visiting Ottawa. These five men, George Taylor Denison and William Alexander Foster of Toronto, Robert Grant Haliburton of Halifax, Charles Mair of Lanark, and Henry James Morgan of Ottawa, were the original members of the "Canada First party," an association that was to have a considerable and almost immediate influence upon the destiny of Canada.

They were men of varied abilities. All but one, Haliburton, who was thirty-six, were under thirty; all had already shown evidence of their promise. Foster, perhaps the most intelligent, was a barrister who wrote on politics for the Toronto *Telegraph* and other journals. Donald Creighton describes him as a man "with literary ambitions and a taste for some of the more blowzy flowers of nineteenth-century rhetoric,"[8] but it was Foster who was to write the pamphlet that became the party's manifesto and whose memory was to inspire a volume of essays and speeches that is still invaluable to the historian.[9] Haliburton, also a barrister, was the eldest son of Thomas Chandler Haliburton of "Sam Slick" fame. He had published several articles and monographs on philosophical, political, and economic subjects, as well as a small volume of verse, and was later to become a leading authority on African and South American anthropology. Denison of the "Family Compact" Denisons of Toronto was also a young lawyer; had led with distinction his Militia unit, the Governor General's Body Guard, during the Fenian raid in 1866; and had already written a number of treatises on military and political affairs.

Foster was in Ottawa on legal business, as was Denison, who had also come to see George Cartier regarding an appointment to a high

[6]In a letter to Morgan's son (MP, Feb. 26, 1927), Mair writes simply "in Quebec," not distinguishing province from city. Probably the place was somewhere near Ottawa where Mair was visiting on business and where Morgan was keeping a speaking engagement.

[7]P. 246.

[8]*Dominion of the North*, p. 322.

[9]*Canada First: A Memorial of the Late William A. Foster, Q.C.*

office in the Regular cavalry. Haliburton was there as a coal-mine owner and promoter of a national tariff policy, and was following up personally the views he had expressed in a pamphlet on the necessity of a "self-reliant policy"—a pamphlet that D'Arcy McGee had discussed in the House of Commons on the night he was assassinated.

Of the five young men who gathered in Morgan's quarters at the corner of Rideau and Ottawa (now Waller) streets,[10] Foster, despite his rhetorical style, was the most conservative, the most capable of subtle humour. Morgan undoubtedly had the widest official acquaintance, the fullest knowledge of things in general and of Ottawa politics in particular. Genial, yet inclined at times to be pompously and patronizingly officious, he was an assiduous writer and cataloguer. Haliburton had the most schooling and the widest general scholarship, and like Foster, was conservative and intellectual. Mair probably had the most imaginative temperament, the most intense idealism, and, despite his experience, the least inclination for practical affairs. But Denison was obviously the dominant personality of the group. Aggressive, self-assured, devoted to his Tory heritage, proud to the point of arrogance, yet capable of kindly humour and consideration, he was to be the man of action in the group. Photographs[11] taken at the time reflect in some measure the individual personalities of its members. Mair, short, with round, healthy face and a mop of curly hair, stands a little self-consciously in what appears to be a new, light-coloured suit far too large for him. Denison, tall, confident in uniform, strikes a characteristic military pose with right knee slightly bent and his hands resting on his sword. Morgan seems passively detached; Haliburton and Foster, though formally posed, give an impression of quiet confidence. But as Denison was to say later, "We must have been congenial spirits, for our friendship has been close and firm all our lives."[12]

[10]This building, so significant in Canadian history, is now the Notre Dame de Sacré Coeur Convent, but to determine this fact was made difficult by the seemingly conflicting evidence that appears in articles and correspondence written by the Canada First members themselves many years later. Morgan writes Denison (DP, 4305, March 11, 1901): "Our place of meeting here was not Salmon's Hotel as stated in the *Week*, but Buck's and Sanger's Hotel, Rideau street, now a convent." But to Mair he writes (MP, Dec. 4, 1899): "Dear old Matthews (you always erroneously made it Salmon's), what happy days we spent there." And the Ottawa Directory for 1868 lists the Revere Hotel as Morgan's quarters. Investigation reveals, however, that Morgan's landlord, Thos. Matthews, sold his hotel in 1867 to Messrs. Buck and Sanger, who renamed it the Revere, and who, in turn, in 1869 sold it to the Sisters of Charity. Morgan then moved to the Salmon's Hotel.

[11]Reproduced in the Toronto *Saturday Night*, April 24, 1909 (see illustration).

[12]*The Struggle for Imperial Unity*, p. 10.

These men were young enthusiasts with a vision, a vision that they felt had not captured the minds and hearts of enough Canadians, as it had captured their own, at a crucial moment in their country's history. In a way, perhaps, they regretted that Confederation had not been forged by a war of independence, by an all-enfolding common cause in which the emotions of the participants were the unifying cohesive of various rational determinations. Confederation had been rather, to use Professor Lower's very apt terminology, a carpentering, not a smelting,[13] of several disparate elements divided by space, race, and creed, by varying political and economic objectives. It had been a rational agreement, characterized by hard-headed bargaining and stimulated by the demands of practicality—mainly the need of the various provinces of *British* North America to combine defensively against *American* North America. As such it could hardly have hoped to arouse much popular enthusiasm. What Confederation implied, however, could arouse an emotional response. In fact, the implication was the emotional response itself—a greater Canadian national sentiment, a proud awareness of the new nation's identity and its seemingly unbounded potentiality. This was the vision of Mair and his friends, this was what they set out to inculcate in the Canadian people. According to Denison, nothing could show more clearly "the hold that Confederation had taken of the imagination of young Canadians than the fact that, night after night, five young men should give up their time and their thoughts to discussing the higher interests of their country."[14]

They were not alone, of course. Much of their inspiration came from D'Arcy McGee's speeches in the House of Commons or from the editorializing of that same patriot in the pages of his appropriately entitled *New Era.* Some of the literary periodicals of the time also took up the cry. But McGee was silenced by an assassin's bullet and the periodicals, as Professor Lower has delightfully paraphrased Hotspur, "could call for the spirit of nationalism to come out of the vasty deep of English Canada, but when called, come it would not."[15] So the group that called itself at this time "the Corner Room," after the place in which they met in Morgan's quarters at the Revere Hotel, considered themselves largely responsible for the task they felt had to be done if Canada were to grow, even, in fact, to live. The apparent inability of the Government to determine a national policy, the

[13]*Canadians in the Making,* p. 290.
[14]*The Struggle for Imperial Unity,* pp. 10–11.
[15]*Canadians in the Making,* p. 294.

annexation rumblings to the south, the unenlightened indifference of England, and the grumbling and weak-heartedness they saw every day more obvious at home led them, once again according to Denison, to make "a solemn pledge to each other that we would do all we could to advance the interests of our native land; that we would put our country first, before all personal, or political or party considerations; that we would change our party affiliations as often as the true interests of Canada required it."[16]

Most important as a first step on behalf of the "true interests" of Canada, said Mair, was the destruction of the main cause of disunity. "Provincialism in the early days of Confederation was rampant," he wrote, "and the very name 'Canadian' was a reproach on both coasts." So the group was to search for every opportunity "to speak and write it down" and to substitute "for its narrow spirit a Canadian sentiment through the operation of which only could we hope to become a nation."[17] Next, he insisted, was the necessity "to inculcate imperialism as our true destiny." The public "was seemingly quite content to set on its 'hunkers', and depend upon the mother country for protection and services at home and abroad." But imperialism "meant expense, and vague perils besides, which 'nobody' could define"; it was, therefore, "not to be thought of, unless by men of foresight, and it wasn't."[18]

There were other aims the achievement of which would help to engender national spirit. Denison, the Militia colonel, for example, insisted that colonialism would remain as long as Canadians were prevented from attaining the higher ranks held only by British officers in Canada. British troops, in fact, should be withdrawn altogether. And Haliburton, the lawyer-businessman, was concerned with a tariff policy more advantageous to Canada. But most significant, perhaps, was the association's repeated insistence that a Canadian national sentiment implied more than the physical and political union of the new nation. Foster was in a year or two to quote approvingly of a contemporary's description of Canada First as "an intellectual movement, as the revolt of educated and thoughtful men against the inanity . . . of what was offered to them as political discussion," and also as "a direct product, in some measure, of that higher culture which the universities and colleges of our land are steadily promoting."[19]

[16]*The Struggle for Imperial Unity,* p. 11.
[17]MP, MS., "Article for *Free Press,*" *ca.* 1905.
[18]MP, Mair to R. G. MacBeth, March 19, 1923.
[19]*Canada First: A Memorial,* p. 77.

Nationhood was to mean a quickened intellectual activity, new achievements not only in materialistic expansion but in Canadian cultural life as well—in science, music, art, and letters. Mair and his compatriots of Canada First had already attained some distinction in literary expression, and the group as a whole well symbolized "the promise which a change to national status seemed to bring of a greatly increased literary activity throughout the country."[20] One of them, Morgan, had, indeed, written only a few months before the five met in 1868 that "now more than at any other time ought the literary life of the New Dominion develop itself unitedly. It becomes every patriotic subject who claims allegiance to this our new northern nation to extend a fostering care to the native plant, to guard it tenderly, to support and assist it by the warmest countenance and encouragement."[21] Morgan merely echoed an earlier commentator, the Reverend E. H. Dewart, who in 1864 had insisted that a national literature was "an essential element in the formation of a national character," and that "without the subtle but powerful cement of a patriotic literature" a people could not be "firmly united politically."[22] It was surely singularly appropriate, therefore, that in the summer of 1868 Charles Mair should be publishing his first book of verse —verse by a Canadian patriot and reflective of the rivers and pineries of his Canadian environment.

An objective analysis of the group and its aims as they were at this early date is difficult. For one thing there is little record by the members themselves—other than the points mentioned above—of what they proposed explicitly. A desire for greater Canadian autonomy while still retaining the imperial connection seems obvious, as is their intention to avoid any party affiliation. Also plain is the insistence upon the "powerful cement" of cultural achievement. And these aims have been found highly commendable by later historians. H. M. Mowatt remarked in 1903 that if those of his own generation who took an interest in national concerns had been old enough at Confederation, "there is not the slightest doubt that we would have been found allied in sympathy and aim with the little party called 'Canada First.' "[23] W. R. Graham has praised their many "prophetic powers,"[24]

[20]R. L. McDougall, "Canadian Periodical Literature of the Nineteenth Century," p. 253.

[21]*Bibliotheca Canadensis*, p. viii.

[22]*Selections from Canadian Poets*, p. ix.

[23]"Greater Canadian Independence," *Queen's Quarterly*, XI (July, 1903), 36.

[24]"Liberal Nationalism in the Eighteen-Seventies," p. 102.

and Donald Creighton their being "the purest and most disinterested"[25] of those seeking a Canadian national sentiment.

But Professor Creighton also emphasizes the group's "naive, confused, and urgent aspiration" towards national unity. Perhaps it was too much to ask these young men, he says, "to describe its characteristics and to indicate how it could be cultivated." Certainly, even at this early period in its formation, Canada First reveals traits that beg for question. Mair and his four friends realized well the advanced quality of their views. They therefore decided, they said, not to work openly in the sense of advertising themselves or of proclaiming their group a new party. Nor did they at this time seek to attract large numbers of followers; "to have vaunted our opinions in the teeth of the bitter acrimonies of the time would have wrecked us at the start," said Mair. Instead, they were to carry out their designs with as little publicity as possibly "until manifest occasion came"; and then they were "to strike and strike hard."[26] Undoubtedly Canada First felt itself on a political tightrope between those who wanted independence from Britain, perhaps even annexation to the United States, and those who accepted, and even desired, the necessity for strong colonial ties with the mother country. But "our opinions" in other respects were far less enlightened. From the very beginning these young men seem to have been completely unaware of their own personal limitations in providing leadership towards a truly unified Canada. Psychologically they were drawn on the one hand by what still amounted to a colonial attachment to Britain and on the other by a growing nationalistic attachment to Canada—a division expressed in their insistence upon both the imperial connection and a greater Canadian autonomy. And the colonial attachment was revealed in "Upper-Canadian" or Ontarian terms. A letter from Denison to Mair written only a few months after their first meeting is significantly illustrative:

> I am pleased to hear you say you will make the English notice you yet before you die. I hope you will live long enough. . . . We Canadians must have more self-confidence—we must look up to England and the English no more as either a superior country or a superior people. I have seen and heard them, I have traversed their country, and I have come home feeling confident we have a finer country, a more intellectual, chivalrous, high-spirited people, and one unspoiled by withering conventionalities.

Of course, he continues, "we must all reverence England for her great history and as the hallowed ground where the dust of all our

[25] *Dominion of the North*, pp. 322–23.
[26] MP, Mair to R. G. MacBeth, March 19, 1923.

ancestors lies buried." But the present-day Englishmen are "merely our brothers," and although

> the country is still the "Mother Country," we Kanucks should resent any assumption of superiority at once . . . , but you can stand being sneered at as a Canadian—I am sure I can. I never felt so proud of Canada as when I was in England and France, and never hesitated to tell people of my country. In France I used to tell them, "Je suis Canadien—de Haut Canada," to which they would reply, "Oui, oui! Colonie Anglais." So you see "colonist" is a term well known to them too.[27]

Here is a two-way pull, but, is is to be noted, not between "Canada" and England, but between "Haut Canada" and England. Denison is representative of the group as a whole in his inordinate, although understandable, sensitivity to England and to England's standards, and at the same time in his resentment of the deep-rooted assumption of superiority engendered by the old colonial relationship. And his naïve insistence upon his Upper Canadianism—even after he has referred to "we Kanucks"—points up strongly the most self-destructive weakness of Canada First. While decrying provincialism it was itself provincial, even parochial. Culturally it was militantly anti-Ultramontane and anti-French. Socially its members represented the "respectable," even, as in Denison's case, the "upper" classes. And with the exception of Haliburton (who was later, significantly, to differ with the others) they were all from Ontario; Foster and Denison, the two main organizers, were both from Toronto, the focal point of English-Canadianism. These were surely factors that could not help coming to light when the group as a whole or anyone of its number should appear from behind the cloak of secrecy they at first felt obliged to assume.

The cloak itself stimulates one or two further questions. Did Mair and his associates really believe that undercover plots and intrigues, followed, when "manifest occasion came," by sudden decisive action, was conducive to national unity? Such planning has implications more of the oligarchic *coup d'état* than of a democratic tolerance for the great variety of attitudes and beliefs characteristic of their country. Future events, even if they were not to answer this question, were certainly to provide exciting commentary. Or was the cloak, partially at least, merely one more indication of the romanticism so characteristic of these youthful visionaries? All of them with the possible exception of Foster, who did not seem to get an opportunity, were to give an

[27]MP, Dec. 20, 1868.

impression that they received an almost melodramatic thrill from engaging in intrigue and subterfuge. Or, at the risk of a charge of unjustifiable psychological probing, can it be suggested that they give evidence of a "group" and "individual" paronoia by which they see themselves as the only true patriots, but are unappreciated as such? The cloak-and-dagger manner then becomes the only one by which they can further their objectives. Certainly the correspondence of Denison, Mair, and Morgan abounds with instances of wounded sensibilities, of unattained preferments, and of aggressively critical denouncements of their "enemies."

There is no satisfactory answer to any of these questions. But it is safe to assume that neither Charles Mair nor his friends appreciated more than superficially the possible repercussions of their meetings at Morgan's. They were not together long enough, indeed, either to discuss thoroughly their programme or to evaluate the mettle of each other—although Mair, characteristically self-confident, the day after they parted in Ottawa saw fit to write a long letter of personal advice to Denison. While admitting to their "short intimacy," Mair advises Denison he will be troubled in soul no longer over thoughts of professional advancement if only he will read the lines Mair quotes from Spenser.[28] Such confidence was very soon to carry Mair into—and out of—far more difficult problems than the giving of friendly advice.

[28]DP, 150, May 21, 1868.

III. Dreamland

CHARLES MAIR'S MAIN PURPOSE in going to Ottawa was to see his volume of poetry through the press. That within a few days of his arrival he had become associated with a group of enthusiastic young patriots whose nationalistic ambitions, politically and culturally, seemed to coincide with his own did not qualify that purpose. The evenings spent at Morgan's quarters in the Revere were to have far-reaching consequences—and towards an understanding of these consequences the emphasis of the preceding chapter has been directed—but it is highly improbable that at the time the five friends viewed the meetings as other than opportunity for some stimulating discussion of their vision of a unified Canada.

This may be stated despite later remarks by Denison and Mair about the pledges and plans they made. Much of the group's correspondence at the time, indeed, reveals that a considerable amount of youthful frivolity, sometimes of a dubious nature, became mingled with the "higher vision." But Canada First was meant to be a way of life, not a career. Before the end of May, 1868, Denison and Foster had returned to their law practices in Toronto (wrote Mair to the former: "Haul down your bunting . . . and run up the parchment"[1]), Haliburton to his legal and mining interests in Halifax, and Mair the medical student, having remained with Morgan the civil servant only until he assured himself that the printing of his book was progressing satisfactorily, had retraced the sixty miles to Lanark.

[1]DP, 150, May 21, 1868.

As a young man venturing to present himself boldly as a nationalist poet, Mair was under no illusions about the reception his book was most likely to meet. The obstacles facing his success had, indeed, been well spelled out by a correspondence acquaintance, the Reverend Edward Hartley Dewart, whose *Selections from Canadian Poets* of four years before had been British North America's first anthology of verse. Himself a strong nationalist, Dewart deplored particularly the fact that the political sectionalism of Canada met no counterpoise in a patriotic, unifying literature. "There is probably no country in the world," he noted, "where the claims of native literature are so little felt, and where every effort in poetry has been met with so much coldness and indifference" as in Canada. The reasons he gives for this neglect have become familiar to every student of Canadian letters. The necessity of hewing wood and of drawing water to the exclusion of the study of poetry and kindred subjects, the false conceptions of the nature and influence of poetry, religious intolerance, booksellers who promote popular British and American, instead of less profitable native works, the colonial mind and heart that can "scarcely conceive it possible . . . that a Canadian Poet might be as highly gifted as some of the favourite names" of the Old Country, are some of the factors that militate against the development of an intrinsically native literature.[2] Charles Mair's hopes, therefore, might have been high, but his expectations probably were qualified.

Dreamland and Other Poems is a slim volume of thirty-three pieces, most of them short lyrics, and some of which had already appeared in journals and newspapers. It was published by Dawson Brothers of Montreal and by Sampson Low, Son and Marston of London, England, an auspicious beginning marred, unfortunately, by a fire in the Ottawa binding house that destroyed all but two hundred copies and made the numerical success of the book impossible to determine. In a modest preface Mair submitted the book "to the ordeal of English criticism," confident, however, that "at the hands of those accustomed to assess the value of literary productions" he would receive candid criticism that would "either be a guide to him in future or induce him to abandon the field of poetry altogether." The dedication to Mrs. William McDougall, wife of the Minister of Public Works, conventional enough at the time, was to be considered significant in the light of later events.

From its title and from those of such "other poems" as "The North Wind's Tale," "Innocence," "Our Beautiful Land by the Sea," "My

[2]Pp. x–xvi.

Love—A Rhapsody," and "Stanzas from the Heart," it may be rightly inferred that the collection is thoroughly romantic. Even the epigraph from Keats—"O Poesy! for thee I hold my pen"—suggests the derivative quality of most of the selections—although it may have prompted one critic to the interesting analogy that "even as Keats forsook surgery to write *Endymion* so Mair quit medicine to write *Dreamland*."[3] Foster, in fact, in a curious and yet characteristic illustration of the colonialism that tempered many of even the most ardent nationalists, referred to Mair as "the Canadian Keats."[4]

But more significant is Foster's further description of his friend as a poet "who tempts us with delicious melody away to the sunny hills of his own *Dreamland*."[5] Here is striking illustration of the sentimental idealism of the nationalist and of what he finds commendable in a poet. Yet, paradoxically, both poet and critic reflect that very colonialism that they hope to eradicate. E. K. Brown has described the colonial attitude of mind as that which "sets the great good place not in its present, nor in its past, nor in its future, but somewhere outside its own borders, somewhere beyond its possibilities."[6] And A. J. M. Smith points out that "a direct result of colonialism may be a turning away from the despised local present . . . towards an exotic, idealized crystallization of impossible hopes and noble dreams." The romantic spirit, he concludes, "is encouraged by a colonial sense of inferiority."[7] Almost any stanza of Mair's title poem may be cited as illustration of such a theory; here is the first:

> We are not wholly blest who use the earth,
> Nor wholly wretched who inherit sleep.
> Behold it is a palace of delight
> Built beyond fear of storms by day or night;
> And whoso enters doth his station keep,
> Unmindful of the stain upon his birth.

In dreamland "bondsmen lift their aching brows no more," men have peace, wives even "may deem their faithless lords are nigh / And maids may kiss false lovers for love's sake." Beyond are "wide plains of amber light," "sunless regions stained with solemn gold," and "empy-

[3]From a clipping from the Ottawa *Journal*, n.d., lent by Mrs. James McLaren of Lanark, Ontario.

[4]*Canada First: A Memorial*, p. 30.

[5]*Ibid.*

[6]*On Canadian Poetry*, p. 14.

[7]"Colonialism and Nationalism in Canadian Poetry before Confederation," *Report of the Canadian Historical Association* (1944), p. 75.

real regions blest." The dream, in fact, becomes an intimation of immortality, an all-enveloping Heaven with Love as guide:

And in our strength and everlasting youth
Arising in clear dawn and light which saves,
We found a realm wherein earth's sorrowings
Were heard no more, where myriad blameless things
Rose from their venal and lethean graves,
And found a resting-place, and called it Truth.

But dreams must end:

That moment there was darkness, and the lists
Of heav'n gave place unto the gloom of day.
Whereat I woke to deadly fears and pain,
To misery of the thunder and the rain,
And crime, and subterfuge, and fierce affray
Of warring creeds and brawling mammonists.

Similarly "Our Beautiful Land by the Sea" is a region of dreams where

. . . ev'ry fair thing which the ocean can bring
Shall be wafted for you and me
By the waves and the winds, till a harbour it finds
In our beautiful land by the sea.

If the theory of Professors Brown and Smith may be applied to such lines it is because they were written when their author was living in an essentially colonial environment. Mair's mother intensely disliked her backwoods life and her son often remarked on her constant references to the homeland. And the literature she prescribed for him has already been noted. "Dreamland" and the "other poems" like it therefore reflect, perhaps, the poet "who thinks of himself as an inheritor of the elaborate tradition of the poetry of the Motherland, and he makes poetry an escape from reality"[8]—not so much because he wants to as because he thinks he ought to.

For in opposition to his mother's influence was that of Mair's own fascination by the out-of-doors, and of his own growing feeling for the country in which he had been born. Lanark village, the beautiful rivers, the towering pines, the seasons, could all be expressed poetically, and thus this collection of early verse reveals a curious combination of sentimental rhapsody on ethereal lands beyond the clouds and a sometimes quite delicate sensitivity to the sights and sounds of the countryside. In "August" the land lies drenched in heat, the beetle

[8]*Ibid.*

"sits and sings / His brassy tune," the chipmunk "whistles out its fear / And jerks and darts along the panneled rails," and

Far o'er the hills the grouse's feath'ry drum
Beats quick and loud within a beechen copse,
And, sometimes, when the heavy woods are still,
A single tap upon a hemlock spire
Dwells with the lonely glades in echoes deep.

In "Winter" when "great pines crack with mighty sound" and "watch-dogs bay the vagrant wind,"

When morn is bleak, and sunshine cool,
And trav'llers' beards with rime are grey;
When frost-nipt urchins weep in school,
And sleighs creak o'er the drifted way;
When smoke goes quick from chimney-top,
And mist flies through the open hatch;
When snow-flecks to the window hop,
And children's tongues cling to the latch,—
Then do I sigh for summer wind,
And wish the winter less unkind.

For the most part, however, the verse is thin and artificial. E. J. Pratt remarks,[9] for example, that one of Mair's often quoted pieces, "The Fire-Flies," though rich enough in detail, is full of stock epithets —"lucid wing," "darkling woods," "bounteous rain," "tremulous lights," "sylphides" and "dreamy glass"—all of which confirm the impression that far too often Mair resisted an inclination to look at things directly and peered instead through a veil of too-well-remembered passages from some Golden Treasury. Keats was obviously his favourite model; Mair's fireflies, for example, are strikingly reminiscent of Keats's gnats:

High overhead they gleam like trailing stars,
Then sink adown, until their emerald sheen
Dies in the darkness like an evening hymn—
Anon to float again in glorious bars
Of streaming rapture. . . .

In "Summer," sleep brings a Keatsian dream

. . . of by-gone chivalry,
Wassailing and revelry,
And lordly seasons long since spent
In bout, and joust, and tournament.

[9]"Canadian Poetry—Past and Present," *University of Toronto Quarterly*, VIII (Oct., 1938), 4.

Rural scenes are often variants of Thomson and Cowper, the forests have the melancholy, brooding note of Bryant, and the landscape as a whole, even in Mair's best verse, has a decidedly Tennysonian quality, as in these lines from "Prologue to Tecumseh":

Ah! now the loneliest very loneliest tarn,
With prickly ash engirt, seems lonelier far
Than when with flushing eve the summer star
Tapered her beams aslant the smooth-topt wood.
And lonelier now seems each wan solitude,
With little lake low-couched among the hills,
And noisy murmurings of hidden rills
Swoll'n with the steady fall of autumn rain.

For some of his lighter lyrics he delved farther into the past. In "Address to a Maid" he praises a mistress in Cavalier fashion:

If those twin gardens of delight
Thine eyes, were ever in my sight
I would no pinks or roses seek,
Save those which bloom upon thy cheek.
I would no pleasant perfume breathe
Save that which parts thy snowy teeth
Or in sweet warblings e'er rejoice,
Save when I listened to thy voice.

And as in Herrick's "Corinna" or "Come with Me," there is in Mair's "Summer" the familiar scolding invitation to enjoy the pleasures of nature:

Awake! Awake! The woods are bright
With mirror-leaves and slumb'ry light.
The streams are singing madrigals,
And bird to bird in gladness calls.

Ye who faint with city moil,
Come and stay with me awhile.
We will find a mossy bed,
With awning branches overhead
And juicy coolness of large leaves,
Much longed for by the swelt'ring beeves,
And, enravished, we will go
Where the honeysuckles grow.

Critics have also found traces of Poe, Longfellow, and Swinburne in *Dreamland*. One of them, herself given to the use of stock epithets, remarks thus on yet another model: "One may note very plainly the influence of the 'Sun-Treader' in a phrase here and there in these earlier poems,—'Orient beams'; 'aerial mountains'; even 'Marmorean hills.'"[10] Mair himself remarked some years later that "there is, of course, some imitative work in *Dreamland and Other Poems*"; Carew and Herrick and Wither, he recalled, "were 'home favourites' when I was a boy and naturally fell into my hands when I emerged from the enchantments of 'Mother Goose' and her kin." But, he insisted, although the forms of such poems as "Address to a Maid" and "Summer" were due to such influences, "the ideas and imagery are my own, and not unworthy, I trust of the old singers."[11]

Mair believed he was writing Canadian poetry: "I have constantly advocated the growth of a native Canadian literature; indeed I think Charles Sangster and myself were almost the pioneers in that field."[12] But *Dreamland* points up well the validity of the question, "What is a Canadian poet?"—a question astutely presented a few years ago by A. J. M. Smith in an address to the Canadian Historical Association.[13] Is a Canadian poet, he asked, one who is "indubitably a *poet* because he has, in sufficient strength, qualities which are recognizably the same in kind as those of the standard poets of the English tongue," and "a *Canadian* poet because he happens to live and write in Canada, to use Canadian place-names, and to mention the flora and fauna of Canada?" Professor Smith did not answer this question directly, but his further comment left no doubt about his attitude. We have called our better poets *national* poets, he said, "because they were recognizably *poets*, judged by the standards of the accepted English masters, and then have pretended to ourselves that they were Canadian." And he emphasized his point by quoting the late Professor James Cappon of Queen's University: "Perhaps our best Canadian poets have devoted themselves too much to an almost abstract form of nature poetry which has too little savour of the national life . . . and is more dependent on literary tradition than they seem to be aware of."[14]

Dreamland is a curious but significant reflection of the attitudes that determined the way poetry was written in mid nineteenth-century Canada. The example set by the English Romantic poets directed it towards the depiction of the native landscape, and although that landscape might be viewed as through an English filter and interpreted by

[10]A. Ermatinger Fraser, "A Poet-Pioneer of Canada," *Queen's Quarterly*, XXXV (May, 1928), 442.

[11]DP, 4317A, Mair to Denison, March 21, 1901.

[12]MP, Mair to Lorne Pierce, n.d., 1923.

[13]"Colonialism and Nationalism in Canadian Poetry before Confederation," *Report of the Canadian Historical Association* (1944), p. 77.

[14]*Roberts and the Influences of His Time*, p. 84.

reference to English models, the poetry was nevertheless considered "Canadian." And herein lies a source of confusion. To be dependent on the literary tradition of England, as Smith has emphasized, surely cannot be a defect; if it is, perhaps all American poets except Whitman are to be dismissed with their Canadian cousins. But in 1868 it was more important that the verse be written by a Canadian than that it be poetry; the comparison was more often between the poet and an accepted English master than between poetry and non-poetry. This approach to criticism is, of course, still with us. Professor Smith wrote in 1946 that "when it is recognized that the claims of nationalism are less important than those of universality and that a cosmopolitan culture is more valuable than an isolated one, our twentieth-century criticism will be prepared to approach contemporary Canadian poets."[15] And as late as 1957 he could remark, "the question of national identity still seems to underlie [our] thinking and haunt [our] imagination."[16]

Mair's confusion of his objectives in 1868 resulted in singularly uneven verse. The literary escapism of "Dreamland" or "Our Beautiful Land by the Sea" is redeemed occasionally by an imaginative sensitivity, by a capacity to see and to depict microscopically the minute details of the animals, birds, and insects of the woods. But far too often Mair's verbosity and his attempts to apply a literary gloss trip him up, and he stumbles. This striving to be "poetic," indeed, results sometimes in lines that are ludicrous and grotesque, in what Desmond Pacey describes as "sudden bewildering descents into bathos."[17] An early sonnet in the *British American* has already provided some evidence of this sort of literary lapse; *Dreamland* gives numerous additional examples. In "Prologue to Tecumseh" the coming of autumn is announced thus:

Call in the last few leaves, yes, call them in,
For ev'ry bird hath ceased its shrilly din,
And all the butterflies are deadly sick.

In "The North Wind's Tale" the wintry blast arrogantly announces himself:

What time I lurk in icy halls
They say 'tis summer, and the earth
Throbs, buds and glows—the fruitage falls;
Each cottage rings with peasant-mirth.

[15]"Nationalism and Canadian Poetry," *Northern Review*, I (Dec.–Jan., 1945–46), 42.

[16]*The Book of Canadian Poetry*, p. 36.

[17]*Creative Writing in Canada*, p. 35.

But, often, ere the tender blade
Hath filled its spike with sappy corn,
I hurtle from my piny glade,
And shout till all the peasants mourn.

A similarly abrupt transition occurs a little later in the same poem:

All night I hunt with snow and storm
The wretched mother, wandering, lost;
And shake with sleet her tender form,
And bind her tears with links of frost.

And when the infant, mute-mouthed, slips
Dead, from the sighing mother's teat,
I freeze the milk which slowly drips
Adown, and steal her bosom's heat.

In "Innocence" a country maiden is praised unstintingly:

Beneath her sloping neck
Her bosom-gourds plumped mellow-white as spray;
Stainless, without a fleck,
The air which heaved them was less pure than they.

And in "To My Photograph" the attempt to attain grim realism is thwarted by a similar over-emphasis:

Yes! wakes to find some men unkind,
And others vain, and others false–
Cold sordid reptiles who would bind
One's very pulse.

And women, too, with paltry shapes
Teazed out of nature's flowing forms–
The early devotees to tapes
And coffin worms.

Such lines, particularly in their mammary emphasis, reflect both the young poet's reading and the more unsophisticated aspects of his early life in Lanark. They certainly help the critic to justify Mair's own comment, made in 1924 when John Garvin was preparing his *Master-Works* edition: "To be sure, there is some immature work in *Dreamland*." But, he added, "really all the more reason why it should be preserved, as illustrating a young poet's imperfections."[18]

One selection in *Dreamland* requires special, if limited, comment– an ode, "In Memory of Thomas D'Arcy McGee." This is the only avowedly patriotic work in the volume and its position in the last few pages implies that Mair was able to have it included only at the last

[18]MP, Mair to Garvin, May 2, 1924.

moment. McGee had been assassinated a month before Mair had come to Ottawa, and the poem was quite possibly part of his original manuscript. But in its elegiac treatment of a fervent nationalist it stands so completely apart from the other verse in the book—from the little wrens, the fireflies, the pines, and so on—that one feels that Mair originally had no intention of including anything even similar to it, and if this is the case, it presents another illustration of the manner in which Mair was influenced by his meeting in Ottawa the other young men of Canada First.[19] It was highly satisfactory to them that one of their own number was exemplifying the poets and writers who would help to inculcate a national sentiment; it was highly appropriate that he should include a tribute to the man who had inspired them most. And thus, perhaps, "In Memory of Thomas D'Arcy McGee" became the first of the many "patriotic odes" that were to beset the path of post-Confederation poetry.

The literary reviews accorded *Dreamland* in the fall and winter of 1868 offer interesting testimony of the kind of criticism a Canadian writer could expect at the time. Most reviewers welcomed the volume as the first significant collection of the new Confederation era. The New York *Albion* of November 25 asked, "Is it not refreshing to find such simple and fresh writing as this turning up in the nineteenth century and the New World?" The Toronto *Leader* of December 29 noted that it signified "that we may hope hereafter to find in native sources a constantly increasing supply of works of original imaginative literature."[20] In a long review on October 19 the Toronto *Globe* said the book was "unquestionably the best collection of poems by a Canadian that has yet appeared," and, although the reviewer did not wish to undervalue the merits of Charles Sangster and Alexander McLachlan, he found "evidence of poetical fancy and power of language in *Dreamland and Other Poems* only surpassed by some among the best known living English and American poets."

Sangster himself wrote a long review in the Ottawa *Times* of February 10, 1869, a review that wittily satirized other notices, but that also revealed the *pique* of a writer who himself, a few years before, had been acclaimed as "the Canadian poet at last."[21] After

[19]A manuscript copy of the poem, dated at Perth on April 11, 1868 (four days after McGee's death) is in PAC, H. J. Morgan Papers.

[20]The reviewer was a Mr. Grahame, whose "grandfather was a well known Scottish poet, author of 'The Sabbath,' referred to in Byron's 'English Bards and Scotch Reviewers'" (MP, Denison to Mair, March 10, 1869).

[21]Sangster had published *The St. Lawrence and the Saguenay and Other Poems* in 1856 and *Hesperus, and Other Poems and Lyrics* in 1860.

Nor far and near seem blent
With hollow merriment
The groanings of the travail of the earth;
And grey-haired grace is old,
And cowered hearts grow bold,
And shameless cheeks are creased with soulless mirth;
And, everywhere, who looks espies
A world's swift tears, or cold, hard-hearted eyes.

Yet as blooms melt in fruits,
Or dead flowers live in roots,
So time may bring the fabled afterage
When knowledge shall be found,
Emboldened and unbound,
And Heav'n shall grow more kind as men grow sage,
And Earth, no longer tempest-tost,
Shall snatch again the grace she once hath lost.

Charles Mair.

Perth, 11th April, 1868.

A page from the copy of "In Memory of Thomas D'Arcy McGee" sent to Henry J. Morgan, April 11, 1868 (Public Archives of Canada).

referring to the "more than mere welcome" that *Dreamland* had received from the press, Sangster turns to the review written by "Deminuendeo"[22] in the Montreal *Gazette*:

> ... one of the author's energetic admirers has gone even so far as to assert that a first measure of poetry had at length been given to the Dominion. "Here," cried Deminuendeo, holding up the book, "is the Alpha of our literary hopes! The lark has risen from the fields, the day has dawned, the sun has peered above the hills; and true poetic light, after long waiting and patient hope, floods the happy skies of 'this Canada of ours'. This is 'the real Simon Pure'; let us rejoice!" And he forthwith went into spasms of admiration and delight, rolling about amongst the fair flowers of rhetoric and figures of speech, like a colt in a clover meadow, or a sleek tabby seriously enjoying its first catnip. There had been a silly fiction afloat, a thread-bare idea which had well-nigh become a legend, that Heavysege had written something which good judges and men of brains called poetry; that McLachlin [*sic*] had published certain lyrics, many of them as charming as the daintiest of the lays of the "old land," that certain of Ascher's poems were in their way equally good; and that Sangster had at one time been a resident of this country, and it was veritably believed that he, also, had written something that passed with certain foolish people for poetry. All these fictions were pretty well grounded into men's minds, until they were really taken for facts, but the new metropolitan luminary soon set things to rights, and "no man's dog" has yet dared to bark at so solemnly-sportive an authority. . . .

This is just the sort of reviewing, Sangster remarks, that is most likely to ruin the sale of Mair's book, and to cause the young poet "to solicit his good angel to save him from his particular friends." The reviews published in Ottawa, he continues, were extremely glowing, "but they were fair and honest, and did not attempt to disparage others at Mr. Mair's expense [*sic*], or to exchange new lamps for old ones." But then Sangster makes it obvious that his chagrin is not entirely due to "Deminuendeo"; "We will not go so far," he wrote, "as to assert that the writer in the *Gazette* took his cue from Mr. Mair's poem 'Night and Morn'; but in the stanza next the last, the Sun 'stands above the watery doom, / And views *our songless shores*.' "[23]

Sangster, however, was too generous, too "fair and honest" himself,

[22]"Deminuendeo" was George T. Lanigan, founder of the Montreal *Star* and himself a versifier ("The Akhoond of Swat"). He sent Mair a sonnet he had composed in honour of the appearance of *Dreamland*.

[23]Commented Mair: "Sangster misunderstood my line 'And views our songless shores,' which was simply classical, as he might have inferred from the context. Sangster was a true Canadian poet, and our native impulse and sympathies were in accord" (MP, written on the envelope containing the review).

not to give *Dreamland* a favourable notice: "No one of taste and discrimination can read these poems," he said, "without admitting that there is sterling poetry in them." Noting that most of the poems had been written before the author was twenty, he asked "if *they* are so mature, what may we not hope for when his muse shall have been dowried with fuller power and his mind has arrived at maturity?" And yet, he continues, there are weaknesses that cannot be overlooked. He finds "many lines of rare beauty" in "Our Beautiful Land by the Sea," but he cannot help thinking while reading it of Poe's "Annabel Lee." Some of Mr. Mair's diction is also doubtful: " 'infant thunder' reminds one of the Indian who informed a missionary that he had climbed a certain mountain where he was sure the thunder lived. On getting to the top, however, he couldn't find the 'big thunder,' but he saw where the little thunders had knocked the bark off the trees 'trying themselves.' " It is therefore to be hoped, remarks Sangster, that it will be only in Mr. Mair's "first installment of poetry" that the reader will find "panting rain," "iron tears," and bees who are "fickle creatures, coy and hard to please." But such blemishes "are mere specks on the sun," and he is confident that "when Mr. Mair favours the public with another volume, it will be . . . of such a character as to fully realise the warmest anticipation of his friends."

Mair was quite pleased with Sangster's review. "You can imagine," he later said to John Garvin, "how a youth's heart has stirred at this bit of praise from the best Canadian poet of the time, in some respects even of time to come."[24]

The absurdities in *Dreamland* went virtually unnoticed by Canadian reviewers. The *Globe* noted instances of "doubtful taste," "false accents" and "obsolete idioms." The Toronto *Leader* thought "Mr. Mair would do well to tone down the warmth of expression in some of his poems, particularly in 'Dreamland,' where the subject could be very appropriately treated without the use of the same fervor of expression which we find fittingly enough in the amatory poetry of Swinburne." But the English critics were not so kind. The London *Saturday Review* of November 28, 1868,[25] devoted this paragraph to the book:

> A volume of poems by Charles Mair requires the excuse of youth which the author modestly pleads. Not that there are no signs of poetic feeling and taste, and of a limited degree of power, but that the author is too prone to allow both his fancy and his rhyme to run away with him; the former

[24]MP, July 8, 1918.
[25]XXVI, 731.

betraying him into the wild incoherences of a dream, the latter into little less than actual nonsense. The critical as well as the creative faculty is necessary to poetry, as to all authorship, and we must say that we have seldom met with a work in which the utter lack of it was so clearly and so naively displayed.

The January, 1869, number of the *Westminster Review* commented:

As usual, the approach of Christmas is heralded by a number of minor poets. Their poems, like Martial's epigrams, are of all kinds, good, indifferent, and bad. Mr. Mair's method of describing a shower, "One shaggy cloud wept / Great puddling drops," is more original than poetical. He certainly, too, goes farther in his Pre-Raphaelitism than an artist should do, when in his minute description of the "chipmunk," he tells us "That should you wag a finger through the air / 'Twill snudge away beneath the balsam bush." In short, Mr. Mair's method of writing poetry may be briefly described as using words which all other people would avoid. . . . We would advise . . . Mr. Mair to take the old advice—*verbum insolitum tanquam scopulum vitare*.[26]

And the London *Morning Star* of March 22, 1869, while admitting that Mair had proved himself "to be the possessor of some at least of the characteristics of a poet," could not say that "these first fruits of a young Canadian poet's reveries" formed an exception to the received rule that "the New World has been strangely barren in original poets."

The derivative aspects were more generally observed than were the lapses in taste, but again the transatlantic attitudes differed. The New York *Albion* insisted that "Mr. Mair is not an imitator," but that "if he were, it would be to his credit that he has turned his back upon the troubled waters of modern poesy for purer and clearer draughts from 'the wells of English undefiled.'" The London *Morning Star* was far less ambiguous. Influences, it said, were "plainly traced" and "unpleasantly marked"; and it was to be hoped that Mr. Mair would be heard of again "in some work of larger and more original scope."

Mair's own Canada First associates offered some of the most interesting commentary. According to Morgan, the opinion was general that *Dreamland* was the finest collection of poetry to have appeared "in any of the provinces of the Dominion." He had not seen the English reviews, but they could not be other than favourable, he assured Mair, considering "the high expression of public approval which the merits

[26]XCI, 138–39. Said Denison: "If that is all the fault they can find, you can stand it, for the word ['snudge'] though uncommon, is expressive, and perhaps the best suited to the idea" (MP, Denison to Mair, March 10, 1869).

of the book has [*sic*] drawn forth on this side of the Atlantic."[27] One can understand, then, Morgan's petulant snappishness when he later wrote his friend: "I suppose you have seen the ill-natured criticism . . . in the *Westminster*. Just like the English, when writing of things Canadian. They do not understand us."[28] George T. Denison, whose poetic sensibilities are indicated by his favouring "The North Wind's Tale," probably the weakest piece in the volume,[29] was also inclined to judge the work on patriotic grounds. "I have told you," he wrote Mair, "of the favourable impression your book has made in our circle." Individual selections such as "The Pines," "Night and Morn," and "Our Beautiful Land by the Sea," he said, "cannot be surpassed," and he had little doubt that the book would be well received in England.[30] Denison's own *Modern Cavalry* was itself currently undergoing the strictures of English criticism, both literary and military. He complained to Mair: "I hear the Army officers . . . are shy about buying it —that is, the mass of them. They think—aw—that—aw—demn'd impertinence—aw—Volunteer—aw—Colonist—aw—aw, etc., etc. Thus logically do they argue against my book." And like Morgan, Denison considered the English literary critics quite incompetent to review Canadian works:

These English papers cannot endure the idea of Canadians interfering in what they conceitedly think they alone are qualified for. I suppose you heard of the way in which the London *Review* attacked me on the ground that I was a Colonist, Provincial, Colonial writer, Canadian, etc.—the same feeling operates against you, but unfortunately for you none of them know enough to appreciate your poetry as we do. I was showing some of your poems to a young Scotch gentleman of literary tastes, and with an evident desire to criticize, what do you think he pitched upon as a fault? Your reference to the Hemlock where you say it "Drunk deeply of mist at the break of a cloud." He said that was not a correct idea as the Hemlock was a small tree. I told him the height of the large Hemlock when he told me he thought they never grew twenty feet high. Giving him "The Voice of the Pines" to read is like throwing pearls before swine— and that, I expect, is a sample of the critics who in England will criticize your book.[31]

A few weeks later Denison consoled Mair: "Critics are proverbially severe on young poets. Lord Byron got his share of severity and lived through it, and I have no doubt you will do the same."[32]

[27]MP, Oct. 25, 1868. [28]MP, April 4, 1869.

[29]MP, Denison to Mair, Dec. 10, 1868. Denison's daughter, Mrs. W. Langmuir, commented to the author of this book: "My father had no poetic feeling whatsoever."

[30]MP, Dec. 20, 1868. [31]MP, Jan. 8, 1869. [32]MP, Feb. 3, 1869.

There is no record of Foster's opinion other than that already referred to. But R. G. Haliburton, both personally and publicly, made some of the most genuine of all the *Dreamland* criticism. Unlike Denison and Morgan, he considered Mair's work objectively—or tried to—as literature. In the Halifax *Daily Reporter* of July 13, 1869, he noted how refreshing it was to find "the sunshine that pervades his poems," and to see "none of that dismal sentimentalism" that seemed to be the current poetic fashion:

Take Tennyson's *In Memoriam* for instance. Everybody vows that it is perfection. To us, while it reminds us forcibly of Moschus' Epitaph on Bion, it is still more suggestive of the poetic tendencies of our neighbour's Newfoundland dog, that keeps us awake by howling all night a canine *In Memoriam* over some departed Towser. We often feel, while in the semi-dreaming state in which he keeps us, ready to swear that that dog must have got that dismal poem by heart, and is trying to set it to music.

Mair, he wrote, was not given to howling: "he sings a cheery strain that seems like an echo of the glad voice of the woods and the waters"; his verse was vigorous—the delineation of the "mysteries of nature" by "an ardent and thoughtful student."

But, also remarked Haliburton, Mair had his faults, "youthful faults of manner, slight affectations, such as are observable in the 'haw-haw' of the sub, and the obsolete archaisms of the young poet." The first great object of all writing, he noted, is to be intelligible to the reader, and "the greatest authority on the sublime tells us that peculiar phrases, unless they have peculiar force, are a blot." When Mair next came before him as a poet he hoped that he would adopt "a more simple style, and that he will speak to living men in the living language of the age."

More important, however, was Haliburton's plea for a valid literary nationalism. Like Denison and Morgan, he wanted to see *Canadian* writing, but unlike them, and unlike Mair himself at this point, he was not concerned with equalling or competing with English models:

In this new Dominion we must bid goodbye to the literary grave-cloths of former years, and strive to create a new school that will interpret the fresh new life of a young nation.

Need we suggest to [Mair] that "Comus and his jolly crew," as emigrants to our woods, are as much out of place as a medieval tournament or Colonial peers would be at Ottawa.

Canada had a fresh, untrodden field for poetry, especially in the West, he reminded his readers. The boundless prairies, the buffalo, the "savage and semi-civilized hunters," the trappers, the half-breeds, were all better worth study "than Swinburne's Atalanta or Milton's Comus." About a year later Haliburton wrote Mair that he had been re-reading *Dreamland*, and, still insisting that "these archaic words set me damning," he repeated his earlier plea:

For God's sake drop the old style. You're living in a new world and you must write in the language of the living to living men. . . .

Most Canadian poets should be published with mild *Eau Sucrée* style of names—such as "Midnight Musings," or what is more to the point, "Nocturnal Emissions!"[33]

The criticism of *Dreamland*, favourable and unfavourable, Mair seems to have taken much more sturdily than did his friends of Canada First. His letters reflect virtually no animosity towards the negative reviews; indeed, fifty years later he was to insist that he had "greatly benefited by their strictures."[34] At the time of publication, however, his thoughts were being engaged in matters far removed from *Dreamland*. The book appeared in late September; but Mair apparently had just enough time to celebrate with a few Ottawans before leaving the capital once again, this time for a place much farther away than Lanark or Perth. Denison, commenting on Mair's "getting so drunk in honor of the issue of [the] book," implied that "out there," his friend must miss such occasions.[35] "Out there" was Red River settlement, Rupert's Land.

[33]MP, Aug. 24, 1870. For some reason J. P. Matthews (*Tradition in Exile*, p. 99) has changed Haliburton's last sentence to "Most Canadian poetry is still dominated by the sugary titles tacked on to them, such as 'Midnight Musings', or what is more to the point, 'Nocturnal Missions' "—surely neither as appropriate nor as expressive as Haliburton's actual words. The last word, of course, was probably misread from an indistinct handwriting, but the exclamation point and a postscript immediately following, commenting on the recent evacuation of Nancy, France, should have provided a clue to Haliburton's indelicate flippancy.

[34]MP, Mair to Garvin, Jan. 7, 1924.

[35]MP, Denison to Mair, March 29, 1869.

IV. Red River

ALTHOUGH CANADIAN HISTORIANS have sketched Charles Mair's activities immediately prior to his arrival in the North-West, they have been mainly concerned with the later, momentous events at Fort Garry. And they either have not heeded or have not known the quite dramatic circumstances in Mair's life that led directly to those events. But for a business recession Mair might have continued at Queen's in 1858 and eventually have engaged in medical practice, perhaps in Lanark or Perth. Instead, he turned his intellectual interests towards writing and towards learning all he could about the North-West. The one led to his appearance in Ottawa in 1868 with a book of verse, and the chance meeting that resulted in the founding of the Canada First party. The other led to correspondence with John Schultz and the decision eventually to join Schultz at Red River. All available evidence indicates that Mair had every intention of returning to Queen's in the fall of 1868. But again a significant circumstance intervened.

During his visit to the capital Mair attracted the attention of the Honourable William McDougall, the Minister of Public Works in the Federal Government. McDougall was the parliamentary member for Mair's own riding of North Lanark and evidently had been befriended by the Mair family; but through the zealous Morgan he became particularly aware of young Charles, and in June, impressed by Mair's intelligence and patriotism, he asked him to undertake some work for him, work appropriate to their shared interest in the North-West. The acquisition by the new Dominion of the Hudson's Bay Company territories—that enormous tract of land drained by the rivers flowing into Hudson Bay and granted by royal charter in 1670 to "The Governor and Company of Adventurers of England trading into Hudson's Bay"—and the settlement of these lands were necessary in the implementing of the Confederation vision of a Dominion extending from sea to sea, and the Canadian Government was taking steps to arrange for the transfer. McDougall and George Cartier were to go to England to treat through the Imperial Government with the Company. It was believed that the negotiations might end in litigation, the Canadian Government maintaining that the Company's rights were titular, not territorial, and confined to localities around its posts. McDougall therefore asked Mair, while he was awaiting the publication of his verse, to return to Ottawa and "to undertake the work of collecting and collating the authorities, the old treaties and others bearing upon the question"[1] in the Parliamentary Library. The work was completed much to McDougall's satisfaction and, having prepared the précis and packed the authorities upon which it was based for shipment to England, Mair was asked by his employer to accompany him to England as his secretary.

Mair's acceptance of the appointment, although it would mean a further delay in his medical studies, was due to a number of interrelated factors. His intention to become a doctor was not strong, being based almost wholly on his father's wish and his own hope of emulating and eventually joining Schultz at Red River. His unexpectedly fortunate connection with McDougall placed matters in a new light. As secretary to the Minister of Public Works at such a momentous time, he would be in an inestimably valuable position to further not only his own interests in Ottawa and in the North-West, but also those of the group to which he was pledged—Canada First. Another factor in his decision was undoubtedly the character of McDougall himself. Mair was in many ways a hero-worshipper. Six years before, the adventuresome and energetic Schultz had become his exemplar, and since the beginning of the summer the proud and masterly Denison had undoubtedly been a dominating influence. Now, another strong personality, that of a man already politically prominent, already selected, it was rumoured, to be the first Lieutenant-Governor of the new western territory, was attracting his attention. Considered somewhat cold-blooded and reserved, McDougall was nevertheless respected as very able; and that he liked Mair and was willing to foster his career is evidenced not only by his placing him in a position of responsibility but also by remarks he made later in correspondence.

[1]MP, MS., "Article for *Free Press*," *ca.* 1905.

Furthermore, the common interests of the two men were not limited to North-West matters: "I was never more surprised," said Mair, "than when . . . the Hon. Wm. McDougall gave me a number of privately printed sheets of his own poems, . . . and excellent they are. He was . . . one of the last men, indeed, whom the public imagined to be given to poetry, yet such was the case."[2] The relationship, therefore, augured well, and Mair must have felt highly elated over the

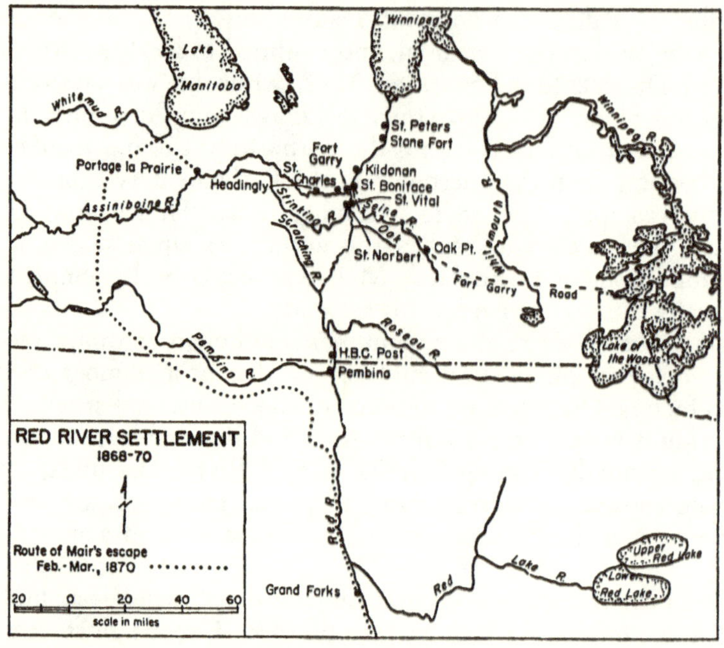

rapid change in his circumstances. Only a year before he had been a merchant in Perth and Lanark; for a few months he had been a medical student at Queen's; then, in quick succession, he had become a member of a group of bright, patriotic young men devoted to an important cause, an author of a highly acclaimed book of verse, and the personal secretary to one of the most promising men in Canada.

But even again Mair's plans were changed by an unexpected event. John Macintyre, his high school tutor, had died in 1859; now, in the

[2]MP, Mair to Garvin, July 8, 1918. The verse, now in the Mair Papers, was written and published by McDougall during a visit to Denmark in 1873. Titles such as "Hamlet's Grave," "The Knave's Cross," and "Grave Questions," and a generally ironic morbidity characterize the collection, which, however, is well documented by scholarly introductions and footnotes.

fall of 1868, his widow, Mair's sister Margaret, was seriously ill and under the care of a specialist in St. Catharines. Mair went to her bedside; and McDougall, who was about to sail, and "whose repeated telegrams to Perth were neither opened nor forwarded by my mother, who expected me by every train,"[3] was compelled to make other arrangements for a secretary. Mair reached Ottawa as McDougall was leaving and had just enough time to be told informally by McDougall what he was to do instead of going to England. The official notification, dated October 1, 1868, recorded that

> . . . the Hon. the Minister of Public Works has been pleased to give you an appointment on the Fort Garry Road under the Superintendence of Mr. Snow, as Accountant and Paymaster. You will proceed at once to St. Paul, Minnesota, and place yourself in communication with Mr. J. McDougall, who has charge of affairs concerning the Road, at that place, and who will direct your further movements—Mr. Snow having, no doubt, left ere this for Fort Garry.[4]

Mair records that he hesitated to accept the new appointment "as this would interfere with my medical studies for a long period."[5] Yet he had only just before agreed to go to England and to risk the possibility of lengthy negotiations over the transfer. Perhaps he felt a little disheartened, as Professor W. L. Morton has suggested, at the prospect of passing the winter of 1868, "not at the heart of Empire, but on the verge of the North-West prairie."[6] He quickly realized, however, that to go to Red River now was merely to accelerate what he had planned to do later. Furthermore, McDougall had made the appointment with careful, if brief, deliberation. He knew that Mair's attitude towards the necessity of western expansion was similar to his own; he knew also that Mair's proficiency as a correspondent could be invaluable. Thus, as Mair related, McDougall "urged me strongly to go, and describe the country, a sealed book as yet to the Canadian people."[7] His Canada First associates were no less aware of the appointment's significance: "At once we saw the opportunity," said Denison, "of doing some good work towards helping on the acquisition of the territory."[8] And Foster was to arrange with George Brown of the Toronto *Globe* that Mair should be the paper's North-West correspondent.[9] By first-hand accounts he would help to advocate the

[3]*Master-Works*, p. lvi.
[4]MP, Dept. of Public Works (F. Brawn) to Mair.
[5]*Master-Works*, p. lvii.
[6]*Alexander Begg's Red River Journal*, p. 20.
[7]*Master-Works*, p. lvii.
[8]*The Struggle for Imperial Unity*, pp. 13–14.
[9]DP, 3881, Mair to Denison, Nov. 29, 1899.

policy that Brown, the editor and proprietor, had in common with McDougall.[10] Influenced by all these factors, Mair consented, and by doing so became the first overt proclaimer of the principles of Canada First.

William McDougall sailed from Quebec on October 3 and Mair, after hasty preparations and a visit to his family in Perth, left Ottawa by rail a few days later. The two men travelled in opposite directions, but their purpose was the same—to help bring about what they felt would be a greater, more unified Canada. Each had talents that seemed to qualify him exceptionally well for his task. McDougall, whose responsibilities were political and legal, had been trained as a barrister and had been in 1867 a "Father of Confederation"—had been made, indeed, a Companion of the Order of the Bath for his part in the framing of the B.N.A. Act. He believed fervently in Canada's need for immediate expansion in the West, and had eloquently and forcefully advocated this expansion at every opportunity. Mair's duties were less precise, less professional. He had neither McDougall's education nor his experience; but he had the same nationalistic spirit, the same enthusiasm for the West. Above all, he reflected promise of being a sensitive observer of life around him and a fluent writer. Both men took pride in the amount of reading they had done about the West; and in this fact there lies, perhaps, the source of one of their common weaknesses. Their conception of the territory and people beyond the Great Lakes was, by necessity, largely academic. It was also characterized by Upper-Canadian nationalistic prejudices. Both men, unfortunately, were to rely upon this conception even after actual experience had indicated they should do otherwise.

It is beyond the scope of this work to deal with all of the many complexities of the Red River uprising of 1869–70, still one of the most controversial episodes in Canadian history. A large part of the controversy, however, is centred in Mair, and any attempt to understand some of the more significant happenings at Red River must take into account his character and personality. Was the part he played a series of acts of high heroism inspired by devotion to his country? Or was it the folly of an ignorant and bumptious young man, causing by his clumsiness irreparable racial antipathies? Historical comment has been contradictory to even this degree, especially when such comment has itself been stimulated by racial, even regional, prejudices.

[10]McDougall, like Brown, was a "Clear Grit." In 1850 he had founded the *North American*, a Reform newspaper that merged with Brown's *Globe* in 1857.

Despite his enforcedly hasty departure from Ottawa Mair began his adventure as best he could. In his pocket he had a letter of introduction from his friend, the Reverend Aeneas Macdonnell Dawson of the Cathedral of the City of Ottawa, to the Right Reverend Monsignor Taché, Bishop of St. Boniface, in which Dawson emphasized that "Mr. Mair's great abilities have commended him to the notice of the leading people" of Ottawa, and that, although "Mr. Mair is not precisely of our communion . . . , Dr. Pusey himself does not surpass him in respect for Catholics."[11] And when he reached Toronto, Mair took advantage of a stopover, as his expense account reveals—"revolver and ammunition, $15.25"[12]—to prepare himself even further for the eventualities of the West.

The letters that Mair wrote to his brothers Holmes and James—letters immediately given to the Perth *Courier* and subsequently copied by the Toronto *Globe* and other papers—provide a detailed record of his trip to Fort Garry as well as considerable critical comment on the land and peoples he encountered on the way. The letters in fact are so full of information and are so enthusiastic about the greatness of the new land that with certain exceptions they were almost certainly intended not for private reading but for newspaper publication as a form of "immigration literature." Until he received official appointment from George Brown of the *Globe*, Mair could by this "private" correspondence carry out the objective of McDougall and his own Canada First group—the extolling of the West as a land of untold wealth and opportunity. For him, indeed, Canada First was becoming more than just a political attitude.

From Toronto he travelled, as did all who wished to get to Red River in less than a month, by rail to Chicago, and thence by a combination of water, rail, and road to Fort Abercrombie, North Dakota, where he hoped to overtake superintendent John Snow and his party. The trip under the best of conditions could only be an arduous one, but Mair, either because of youthful enthusiasm or because of his patriotic obligation, reveals little if any sense of hardship. Petty annoyances are not mentioned or are treated humorously, and the more obvious deprivations concomitant with travel through a primitive West are either understated or are exploited as intrinsic to the romance of the great new land. The letters in fact continually emphasize the ease and comfort that the new settler would experience once he has left his Ontario town or farm. In the Montreal *Gazette* of

[11]MP, Oct. 6, 1868.
[12]MP, "Statement in detail of travelling expenses," 1868.

December 25 (and the Toronto *Globe* of the 27th), Mair reported that after three days on the train to Chicago and LaCrosse, he journeyed by "immense" steamer up the Mississippi to St. Paul, "a splendid two day's sail" made constantly enjoyable by "magnificent and striking" scenery. A further seventy miles by rail brought him to St. Cloud "in time to attend Judge Donnelly's political meeting"; and "four splendid horses, changed every fifteen miles," pulled his stage-coach to Sauk Centre, fifty miles farther west. There, "after great difficulty" (which he does not detail) and "valuable fact! only on account of being a Mason," he obtained a driver to take him to Abercrombie, another 125 miles, "where I found Mr. Snow, the Surveyor, waiting for me."

Mair and Snow then travelled together the 225 miles to Fort Garry, this time by a horse and buggy bought by the latter at St. Paul and with "every luxury, even *condensed milk*, an admirable thing." The record of this part of the journey reads like an idyllic travelogue:

We passed through a most beautiful country, parts of which were perfect paradises of lakes and hills, swarming with ducks, geese, brant, and every species of game. The prairie chickens were literally in millions, and occasionally a large elk would bound away and then stop and stare at you and begin eating quite unconcernedly. This was the greatest place for game I ever saw, and wherever we stopped for meals at the little outposts we had invariably elk roasts or steaks. Some of the lakes were extremely beautiful—one especially, Pelican Lake, surpassed in loveliness of outline and colour anything I had ever heard or read about; it baffles description.

In the Perth *Courier* of January 14, 1869, he writes of the same trip, and with the same modest estimate of his abilities to describe it:

No description of mine can convey to you an idea of the vastness and solitary grandeur of these prairies. Sometimes for a whole day you will drive through a perfect ocean of luxurious grasses now yellow and decaying, and perhaps the next day your tracks will be through an immense expanse of inky soil where the prairie fires have consumed the herbage. The prairies are a dead level, and the traveller drifts along in a sort of dream between earth and sky over roads as solid and even as marble. There are no such roads in the world as those which nature has provided here, and when one begins to be cut up, all you have to do is to go off a few feet over the prairie and trot ahead at top speed. You can drive in any direction, north, east, west and south, at full gallop with a carriage and four, if you wish. . . .

Mair and Snow reached the edge of the Red River settlement one evening in late October just in time to hear "the convent bells of St.

Boniface sounding sweetly over the water"[13] and within a few minutes had registered at "Dutch George" Emmerling's hotel.

But Mair's stay at Emmerling's was brief, for he lost little time in finding his correspondence friend, John Schultz; and for the few days prior to his leaving with Snow to set up road headquarters at Oak Point, thirty miles to the east, he lived with Schultz at the latter's combined medical dispensary and trading store. There is no extant correspondence between Mair and Schultz prior to 1869, and it is therefore difficult to determine whether or not Mair had more than superficial knowledge about Schultz's standing in the Red River settlement. This point is of some importance because historians have emphasized the "error" committed by Mair and other "Canadians" in intimately associating themselves with Schultz.[14] To Mair especially, however, such association was not an "error"; he had long before established at least a correspondence acquaintanceship, had found a kindred spirit, an ideal, indeed, by it, and now quite naturally wished to know Schultz personally. If Mair was aware before he arrived at Red River that Schultz was extremely unpopular among the great majority of the settlement, it must be concluded that he would have discounted such an attitude as being unreasonable and short-sighted, for Schultz represented to him an *avant-coureur* and agent in Red River not only of his own theories on North-West expansion, but also of those of the Minister of Public Works and of the Canadian Government itself. In any case the two men immediately became close friends.

An understanding of the basis of Schultz's unpopularity requires at least a summary account of the state of affairs that had been developing at Red River during the few years prior to Mair's arrival—a state of affairs in which Schultz was only one, if an important, factor.

Central, of course, were the *métis*, whose leader, Louis Riel, was to give his name to the uprising of the following year. A people of mixed French and Indian blood and the product of an already old partnership between trader and native, the *métis* in 1868 accounted for about one-half of the population at Red River. Whether they were still, as Professor G. F. Stanley sees them, a primitive people living mainly as nomads by hunting and trading, or almost the opposite, as Professor W. L. Morton maintains, an already civilized society about to evolve completely from nomadic to settled existence, it can be agreed that the *métis* were an ethnic and political entity

[13]Toronto *Globe*, Dec. 27, 1868.

[14]See, for example, W. L. Morton, *Begg's Journal*, p. 23, and G. F. Stanley, *The Birth of Western Canada*, p. 54.

zealous of its rights as a people—as a "new nation." Endangering those rights was the impending transfer of the North-West from the government of the Hudson's Bay Company to that of the Dominion of Canada. The transfer itself need not have been cause for alarm; it had been regarded for some years as inevitable by most inhabitants at Red River, including at least the *métis* leaders. But by 1868 there were strong indications that the terms and conditions by which the transfer was to be effected would seriously affect the *métis* as a corporate entity. Foremost of these indications was the acknowledged purpose of the Dominion Government to open the North-West to the settlement of great numbers of immigrants from eastern Canada; but even as late as the time of formal negotiations for the transfer there had been no attempt on the part of any authority—Imperial, Dominion, or Hudson's Bay—to inform the *métis* of their place in the new province. There were further reasons for their anxiety, which can be more properly examined in reference to the other factors that complicated the situation at Red River; but the *métis* were pivotal amidst a number of other groups that eventually resolved themselves into two factions—that supporting the transfer and that opposing it.

Of this latter group the most altruistic were undoubtedly the Roman Catholic clergy. These men had been working valiantly for many years to bring the *métis* into the Church and to extend the formation of French culture in the West; they therefore quite naturally feared the sudden and—to them—premature influx of Anglo-Saxon Protestants into their parishes. As intelligent, well-educated men they realized that the civilizing of the North-West was inevitable, but they were neither ready for it yet nor pleased about the form it appeared to be assuming.

For the officers of the Hudson's Bay Company at Red River the transfer had implications far more personal than it had for the clergy. For them it meant the end of a rule, of a system by which they had enjoyed almost caste-like privileges. And they well knew that to many easterners, William McDougall among them, their employer was the *bête noire* obstructing the progress of Canadian nationality in the West, and that when the new government assumed control they themselves could expect little charity. The transfer would also mean competition, even disruption, in the fur trade over which they had so long enjoyed, if not a monopoly (which they had in theory by charter), certainly a secure supremacy. These officials, therefore, could easily sympathize with the *métis* even though they might not actively support them.

Another group not favouring the transfer were the Americans both in the settlement itself and across the border in Pembina and St. Paul. These men, either actively or passively, were annexationists. Those in the settlement were generally willing to await what they considered inevitable—the incorporation of the North-West into the American republic. But those at the border and in St. Paul, particularly one Enos Stutsman, had for some time made it plain that they would actually aid any resistance to Canadian expansion in the North-West. To Canadian nationalists generally and the Canada First group especially, these men would represent the direst threat of all—continental union with the United States.

The *métis*, the Roman Catholic clergy, the resident officers of the Hudson's Bay Company, and a few Americans were therefore the main elements that viewed with various degrees of apprehension either the intention of the Canadian Government to take over Rupert's Land or its means of executing that intention. And they, with certain free traders and a considerable number of English-speaking colonists —mainly Scots and Irish— who approved of the transfer only on specific terms, constituted by far the major part of the Red River settlement. As a whole, they were a complex group of varying loyalties, but if any one element was actively to resist the transfer the others could be depended upon for at least moral support.

Concentrated against them were the so-called "Canadian party"—or "loyalists," as they described themselves—a small band of men who not only fully approved of the transfer but also openly advocated its necessity. Some of them, English-speaking colonists and free traders, had counterparts on the opposing faction. The "loyalist" colonists, however, regarded the transfer as a matter of simple allegiance to the flag. Some of them, like Sgt.-Major Michael Power, were British Army pensioners, or like Murdoch McLeod had come from as far as the Hebrides to serve with the Hudson's Bay Company and had afterwards entered farming and free trading. Among this colonist group was also a number of Canadians from Upper Canada who had followed the exploring parties of S. J. Dawson and H. Y. Hind in 1857. The free traders of Winnipeg, however, were the most significant element of the Canadian party. Unlike their counterparts of the opposition, they were bitterly hostile to the Hudson's Bay Company, but their antagonism was not only that of the independent trader against a powerful business competitor. These men resented the Company's commercial position, but far more odious to them was its title to millions of acres of land and its governmental control over that land's inhabitants. And their most active and outspoken representative was John Schultz.

Dr. John Christian Schultz had had a stormy career at Red River since his arrival there in 1861. Perhaps he had never really intended to practise medicine, for within a year he had established a lucrative fur trade and a thriving general store. In 1865 he had acquired control of the settlement's only newspaper, the *Nor' Wester*, and had continued with ever increasing frankness the policy on which that paper had been founded—the necessity for ending Hudson's Bay rule and for opening the country to settlement. Because of this and other factors, by 1868 he had emerged as the most notorious figure in Red River. In 1864 he had been instrumental in forming a Masonic Lodge; in 1867 he had married a Miss Anne Farquharson just in time to prevent her conversion to Roman Catholicism; and in early 1868, after refusal to pay a debt in favour of his half-brother and partner, Henry McKenney, he had had to be taken to jail by force. In this affair even his release was dramatic. No sooner had he been carried off by cariole than his bride of a few months "forthwith caused all the doors and windows to be barred and secured with nails and spikes, so as to guard the shop against a fresh entry on the part of the Sheriff." Then,

> towards one o'clock on the Saturday morning about fifteen persons, among whom was Mrs. Schultz, forcibly entered the prison where Schultz was confined, overpowered the constables on duty, and, breaking open the door leading to his cell, liberated him. This done, the party adjourned along with him to his house, where report says "they made a night of it."[15]

The special *Nor' Wester* of the following day not only presented Schultz's side of the story but also took the occasion to point up the complete incapacity of the Hudson's Bay Company as both a judicial and executive authority.[16]

Schultz is one of the ambiguous personalities of Red River history. He obviously had many qualities of the natural leader: he was strikingly handsome, of great physical strength, aggressive, ambitious, decisive, and intelligent. He was also known as a man of kindness and reserve, even of scholarship; articles he wrote on Red River botany had been recognized by the Botanical Society of Canada and those on primitive western fortifications and on the Eskimo later led to his election to the Royal Society of Canada. Certainly among his devoted

[15] J. J. Hargrave, *Red River*, p. 426.
[16] *Ibid.*, app. G, p. 504.

Canadian party associates he was an almost archetypal figure of the national patriot and champion against tyranny. Professor Morton fairly concedes: "He sincerely sought to develop the North-West; he saw its possibilities with the vision of the statesman as well as the eye of the speculator."[17] Schultz's enemies and many other historians, however, saw not the visionary statesman but only the arrogant speculator. The *métis* and clergy disliked his Masonic Protestantism and feared his bold expansionist policies; the Hudson's Bay Company resented his abusive vilification of its authority; and those traders and colonists of the settlement who opposed the transfer found it easy to distrust him as a selfish, unscrupulous adventurer. Even today Schultz's character continues to stimulate opinion ranging from honest fascination to prejudiced or sensational acrimony. To W. L. Morton he was "a sinister paradox,"[18] to R. E. Lamb, a "bellicose . . . contemptuous . . . carpet-bagger,"[19] and to Joseph Kinsey Howard, "an ambitious meddler . . . ruthless and bigoted."[20] Before he died he was also to be Sir John Christian Schultz, F.R.S.C., F.B.S.C., Lieutenant-Governor of Manitoba and a very wealthy man.

Charles Mair's immediate association with Schultz at Red River was not in itself a matter of resentment to the anti-Canadian group. He himself records the warmth of welcome extended to him by representatives of both the main factions: "We had a very pleasant stay at Fort Garry and received all sorts of entertainment," he reported in the *Globe* of December 27; "they live like princes here"—even to the extent of "nuts of all kinds, coffee, port and sherry, brandy punch and cigars, concluding with whist until four o'clock a.m." Schultz gave a party, he wrote, at which "there were three English Church clergymen, including the archdeacon, and a number of young ladies with music, chess, and what not." And at the home of Alexander Begg, an anti–Canadian party free trader, the *Globe* of January 4 recorded, he was offered "hospitalities to my heart's content." Begg himself easily recalled a few years later that the young poet from Canada "received the hospitalities of many families" during his early days at Fort Garry.[21]

But such initial relationships were soon put to test. Mair and Snow made their headquarters in a log and mud hut at Oak Point and prepared to build their road. As Mair reported in the *Globe* of December 27, however, "I have bought a splendid train of dogs and can

[17] *Begg's Journal*, p. 22.
[18] *Ibid.*
[19] *Thunder in the North*, pp. 10–11.
[20] *Strange Empire*, p. 88.
[21] *The Creation of Manitoba*, p. 17.

ride into the Fort in seven hours easily" (although "seven hours" hardly seems "easily"); and by Christmas his intimacy with Schultz and his support of the Canadian party had become obvious enough to cause resentment where previously there had been friendly acceptance. Begg, who had been one of Mair's hosts, now noted that both Mair and Snow had "severed the confidence there may have been felt in them by the respectable settlers" by their "joining hands with this ultra and dangerous party."[22]

The activities of the road party itself were also a matter of concern, particularly to the *métis*. Actually, the Canadian Government had as yet no right to construct a road over what was still the territory of the Hudson's Bay Company, although some authority for the project did exist in the oral permission Snow had received from Governor Mactavish. To those *métis* and settlers, however, who were suffering famine following a grasshopper plague of the previous summer, the announced intention of the road party to provide money and provisions in return for work was more than welcome. But the first trees were hardly felled when news of trouble was reported back to Fort Garry. The relief programme had proved a disappointment: fewer men than expected were hired, and these few (about forty) claimed their wages were low. In addition was the more serious charge, according to J. J. Hargrave, "that Messrs. Snow and Mair were purchasing from the Indians portions of land to which the actual occupants laid a pre-emption claim."[23] The actual occupants were *métis*, and such was their indignation, said Hargrave, that "Mr. Mair was brought to Fort Garry under compulsion of an excited crowd of French half-breeds who required he should forthwith quit the country as he was, in their opinion, a man likely to create mischief."[24] Governor Mactavish intervened, however, and "after some altercation" Mair was permitted to return to work. Snow was not quite so fortunate. For having sold liquor to the same Indians he was fined ten pounds in Petty Court and later accused by Riel of trying "to seize the best lands of the *métis* . . . at Oak Point."[25]

Because of the welter of conflicting evidence and bias it is difficult

[22]*Ibid.*, pp. 20–21.

[23]*Red River*, p. 458.

[24]*Ibid.* Hargrave, however, confused this episode, perhaps intentionally, with another; see p. 74. Bishop Taché in his deposition (Report of the Select Committee, Canada, *Journals of the House of Commons*, VIII, app. 6, p. 9) stated: "Mr. Snow's companion then came to my house to see me, and to ask me to interfere. He also stated that he had requested the half-breeds of Point du Chêne to come with him to me, and that they refused to do so. . . ."

[25]Morton, *Begg's Journal*, doc. XXVII, "Memoir by Louis Riel," p. 528.

to determine the truth of these charges. Hargrave, nephew and secretary of Governor Mactavish and no supporter of Mair, admits that the episode he himself reports was the result of a "misunderstanding about payment" for work on the road.[26] The Mair Papers include "private vouchers" from Mair to Alexander Begg for considerable quantities of brandy and gin, but such transactions between a trader and the paymaster of a road party would hardly be unusual. Snow's sale of liquor was proved; but surely it is irresponsible to state blandly, as Joseph Kinsey Howard has done, that "Snow started dickering with the Indians for property . . . and one of his favorite mediums of exchange was whiskey."[27] Professor Morton suggests instead that there may have been "some *treating* of Indians to induce them to tolerate the claim-staking."[28] In any case these irritations might have been forgotten or pardoned if they had not been aggravated by Mair himself, not only by his association with Schultz, but also by what Begg described as his "preaching a doctrine sufficient of itself to cause distrust in the minds of the Red River people."[29]

This "doctrine" was contained in the supposedly private letters Holmes and James Mair gave to the newspapers and in those Mair himself later sent when he was appointed special correspondent. And that the young poet from Ontario either did not realize that his commentary on the West would "cause distrust in the minds of the Red River people" or, if he did, was indifferent to such a consequence, offers a further reflection of his character and personality. In either case he saw himself as a professional writer from the East with a responsibility both to his own newly acquired reputation as a man of letters and to his special appointment as a governmental agent. Certainly, Mair's correspondence as it eventually appeared in the *Globe* and *Gazette* offers some of the most vivid descriptive prose ever written in Canada. It is an effortlessly fluent prose, revealing a rich vocabulary and indicating occasionally that same sensitivity to sights and sounds that mark the better lines of *Dreamland* (Mair's notebooks give ample evidence of his propensity to jot down whatever interested him at a particular time). The letters are lengthy—in some cases over 2500 words—but they are consistently stimulating. A description of the prairie may be followed by historical or even geological comment. That of "a genuine out west political meeting" includes the humorous "tall tales" related by the speakers and the earthy, sarcastic observations of their listeners. Begg and the anti-Canadians of the

[26]*Red River*, p. 458.
[27]*Strange Empire*, p. 87.
[28]*Begg's Journal*, p. 528, n. 5.
[29]*The Creation of Manitoba*, p. 21.

settlement could not have objected to Mair's graphic account, for example, of Judge Donnelly addressing the voters of St. Cloud, Minnesota:

The court room was a very republican affair indeed—a cheerless, bare room fitted with undressed, unbacked deal seats, and a sort of low bar-room counter at the upper end, behind which were an ordinary chairman and Mr. Donnelly. Mr. D. had risen even physically with his argument and a decided change had been wrought in his face by dint of assumed or real earnestness. The massive head rolled proudly over the short, stout body, and not only in the eye, but in the whole countenance, there was something which reminded one strongly of McGee. But the eye lacked the melancholy light, and the countenance the kindly clumsiness of the man of genius. . . . Sometimes his language was brutally coarse and vindictive and his anecdotes horrible. But it was evident enough that this was merely the sop to Cerberus, an obscene rhetoric addressed to the groundlings. Speedily casting aside the garbage of the demagogue, he clothed clear and incisive thought in chaste and elegant language and illuminated all by illustrations drawn from the purest sources. The whole man became transfigured. The voice, a powerful one, an admirable instrument, was by times sonorous or gentle, according to the agitation of his thoughts; so accurate was the accent, so admirably poised the manner that no discrepancy whatever existed between the idea and its expression. His denunciation of slavery, a subject upon which our language has rotted and festered for ages, was unique and terrible; not in a pollution of epithets, but in condensed thought, ribbed with language as with fire. It was perfectly charming to listen to this man forgetting himself and his audience, and perfectly horrible to think that after all he was a demagogue, and a mere instrument in the hands of others. He seemed to feel the degradation, and suddenly swooping like an eagle upon carrion, he again regaled his audience with malignant sarcasm, and anecdotes redolent of the slums. In this he touched the level of his auditory, who, men and women, laughed and applauded vociferously.[30]

This passage not only describes Judge Donnelly; it also reflects much of Mair himself. The style is vivid and forceful, but quite self-consciously so. It is that of a writer who seems capable of giving

[30]Montreal *Gazette*, Feb. 27, 1869. Judge Ignatius Donnelly (1831–1901) was one of the most brilliant—and unconventional—personalities in nineteenth-century America. A prominent politician, he was also a remarkably erudite and prophetic writer. Among his more notable literary works were *The Great Cryptogram* (1888), in which he presents the thesis that Francis Bacon wrote the Shakespearian plays, and *Cæsar's Column* (1890), a novel in which he forsees (in Baconian fashion) many of the marvels and horrors that the twentieth century has actually experienced.

detail but who is more at ease with the broad stroke, the generalized, the even caricatured, impression. It abounds with open vowels and rolling phrases; it approaches the rhetorical in its use of metaphor and simile—"the sop to Cerberus," "the garbage of the demagogue," "rotted and festered," "pollution of epithets," are only some of the terms Mair uses to describe language. But the passage is characterized by not only a romantic style. Mair's attitude towards Donnelly and "the groundlings" is highly critical. He views these people almost as anthropological oddities quite removed by customs as well as by miles from the norms of eastern society. And in some respects, of course, they were; fact and folk-lore often merge in the history of the West. But Mair never fails at least to imply the role in which he wishes to be seen by the reader. He is aloof from this society; yet he can understand it—and judge it.

But by such interpolated accounts of the incidents and events that befall the frontier traveller or the immigrant, Mair made his pictures of the West more vivid to the eastern reader. The river steamers, the mule trains, the Red River carts, the Indians, the half-breeds, even the white settlers, are richly portrayed as features of a strangely grand new country quite beyond the experience, if not the romantic imagination and yearning, of the inhabitant of civilized Ontario. It is when Mair's depictions seem particularly exaggerated, a little too lush, even though always maintaining a tone of sincerity, that the reader is reminded that the letters were written not just for their own sake nor, as Hargrave rather innocently—or ironically—suggested, "to vary the monotony of existence in the backwoods."[31] As the *Globe* of May 28, 1869, remarked on one of them: "the very clever and interesting letter of our correspondent in the North-West is animated by a spirit of Canadian patriotism worthy of admiration." That patriotism was directed towards convincing Canadians in the East of the desirability of settlement in the North-West and of the great possibilities there for a rich future.

So far as he had yet seen, Mair informed his *Globe* readers,

> the country is *great*—inexhaustible—inconceivably rich. Farming here is a pleasure—there is no toil in it, and all who do farm are comfortable, and some wealthy. What do you think of a farmer within a bowshot of here, being worth seven or eight thousand pounds sterling, and selling to the Hudson's Bay Company last week £5,000 stg. worth of cattle: a man who came from Lower Canada nineteen years ago, not worth sixpence?

[31]*Red River*, p. 451.

Or what would the young farmer back in Ontario, "ploughing and cursing among his rocks," think if he were told

he could run a furrow for miles through a vegetable loam two feet deep? He has heard of Minnesota, perhaps, and its boundless prairies, but Minnesota is *sand* compared to this. . . . What would he think of the puzzle-headed and very unscientific Mr. Amable Ducharme (the ignorant, yet something agreeable old fellow from whom we rent our headquarters) reaping, two summers ago, fifty-seven bushels of wheat for two and three-quarters planted?

Care and science are indeed unnecessary "in a land, which, as Douglas Jerrold was wont to say 'When tickled with a hoe, laughs with a harvest,'" in a land "upon whose bosom has withered the enriching and procreant vegetation of centuries—land which drops fatness, as if in the fulfilment of prophecy; at once generous and abundant and more durable than its tiller." Beyond Red River is the prairie:

There the awful solitude opens upon the sight and swells into an ocean, and the eye wanders over the "silent space" of the West. The man must be corrupt as death who, unaccustomed, can look unmoved upon this august material presence, this calm unutterable vastness. Man is a grass-hopper here—a mere insect, making way between the enormous discs of heaven and earth.

Portage la Prairie is not just a thriving settlement; it is really a *portal*, through which will flow "the unspeakable blessings of free government and civilization." It is there that the Canadian "for the first time clearly recognizes the significance and inevitable grandeur of his country's future." Far behind him are "his glorious old native Province[s],[32] the unsullied freedom of the North, the generous and untiring breed of men." Before him "stretches through immeasurable distance the larger and lovelier Canada—the path of empire and the garden of the world." And many Canadians are needed—"manly, intelligent, industrious young Canadians from all parts of the Dominion"— to lay the foundation of Canadian feeling,

and to extend to the further ocean the warmth of a purely indigenous sentiment without which we can never become eminent as a nation. Canadians have but to come here, and look upon inexhaustible resources, sleeping on the lap of a domain which is boundless, to imagine the possibilities of our future. Let our brain-work be wide ranging, sustained,

[32]Thus Mair corrected his own copy of the *Globe*; but it is highly likely that his letter read simply "Province," as the newspaper has it.

earnest and truthful, our handiwork dexterous, thorough and effective, and this generation of Canadians may yet look upon our country elevated from the humble condition of a mere dependency to that of a notable Power in the most notable Empire in the world.[33]

The letters seemed to justify the high hopes of McDougall and Mair's Canada First friends when they had urged him to open "the sealed book" of Rupert's Land. The Toronto *Globe* of June 11 remarked that "the greatest interest has been manifested in every section of Ontario in the letters . . . from Mr. Charles Mair," and emphasized with some specificity Mair's call for settlers; "We hope to see," it said, "a new Upper Canada in the North-West Territory—a new Upper Canada in its well-regulated society and government—in its education, morality and religion." Denison wrote Mair of his pleasure in reading "such good accounts . . . of the great North-West," and added, characteristically, that "together we the Men of the North (as Haliburton says) will be able to teach the Yankees that we will be as our ancestors always have been, the dominant race."[34] Morgan complimented Mair on his "good service in attracting attention to the country," and added (just as characteristically) that the letters had at the same time brought Mair himself to prominence: "I have heard great praise bestowed upon them, from men whose praise is worth having—men like Tilley, Gray, Dawson, S. J. Morris, Haliburton."[35]

In the same letter Morgan remarks *en passant* that Governor Mactavish had commented while on a recent trip to Brockville, Ontario, that Mr. Mair had been "too lavish of praise of the country." Said Morgan: "sour grapes"; but Mair referred to the charge in his letter to the *Globe* of May 28. Governor Mactavish, he maintained, would not dare to speak like that in the West: "It is one thing to be the chief of a fur-trading monopoly and an enemy to Canadian extension. It is another thing to be a Canadian with no personal interest to serve, but jealous for the prosperity of Canada, and anxious, like thousands of others, that something good and great may be made out for her." This relatively unimportant literary exchange reflects dramatically not only a number of attitudes and biases towards the transfer of the North-West but also the manner in which they were coming into conflict. Morgan's assessment of the Hudson's Bay Company's position as "sour grapes" is superficial. Mactavish's charge of exaggeration

[33]Toronto *Globe*, Jan. 4, Feb. 16, May 14 and 28, 1869.
[34]MP, March 10, 1869. [35]MP, April 4, 1869.

typifies the attempts made by the Company to call into question the agricultural possibilities of the North-West and at the same time, in conjunction with Mair's reply, exemplifies growing personal antipathies. Most significant, however, is Mair's bold invitation to "him or anybody else" to take issue with his reports, for only a few weeks before he had undergone what was meant to be a humiliating experience.

The *Globes* containing the first two or three of Mair's letters had begun arriving in the settlement some time in January, 1869. To a people already tense over recent events and the implications of the approaching transfer, the letters were little short of sensational. Their glowing accounts of the possibilities of the West were in themselves enough, as Begg states, to cause "distrust" among the settlers and natives. But such accounts were only part of the "doctrine" to which Begg objected; certain passages of a more personal nature were far more infuriating. The *métis*, said Mair, "are a harmless obsequious set of men and will, I believe, be very useful here when the country gets filled up." But, he continued, they are "a strange class"; they "will do anything but farm, will drive ox-trains four hundred miles—go out on the buffalo hunt—fish—do anything but farm." The *métis*, indeed, said Mair—and this annoyed many settlers receiving or awaiting assistance as a result of the famine—"are the only people here who are starving"; of the rest, "not one of them requires relief other than seed wheat which they are quite able to pay for." To add to this impression of a lazy, self-indulgent *métis* and to that of himself as a rather superior being viewing the lower orders with disdain was one especially offensive paragraph:

After putting up at the Dutchman's hotel . . . I went over and stayed at Dr. Schultz's after a few days. The change was comfortable, I assure you, from the racket of a motley crowd of half-breeds, playing billiards and drinking, to the quiet and solid comfort of a home.** I was invited to a dinner-party at Beffs [*sic*], where were the Governor's brother-in-law, a wealthy merchant here, Isabister,[36] and other Nor' Westers. Altogether, I received hospitalities to my heart's content, and I left the place thoroughly pleased with most that I had met. There are jealousies and heart-burnings, however. Many wealthy people are married to half-breed women, who, having no coat of arms but a "totem" to look back to, make up for the

[36]Mair's handwriting was unusually beautiful and clear, being characterized by a firm, even stroke. But the printer evidently had difficulty with "Begg" (Beff) and "Inkster" (Isabister). The Governor's brother-in-law was A. G. B. Bannatyne, Begg's trading partner. Inkster was either John or his son Colin, both prominent "Nor'-Westers."

deficiency by biting at the backs of their "white" sisters. The white sisters fall back upon their whiteness, whilst the husbands meet each other with desperate courtesies and hospitalities, with a view to filthy lucre in the back-ground.**[37]

Mair surely never intended that such lines would be made public and had hoped his brother Holmes would use greater discretion in giving them to the papers. He later defended them as the reflection of "the usual freedom and flippancy of a private letter to a friend," and himself as a victim of "an unpardonable indiscretion" that "allowed the letter to be published *verbatim*." No one, he insisted, could possibly have felt more sincere regret than he did when the letter appeared in print: "I had received much kindness in Red River, and certainly bore no feelings of dislike or ill-will to anyone. But political and monopolist antagonisms ran high, and . . . this letter . . . , amongst sensible people, at any other time would have only provoked a smile."[38]

The offending letter Professor Morton describes as "in execrable taste";[39] to anyone familiar with Mair's previous career it reveals interesting echoes not only of the lapses in *Dreamland* but also of Mair's youthful intractability and self-confidence. J. J. Hargrave, indeed, noted that the only review of Mair's poetic work he had seen was the short, uncomplimentary paragraph in the *Saturday Review*, which "set forth certain characteristics of the poet which have recommended themselves as true to a number of people who have enjoyed the opportunity of observing his public conduct under prosaic circumstances."[40] But the question of taste, "execrable" or otherwise, is here really only part of a larger issue. Mair, as an aspiring young literary figure and member of a group of Toronto and Ottawa notables, was very conscious of the niceties of social decorum; Haliburton's criticism in respect of the "haw-haw" of the subaltern points, indeed, to Mair's rather superior opinion of his own graces. And it was partly because he considered so many people of Red River to be without the refinements of manners he respected as *de rigueur* in Ontario that he could write such a letter. All of Mair's early correspondence, in fact, and not only this one letter, reflects a young man who feels himself to be superior, socially, culturally, and politically, to the inhabitants of the West, and who is writing to other Canadians like himself, prospective immigrants of "the right class."

[37]Toronto *Globe*, Dec. 14 and 27, 1868; Jan. 4, 1869.
[38]Letter to the Saskatchewan *Herald*, March 15, 1880.
[39]*Begg's Journal*, p. 19. [40]*Red River*, p. 450.

The tone throughout the letters is of condescension or of tolerant amusement; but it reflects a writer whose social pretensions limit his art. For if Mair had actually been what he thought himself to be, his writing would have been mannered, temperate, more dispassionately satirical—that of the cultivated man. His depictions of western society, however, reveal him as a young snob, and are couched in language sometimes quite as vulgar as the scenes purportedly being described.

And yet it is quite likely that any other member (perhaps excepting Haliburton) of the Canada First group would have, with equal literary talents, written just as Mair wrote. And so might any number of other Upper Canadians of similar background and attitude. Unfortunately for Mair, he was the one who took it upon himself to imply that the blessings of the civilization he represented would soon effect a change in the West. When the monopolistic paternalism of the Hudson's Bay Company was extinguished, real progress would begin, a progress that would incorporate people such as the "harmless" *métis* because they were "very useful," but would not accept them as equals. And despite Mair's references to "manly, intelligent, industrious young Canadians from all parts of the Dominion," the letters leave no doubt about who should settle the West. The new land must be populated by British stock because, first, it was simply superior, and second, such expansion as resulted would accelerate both the unification of Canada and the consequent assumption of her rightful place in the Empire.

The punishment Mair received for expressing his views on Red River society was even more debasing than any meted out to him twenty years before by dominie Mason. Hargrave records that one of the first reactions was that of "Dutch George" Emmerling, who "threatened that should the author of these philippics ever enter the house he had maligned, he should be expelled."[41] Much more severe was the anger of the Red River ladies:

> One lady pulled the poet's nose, while another used her fingers rudely about his ears. A third confining herself to words, said his letters would be productive of serious mischief by circulating doubts about the reality of the destitution, of which they gave an account highly calculated to mislead and to paralyse the efforts being made to raise money abroad for the relief of the suffering poor. She therefore recommended that, as the poet had obviously overstepped the limits of his privilege, he should be treated in the same way as are dealers in stimulants of another character under similar circumstances, and have his license taken away.[42]

[41] *Ibid.*, p. 456. [42] *Ibid.*

The scene at the settlement post office, as recorded by Abbé Georges Dugas, the Roman Catholic director of St. Boniface College, was even more violent:

Mair, having committed the indelicacy of writing, in the Ontario papers, some words offensive to the women of Winnipeg, underwent the humiliation of being horse-whipped in the town post-office, by the wife of one of the most notable citizens, Mrs. Bannatyne.[43] She asked the clerk of the store in which the post-office was located to let her know when Mair came at his regular time on Saturday at four o'clock in the afternoon, when the store was full of people. Daniel Mulligan, the clerk, seeing Mair coming, ran to tell Mrs. Bannatyne. She quickly threw a shawl on her head and arrived like a bomb at the post-office; she held a large whip in her hand. Without hesitating, she seized him by the nose, and administered five or six strokes of the whip to his body: "There," she told him, "you see how the women of Red River treat those who insult them."

The scene lasted only half a minute. But it seemed long to Mair who hastened to leave, daring neither to speak nor retaliate. That evening the episode was known throughout the district.[44]

Also that evening, according to Hargrave, "Mr. Mair had a somewhat stormy interview" at the same post-office with some of "the husbands who meet each other with desperate courtesies and hospitalities with a view to filthy lucre in the background." Mair tried to explain that the letters were private correspondence, but this served only to emphasize the sincerity with which he had described the settlement. And the asterisks following the most insulting statements "opened up long, dim vistas of uncertainty and surmise" in respect of what else he might have written, comment that his brother had decided should be suppressed. At the same time Mair hinted that he expected a more objectionable letter to arrive momentarily, unless a warning to his brother had reached Perth in time. For several weeks "the arriving 'Globes' were carefully scrutinized by an interested circle of acquaintances in hopes of seeing the poet's apprehensions justified. Their anticipations were, however, disappointed, in consequence either of the means taken by Mr. Mair to stop the publication having been successful, or of some other deterrent cause unknown."[45]

The unfortunate affair made Mair the object of all the resentment that the majority of the populace felt for the Canadian party. A

[43]The wife of A. G. B. Bannatyne, the Governor's brother-in-law, and almost certainly a guest with her husband at Begg's dinner-party.

[44]*Histoire véridique*, p. 27. The quotation is translated from the French of Dugas.

[45]*Red River*, pp. 455–57.

"French gentleman" wrote to his friend Hargrave: "The indignation against Mr. Mair is going on furiously."[46] According to another witness it was so great "that he was ordered to leave the territory," but through the intervention of Governor Mactavish he was allowed to return and remain "after apologizing to the leading half-breeds and promising that he would write no more letters of such a nature."[47] This latter report probably inspired Joseph Kinsey Howard's glib, spiteful, *and* inaccurate comment that Mair "apologized abjectly, abandoned journalism, and thereafter confined himself to epic verse."[48]

Mair's enemies made certain that their impressions of his early conduct at Red River would never be forgotten. Hargrave, Begg, and Dugas were not only antagonistic participants or spectators in the events of this time and afterwards; they were also, to varying degrees of proficiency, journalists, and some of their works have become basic documents. Begg in particular carried on a form of literary harassment, and among his many writings is what is considered the first historical novel of the North-West, *Dot-it-Down*, a smugly naïve and rather clumsy satire in which Mair plays a notorious role and for which—by his propensity for note-taking—he even provides the title. In the work other prominent personalities are thinly disguised by similar pseudonyms.

Dot, "a stout, dumpy, little fellow," enters the story during a performance of some Red River theatricals, where he "appeared to think himself of more importance than the whole of those in the room put together" and where "by his loud remarks, and sometimes sneers, he made himself so disagreeable that at last the door keeper was obliged to admonish him to keep a little more quiet" (pp. 252–53). The next day, while confined to his room "from the effects of a debauch at the Everling Hotel," he is visited by Cool (Schultz). Cool tells him that his party "wants someone of influence to strike a death blow at that great monopoly, the Hudson Bay Company," upon which Dot cries, "I am the man; for I know all about that from the time of the charter down to the present day. I've made it a study." Thus "Cool and Dot became fast friends from that day forward" (pp. 274–75).

As Begg describes Dot, he is a bumptious and cocksure young man constantly trying to impress the modest, hospitable Red River folk with his social and literary prowess. He is also depicted as a would-be

[46] *Ibid.*, p. 455.
[47] Thomas Spence, deposition, Report of the Select Committee, Canada, *Journal of the House of Commons*, VIII, app. 6, p. 133.
[48] *Strange Empire*, p. 86.

gallant, too free with both wine and ladies. At a dinner-party given by Mr. Bon (Bannatyne?) his drinking leads to the following scene, some details of which were probably inspired by Mair's comments to the press and their consequences:

... he happened to be sitting in a corner of the room in close conversation with the young lady to whom he had taken such a violent fancy.

"Haw (hic), he said, "what a lucky dog am I, to be in such an (hic) enviable position. What pleasure it gives me to be able to sing the praises of the Red River belles in their primitive (hic) loveliness! Ah me! I will represent them on the banks of the winding streams—their wigwams beautifully (hic) sit-situated beneath the noble, spreading branches (hic) of the stately oak; their (hic) flowing tresses will (hic)—Haw! my dear!" Here followed a huge wink, and then the loud report of a hard slap could have been heard across the room, and "Dot" realized, as well as he could at the time, that it was no joke making fun of the Red River ladies, for his cheeks burned and his eyes blinked from the effects of the blow administered by the indignant girl.

Dot, repressed momentarily, soon recovers, and eventually brings the party to a crashing finale when, "in trying to stand upon his head, his heels came in contact with the table, overturning it, and dashing wine glasses, tumblers and decanters in a heap upon the floor" (pp. 280–82).

Begg saves his most uncharitable insinuations, however, for the depiction of what was undoubtedly his own dinner-party—the same one to which Mair had referred in his letter to Holmes. "We find him in a gentleman's house," he relates, where

great pains had been taken by the host to prepare a creditable repast on the occasion. Several of the prominent men in the settlement were invited to meet the correspondent and his friend [Snow?], and there was every reason to expect a pleasant evening.

The dinner passed off very well, "Dot" however, carrying on the principal part of the conversation, chiefly in sounding his own praise, etc. etc. "Dot's" friend said very little, being a man of few words, with, moreover, a great respect for "Dot's" fund of learning; he consequently felt somewhat fluttered in expressing himself before the great correspondent. After dinner a quiet rubber of euchre was proposed, and a couple of sets were immediately formed. "Dot" insisted on playing for stakes, although it was objected to by several in the room.

... "Dot" found that he had old hands to deal with, and when he rose from the table he was several pounds sterling poorer than when he commenced. After the game of euchre, "Dot" nearly got himself into serious trouble, for he was discovered by the hostess in the kitchen making violent love to one of the domestics belonging to the house; a pretty girl be it said, to "Dot's" credit as a connoisseur.

"I fear you have made a mistake, sir," said the lady of the house. "This is the kitchen."

"Haw! yes, deuce take it, but what's the odds. I am travelling for information."

"Surely not in a culinary way," replied the hostess, smiling.

"Not particular, my dear madam, anything now-a-days will satisfy the public taste in Canada. I should like to describe how the people live; that will be interesting I am sure; besides," he continued, "this little dear," (chucking the girl under the chin.[49]

"If you have no more respect, sir, for me in my own house than to make love to one of my servants before my face, I will call my husband. You had better, I think, join your friends in the sitting room."

"Deuce take the people in Red River," muttered "Dot", "they are confoundedly particular about trifles." With this he left the kitchen.

"Dear me," said the lady, "if this is the way newcomers are going to behave themselves, I don't want to see any of them here again."

Once again the affair ends in debauch at "Everlings," but the next day Dot reports the dinner-party in a letter to the press—leaving out, of course, says Begg, "the scene in the kitchen." When "the gentleman who had shown the hospitality" read the account later, he was "highly indignant, and resolved to be more careful in the future when asking strangers to dine with him" (pp. 286–88).

Soon Dot's only friends are Cool and Sharp (Snow); but after several brushes with the law and the righteous folk of Red River—one is over claimstaking—these three are reduced to utter disgrace and leave the settlement. "Ah! Canada, how your champions suffered for your sake! Ah! Canada, how you have also suffered by their deeds." Sharp becomes the proprietor of "a third-rate boarding house" in St. Paul; Cool disappears to some other community where "assuredly there was trouble in store for them"; and Dot,

the unfortunate correspondent, found to his cost that he had got into bad company, and felt that he was consequently a loser by the connection. His land speculations were frustrated by the action of the settlers in the matter. His expenses while in Red River had been enormous, through his extravagance, and he found that he possessed few friends on account of his untruthful letters to Canada. He, therefore, decided to follow in the footsteps of Cool; and it is to be hoped when he reached Canada he tried to make some reparation for the evil he did while in Red River. But we fear

[49]The half-line and missing parenthesis is unexplainable except by faulty proofreading, although one is tempted also to suggest censorship.

his malady, so far as speaking slightingly of the North-West people, was beyond redemption. Some unknown wag presented "Dot", on the day of his departure from the settlement, with a leather medal, on which were inscribed the words—

"For Services in the North-West,
"Haw!
"Dot that down!"

(pp. 354–56)

How much of all this can be accepted as a realistic depiction of personalities and events at Red River is difficult to determine. Begg certainly deviates from fact when he disposes of his villains: Mair, Schultz, and Snow were to play even more dramatic roles in the near future. His characters and situations, although they may have historical basis, are mainly caricatures—Begg did not have the skill to make them otherwise—and must be accepted, as Professor Morton remarks, at a judicious discount.[50] The pseudonyms Begg employed also allowed him to express a personal resentment—hardly conducive to objectivity—and to express it in perfect safety from charges of slander.[51]

The fact remains, however, that Begg had basis for his satire. And unfortunately for Mair, his own friends have helped to confirm the impression that Begg created. Haliburton, in his review of *Dreamland*, refers to him as appearing "as brimful of fun and frolic as a schoolboy . . . as if cricket or croquet, boating and flirting, were more likely to be engrossing his thoughts, than the quiet mysteries of nature."[52] Foster, fearing that Mair's "residence in the West . . . has destroyed . . . an appreciation of intellectual supremacy," notes Mair's "unfortunate if not immoral" recollections, in one of his letters, of their evenings together in Ottawa: "Chambermaids! Orgies! Ah me! Morgan, Mair, Denison. Oh me!"[53] Morgan writes that he trusts Mair has resisted "temptation in the shape of women and whiskey,"[54] and later, referring to an "interesting document" he has received from Mair, remarks:

—interesting in more ways than one, as the feather which you enclosed will testify. I have it still (the feather) and will carefully preserve it as a

[50]*Begg's Journal*, p. 20.

[51]In 1885, however, appeared *The Story of Louis Riel*, a fictitious history of no indicated authorship (but written by Joseph Edmund Collins, a "friend" of Mair) in which Mair is named and his letters made far more sensational than they actually were.

[52]*Halifax Daily Reporter*, July 13, 1869.

[53]MP, Foster to Mair, June 10, 1875.

[54]MP, Oct. 25, 1868.

trophy of your prowess in the land of the Dacotah. . . . In your next you must tell me something of the society at the Settlement, and of the number of pretty girls on the census roll. Speaking of girls reminds me that information has reached here of a little mishap on your part with a little feminine Nor' Wester. Haliburton and I had a good laugh over it, but the elderly gentlemen frown dreadfully, and say all sorts of things against you.[55]

Denison recalls that the last time he had seen Morgan and Mair together, "you had both taken the pledge—and the next I hear of you and see of Morgan is a 'bust' in each case. But such is life."[56] From Denison also comes a picture of Mair cutting a gallant figure on the main street of the settlement by means of the latest Toronto fad:

You ask me to buy a velocipede for you and send it up to you—I have not done so for several reasons—

(1) A really good one costs I believe more than you mention.

(2) The express fare and *duty* on entering the States would add largely to the cost.

(3) Perhaps you are not aware of it but they are of no practical use out of doors in this country. They require a very smooth hard road or pavement; they are used here mainly in schools or rinks boarded over and people go and ride on them as they skate in the winter time—In Paris I saw them in use on some of the quiet streets, but there the streets are as hard and smooth as a floor.

(4) None have yet been made with a place for the bottle of grog and the Sandwich.[57]

Mair's friends in the East treated his adventures with the good humour and tolerance that acquaintanceship and distance could allow. They remembered the youthful larks of the "Corner Room" at the Revere Hotel and they sympathized with Mair in his self-imposed banishment. As Denison said: "I do not doubt that you are lonely enough out there, and you ought to have some friends—white folks—with you. It is not right you should be entirely alone among those wretched, half-starved half-breeds."[58] The comments of Mair's western companions, however, reflect their awareness of the settlement's resent-

[55]MP, April 4, 1869.

[56]MP, March 10, 1869.

[57]MP, April 22, 1869. The velocipede or "bone-crusher" was the fore-runner of the modern bicycle. The Kingston *Daily News* of March 23, 1869, reported that in that city the two riding schools (one in the city hall) were doing "a flourishing business," but that operating a velocipede seemed to be a "work of much difficult labour" and that those "aspirants who are the most reckless appear to have the best success."

[58]MP, March 29, 1869.

ment towards him. Returning from a visit to Mair's Oak Point headquarters a few days after the inflammatory *Globes* had reached the settlement, Schultz reports that when his party sought quarters for the night at a previously friendly half-breed's, "much to our surprise we were refused admittance—refused in fact point blank until the young lady in charge was assured that Monsieur 'chuchacheese' was not with us."[59] John Snow, on the way back to Ottawa, writes from St. Paul: "Contrary to our understanding, I find the St. Paul people know all that has transpired at Fort Garry as well as ourselves; everything has been duly reported, even Mrs. B's attack on you. . . . Do try to keep quiet and out of harm's way."[60] Obviously nervous, Snow repeats his warning a few weeks later, this time from Hull.[61]

From Mair himself there is little even to be guessed concerning the charges against him. The liquor vouchers in the Mair Papers are doubtful evidence; other documents are similarly ambiguous. Three days after Mr. John Garrioch had reported from Portage la Prairie that there was "a perfect misunderstanding" between Mair and the Indians over what land "they would allow immigrants to occupy,"[62] Mair wrote to McDougall that he had applied "a modest pressure" upon the Indians by "pointing out their insignificant numbers compared with the incoming multitude and the obvious necessity, hence, of acting friendly and honestly."[63] In the same letter, however, he decries the methods used by certain land-seekers and advises McDougall that one of the greatest problems will be "to devise a method of distributing Indian annuities in such a manner that they shall be of real service to the recipients and not find their way into the pocket of the rum-seller as soon as paid." The only indication of Mair's personal acquisition of land is a quit-claim deed between himself and one Charles Demerais, with Schultz as witness, by which he bought a thousand square chains of property at Portage for eighty pounds sterling—a quite reasonable price.[64]

The memory, certainly of his humiliation at the post-office was to haunt Mair for many years; some of the enemies he had created at Red River were to ensure that it did. But in the first months of 1869 he must have felt beleaguered by friend and foe alike. Admittedly, his

[59]MP, Schultz to Mair, Jan. 12, 1869. [60]MP, Snow to Mair, March 29, 1869.
[61]MP, May 19, 1869. [62]MP, Garrioch to Mair, June 18, 1869.
[63]PWF, series 98, subject 429, Mair to Minister of Public Works, June 21, 1869.
[64]MP, July 2, 1869. Schultz, however, eventually owned much of the most valuable land in Winnipeg. Principal Grant of Queen's wrote to Mair (MP, May 11, 1882): "The Schultz lots given to us two years ago and assessed at $30.00 for the three have been sold by us for $1500.00."

Canada First friends treated his indiscretions with good-natured levity. But they had no real conception of the increasingly tense situation in the North-West. There was another friend, however, whose whole future depended upon the manner in which the transfer of the territory was effected, and who had to view the conduct of one of his employees, even though a friend, from a different perspective from that of Denison and company. This was the Honourable William McDougall, who shortly after his return from England wrote to his paymaster-*cum*-correspondent:

I have at last got an Order-in-Council to go on with the roads without waiting for the actual transfer. . . . Mr. Snow takes this letter to you and will explain everything needful to my powers and intentions.

Your letters have created great interest and will no doubt bear fruit. I am flooded with communications of intending emigrants from all parts of the Dominion, partly because of a general rumour that I am to go out as Governor. . . . It will probably be late in the season before the final legal changes are effected. In the meantime the H.B. authorities exercise jurisdiction, but with new views, feelings and interests. It will be your duty while you are in Govt. employ to cultivate the most friendly relation with them. Where there was antagonism there must now be cooperation. . . . I apprehend no serious difficulty for it will be their interest to live on good terms with us. . . .

As to your personal position, salary, etc., I can only say that as your employment is exceptional and temporary I shall deal as liberally with you as I can in justice to the public and the Govt. I regret to have heard some rumours, which upon enquiry I found too true, that prevent me from doing all I had intended in your case. I need not be more precise, but you will at once admit—your own good sense will tell you—that full confidence cannot be placed in one who sometimes forgets himself, and what is due to those who become answerable for his conduct. I hope for the best. Your future is in your hands. You have talents and genius of a high order—don't follow bad examples, or the end will be like theirs. I write you as a friend who is willing and may be able to do you service, but not if you become your own enemy.[65]

There was also another correspondent, but one who obviously did not write "as a friend," and who expressed his opinion publicly in the pages of the Montreal *Nouveau Monde* of February 25, 1869:

Red River, February 1, 1869.

MR. EDITOR:

Please be so good as to give me a little space in the columns of your journal, in order that I too may write of Red River.

[65]MP, June 13, 1869.

I cannot resist that desire since I have read the enormities which a journal of Upper Canada, the *Globe*, has just uttered, in publishing a letter of a certain Mr. Mair, who arrived in Red River last fall. This gentleman, an English Canadian, is, it is said, gifted in making verses; if such is the fact I should advise him strongly to cultivate his talent, for in that way his writings would make up in rhyme for what they lack in reason.

Scarcely a month after his arrival in this country, Mr. Mair desired to describe it and its inhabitants. He succeeded rather like the navigator who, passing by a league from the coast, wrote in his log: "The people of this country seemed to us to be well disposed. . . ."

I know some men who have more than two weeks' experience and who say the opposite to this gentleman. He says finally: *the city of Portage la Prairie is destined to become one of the most important in the country: however, I shall not speak to you of it until I have seen it.*

And why not? You speak of a great many others things that you have not had time to see or know; that would be worth as much as the remainder of your letter; as much as the scarcely courteous terms, I will even say barely civilized, which you use in speaking of the ladies of the country, who certainly by all reports are quite equal to the ladies of your country.

Be it said in passing, Mr. Mair, if we had only you as a specimen of civilized men, we should not have a very high idea of them. If I wished to amuse myself by wielding the pen as you do for the sole pleasure of uttering follies to the world, I should have some amusing things to say on your account. . . .

L. R.

The editor of *Le Nouveau Monde* noted that the letter had been written "by a half-breed . . . rightly indignant of the stupidities which a certain Mr. Mair" had published. If "L.R." was "almost certainly" Louis Riel,[67] he would later have an opportunity to show his indignation in a much more forceful and personal manner.

So Charles Mair, within ten months after he had set out for Ottawa with a manuscript of verse intended to sound a keynote of a new unified nation, had, ironically, by his pen helped to create a situation of potential danger to Confederation itself. By his friends both in the settlement and in Ontario his letters were regarded as part of the propaganda necessary to make an indifferent population aware of their great country; Mair's social conduct they considered unfortunate, but certainly not monstrous. But this Upper Canadian had brought to the

[66]This translation and the original appear on pp. 399–402 and pp. 567–9, respectively, of Morton, *Begg's Journal*.
[67]Morton, *Begg's Journal*, p. 399, n. 2.

West those attitudes and prejudices that had been formed over a period of thirty years and then sharpened by his alliance with a particularly aggressive group of other Upper Canadians; one of them, McDougall, was even a Father of Confederation. In Ontario such pro-British, Protestant attitudes and prejudices could thrive with comparatively little, if any, opposition. In the melting pot of the new West, however, they were bound to provoke conflict.

V. Red River: Insurrection

1. FORT GARRY

THE NEGOTIATIONS for the transfer of the North-West Territory to the Dominion of Canada were completed in March, 1869. As had been expected, they had not gone smoothly, but had been marked by bitterness and by grudging compromise on both sides—especially the Hudson's Bay Company. The main provisions were the surrender by the Company of all its rights and privileges in Rupert's Land, the payment by Canada to the Company of £300,000, a grant of one-twentieth of the land in the fertile belt as well as of acreage around the Company's posts, and the right of the Company to continue trading. When the vastness of the territory involved is considered, the terms were extremely favourable to Canada; but the Company undoubtedly recognized that both time and the spirit of Canadian expansion were against it and that it must salvage what it could. The Canadian Parliament ratified the terms; the date of the transfer was fixed for December 1, 1869, and the Honourable William McDougall, C.B., in recognition of his unceasing efforts to bring the North-West to Canada, was appointed Lieutenant-Governor.

The news of the transfer began reaching Red River towards the end of April; the reaction to it points up the various antipathies and divisions that had been growing for almost a year. It was certainly not hailed, as Denison stated, "with universal joy by all classes of the population of Red River"; nor did the "French, as well as English, look upon it as the consummation of the hopes and wishes of years."[1]

[1] *Reminiscences of the Red River Rebellion of 1869*, p. 3.

To most of the settlement, indeed, this news, which determined their future and which reached them in no official way whatever, meant only an increase in the already obvious tension.

But the Canadian party had every reason to be elated. Some of them had long awaited this momentous event. Schultz, visiting Denison in Toronto a few weeks before the announcement, had written to Mair: "It does one's heart good down here . . . to hear the Hon. H.B. Co. raked up—all classes unite in cursing the monopoly that keeps that great country from Canada. And if the Company *had* a body to kick, many a Canadian shoe would be battered in the service."[2] Shortly afterwards he had emphasized that "Canada *must* have the country —if not by peaceable adjustment in England, then in any way it can be got."[3] Such a feeling of urgency may partly be accounted for by his noting at St. Cloud that "many Canadian emigrants" are on the way "and others fully determined to come" and that "we may expect a considerable immigration and of the *right class*."[4] To John Snow the early demands of the Company for better terms were "monstrous." Far better, he wrote Mair, "leave the old rotten hulk to die a natural death. . . . The event might be hastened by the introduction of a few thousand Canadian emigrants of the right staunch."[5] But in less than two weeks he was able to write his friend with obvious enthusiasm: "The HBC have accepted the terms. . . . *The whole country is now to all intents and purposes ours!*"[6]

To the Canadians of the road party the announcement was particularly welcome. For a number of reasons their work had come to a virtual halt. The first appropriation for the project had been expended; the winter break-up had brought encumbering mud, and perhaps most important, the growing resentment towards their activities—both semi-official and personal—had caused among some of them a state of nervous uncertainty. In May Mair wrote to McDougall that he was forced to employ a man "to continually pass over the track, because numerous fires have lately taken place in the woods," which threatened to attack their bridges and works.[7] In June he reported that the fires had done "immense injury to standing timber," but that it was difficult to ascertain their cause:

The Indians forsake the woods in summer, and the settlers at Point du Chêne protest that they never leave camp-fires burning when cutting

[2]MP, March 6, 1869.
[3]MP, March 19, 1869.
[4]MP, April 1, 1869.
[5]MP, April 3, 1869.
[6]MP, April 14, 1869.
[7]PWF, series 98, subject 429, Mair to Minister of Public Works, May 25, 1869.

timber for their own use. Whatever their origin may be, it is plain enough that stringent measures for protection will have to be taken in order to arrest the agency which threatens the total destruction of the valuable standing timber between Oak Point and the Lake of the Woods.[8]

It is hardly surprising, therefore, that in the midst of what Schultz termed "a silence almost ominous"[9] Mair should turn to the best source of relevant advice he knew—his militant friend, Denison. The colonel's reply is serio-comic, but by its detail probably reflects Mair's concern;

You ask me for some military advice; I shall give it with pleasure. You seem to have all the munitions of war requisite for the size of the garrison. Your magazines of supplies also appear to be ample. The only weak point is the disparity of numbers, the garrison being as small as ordinary circumstances would admit of.

One great difficulty from a military point of view in your position is that your line of communication is so long that it cannot be kept open and is liable to constant interruption. The force of the enemy would also be probably large enough to outflank you and in fact surround you.

The history of war teaches us, however, never to despair, not even in this apparently hopeless condition. Napoleon was somewhat similarly situated in Egypt—and in the midst of a semi-barbarous race. His genius was equal to an emergency. He immediately formed hollow squares, put the provisions, etc., inside, and bade defiance to attacks. Profit by his illustrious example. When you are attacked, form yourself into a hollow square, put the whiskey and provisions inside, and tell them to come on if they dare. If that don't "circumvent" them I know no method of doing it on military principles.

Joking aside, I will send you by post my manual of outposts with instructions for the defence of detached houses, etc. Even if you never require it it will be interesting reading. . . .[10]

Schultz also had been discussing with Denison the possible necessity of military defence at Red River. When he visited Denison in March he insisted that "a corps of Mounted Rifles . . . should be sent there" by the Government "for the protection of Red River Territory as well as for the maintenance of order in it."[11] There was further significance to Schultz's visit: "When I meet a damn good 'Kanuck' like him," said Denison, "I like to see more of him for that is the side I am on."[12] And since Mair had advised it, Schultz was enrolled in Canada First: "Haliburton happened to be in Toronto at the time,"

8*Ibid.*, June 21, 1869.
9MP, April 1, 1869.
10MP, March 29, 1869.
11MP, Denison to Mair, Aug. 11, 1869.
12*Ibid.*

Denison later recorded; "I introduced Schultz to him and to W. A. Foster, and we warmly welcomed him into our ranks. He was the sixth member."[13]

By the end of June work on the road was resumed in earnest, and Mair, perhaps now doubly anxious to please his chief, was able to forward to him a series of generally favourable reports on its progress. He was also gratified to see that large numbers of Canadians were daily arriving, to whom "I have given such aid as lay in my power."[14] The Queen's birthday had been celebrated by a gathering of settlers in Winnipeg, "where they had horse races and other sports,"[15] and "Dominion Day we celebrated by firing a number of shots out of an anvil, hoisting the ensign, and by a bon-fire in the evening."[16] He was sorry to have to add that he understood "the Americans here are to celebrate the '4th' out of the H.B.Co.'s cannon, which . . . were silent both upon the Queen's birthday and Dominion Day." But these and other activities would be fully recounted by Dr. Schultz when he visited McDougall in Ottawa, and by whom Mair was sending "an Indian Chief's dress of antelope skin—beautifully made by the same persons that provided suits to Lord March, Dr. Cheadle and other English gentlemen who have been in this country."

The correspondence and other recorded commentary of Denison, Snow, Schultz, and Mair at the time are a further illustration of the social and racial prejudices that characterized their collective attitude towards the transfer and the various factions involved in it. It is highly unlikely that Denison could really believe as late as 1873 that the news of the agreement had been received "with universal joy" and as a promise of "the consummation of the hopes and wishes" of both French and English. The statements were made in his preface to a slim collection of newspaper articles written mainly by his own friends and acquaintances and reflective of their particular biases. But the articles—especially one by Mair himself—must have indicated to him that "all classes" did not look forward to the transfer. It is quite safe to assume, therefore, that Denison could become blind to the facts when they were unsuited to his own attitudes and objectives; and his remarks, typical, in their bold positiveness, of the man himself, become an early illustration of the sort of propaganda that has influenced English Canadians and the writing of their history texts for years. The colonel's opinion of the *métis* is made explicit enough in his letter of military advice: they are "semi-barbarous," to be sub-

[13]*The Struggle for Imperial Unity*, p. 15.

[14]PWF, series 98, subject 429, Mair to Minister of Public Works, June 21, 1869.

[15]*Ibid.*, May 25, 1869.

[16]*Ibid.*, July 3, 1869.

jugated like the Mamelukes in Egypt or, one can imagine, like the Zulus or the Sudanese Fuzzy-Wuzzies. His entire attitude is in the tradition of the type of imperialistic militarist to whom war is a sort of Public School boy's game, but the boys are in the Mounted Rifles and drink whiskey.

Mair's colonial Canadianism is curiously illustrated by his reports to McDougall. The Queen's birthday, Dominion Day, the Americans and "the Fourth," the Hudson's Bay Company, are all placed into relationships significantly reflective of his prejudices; and his comments on them, one feels, could not have been more appropriately highlighted than by his almost obsequious reference to the dispatch of the Indian costume that had been made by "the same persons that provided suits to Lord March, Dr. Cheadle and other English gentlemen."

More ominous, however, are the remarks of Schultz and Snow. The former's thinly veiled reference to armed force, the latter's proclamation that "*the whole country is ours*," their common insistence on immigrants of the "right class," are manifestly indicative of the imperialistic quality that the nationalism of these men could assume while they were intensely awaiting or exultantly celebrating the outcome of the negotiations. As unrest in the settlement grew, such men could be depended upon to take a decisive stand.

The weeks following the announcement of McDougall's appointment passed uneventfully into those of the summer of 1869. Mair continued to write his letters to the *Globe*, letters no less enthusiastic than before in their praise of the West's natural resources, but now far more reticent in their commentary on the West's peoples. None of his correspondence, however, whether public or private, gives any indication that he attached any significance to the arrival of Louis Riel in the settlement or that he was aware Riel was taking a leading role in the discussions of the increasingly unsettled *métis*. He does record that he engaged in conversation with Riel in June and that the young half-breed visited Pointe du Chêne in July, perhaps to watch the activities of the road party.[17] Mair's duties on the road and with the growing number of immigrants, however, demanded nearly all of his attention, and July and August went by in peaceful, if busy, preparation for the transfer.

[17]Louis Riel had been born in St. Boniface in 1844, had been sent by Bishop Taché to college in Montreal in 1858, and from some time in 1866 to the summer of 1868 had been employed as a clerk in a dry-goods store in Minneapolis or St. Paul. According to Mair (MP, "Red River Memo"—the handwriting of which indicates a date of 1923 or later), "Riel had been clerking at Langevin's store in St. Paul."

Another, more recent, arrival in the settlement Mair came to know well almost immediately. Colonel John S. Dennis arrived in August, authorized by McDougall to begin surveying operations and the staking-off of lands for immediate settlement. Mair may have heard (particularly from Denison, who had served with Dennis) that the surveyor-soldier's previous career had been anything but illustrious—had even been tinged by charges of cowardice during the Fenian raids of 1866; but he quickly accepted him as a friend because Dennis, like himself, committed the "error" of associating with Schultz and the Canadian party.

Dennis's allying himself with this hated group was probably just as reprehensible to the *métis* as his using a surveying system that traversed their long ribbon-like holdings. For, as the official date of transfer approached, such association was further evidence to them of the close connection between Mair, Schultz and other "loyalists" and the incoming Government of Canada. And on October 11, 1869, the *métis* decided to challenge that authority. A party of surveyors near St. Vital, wishing merely to cut across the rear or "hay privilege" of André Nault's farm for the purpose of determining a meridian line, was challenged by Nault and almost immediately afterwards by a group of neighbours led by Riel. The surveyors withdrew, and the first overt act of resistance to the authority of Canada had occurred.

The succession of events that followed the St. Vital episode has been minutely described by Canadian historians, and there is no need to relate it once again here. Relevant, however, is the contribution of Mair's recorded comments, elliptic and disconnected though they sometimes are, towards a fuller appreciation of those events. There was, for example, no doubt in his mind about the purpose of Nault's halting the surveyors. Over half a century later he wrote to his friend, R. G. MacBeth:

I see André Nault is dead at the great age of ninety-five. I knew him well. . . . André at heart was not disloyal to the Queen and was certainly not an Annexationist. . . . Obfuscated by Riel and his gang of Fenians and Annexationists who knew perfectly well that Col. Dennis's running of base and meridian lines would not interfere with any settler's rights and boundaries, through sheer misunderstanding was instrumental in putting an end to the Colonel's work, just as with no occasion whatever for misunderstanding, the same influences put an end to our immigrant road-building. . . .[18]

[18]MP, March 14, 1925. Mair here refers to the *métis* antagonism that was a factor in stopping road construction in the spring of 1869. Operations were resumed, as has been noted, by June.

Particularly noteworthy here (and this is a matter more comprehensively discussed in subsequent pages) is Mair's analysis of Nault's action. The surveyors undoubtedly offered merely a pretext for Riel to take a stand against the Queen's authority. But that stand, as Mair sees it, is not on behalf of *métis* rights. Riel is the leader of a "gang of Fenians and Annexationists," that is, representatives of forces far more dangerous to Canada than the discontent of a people he had called harmless and obsequious.

Whatever his view of the episode, however, Mair was far from St. Vital when it occurred. For him, certainly, as he later remarked, "Events were moving swiftly in Red River."[19] McDougall's appointment as Governor had been made official on September 28; on that same day Mair had telegraphed his chief from St. Paul offering his services pending the arrival of the official party some time in early October. St. Paul is over six hundred miles from Winnipeg, and although Mair was undoubtedly anxious to welcome McDougall, he would not likely have gone so far to do so if another factor had not been influential. He was on his wedding-trip.

Mair's marriage to Elizabeth Louise McKenney was a romantic episode in two careers already excitingly varied. Eliza McKenney was from Amherstburg, Ontario, and could trace her ancestry to at least the first French settlement on the Detroit River by Cadillac in 1701. Her father, Augustus McKenney, was a prominent merchant in Amherstburg, but in 1862 he went to Red River and entered the fur trade. Soon afterwards his health failed, and with his family he returned to Amherstburg—but not without adventure. In 1862 had occurred the notorious Minnesota Sioux massacre in which hundreds of whites lost their lives, and which was allegedly caused by American governmental laxity. Canadian travellers often surrounded their carts with Union Jacks, evidently respected by the Sioux; such identification, according to Mair, saved the McKenneys at Detroit Lake when, surrounded by Sioux, they showed the flag and were consequently "treated . . . with the greatest kindness and hospitality." A party of the Sioux, indeed, "accompanied them for a long way" and they arrived home, "having neither been robbed or molested . . . in the slightest way—Dr. S. being one of the party."[20] "Dr. S." was John Schultz, half-brother of Augustus McKenney and uncle of Eliza.[21]

[19]*Master-Works*, p. xxxvi.

[20]MP, fragmentary notes dictated about 1921 by Mair to his daughter, Mrs. E. J. Cann, and hereafter referred to as "Notes on Early Rebellion."

[21]Mair's father-in-law was not H. O. McKenney, as stated in Morton, *Begg's*

In 1867, when Schultz married Anne Farquharson, he took her to visit his old home at Amherstburg; on their return they were accompanied by Miss McKenney, now eighteen. As Mair later described her, she was a very attractive young woman of medium height, "of an eminently beautiful cast of countenance—liquid brown eyes—very luxuriant dark hair—a graceful figure, and a heart full of tenderness and affection."[22] He has left no record of exactly when he met her and no details of their courtship except that "at this time a great happiness had come into my life."[23] The first meeting, however, might well have been at that early "party at Schultz's" where there were "three English clergymen, including the Archdeacon, and a number of young ladies, with music, chess and what not."

The wedding ceremony was conducted on September 8, 1869, by the same Archdeacon McLean in the old Cathedral of St. John's, and after the wedding breakfast the young couple set out with a single pony and democrat for a camping trip on the plains—a trip that was to culminate in their joining McDougall's vice-regal procession from St. Paul.[24] On September 28 they reached that city, and Mair, after telegraphing McDougall that cart-trains were arriving in St. Cloud in order to transport his party's luggage to Fort Garry, took rooms at the Merchant's Hotel. Within a few days all were together on the way to the settlement. By October 11, the day on which Nault and Riel had challenged the surveyors, they were at St. Cloud, awaiting the transfer of the luggage from the train to the many rigs and carts. Shortly afterwards they were making the long trek across the Minnesota plains. Mair records that "it was a pleasant, happy trip"[25]—although there was a severe storm the day they met the Honourable Joseph Howe, Secretary of State for the Provinces, who was returning from a very brief, unofficial visit to the settlement—and on October 30 the party reached the border village of Pembina. There a *métis* handed McDougall a note from Riel: "Le Comité National des Métis de la Rivière Rouge intime à Monsieur McDougall l'ordre de ne pas entrer sur le Territoire du Nord-Ouest sans une permission speciale de ce Comité."[26]

Journal, p. 166, n. 1. Henry McKenney preceded his brother Augustus to Red River in 1859; both were half-brothers of Schultz.

22MP, "Notes on Early Rebellion."

23*Master-Works*, p. xxxvi.

24Perhaps such a honeymoon trip was not unusual in a community where wedding festivities sometimes lasted for a week. An interesting side-light on the Mairs' trip is revealed by a bill he submitted to the Dept. of Public Works: "Sept. 7, 1869, for brandy, tent, bacon and cash paid for horse—£28, 7s, 6d—to Hudson's Bay Company" (PWF, series 98, subject 429, Mair to Minister of Public Works, March 14, 1871).

25*Master-Works*, p. xxxviii.

26Canada, *Sessional Papers*, 1870, V(12), 11.

McDougall was allowed to spend the night at the Hudson's Bay Post across the border, but the next day he was made to return to Pembina. His Secretary of Council, J. A. N. Provencher, and his chief of military affairs, Captain D. R. Cameron, son-in-law of Charles Tupper, got as far as St. Norbert—ten miles from Fort Garry—but they also were escorted back to Pembina. As Mair's daughter long afterwards recorded her father's memories of the event, Mair stayed with McDougall the night of October 30, advising him to act on the instruction of William Hallett, an old English half-breed and guide to the party with whom Mair had been devising a scheme to get McDougall through the *métis* to the "loyal Portage district." McDougall, however, had been told by Colonel Dennis that "an envoy was to come to take him into Fort Garry" and he decided to remain at Pembina. Mair and his wife were allowed to proceed, meeting on the way the returning Cameron, who advised them not to go on. They did so, however, and shortly after, at Stinking River, met an armed band of *métis* led by Ambroise Lépine—"the supposed envoys"—who stopped them, but eventually allowed them to go on because, stated Mair, he was well known to Lépine and his men, "as they had worked on the road." But at St. Norbert, recalled Mair's daughter, "a guard (Lavallée) called, 'halt' . . . , came forward—Pater knew him also—bars were let down—Mater taken to convent, Pater to Priest's house (Father Ri[t]chot)."[27]

By November 2, therefore, all of McDougall's party was under some form of detention. On that day, also, Riel occupied Fort Garry. No resistance was offered by the Hudson's Bay Company staff in charge, and as a result of initiative and resolute action, Riel was in control at Red River. He unquestionably seized the fort to prevent a similar occupation by the Canadian party; Mair was later to recall that a petition was sent to Governor Mactavish, "setting forth the evil influences at work to thwart us . . . , praying that action be taken by him to restore order," and "offering their [i.e. the Canadian party's] services to garrison Fort Garry." But the offer was "refused" and the post was taken "by Riel and men without resistance and £100,000 worth of supplies."[28] Thus the *métis* leader had not only challenged Canada's right to send officials—surveyors *or* Governor's party—he had also placed himself in a position from which only a well-armed force would dislodge him. Such a force might come from Canada; but it would require many weeks of preparation and travel. The United States might intervene; but Riel would not regard such intervention

[27]MP, "Notes on Early Rebellion."
[28]MP, "Red River Memo."

as unwelcome. Only a general rising of the many English-speaking settlers from districts such as Portage could be a real threat in the immediate future. And on their not taking up arms against him—at least not before the *métis*' case had been properly considered—was the gamble Riel took on November 2, 1869.

Mair was detained in the presbytery of the Reverend N. J. Ritchot, curé of St. Norbert, and since the same rooms were being used, with Ritchot's approval, as the headquarters of those *métis* guarding the barricade, he had ample opportunity to discuss the recent turn of events, both with them and with the priest. With Ritchot he evidently engaged in "arguing over going against the law," the priest even maintaining, "in the heat of an argument, that they had their authority and advice and acted with the knowledge of the Can. Gov^{nt} (the French element—Sir H. Langevin, Caron, and others)."[29] With his *métis* captors Mair's conversations had a more personal note: his own immediate future. The *métis* considered him far too important, in the light of his previous activities in the settlement, either to liberate or to evict from the country. Riel himself had to decide. So for four days, until November 4, Mair remained with priest and *métis*, until "finally, Riel appeared and asked Pater if he asked him to leave country would he go peaceably." Mair agreed, asking only to be allowed "to settle his affairs up";[30] he and Eliza were released and reached Winnipeg the same day.

Whether or not he actually intended leaving the country and just what affairs he wished to settle are questions to which Mair has left no answers. But it is highly unlikely that in the circumstances he would argue with Riel and thereby lose what was surely an unexpected opportunity to return to the settlement. Nor would Riel, an intelligent and understanding man, be indifferent to the claim of a road-party paymaster that he had professional responsibilities to dispose of before he left. There was also the matter of some poetry manuscripts that Mair had brought from Canada and had been preparing for publication:

I had one completed poem (founded on some incidents of the early life of Zoroaster), only awaiting revision for publication and which it was my

[29]MP, "Notes on Early Rebellion." Hector Langevin was then Secretary of State for Canada and Henry J. Morgan's departmental superior. He later succeeded McDougall as Minister of Public Works. "Caron" may have been R. E. Caron or his son, Adolphe, neither of whom was a member of the Dominion Government in 1869. They were, however, eminent French Canadians, Adolphe later becoming Minister of Militia.

[30]*Ibid.*

intention to publish after my return from Red River. I had spent five years over this poem. . . . Another, founded on Ponce de Leon's discovery of Porto Rico, I had begun and made considerable headway in . . . and some prose tales and scattered verses.[31]

Mair does not record that he appealed to Riel's own interest in poetry (the *métis* leader had written considerable verse in the manner of Lamartine); he probably felt, indeed, that the less said about literary matters the better.

Once at Winnipeg, Mair determined to remain. He quickly rejoined his friends of the Canadian party, whose main objective now was to effect McDougall's entrance into the settlement and Riel's ejection from Fort Garry. When Governor Mactavish's proclamation to this purpose was virtually disregarded by Riel the Canadian party saw two courses open to McDougall: he could issue his own proclamation, and he could await a show of force by the English-speaking settlers. Snow thought the first course would be sufficient; "Issue Proclamation," he advised, "and then you may come fearlessly down."[32] But Mair, supremely confident of his chief's authority and of the force of "loyalist" arms, wrote, "The English have not risen, because they have not been called upon. . . . Issue your proclamation and it will be responded to by five hundred men."[33] He did not seem to realize (or perhaps, to care) that McDougall had no legal right to issue such a proclamation; the Governor-designate's tenure did not officially begin until December 1. McDougall, therefore, could only wait as patiently as possible for that date and hope that in the meantime his allies in the settlement could dislodge Riel or do something to undermine his power.

And the opportunity for action by the "loyalists" was not long in coming. Towards the end of November there occurred what the sympathizer with the Canadian party would describe as a decisive stand against odds. To others with perhaps a taste for comic-opera, it was the case of the "Government pork." Recently arrived supplies for the road and survey parties had been stored in Schultz's warehouse. Riel wanted them and so did Schultz. While the former tried to decide whether or not to seize the pork, the latter invited Mair and his wife (who were now staying with the Schultzes) and about seventy other Canadians to barricade themselves in his store and living quarters and there to defy Riel until the *métis* leader bowed to the Queen's authority on December 1.

[31]DP, 725, Feb. 20, 1878.
[32]Canada, *Sessional Papers*, 1870, V(12), 39. [33]*Ibid.*

According to the fragmentary notes later compiled by Mair's daughter, Riel had perhaps foreseen the possibility of his enemy's taking such a stand. Just before the fencing over the Government supplies began,

> . . . with a body of his armed halfbreeds he called at Dr. S. house, Dr. S. and Mr. Mair, who happened at that time to be absent—in the lower parishes attending a loyalist meeting. The only occupants of the house being Mrs. Schultz and Mrs. Mair . . . , Riel entered with a body of armed men with fixed muskets, ascended the stair leading to the drawing room. Mrs. S. being ill in bed [they] were met at the head of the stair by Mrs. Mair who demanded their authority for entering a private house in such a way—it being after dark. She got hold of a little old pistol without a lock and demanded of Riel what his object was. . . . He said he had come to arrest Dr. Schultz. "Why," she said, "if you had known that Dr. Schultz was here, you wouldn't have dared to enter this house." He seemed to be completely cowed and his followers to be thoroughly ashamed—so they turned tail and went off.

Even after the garrisoning of the house by the Canadians, Riel seemed reluctant to take strong measures to dislodge them. The *métis* patrols engaged in games and running races, and Mair recalled that one of the defenders, Thomas Scott, became a part-time bartender at the Red Saloon across the way—a place frequented by Riel, *métis*, and Fenians—in order to spy upon them. On one occasion, apparently, Scott was confronted at the saloon door by Riel and asked what business he had inside. "Scott said he knew best what his business was and brushed Riel aside." According to Mair, "This afterwards cost him his life, for he made Riel his implacable enemy." Eliza Mair, whose "determined courage was the admiration even of the enemy," also showed her disdain for Riel once again. When it was felt really necessary that a number of rifles be brought from Schultz's surgery "she undertook this mission, believing they would not fire upon a woman, and carried the half-dozen rifles to the house and in sight of them all." With such arms and the protection afforded by walls "lined with plates from stoves in the store so bullets couldn't go through," her husband, her uncle, and their fellow "loyalists" were determined to withstand Riel.[34]

McDougall, meanwhile, decided to take desperate measures. Some hours before dawn on December 1 he slipped across the border, and while an aide unfurled a Union Jack, to the wind and snow swept plains he read aloud his proclamation of Governorship. At the same

[34]MP, "Notes on Early Rebellion."

time, and as a more concrete step, he authorized Colonel Dennis "to raise, organize, arm, equip and provision, a sufficient force" to "attack, arrest, disarm, or disperse the . . . armed men so unlawfully assembled and disturbing the public peace; and for that purpose, and with the force aforesaid, to assault, fire upon, pull down, or break into any fort, house, stronghold, or other place in which the said armed men may be found."[35] These measures virtually ruined McDougall's career. Unknown to the incoming Governor, the transfer had *not* taken place on the date originally designated, because Sir John A. Macdonald had decided that peaceful occupation should first be assured. McDougall's proclamation, therefore, was meaningless to all but the English-speaking settlers and the Canadian party, who not only believed in its validity but continued to insist that the "Governor" be allowed to proceed to Fort Garry.

Dennis's commission was greeted most enthusiastically by the Canadians barricaded in Schultz's store. Well known, Mair said, was the fact "that under the leadership of William Dease [a "loyalist" half-breed], about a hundred of the most respectable French half-breeds were in sympathy with the English loyalists. . . ." Therefore, "failing peaceful proposals, an immediate attack upon the fort was counselled by Dr. Schultz and other leaders."[36] But Mair's hopes, like those of his patron, everywhere proved unjustified. Dennis, instead of listening to "Schultz and other leaders," went about the surrounding parishes, recruiting English-speaking settlers and "loyalist" Indians, and having made the Lower or "Stone" Fort, twenty miles north of Fort Garry, his headquarters, began drilling them for *possible* action. Even this modified plan, however, met a response disheartening to Mair and his besieged comrades. The settlement as a whole had no desire for bloodshed, the possibility of which was definitely implied in Dennis's order, and instead of running to arms, most of the settlers remained in their homes. In the light, therefore, of his earlier ringing exhortation to McDougall, Mair must have been both embarrassed and chagrined to admit that "the apathy of Scotch settlers through dread of Fort Garry" seemed "more typical than peculiar."[37] He may have felt a measure of satisfaction in the party's disobeying Dennis's order to join him at the Stone Fort, but even this dubious consolation was short-lived. The division of leadership not only made Dennis's

[35]Canada, *Sessional Papers*, V(12), 105.

[36]Review by Mair of Denison's *Soldiering in Canada*, Ottawa *Citizen*, Oct. 6, 1900.

[37]MP, "Red River Memo."

commission virtually meaningless; it also made the Schultz party's position completely hopeless.

Many years later even Mair himself could not permit Robert Norwood, in a biographical sketch, to compare the stand of the "loyalists" with that of the Spartans at Thermopylae; Riel as Xerxes and Schultz or himself as Leonidas, he conceded, "would, I fear, have been looked upon as bathos."[38] But his own comments on the siege reveal that he nevertheless saw it as an affair in which the highest ideals of honour and loyalty were at stake, the very ideals, indeed, upon which he considered the British Empire itself to have been built. The party's food, water, and fuel gave out; Riel surrounded them with three hundred men armed with rifles and cannon and threatened to "reduce the house to flames."[39] When Bannatyne brought an agreement of surrender, Mair refused to sign it[40]—perhaps maintaining, in the light of his promise to Riel, that he was only *visiting* Schultz. But by now he was alone in his determination. All the others signed, and he had no alternative but to file out with them under the guns of Riel's men. Mrs. Schultz, still ill, "fainted and went into hysterics,"[41] and was taken in a sleigh by her husband to Fort Garry. Mair and Eliza followed, "all their clothing and effects being left behind," including Mair's manuscripts.[42] As they entered the gate they heard the *métis* fire a great volley of rifle-shots in jubilant signal of success.

Even within the confines of the fort the seemingly indomitable Mair would not at first acknowledge defeat. Admittedly, the Canadian cause had been deprived of the Schultz group—surely its greatest asset in terms of enthusiasm and reckless courage—but he regarded Dennis's position as still strong; "he had arms, ammunition and provisions . . . and could have defended the Stone Fort . . . and maintained it as a nucleus of resistance and a rallying point."[43] In addition, William Dease was supposedly awaiting only Dennis's order to attack Fort Garry. Dennis by now, however, had decided that the situation was one for discretion instead of valour, and having issued a proclamation ordering the disbandment of the forces he had recruited, he joined McDougall at Pembina.[44] From there, on December 18 and

[38]GP, Mair to Garvin, Jan. 6, 1926. [39]MP, "Notes on Early Rebellion."

[40]*Ibid.*, also Victoria *Daily Colonist*, Sept. 20, 1925: "Charles Mair was the only one of the seventy or eighty who refused to sign the terms."

[41]Begg's own statement in Morton, *Begg's Journal*, p. 216.

[42]MP, "Notes on Early Rebellion."

[43]Ottawa *Citizen*, Oct. 6, 1900.

[44]According to Mair, "the d–d coward" slipped away in disguise (DP, 4124, Sept. 14, 1900).

after waiting in vain for Riel to answer McDougall's request that the *métis* leader meet with him, the "Conservator of the Peace" and the man who would never be Governor of the North-West set out on the long return journey to Canada.

Mair and the Schultz group were now completely on their own. Because the fort was already swarming with *métis*, it could not accommodate all the prisoners, and Mair, Schultz, and about thirty others were taken to the courthouse outside the fort walls and there placed in cells. Through the intervention of J. H. McTavish, an accountant of the Hudson's Bay Company, Riel gave permission for the married men to be with their wives in McTavish's quarters inside the fort; but Mair steadfastly declined, saying "he would not separate from his friends."[45] Eliza Mair attempted to visit her husband but was brought back by armed men; yet, on another occasion, she went to the Schultz house "to get some things, and did without escort or guard."[46] That she did manage to see her husband of three months at least twice, however, is recorded by Mair himself[47] and implied by Begg's *Journal* entry for December 21: "Mrs. Mair is not allowed now to see her husband—this, it is said, has been brought on by her abuse of the French guards around the Fort."[48] It was probably about this time that she was allowed to move outside the fort to Clover Cottage, the home of her friends, the Drevers, and one would infer that Riel was only too willing to be relieved of the redoubtable Eliza Mair.

To Charles Mair, Christmas day, 1869, meant sharing pemmican and tea with two other prisoners in a jail cell, a small dirty room made freezing cold by their having broken the window to obtain ventilation. It also meant separation from his bride, the memory of which was made more bitter later when he learned that Riel had eaten Christmas dinner from plates that he and Eliza had received as a wedding gift. Perhaps the irony of the situation reminded Riel of his conversation with Mair a month before. A few days after Christmas he called his prisoner into the courthouse upstairs and there accused him of having lied to him at St. Norbert. Mair

> asked him how he had lied to him at St. N. and Riel replied that when he and Mrs. Mair were driving off in their rig he stopped them and said he had but one request to make, and that was that he wouldn't take up

[45]MP, "Notes on Early Rebellion." Begg remarks that Mair "was separated from his wife chiefly through his own mismanagement" (Morton, *Begg's Journal*, p. 218).

[46]"A Notebook of James Ross," in Morton, *Begg's Journal*, p. 443.

[47]*Master-Works*, p. xxxviii.

[48]Morton, *Begg's Journal*, p. 236.

arms. Mr. Mair denied this and said . . . that when Riel asked them to leave the country he said he would do so—"and now, he said, I am willing to do so."

At this reply "an altercation took place" and Riel, slapping Mair on the shoulder, said, "I am very sorry, Mr. Mair, but we can't save you; you must prepare to die." He "then bounded off in a high state of excitement," and Mair was escorted back to his cell by a guard, "who expressed sympathy and gave . . . [him] a drink from a cask."[49]

Mair then suggested to his fellow prisoners that his execution would not be the only one, and as a result, "we decided then and there . . . to escape." In the cell across the hall, a cell to which Mair and his two companions had access, Peter McArthur had filed the window bar "so that it could be taken out when required."[50] On the night of January 9, 1870, Mair and a few others were allowed to go "into the guard room and dance," and at midnight, when the sentries outside entered "to rouse their relief, who were asleep" or watching the dancers, twelve prisoners managed to slip away. One by one they were shoved through the narrow opening—so narrow they were unable to take their coats into a bitterly cold night—and after passing through a gap in the stockade, disappeared to various hiding places. Mair "lit on his head, picked himself up," and after a moment's hesitation "decided to walk right down the cart track" to the Drevers' cottage.[51] Begg recorded that he "was very excited" and, "asking for something stimulating to drink—which he got—he then bought a cap and coat, neither of which he had."[52] Mair later told his daughter, however, that although the escape by now was known he had "time to kiss Mater good-bye."[53]

Mair's objective was the English settlement of Portage la Prairie, sixty miles distant, and by 12.30 A.M., with a sled and pony borrowed from Drever, he was on his way across the winter plains. Almost immediately he got off the track and wandered into the "rebel settlement of St. Charles," but fortunately the place was "all asleep and in darkness." Back on the main road, he had just passed Headingly—twelve miles west of Winnipeg—when he met some twenty sleds of *métis* recruits, led by, once again, Ambroise Lépine. He "jogged along, not hurrying or whipping his horse, only turning aside for them," and paid no attention when the last *métis* called "arrêt!" It was "a critical moment," Mair recalled, but the man presumed he was "some settler going to trade at Lane's Post, and drove on."[54]

[49]MP, "Notes on Early Rebellion."
[50]*Master-Works*, p. xxxix.
[51]MP, "Notes on Early Rebellion."
[52]Morton, *Begg's Journal*, p. 256.
[53]MP, "Notes on Early Rebellion."
[54]*Ibid.*

Mair reached Portage some time during the day of January 10, and at a saloon kept by an American named House he found members of Dennis's surveying party—Captain Boulton, Major Webb, and Mr. W. B. Hall. A "jolly bout of hot brandy and water" was followed by an evening of whist, although not before Mair had sent for his wife, whose value as a hostage Riel would not overlook. Disguising herself as a half-breed, Eliza Mair eluded the *mêtis* patrols, and was brought by one Sam Bannerman in "a marvellous drive of ten hours" to join her husband in Portage.[55] There, first with John Garrioch, and then with the Reverend Henry George, the Mairs had their first opportunity to establish at least a modicum of domestic life—a modicum because it was to last only a month.

By mid-January, 1870, therefore, Canadian national expansion in general and Canada First in particular had suffered a severe blow. The Governor-designate of a territory that was to be transferred with no more inconvenience than the writing of signatures at a conference table was in ignominious retreat, his career virtually ruined. With him was his "Conservator of the Peace" whose survey lines had provoked the first act of resistance. The principal emissaries of Canada First within the settlement were likewise incapable of opposition to the man who had defeated them—a mere half-breed, at that. John Schultz was his prisoner and Mair, with a price on his head, had barely managed to flee across the frozen prairie to "loyal" Portage.

2. THE PORTAGE EXPEDITION

WITH HIS ENEMIES either in prison or in retreat to opposite points of the compass, Riel was, during the first few weeks of the new year, at the peak of his power in Red River. Even the arrival of Donald Smith, appointed by Sir John A. Macdonald as a Special Commissioner to inquire into the grievances of the settlement, did not qualify the *métis* leader's authority. When the shrewd Smith was able to institute a system of checks and balances in the settlement by which a representative Convention of Forty would negotiate with Canada, Riel resorted to outbursts of temper and threats of force; by February 10 he had made the settlement recognize his Provisional Government and himself as its President. But on the evening of that day, amid the jubilation of noisy Riel supporters gathered in the saloons, someone abruptly announced that a force of hundreds of men was at that moment on its way from Portage la Prairie to attack Fort Garry.

The "Portage expedition," like the previous militant schemes

[55] *Ibid.*

of the "loyalists," was characterized more by reckless zeal than by prudent deliberation. And once again, as in the case of the "plotting" in the "Corner Room" or the "stand" at the Schultz house, the impression given by Mair and his patriotic friends is of a group of grown men behaving like characters in a schoolboy's novel. From planning to final episode the "expedition" is replete with cloak-and-dagger meetings, complicated plots, enemy spies, truce parties—even the tearful pleas of women. Only the element of real tragedy that eventually entered confirms the fact that these men were in dead earnest.

When Mair arrived at Portage, "a secret meeting had been held at the home of an Orangeman called John Connor" for the purpose of organizing a force to liberate the Fort Garry prisoners. "I attended the next one," he stated, "and took an active part from that on." Specific leadership seems to have been lacking, although Mair himself evidently exerted some authority. Under his auspices, for example, Captain C. A. Boulton was "let into the scheme at the last moment and after everything had been prepared," despite the feeling of other "loyalists" that Boulton "lacked back-bone" when he had left the Schultz house during its siege.[56] But even Mair might have questioned Boulton's suitability if he had realized the Captain wished to join the group because he feared "a rash act might bring trouble upon the country."[57] The operation contemplated by the "loyalists" required, indeed, a leadership characterized by experience and discretion; but once again it was to be coloured mainly by the impulsive aggressiveness of John Schultz. For, in storybook fashion, that redoubtable "loyalist" had escaped from the courthouse jail on January 23 with the help of a gimlet and knife concealed by his wife in a pudding. He had injured his leg in the drop from his cell-window, but finding refuge at the home of Robert MacBeth in Kildonan while *métis* scoured the area, "he sat upstairs, revolver in hand, determined not to be taken a second time."[58] Since then he had "moved about from St. Andrew's to St. Peter's . . . and so on," organizing the English-speaking settlers for action once more against Riel.[59]

The attack was to be made by forces converging on the fort from three directions—Mair's (or Boulton's) party from Portage, Schultz's

[56]DP, 5557, April 23, 1909.

[57]C. Boulton, *Reminiscences of the North-West Rebellions*, p. 101.

[58]Morton, *Begg's Journal*, p. 101.

[59]MP, "Murdoch McLeod." This document and two others, "J. Dilworth and Self," and "Notes on Early Rebellion" (all in MP), provide the basis for the account that follows.

from St. Peter's, and the still loyal William Dease's from the south. On February 10, the Portage group had reached Headingly; and here occurred what should have made the whole operation appear hopeless even to the participants themselves. For four days they were compelled by a severe blizzard to remain in Headingly church and the only element that augured any success for the expedition, that of surprise, was lost. Even so, however, the "loyalists," obviously feeling compelled to justify somehow their arduous march, boldly trudged through Winnipeg and past the walls of Garry itself, Thomas Scott going so far as to enter a house and search for Riel. At Kildonan they joined Schultz, "occupied the schoolhouse . . ., hoisted the union jack," and sent Thomas Norquay with a demand to Riel that he release the prisoners. This alliance with Schultz encouraged the force to determine once again to attack the fort, whether the prisoners were released or not. Boulton and especially the English clergy tried to dissuade the men, but to no avail. On the morning of February 16 a force of over five hundred men, armed with ladders, swords, clubs, rifles and cannon, was prepared "to move on St. Boniface, plant the cannon there and breach the walls of Fort Garry."[60]

The stage was now set for the final act of tragi-comedy. But the action that occurred was not that of brave men storming a battlement in the name of their Queen; rather it was an episode that should have forcefully revealed to the "loyalists" the realities they evidently could not see. It began when Norbert Parisien, a half-breed "spy" captured the previous night and kept in the schoolhouse, "asked to be taken out to go to a water closet." It ended with the first bloodshed of the insurrection, when Parisien escaped, seized a shotgun, and killed Hugh Sutherland, a youth of seventeen who had come over from East Kildonan "perhaps to see what was going on." Parisien was almost immediately captured by the enraged "loyalists," but his precipitate act became the ironic means by which their own rashness was halted.

For the entreaties of the clergy were now joined by the implorings of the parish women, who, led by young Sutherland's mother and frantic with fear, begged the men to return to their homes before all were murdered. This reaction was completely unexpected by the "loyalists." According to Mair, they had believed Sutherland's death "would fire the blood of every man"; instead, they were presented with "an extraordinary scene, pitiful beyond description—exhibiting

[60]The "loyalists" presumed that the *métis* would not fire towards their own houses in St. Boniface.

as it did a poltroonery on the part of the Kildonan people utterly astonishing." As a result, he said, "The Portage party was deserted and left sixty miles from home, without provisions or bedding and Fort Garry to pass."

This belated concern for the possible consequences of the march from Portage proved justified. Nor did Mair, for one, believe Riel's assurances—brought by an intermediary named "Flat Boat" McLean—that the party could return in peace. He and three others departed almost immediately, having advised the now approximately fifty men to strike out at once across the prairies and not to tempt fate again by passing almost under the walls of Garry. Even Schultz conceded that without organized support his own situation was precarious, and he too avoided the fort, heading southeast towards the American border. But the others, after resting overnight and with Boulton still in nominal command, had proceeded no farther than a point opposite the fort when they were intercepted by a band of about seventy *métis* horsemen. For a moment or two the more aggressive "loyalist" spirits prevailed, but Boulton was by now completely convinced that the Portage cause was hopeless and that resistance would be suicidal. Within the hour, forty-eight prisoners were herded into the cramped cells of Fort Garry and Boulton and Murdoch McLeod put in irons. *Métis* patrols were again dispatched to search for the hated Schultz and Mair, and the "Portage expedition" was over.

But even if once more Riel had thwarted his enemies, forces were already in motion which were to effect his downfall. Beyond Winnipeg Schultz and Mair had determined to return to Ontario to urge a military expedition. Within the walls of Fort Garry itself Riel committed himself to actions that supported their cause. Shortly after his capture, Boulton was condemned to death and was saved, according to McLeod, only by the plea of young Sutherland's mother.[61] Perhaps too it is significant that Begg notes in his *Journal* for February 24 that "Riel was taken very ill this morning . . . being threatened with an attack of brain fever."[62] For, although by the 27th the *métis* leader had supposedly recovered, a few days later he shocked the settlement by announcing that one of his prisoners, Thomas Scott, had been tried by court-martial and was to be shot. And this time intercession was not heeded. On the morning of March 4 Scott was put to death by a *métis* firing squad.

[61]MP, "Murdoch McLeod."
[62]Morton, *Begg's Journal*, p. 321.

Such a summary act is far easier to explain than to justify. The charge against Scott, insubordination and striking his guards, seems inordinately inconsistent with the penalty, and to this day even many of Riel's sympathizers have been compelled to regard his orders as a crime. As a political necessity Boulton's execution would perhaps have been justified, but Scott's, even when the most extenuating circumstances are taken into account, must at the best be considered as manslaughter. And there were undoubtedly extenuating circumstances. Scott had first been imprisoned by the *métis* during the siege of the Schultz house—not long, in fact, after his brush with Riel in the Red Saloon. With Mair he had escaped on January 9 and with him had been one of the main organizers of the ill-fated Portage expedition. It was Scott, also, who led the search for Riel on the night the party passed through Winnipeg. Only after his second imprisonment on February 17, however, did he make himself particularly obnoxious. Not only did he use defiant and abusive language to the guards, he probably also struck them on more than one occasion. He and McLeod were reported to have smashed down their cell doors (probably after they had used their window sash as kindling in order to keep warm), and had threatened to burn down the whole building.[63] But most provoking, perhaps, was Scott's defiant refusal to support the appointment of one Dan Shea, "a notorious Fenian," as English delegate to Riel's Provisional Government. According to McLeod, he shouted, "Boys, you can do what you like, but I won't consent," and was consequently "ironed with irons which had been taken off Boulton."[64] Scott was considered even by the Canadians to be an impetuously bold, aggressive man—only a few months previously he had been fined in General Quarterly Court for assaulting John Snow, his road party employer—and to Riel he had become unbearable.

By Scott's death, it has been suggested, Riel thought to frighten the enemies of his Provisional Government into submission. Ironically, however, the shooting of Scott, although it brought a fearful tranquillity to the settlement, was also the means by which those enemies were able to stir Canada to take action against him.

The enemy who was, with the possible exception of Schultz, the most dangerous to Riel was taking every possible precaution that he would not again be captured by the *métis* leader. Having grossly miscalculated the temper of the English-speaking settlers—"apathy" and "poltroonery" are themselves epithets reflective, perhaps, of a

[63]MP, "J. Dilworth and Self."
[64]MP, "Murdoch McLeod."

continued lack of perception—Charles Mair nevertheless realized that in the West he was now of no use to what he considered to be the interests of Canada. He had reached Portage la Prairie on February 17, but suspecting that Riel had made him a marked man, he remained there only until the 22nd. Then, leaving his wife with friends,[65] he set out with John J. Setter,[66] two guides and two dog trains, on the long, circuitous route towards the southwest and St. Paul, Minnesota.

The early part of the diary Mair kept of the trip[67] reads like an account of an enjoyable camping tour—even in the height of winter—and once again, as from the letters to his brothers, the reader receives an impression that Mair intended that his observations would eventually be published. The Bad Wood Hills, for example, "have a picturesque roll resembling the hilly country between Lakes Osaki[s] and Breckenridge in Minnesota without the Lakes and streams to vary their outline or color." The view from the hills "is very grand, and one can imagine the time not far distant when the wealthy denizen of the plains will seek the Hills in summer to vary the monotony of the prairie and cover their gentle and beautiful slopes with villas and residences." Near the Tiger Hills the men encountered an Indian family who "were just out of provisions when we reached them and were boiling their last morsel, viz., the lungs of a moose, in a pot over the fire." For a pair of moccasins Mair "made a trade with the younger Indian of a pair of snow-shoes, in which he screwed me most confoundedly"; after eating a large portion of their supplies, "the old fellow began to speak politics . . . [and] told us that Riel was ruining the Indians [and] that he wanted the Canadians to come in." Mair closes his diary for this day with the remark that they escaped the old Indian and his family as quickly as possible, "inasmuch as their inroads upon our supplies had already carried dismay into our souls and a conviction that another day's delay at the barren lodge would be our ruin."

On March 3 Mair records that they found enormous fresh bear tracks, and adds facetiously that "as we had no arms and hadn't lost

65In the account written for Garvin's *Master-Works* Mair states that on his arrival at Portage he immediately sent for his wife in Winnipeg (p. xliii). But he evidently had forgotten in 1924, when he wrote the account, that Eliza was already in Portage and that he had sent for her after his escape in January.

66Setter was a brother-in-law of John Norquay, Premier of Manitoba 1878–87.

67MP, "Diary of C. Mair."

any bears we did not pursue them." He further comments that the spring-like weather had tempted the bears out; but "Alas! How miserably were they and we mistaken." For on March 7, after the party had travelled 250 miles with little hardship, it was suddenly struck by a fierce blizzard, and by the end of the day Setter was snow-blind and in great pain. Since their provisions were giving out, the men could not pause, and on the 9th they were reduced to two meals a day, these consisting simply of flour mixed with butter and snow and made into a paste over the fire. By the 11th they had reached the Red River and the tiny settlement of Grand Forks, "where to our inexpressible joy we found our friends, Dr. Lynch and Wm. Drever, on their way from Fort Garry to Canada."[68] Here also was food "for men and dogs [and] we regaled ourselves . . . to our hearts' content." The guides were sent back to Portage and the four Canadians resumed their trip together.

But the worst weather was yet to come. For three days after March 14 the men were forced to huddle around their fire in the woods while a "fearful storm" raged about them. Setter left camp to search for a hut, and "the whole day passed away in the utmost anxiety and suspense"; he returned at dark after wandering all day on the prairie and when he had been quite given up for lost. The horses that they had exchanged at Grand Forks for their dogs and sleds gave out on the 17th, and Mair became exhausted, "as I had walked all day without snow-shoes." By the 20th, however, they were within forty miles of Fort Abercrombie and encountering the huts and hamlets sparsely dotted along the snow-obliterated cart track. At a Mr. Probsfeld's, "[we] had several horns of good whisky and enjoyed ourselves hugely," and a month after leaving Portage or Winnipeg the weary quartet walked into Abercrombie. From there, after resting for two days, they were able to take a stage to St. Cloud, whence they boarded the train to St. Paul.

The journey from Portage la Prairie to Fort Abercrombie was a really remarkable feat. For nearly 450 miles Mair travelled by foot and dog-sled and for the most part across desolate, blizzard-swept prairie or through North Dakota wilderness. One of his guides, David Halcro, was a replacement for another who early returned to Portage

[68]Dr. Joseph Lynch had come to Red River from Ontario in 1869, and was a friend of Schultz and Mair. William Drever was the "loyalist" of Clover Cottage who aided Mair after his escape on January 9. Both were pursued by Riel's troops as far as the border.

for supplies and then refused to return to the party because of the dangers involved in the trip.[69] Riel's buffalo-hunters, whose natural habitat was the prairie, were searching for them. The Indians, especially the Sioux, were not all "friendly," and could not be depended upon to distinguish between American bounty-hunter and Canadian refugee. The rigorous weather, indeed, may have saved Mair's life.

Three aspects of Mair's short stay in St. Paul and the trip thereafter to Toronto are worthy of note. A singular coincidence "was the arrival of Dr. Schultz . . . not long after our arrival there. . . . We must have been at one time 700 or 800 miles apart, both parties traveling on snowshoes and arriving almost at the same time."[70] Mair also notes in his diary that he was interviewed by the St. Paul press and that he and Setter made a point of calling upon the St. Paul *Pioneer* "and explained matters *in re* Red River." Perhaps more stimulating to Mair, however, was the fact that on March 30 he boarded the train with Donald A. Smith, also en route to Canada from St. Paul. For over one thousand miles Mair had opportunity to discuss recent events with Smith, and even the meagre record of their conversation that he made in his diary is interestingly reflective of the different personalities of the two men. It is obvious, for example, that Mair seized upon the occasion to revile "the grasping stockholders" of the Hudson's Bay Company; but Smith apparently parried Mair by noting merely that "the expressed enmity of young men in [the] HB Co office towards [the] stockholders" was "not at all entertained . . . by himself, save the mark!"[71] Mair also, and probably with Father Ritchot particularly in mind, evidently condemned the Roman Catholic clergy's support of Riel. Smith, however, told him "it was unwise to accuse [the] priests and that it was even doubtful whether they were implicated." Just as reprehensible to Mair would be Smith's assertion that he was not certain Scott's death was murder—an attitude perhaps made even more invidious to Mair by his impression that when Smith "reached Ontario and found the country was ringing with indignation he changed his note."[72] Mair never trusted Smith.

[69]The guides, Richard Favell and David Halcro, were half-breeds—the latter of English descent—and were paid six and seven shillings per day, respectively, for their services (PWF, series 98, subject 429, Mair to Minister of Public Works, March 14, 1871).

[70]*Master-Works*, p. xlv.

[71]The handwriting of this section of the diary is at times illegible, perhaps because Mair, in "dot-it-down" fashion, was attempting to write on the rocking train.

[72]MP, W. F. James to Mair, March 5, 1902. A break in the diary followed by particulars of Scott's death might have been intended for Smith's comments on the episode.

Beckles Willson's laudatory biography of Smith he termed "the most nauseating pack of purchased lies and slander yet put forth";[73] even when Smith died in 1914 at the age of ninety-four, the best eulogy Mair could express was that "the old sinner Strathcona died hard."[74] The calculating shrewdness of a politician like Smith was simply intolerable to the direct, assertively loyal Canada Firster.

3. TORONTO

WHEN MAIR ARRIVED in Toronto on April 6, 1870, Canada First was about to become an important factor in national policy. Mair had been purposely sent to Red River to express the group's message of the necessity for an expanding and unified Dominion; but even his colleagues had hardly envisaged that his enthusiasm would help to foment a "rebellion" from which he himself and another Canada First member, Schultz, would barely escape with their lives. And the group's reaction to this turn of events serves to illuminate, even more, perhaps, than does Mair's conduct in the West, the way in which their fervent "nationalism" was strongly qualified. Their Upper-Canadian provincialism, their aggressive sense of superiority, their self-indulgent concern for their own unrecognized merit, their inclination towards the melodramatic—all are reflected in the action they took almost immediately after the return of Mair and his fellow "loyalists" to Ontario.

To Canada First the most urgent matter was that of sending a military force to restore order in Red River and to avenge what the group insisted were grave injustices, even murder, perpetrated against loyal Canadians. And here there was no longer a necessity for working secretly; this was a moment "to strike and strike hard." Denison had organized a committee from the Canada First group (which now numbered twelve)[75] when the news of Mair's flight and Scott's death had reached Ontario, and these men proceeded, as Denison himself proudly reported, "to arouse the indignation of the people, and foment a public opinion."[76] George Kingsmill, the editor of the Toronto *Daily Telegraph*, at Foster's suggestion printed his paper with "turned rules" as "a mark of respect to the memory of the murdered Scott."[77]

[73]DP, 4749, Nov. 19, 1902.
[74]DP, 6122, Jan. 22, 1914.
[75]The additional six were George Kingsmill, James D. Edgar, Dr. William Canniff, Richard Grahame, Hugh Scott (brother of Thomas) and Joseph McDougall (brother of William).
[76]*The Struggle for Imperial Unity*, p. 22. [77]*Ibid.*

Foster wrote a series of articles marked by patriotic fervor and indignation and published as "editorials" in the same paper. While what Denison called the "Government organs" were trying to calm public excitement, Canada First did everything in its power to arouse it. When, at a committee meeting, cooler heads suggested that any reception of the refugees as heroes should await fuller information—that, indeed, Mair and his friends might have acted indiscreetly in the West—they were vehemently denounced by the fiery Denison:

I said that these refugees had risked their lives in obedience to a proclamation in the Queen's name, calling upon them to take up arms on her behalf; that there were only a few Ontario men . . . in that remote and inaccessible region, surrounded by half savages, besieged until supplies gave out. When abandoned by the officer who had appealed to them to take up arms, they were obliged to surrender, and suffered for long months in prison. I said these Canadians did this for Canada, and were we at home to be critical as to their method of proving their devotion to our country . . . ? They had escaped and were coming to their own province to tell of their wrongs, to ask assistance to relieve the intolerable condition of their comrades in the Red River Settlement. . . . Is there an Ontario man who will not hold out a hand of welcome to these men? Any man who hesitates is no true Canadian. I repudiate him as a countryman of mine. Are we to talk about indiscretion when men have risked their lives? We have too little of that indiscretion nowadays and should hail it with enthusiasm.[78]

Denison's references to "Ontario men," "these Canadians," "our country," "true Canadian," "countryman of mine," and "half savages" require little comment; they speak eloquently for themselves. In the West the attitudes they reflect had helped to cause an insurrection. In Toronto, however, Denison could state, "I soon had the whole meeting with me"; and the result was a proclamation by the Mayor for a public reception. On the evening of April 6 a thousand people met the refugees at the station; at least five thousand tried to get into St. Lawrence Hall to hear them. When the auditorium, according to the *Globe* of April 7, "was packed from roof to ceiling [*sic*]—literally—for some adventurous perched themselves on the cornices," the Mayor was forced to adjourn the meeting to the City Hall square. There, speeches by Mair, Schultz, Lynch, and Setter aroused the huge crowd to a pitch of patriotic zeal and excitement.

Mair's address was by far the longest, and for the purpose was perhaps not as effective as it might have been; for, once again, as in

[78]*Ibid.*, pp. 24–25.

the instance of his remarks on Judge Donnelly, it appears that Mair was more concerned with drawing attention to himself than with his purported subject-matter. In a sustained rhetoric that required two long columns of the *Globe* for its recording, he impressed upon his listeners both his comprehensive knowledge of North-Western history ("I am the man," said Dot, "for I know all about that from the time of the charter to the present day. I've made it a study.") and the part played by himself and his comrades against "Riel and his cutthroat followers." The historical review, he explained, was necessary to an understanding of "why the most bigoted portions of the inhabitants should be able to overcome those possessed of property and intellect"; and although "it was not his intention to-night to indulge in any melo-dramatic statements," he believed his audience would agree that the actions of himself and his friends "were not melo-dramatic in Red River."

Whatever the subject, however, whether Lord Selkirk's settlement or the siege of Schultz's house, Mair gave ample evidence that he was aware he was a thousand miles from Red River and among the English Protestants of Ontario. When the Hudson's Bay Company began extending its operations into the interior, he said, it had difficulty in competing with traders from Montreal "because the French have an aptitude for falling into the modes of savages (laughter)"; and the *métis* who occupied Fort Garry were particularly gratified with the supplies found there, because, said Mair, "the French at Red River delight in having all the whiskey they drink and as little to do as they could possibly have (laughter)." That very "capture," he said, was a result of treachery on the part of Company and clergy; Riel, "probably sent for by the hierarchy at Fort Garry," became "the life and soul of the secret meetings, acting with the support and under the influence of the priests, who held the crucifix up before the people and told them if they fought against Riel, they fought against that." Everyone knew three days before the capture, he insisted, that it was going to take place—a Mr. Hyman, indeed, had been willing at the time to swear out an affidavit reflecting Mactavish's compliance, but through the "sinister" influence of "Mr. Sandford [*sic*] of Hamilton (hisses)," he reconsidered, and the fort was literally given away by the Company.

Besides repeating his charge that "the French at Red River" (he does not refer to them as *métis*) would "do anything but farm"—and one infers from the phrasing of his statements here that he had been preparing for his address by reading his own letters to the press

—Mair emphasized the additional one that they lacked courage. When the Canadians barricaded themselves with Schultz, "Riel immediately surrounded the house with his men, but he was unable to bring them to the scratch. They walked around the house and pointed their guns at the inmates, but did nothing else, and after a while went away (laughter)." Mair could understand, he said, the reluctance of the English-speaking settlers to rise against Riel; "living beside the French on terms of amity," it would be "injudicious to take up arms against them, for if they did so and were unsuccessful, their families would be butchered and their property destroyed." But outweighing this factor, Mair insisted, was another that the Canadians felt would influence the settlers; "an emergency had arisen in which their honour was concerned . . .; it was imperatively necessary that they should take a decided stand." But when the expected support did not materialize, the Canadians, "worn out by want of sleep and proper nourishment," had to surrender:

They did so unconditionally with the alternative of being all butchered. They and even their wives were then taken to Fort Garry, where 27 of them were shut up in a room 14 ft. by 12 ft. in size, and swarming with vermin; a room which reminded them more of the Black Hole of Calcutta than of anything else (Groans). These sufferings were borne cheerfully enough; they turned them into amusements rather than anything else, knowing that being far from home it was necessary to bear up under any calamity.

From this emotive account, in which he also included the escape of himself and "poor Scott," Mair turned to commentary on the expedition from Portage—"a noble [settlement] . . ., never under the influence of the Hudson's Bay Company." Riel, he insisted, had released his prisoners because of fear of attack by the Canadians—"(a voice: 'You want Canadians up there to settle them!')"—but the *métis* leader was able to "wreak vengeance" by means of "poor Scott, whose blanket the speaker had shared for five weeks."

On this personal note "Mr. Mair resumed his seat amid loud cheering." But almost immediately he was brought to his feet to make what for him must have become, in the past year, a rather familiar gesture—the attempt to explain certain of his statements. For John Schultz, as the next speaker, prefaced his remarks by praising the *loyal métis* of Red River. At once, from the crowd came "What did Mr. Mair say?" Mair was then obliged to point out to his audience, as he had been obliged before to a group of irate settlers, that "his remarks must have been misunderstood." There was, he admitted, "a very considerable section of the French people who were industrious and in comfortable circumstances and that section had been loyal." When he mentioned the French, he said, "he referred only to those of Riel's party."

The crowd by this time, however, was in no mood to quibble; Mair's appeal to their anti-French, anti-Roman Catholic prejudices had been effective enough, even without his adding, as reported by the Toronto *Leader* of April 7, a slogan of "Death to the murderers and tyrants of Fort Garry!" From then it was virtually a matter only of time before Canada First had obtained vigorous popular support for its proposals.

Of the original five members, all but Morgan (who was sensitive about his position as a civil servant) worked incessantly to make a hesitant Government take immediate steps on behalf of "the people of Canada." Leaving Foster to continue his articles, Mair and Denison, accompanied by Schultz and Lynch, set out to see Sir John A. Macdonald, but not before they had sent word "to friends at Cobourg, Belleville, Prescott, etc., to organize demonstrations of welcome to the loyalists."[79] At Belleville the excitement was particularly intense because Thomas Scott had lived in Hastings county and was a locally well-known Orangeman; and Mair was induced to detrain there and address the large crowd in the railway round-house. So well received, indeed, were Mair and the relation of his adventures, that he returned on August 5 and delivered another lecture. As he proudly recalled many years later, "The Mayor presented me with a valuable watch, especially unique from being made of Madoc gold, accompanied by an illuminated morocco bound volume containing 70 signatures of the principal professional and business men of the city and country."[80]

The Canada First delegates to Ottawa, however, were less effective. One of their main objectives was to make the Government refuse to receive Father Ritchot and Alfred Scott, Riel's Provisional Government emissaries. To Denison these men were the representatives "of those who have robbed, imprisoned and murdered loyal Canadians, whose only fault was zeal for British institutions, whose only crime was devotion to the old flag,"[81] and official recognition of them was tantamount to treason. But when it came to in-fighting, the impetuous

[79]*Ibid.*, p. 26.
[80]*Master-Works*, p. xlvii. The commemorative volume is now in the Perth Museum.
[81]*The Struggle for Imperial Unity*, p. 26.

Denison was no match for Sir John A., and despite his resorting to varied tactics and expedients, the soldier was finally outwitted by the politician. After an initial rebuff by Macdonald, Denison and Co. decided that Lynch, as a former Riel prisoner, should address Sir John Young, the Governor General. Denison drafted the document, Lynch wrote it out, and together they delivered it to Government House. But this expedient failed; so, on Foster's urging, Thomas Scott's brother Hugh swore out a warrant in Toronto for the delegates' arrest. But the Government advised Ritchot and Alfred Scott to avoid Toronto on their way to Ottawa, and when the warrant was forwarded to the Ottawa Chief of Police he denied having received it. Denison then insisted that "there was some underhanded work, and that we would give the information to the Press, and that it would arouse great indignation." Thereupon, he said, the warrant turned up, having been diverted by Sir John, and on April 14 Ritchot and Scott were arrested. But even then the delegates were released (because a Toronto warrant had no authority in Ottawa), re-arrested on a new warrant sworn out by Hugh Scott (who came to Ottawa for the purpose), and then discharged on April 21 for lack of evidence. Ritchot and Scott were treated as legal envoys, and Denison had to find consolation—perhaps, to him, considerable—in having "nothing to do with Macdonald until many years later when Sir John came out boldly for the Empire and side of loyalty under the well-known cry, 'A British subject I was born, a British subject I will die!' "[82]

There now remained the most important question of all—that of sending a military expedition to Fort Garry. To Canada First this was not only a matter of revenge or of the safety of "loyalists" still at Red River, now jeopardized by "the recognition and endorsation of the murderers,"[83] but also of a possible move by the United States at a time when both the Canadian and the Imperial governments seemed incapable of resolute action. To Mair, and to Denison in particular (for whom the memory of the Fenian invasion was a constant goad), *métis*, Fenians, French Canadians, and Yankees were generally tarred with the same disloyal brush, and only a show of force could save Canada. To Mair, also, the thought of British troops marching down the main street of the settlement undoubtedly helped to assuage the memory of personal ignominy he had suffered there a year before. And the outcry they both helped to generate in Ontario was placing

[82] *Ibid.*, pp. 28–32.
[83] *Ibid.*, pp. 36–37.

the Government in an increasingly difficult position. The *métis* had the support of Quebec, and the "loyalists" that of Ontario. Ottawa had to satisfy both and at the same time keep a wary eye upon the United States.

In its desperation the Government found a clever compromise. By the Manitoba Act the rights of the *métis* were to be recognized when a new province was created on July 15, 1870. At the same time a combined force of British Regulars from Quebec and Canadian Militia from Ontario was to be despatched to Red River, both as an appeasement to Ontario and as a warning to the United States. A. G. Archibald of Nova Scotia, the new Lieutenant-Governor, would assume office in August, probably just before the arrival of General Wolseley and his troops; until then Riel was to continue his Provisional Government.

But in this delicate balancing of olive branch and sword, the sensitively suspicious Canada Firsters immediately believed that they recognized deception. It was all very well to show the sword, they protested warmly, but once at Red River Wolseley should make some use of it; otherwise Archibald would establish his civil government and Riel and his murderers would escape their rightful punishment. In addition, Canada First did not believe that the Government really intended the expedition to reach Fort Garry; it was sure that Riel would be granted an amnesty by the Imperial Government and Wolseley recalled, Ottawa the while maintaining that troops were no longer necessary at Red River. How this bent for blood became mingled with patriotic concern for Canada's future in the North-West is well illustrated in the final episode of Canada First's campaign for national unity and sentiment.

Haliburton, who until now had taken little part in the excitement over Red River, about July 18 happened to be in Niagara Falls on his way to New York and England. Upon learning that Sir John Young was at the Clifton House, he decided to stop over "and see him about an important point that had apparently not been thought of, viz., the danger that the French laws of Quebec would be introduced into the North-West";[84] but when he discovered that the vice-regal party had moved to a smaller, more sequestered hotel, he "felt convinced that there must have been something at the bottom

[84]The quotations relevant to this episode are from "How a Cabinet Secret leaked out, and the Result," privately printed by Haliburton in 1899 and now in the Mair Papers. Denison quoted the article in full in an obituary of Haliburton, published in the *Canadian Magazine*, XVII (May, 1901), 126–30.

of this odd move." The following morning Haliburton found Young, and carefully veiling his suspicions by casual conversation, was eventually startled to hear Young remark that he expected Sir George Cartier, Bishop Taché, and Governor Archibald to arrive almost momentarily. At once, said Haliburton, "the whole truth flashed upon me—'His visitors will be on their way through the United States to Fort Garry, to head off Colonel Wolseley with an amnesty. The place of meeting is a safe one for them, as in a minute or two they can skip over to the United States and be out of reach of the people of Canada.'" He immediately communicated to Schultz in London, Ontario, that "mischief is afloat" and begged him "to notify the Twelve Apostles at Toronto (the leaders of the Canada First party) to be ready to strike a blow" the moment they confirmed his belief.

The consequences in Toronto were almost immediate. Denison wrote to Wolseley, urging him to press on and to discourage any communication from the rear. At the same time the Ontario officers in the force were exhorted that if Wolseley's Regulars should be recalled they should "take their boats and possessions and go on at all hazards."[85] When it was learned that Cartier and Taché were to pass through Toronto on their way to meet Young at Niagara, Denison informed the Deputy Adjutant-General that a hostile demonstration of "loyalists" would result, and that if any ceremonial reception were to be attempted, "we would take possession of the armoury that night, and that we would have ten men to his one, and if anyone in Toronto wanted to fight it out, we were ready to fight it out on the streets." On being told that he was threatening revolution, Denison replied, "Yes, I know I am, and we can make it one. A half continent is at stake, and it is a stake worth fighting for."[86] Cartier and Taché avoided Toronto, just as Ritchot and Scott had done three months before; but on July 22 an immense public rally was held in the city to protest against any possibility of the Government's recalling the expedition and of Archibald's travelling to Red River via the United States. "Will the volunteers accept defeat at the hands of the Minister of Militia?" "Shall our Queen's Representative go a thousand miles through a foreign country to demean himself to a thief and a murderer?" "Men of Ontario! Shall Scott's blood cry in vain for vengeance?"—these were characteristic slogans shouted by the indignant Toronto loyalists.[87] Even the Honourable William McDougall was called upon to help inflame the huge crowd.

[85]*The Struggle for Imperial Unity*, p. 37.
[86]*Ibid.*, pp. 37–38.
[87]*Ibid.*, p. 42.

It became a matter of history, according to the Canada First group, that in consequence of the furious meeting Sir John Young did not dare to send Archibald through the United States to Fort Garry.[88] And on the morning of August 24, 1870, or nine days before the Lieutenant-Governor, Wolseley and his troops reached Winnipeg after their truly remarkable march. Captain Redvers Buller, one of Wolseley's officers who was destined to go on to greater achievements,[89] described the scene in a letter to his sister in England:

We rowed to within 1½ miles of the fort and then all landed and in the pitiless rain marched to the attack; B Company skirmishing in front, H behind, the remainder—Guns, Staff and foot—in the middle: Up to our knees in thick, sticky, slippery black mud we splashed our way; cutting through the corner of the town of Winnipeg, a scattering collection of indifferent wooden houses on a muddy road where we were enthusiastically greeted by a half-naked Indian, very drunk. We marched across half a mile of prairie and reached the back door of Fort Garry just as Riel and O'Donoghue . . . walked out of the front door. Finding the back door shut we marched round to the front one, which we found open. We formed line, fired 21 guns, presented arms, gave three cheers for the Queen, and stood at ease in the rain, and so ended the attack and capture of Fort Garry.

Buller states that at this moment his attention was drawn to Riel and O'Donoghue, who were standing on the opposite side of the river and watching the troops, but who "in about ten minutes mounted their horses and rode off." Shortly afterwards, Wolseley's men marched into the fort, "the band playing the Regimental quick-step," and took up quarters recently vacated by "Riel's gang." The officers went into Riel's house,

which we incontinently proceeded to loot. He evidently was rather hurried in his departure as we found his breakfast served on the table still warm and only half eaten; we finished it, having had none ourselves, turned the house upside down, found nothing worth taking unless perhaps I should mention this elegant paper of sorts on which I am writing.

Buller probably never knew that the "elegant paper" belonged to John Schultz.[90] But he very likely expressed the sentiments of many when he termed the expedition "an utter farce," a "political job of that

[88]Historians, however, are still undecided on whether or not Archibald even intended arriving before Wolseley. He gave Bishop Taché the impression that he was at least going to try to do so; yet he later testified that Cartier had advised him not to (Morton, *Begg's Journal*, p. 142).

[89]General the Rt. Hon. Sir Redvers Buller, V.C., G.C.B., G.C.M.G. Buller's disastrous campaign in the Boer War, however, brought an unhappy end to an otherwise distinguished career.

[90]Queen's University Library, Redvers Buller to Henrietta Buller, Aug. 24, 1870.

scoundrel Cartier's," that might be redeemed, however, "if they were to hang a few priests up here." It did so disgust one, he concluded, "to have to come all this way for the band to play 'God Save the Queen.'"[91]

Canada First's appraisal of the "capture" of Fort Garry was entirely different from Buller's. Haliburton reflected in 1899 that if he had not acted promptly that day in Niagara Falls, "the future of half a continent would have been mortgaged; Colonel Wolseley would have been made a laughing stock, and might never have won his peerage; while a race war might have grown out of these questions, compared with which, that in South Africa would now seem a trifle." Even Young would never have ascended to the peers as Lord Lisgar, he maintained, if it had become known at the time "that Sir John Young's chatter had saved the North-West."[92] Haliburton's incongruous mingling of possible consequences seems curious, especially in the light of the perceptiveness he revealed in criticizing Mair's verse; but the young Nova Scotian is here merely once again representative of his Canada First friends in his nationalistic concern on the one hand and his colonial subservience on the other; the loss of half a continent and the possibility of a race war are matters of supreme importance, but so are ascensions to the peerage. Denison probably agreed on all points with Haliburton, but he chose to emphasize one in particular. But for the expedition, he said, that great western country would not have been opened up for generations; indeed, it might well have been absorbed by the United States.[93] Mair was more explicit: "When the Union Jack replaced the Fenian flag," he told a friend, the country was saved from being "swarmed over by Fenian and American desperadoes."[94] Hamilton Fish, the American Secretary of State, he charged, was part of "the most dangerous plot since 1837 to destroy British connection and Canadian autonomy," and "to further which

Buller's letter is not part of the Mair Papers but was a single presentation by his daughter to the university in 1934. When reading the letter, the author suddenly realized it was written on the same notepaper—monogrammed "J.S."—that Schultz used in his letters to Mair. Riel evidently had expropriated the paper with the other effects of Mair and Schultz.

[91]A diary, now in the author's possession, of Lieutenant H. W. Snelling, a member of the 60th Rifles, frequently reflects the punitive temper of Wolseley's troops.

[92]"How a Cabinet Secret Leaked Out."

[93]*The Struggle for Imperial Unity*, p. 48.

[94]MP, Mair to J. B. Allen, Nov. 23, 1923. O'Donoghue hoisted the Fenian flag, Riel, the Union Jack. After bitter argument the two leaders compromised by flying both flags.

a considerable sum had been placed in American hands in Winnipeg."[95] The sending of Imperial troops to Winnipeg was a warning from Britain herself; without them "the country would have been lost, just as Oregon and Washington were lost."[96]

Mair's fear of American annexation designs—Lanark "Training Day" had been an early manifestation—was almost as obsessive as Denison's, and although the action at Red River was restricted to a conflict between peoples who were all British subjects, the menace of American intervention was constantly impressed upon him. He somehow managed to obtain, for example, a letter from Henry Eck, an American sympathizer in Winnipeg, to Enos Stutsman, the most active of the St. Paul annexationists, in which Eck notes with satisfaction that "there will be a fight sure, and . . . everything will become so complicated, and can be made so, that Uncle Sam must interfere." The concluding lines of the letter provided a fillip: "Vive la 4th of July! Had a good time on British soil and made some people sick; fired a salute of 13 guns in the morning; at 4 o'clock, and 12, 37 guns; and at dusk 13 more; small arms were fired all day." This demonstration, along with decorations "printed by your humble servant" and two great bon-fires, put to shame, Eck was happy to observe, that of Dominion day, when only "a small flag about the size of a pocket hankerchief [*sic*] made its appearance—the Union Jack, awfully mean and loyal."[97]

Against this background of possible continental war, Riel and his attempts to gain recognition of *métis* rights were as a pawn to be manipulated according to the hopes and fears of various individuals and groups. Mair, however, saw himself as one of a gallant little band that was determined Canada should not be deprived of her destiny in the West by aggression from without and treachery within; the interests of the Hudson's Bay Company, the *métis*, the priests, the disloyal settlers at Red River, were all secondary, and, if necessary, should be sacrificed as such. Amid the excitements of imprisonment, the Portage expedition, the escape across the plains, the shooting of Scott, and the vengeful outcry of Ontario, Riel naturally became Mair's main focus of enmity; but later, on the several occasions when he attempted to analyse the causes and implications of the Riel insurrection of 1869–70, although it is evident that he felt personal animosity towards, even feared, the *métis* leader, Mair never represented him as more than a tool of other, far more dangerous interests.

[95]MP, Mair to R. G. Macbeth, March 19, 1923.
[96]MP, Mair to Allen, Nov. 23, 1923. [97]MP, July 9, 1870.

In a lengthy statement published shortly after his return to Ontario and titled simply "Insurrection in Red River,"[98] Mair placed almost the entire blame at the feet of "The Old Lady of Lime Street"—the Hudson's Bay Company. For years, he said, the Company had kept the North-West hermetically sealed to the outer world and had ruled half-breed and settler alike with exclusive authority. When anyone had independence enough "to speak out and advocate progress and material improvements," he was consoled for the absence of both by a seat on the Company-constituted Council of Assiniboia "or by a sum of money in proportion to the sum of his influence." Part of the Council was a group of English-speaking settlers, a clique "which believes in mosquitoes, grasshoppers, frosts and Crown colonies; which envelopes the stranger, especially the English stranger, in Red River, keeps him carefully from the people, and sends him away with an idea that the country is a swamp, with only a mere riband of dry land along the river." These parasites of the Company, Mair ironically continued, believed "that the only cure for immigration is a Crown Colony," for thereby the *status quo* would be preserved, and immigrants, "instead of pouring into the country as they are so absurdly doing into the North-Western States . . . would not come in at all, or at all events, would drop in one by one, and be amenable to reason."

Mair was obviously recalling here his own early experience at Red River and how he had run afoul of Messrs. Bannatyne and Begg. Bannatyne, he charged, had become "a most useful tool and instrument" of the Company; such, indeed, was his character for treachery that the half-breeds "who have been used and then deserted by him upon former occasions" no longer trusted him. Begg "vehemently ran down his own country, actually advocated annexation to the United States . . . and in consequence attracted Mr. Bannatyne's favourable consideration." As a merchandising partnership they had furnished supplies to Riel and as local postal authority had rifled the mail for him. When there was a danger that their party might be outvoted by the Canadians "whilst meetings and elections were the order of the day," it was undoubtedly a great relief to the "B + B" firm to have the entire body removed and "placed under lock and key at Fort Garry." As a result, "Bannatyne, Begg, the Yankee, the Company and the priests had a fair field," and the other loyal, but less aggressive, English natives were cowed into submission. Mair's duty—and tempera-

[98]Toronto *Globe*, May 7, 1870; an excerpt is reprinted in Denison, *Reminiscences of the Red River Rebellion*, pp. 1–7.

ment—precluded submission, either in December, 1869, or a year earlier; the antipathies he thereby engendered are quite possibly better explanation for Mrs. Bannatyne's horse-whipping and Begg's *Dot-it-Down* than are an indiscreet letter and tactless conduct at a dinner-party.

The priests Mair considered disloyal because they were Roman Catholics and owed allegiance only to Rome. As French Canadians also they were antipathetic to British rule, since it was still too early, he felt, to expect loyalty from a conquered race. Orangeism, however, Mair loftily despised, notwithstanding its support of the Wolseley expedition and his own friendship with Thomas Scott: "A coarse brawling pack of vulgar ruffians and imposters," he classified them; "God help Protestantism in Canada if it has to be defended by that contemptible trash."[99] Jesuitism he regarded as aggressively dangerous, but among the other orders he had friends with whom he corresponded for years—Father Aeneas Macdonell Dawson, for example, who had introduced him to Bishop Taché.

One additional charge made by Mair warrants some brief consideration here, mainly because it implicated a famous Canadian statesman, but also because it was evidently to have an influence upon Mair's literary activity many years afterwards. In his *Globe* article he relates in detail the arrival of the Honourable Joseph Howe at the settlement in advance of McDougall. Howe, he charged, "through a natural proneness to sedition" and the instrumentality of Mr. Sanford, a merchant from Hamilton, Ontario, who accompanied him, "fell completely into the hands of the Bannatyne faction." Because of this it was difficult for any Canadian in Winnipeg to get more than a momentary interview with Howe. When anything further was attempted, Sanford, "who acted as general toad-eater and bodyguard," immediately became "excited, fussy and self-important" and managed to keep Howe at a distance from the Canadians: "Imagine then the indignation of these men when it became evident that Mr. Howe had come to Red River, not as a friend of Canadian autonomy, but as its enemy." The theme of Howe's conversation with others, however, was

that England had lost all affection for her Colonies and looked upon them as a species of barnacles which could not be too speedily rubbed off. As for the North-West Territories, their interests were manifestly with the United States; but aside from this he doubted very much whether Canada was rich enough or powerful enough to govern so extensive a country. Not,

[99]DP, 1733, Aug. 13, 1889.

for that matter of it, that it was not [*sic*] so very much a country after all, for it seemed to him a very cold and miserable country, though the soil he had observed in his travels in the Territory . . . was good enough.

Nevertheless, Howe is reported to have said, if there were any in Red River who differed with him in these general opinions and who wanted rights and privileges, "let them do as the Nova Scotians had done—let them clamour for them and they would get them."

Mair's charge was only part of a widespread denunciation of Howe and his trip then prevalent in Ontario. McDougall himself published a series of open letters to Howe in which he accused the statesman of being "the chief abettor if not the chief instigator"[100] of the Red River insurrection, and in a speech to his constituents at Dalhousie, reported in the Perth *Courier* of July 1, 1870, McDougall stated that "after the most conclusive evidence" he had decided that Howe was "a disloyal man"; he even accused him of negotiating in Ottawa with an American Government spy he had met at Pembina. Howe had answered such charges even before they were made. In a personal letter to McDougall, who at the time was still waiting at Pembina, he protested against "the reports of certain persons," and flatly denied having even seen any of "the leaders of the insurrectionary movement."[101] There is no record of his reaction, if any, to Mair's *Globe* article; and Mair did not repeat his charge, either in published work or private correspondence, until he was a very old man. By the time of Howe's death in 1873 the matter seems to have been generally forgotten; even the excerpt from Mair's article that Denison reprinted that year in his *Reminiscences of the Red River Rebellion* omits it entirely. And Canadian historians have been able to accept without much discussion Howe's denial of complicity in the insurrection. Professor G. F. Stanley maintains that there is no authority for the charge, that it was merely "the result of personal vindictiveness and political partisanship";[102] while Professor W. L. Morton states that "there is no reason to doubt that [Howe] meant, not to foster rebellion . . . , but only to re-assure those anxious about the future."[103]

But historians have generally supported one aspect in particular of Mair's analysis of events at Red River—the danger of American expansion and annexation. The despatching of the Wolseley expedition

[100]*The Red River Rebellion: Eight Letters to Joseph Howe*, p. 6.
[101]PAC, McDougall Papers, 60, Dec. 11, 1869.
[102]*The Birth of Western Canada*, pp. 64–65.
[103]*Begg's Journal*, pp. 44–45.

undoubtedly created and increased antipathies, and a Government more beleaguered than that of Canada at the time could hardly be imagined. French-speaking Quebec, sympathetic to the *métis*, decried the force. English-speaking Ontario, crying for revenge upon the "murderers" of Scott, demanded it. And, as Mair had good reason to know, the United States were watching the whole affair with the keenest of interest. Thus the expedition became a concrete indication to the United States that Britain was really supporting Canada in her expansion westward and, as Professor Creighton affirms, Secretary Fish reluctantly concluded that "there was little prospect of getting half a continent for the *Alabama* claims."[104] History may concede, therefore, that Mair and Canada First, in their naïve, clumsy, and often unthinking way, by their role in assuring that troops be sent, went far to repair the breach their own precipitancy had helped to cause. The tragedy lies, of course, in the fact that such an expedition should ever have been necessary. And although it served its purpose, it could not redeem the losses that had been inflicted upon the cause of national unity, upon personal aspiration, upon human life itself.

The momentous events that took place at Red River in 1868–70 were to inform Mair's whole later life. It is, in fact, almost impossible to surmise what his career would have become without their influence. That he was chastened by his experience there is little doubt, although to what extent is difficult to determine; he himself invariably gave an impression of complete assurance regarding the correctness of his conduct. The presentation speech he made at Belleville in 1870, for example, could be ascribed to any year of his life thereafter. At that time, as reported by the Perth *Courier* of August 19, 1870, he rigorously extolled "that devoted little band" who, when "they saw the flag which is the symbol of liberty and justice insulted and defiled," determined "to defend it with their lives." And yet, even though he was not quite the ridiculously superior egotist causing by his folly a series of tragic events, as Begg saw him, he also was not always the zealous patriot acting from high-minded motives. Somewhere between these extremes was the Charles Mair of 1870, who, like the new Canada he undoubtedly cherished, had been put to a test. From that test he had emerged whole, but not unscathed.

[104]*Dominion of the North*, p. 319.

VI. Canada First
Transition and Decline

THE GRIEVANCES that had stimulated Louis Riel to resist the authority of Canada did not disappear with his departure from Fort Garry in August, 1870; they were only temporarily and partly appeased. Fifteen years later they would reappear and cause an authentic rebellion, not just a "resistance," an "uprising," or an "insurrection." Nor was the bitterness of the interim confined to the defeated *métis*. The despatching of the Wolseley expedition may have saved Canada from annexation by the United States, and it may have re-established the programme of western development; but to those who most ardently demanded and supported it the following months brought indication that it may have been a hollow victory. The bungling that had characterized the negotiations of the Canadian and Imperial governments to effect the transfer of the North-West could not be expunged so easily.

From Charles Mair himself there is little record of the disillusionment felt by his former comrades of the Red River. But in their frustration at what they considered the ungrateful attitude of the Government may be mirrored his own. As early as February, 1870, or three months before the Wolseley force was sent, Mair's former superintendent, John Snow, wrote to him from Ottawa that although Canada had "in her official capacity blundered and made a mess of the whole affair," the disposition seemed to be "to shift the blame from one to another," and to select Mair and himself "for a large share of abuse."[1] Later, from John J. Setter, Mair's companion on the long trek across the frozen plains, came a resentment more explicit. Setter had been rebuffed at Ottawa, "while the low rabble at Fort Garry sent rebel representatives"; he had left his family and occupation to take up arms for Canada and had offered his life "in defence of her flag." At a time when many Canadians were thrust into prison and subjected to the most inhuman treatment, "sufficiently so as to deprive one of them of reason,"[2] he had helped to liberate them. Then, through "the treachery and villany [*sic*] of the thieves at Fort Garry," he had been compelled to flee, only to find a greater treachery at the hands of the Government for which he had fought. "If trouble arises again," he said, "I shall know which side to join."[3] Captain D. R. Cameron, Sir Charles Tupper's son-in-law, expressed to Schultz his "intense disgust with the treatment" accorded by Ottawa to the rebels;[4] and when Riel himself, having quietly returned to the settlement, was publicly thanked by Governor Archibald for rallying his men against the danger of a Fenian invasion led by his former lieutenant, O'Donoghue, loyalist resentment flared anew. "Imagine the feelings of some here," John F. Bain wrote indignantly from Winnipeg, "when they knew the Governor had shaken hands with Riel!" The only consolation Bain could offer, by way of a postscript, was that "The B + B firm have dissolved; cause—the junior partner [Begg] swipes too much."[5]

Even the redoubtable John Schultz was still encountering reverses. Although he was later to serve long terms in both Commons and Senate, in 1870 he was defeated in Manitoba's first election by none other than Donald A. Smith. As interpreted by Denison, this defeat meant "uphill work for loyal Canadians, British Canadians, for years to come."[6] And Schultz, like his friends, felt only bitterness about the Government's policy towards his former enemies. During the investigation of the Select Committee into the "Difficulties in the North-West Territory" he commented to Denison that among the witnesses

[1]MP, Feb. 1, 1870.

[2]William Hallett, the old plains hunter who had sought to advise McDougall at Pembina; "His mind was a wreck and about the time we got to Headingly he took his life by shooting himself" (MP, "Murdoch McLeod").

[3]MP, July 15, 1870.

[4]MP, Oct. 15, 1870. Cameron's bitter letter is marked "strictly confidential," but was, nevertheless, given to Mair.

[5]MP, Oct. 21, 1871. [6]MP, Jan. 22, 1871.

called to testify—men such as Taché, Ritchot, Bannatyne, and Hargrave—no "greater set of rebels could be found." He felt certain that "these beggars will all state that myself, Scott and the other Canadians there caused the rebellion"; and he added, even more prophetically, "we may go down to posterity, embalmed in a Blue Book."[7] Canadian historians know well that Schultz's fears were justified.

More important to Mair personally was the downfall of his former patron, William McDougall. Exhausted physically by an attack of smallpox—which, Morgan knew "*for a fact*," had been deliberately given to him "in the reading room of the House of Commons"[8]—and spiritually by the crumbling of the hopes he had cherished so long, McDougall was thoroughly beaten; "Poor man," said Snow, "he does not seem to have any friends in the House, and many outside say he was cold and heartless always."[9] The enemies of the former Cabinet Minister and Governor-designate were having their day, and there was little he could do for one who was himself a target for their abuse. Henceforth the young poet would be on his own.

The energy and initiative that had already taken Mair both into and out of many adventurous situations were, however, to characterize his actions in the summer of 1870. Notwithstanding the growing conviction of his friends that much of their effort had been in vain, he vigorously continued his speech-making throughout southern and eastern Ontario. And somehow he managed to include even a long journey to the Red River and back during the months of June and July. His correspondence reveals that although he was in Perth on June 1, he was in St. Cloud by June 14, perhaps in Winnipeg about July 2, and in Perth again by July 25. Denison's comment that while he was in St. Cloud Mair could "hear what is going on in the settlement"[10] might imply that he had meant to act in liaison with Wolseley; but a better reason can be offered.

Mair had last seen his wife, Eliza, on February 22, 1870, the day he had set out from Portage la Prairie for St. Paul. Since then she had borne hardships of her own. Shortly after her husband's departure Riel sent an armed band to search the Portage area for "loyalist" refugees. On learning of Mair's escape, the *métis* decided to take Eliza back to Fort Garry, but their scheme was defeated "by the ingenuity of Mrs. George," the wife of the Reverend Henry George, who was able to conceal her (in a manner unrecorded) from Riel's troops. Not long afterwards, "when things had somewhat quieted

[7]DP, April 23, 1874.
[8]MP, June 14, 1905.
[9]MP, March 21, 1870.
[10]MP, June 14, 1870.

down," Eliza went to Winnipeg to search for the manuscripts her husband had left in the Schultz house, but was unable to find them.[11] On this same day, March 4, Thomas Scott was put to death; and again fearing for her safety she sought refuge with the Drevers. Commented Colonel John Dennis: "My heart is sore for that little woman. I hope she may survive all she has had to undergo during the past winter."[12] Eliza not only survived; on July 2, 1870, at Clover Cottage, she gave birth to Maude Louise Mair, the first white child of British parentage born in Winnipeg after the passing of the Manitoba Act,[13] and Mair's haste to return to the country from which he had so recently escaped was probably due to the approach of this event. A popular magazine article states he did not see his daughter until she was three months old;[14] Denison hoped in November that "the baby did not scream when she saw you";[15] but the St. Cloud correspondence indicated that Mair was determined to be at least as close as possible to Eliza when their child was born.

In any case, when order had been restored in Manitoba Mair joined his wife and daughter at Portage la Prairie, where upon the land bought from Charles Demerais exactly one year before their child's birthday, Eliza had had John Garrioch build a store and house. If Mair had ever entertained any thoughts of returning to his medical studies at Queen's they were gone now; the West that he had extolled, even to the point of endangering his life, was to provide his livelihood —and by those specific means he knew best from his earlier days in Lanark and Perth, by general merchandising and trade. And Portage seemed to offer opportunity far greater than even the Ottawa Valley had offered his grandfather and father before him. Here was a new town at the very gateway to a vast new land, through which, as he himself had said, "will flow the unspeakable blessings of free government and civilization." And through which, he might have said, will flow the thousands of immigrants eager to buy land and supplies. The lessons Mair had learned from his astute Scots parentage had been confirmed, even if their application had been interrupted, by John Schultz. Schultz the missionary-speculator had chosen Winnipeg to begin his rise to fortune; Mair chose Portage la Prairie. The Toronto *Globe* of July 19, 1870, offered this revealing editorial comment on

[11]MP, "Notes on Early Rebellion."

[12]MP, April 2, 1870.

[13]Emily Weaver, "Elizabeth Louise Mair—A Red River Pioneer," *Canadian Home Journal*, Dec., 1924, p. 63. Clover Cottage was on the corner of what are now Portage and Main streets, Winnipeg.

[14]*Ibid.*

[15]MP, Nov. 10, 1870.

an advertisement captioned "Ho for the Assiniboine!" that Mair had placed in its columns:

Mr. Chas. Mair, of Red River, proposes to form an emigration party for the North-West this summer. To this end, in conjunction with a firm in Montreal, he has made special agreements with the western railway companies for through and reduced rates to St. Paul, for passengers and freight, and with other parties engaged in waggon transportation over the prairies of Minnesota and Dahcota in a similar manner. The trip will occupy some 20 days, and will be effected with perfect regularity at or near the English Settlement of Portage la Prairie, which is in the very heart of a splendid country, with abundance of wood and water; and on arrival at Fort Garry suitable arrangements will be made for transport to that point.

But Mair was doing only what anyone with similar experience and obligations might have done. He was a store-keeper by trade; and although he may have had talents of a higher order, as McDougall had told him, who would buy them? For the present at least he would have to do his best as a businessman.

Mair's settling in the West marked the beginning of the end for his family in Lanark. In 1871 Holmes Mair sold out and followed his brother to Manitoba to open a store in Westbourne. Margaret Holmes Mair, the mother to whom Charles was so devoted, died in that year, and James, the only other brother still in Lanark or Perth, died suddenly in the spring of 1872. From then until his own death, Charles Mair would be joined to Lanark's lovely hills and quiet river only by indirect relationships, by a few friendships, and by his memories. Even the two or three visits he made in later years were brief, perhaps because his friends of youth, like himself, had left the little village whose prosperity began to decline with the timber trade upon which it depended. A legend still extant in Lanark relates that while Mair and Joshua Fraser were students at Queen's they placed under a boulder near the Clyde a coin talisman that was to be claimed by whichever in later years should return first. Fraser supposedly did not return, dying in a fire at Sharbot Lake in 1883; it is therefore a matter of apparently mystic significance to the very old residents of present-day Lanark that when Charlie Mair sought the talisman in 1906 it had disappeared and that he himself never again returned.

In the fall of 1870, however, the necessity of making a living was uppermost in Mair's mind. A legacy from his sister Margaret Macintyre (whose illness in St. Catharines had prevented his joining McDougall) aided him moderately in 1873, but there is no evidence before that time of any considerable capital by which he might begin merchandising. Immediately upon his return from Red River in July, 1870, he had submitted to the Government a claim for £101 "for expenses incurred and services rendered" while collecting and collating documents during the summer of 1868. A year later, not only had he not received this money, he had also not received satisfaction in respect of another claim. To Hector Langevin, the new Minister of Public Works, Mair complained that "with the exception of some of my wife's clothing returned through the good offices of Bishop Taché, and a table, washstand, bed-stead and sofa . . . restored in ruinous condition," Riel had confiscated and scattered some $3000 worth of his effects. Since this "sore and entirely unjustifiable calamity" had occurred while he was "an officer of the Canadian Government," surely he could expect compensation.[16] Mair's subsequent silence in the matter indicates payment, probably in 1872; and the money received might have been used to repay the wholesalers who backed his Portage venture.

By 1873, certainly, Mair showed signs of becoming a substantial citizen in a growing Portage la Prairie. His papers reveal he had begun to follow Schultz's example of buying and selling land—to the extent that the Winnipeg *Free Press* of February 28, 1873, could report that "Mr. Charles Mair gave a beautiful three-acre lot for a church site at the Portage"; for the church itself he also evidently made frequent contributions of both time and money. Some indication of the manner in which land speculation was conducted is revealed in the confidential correspondence of one of Mair's friends, advising Mair to acquire certain properties that the company employing the friend was anxious to buy.[17] This combination of astuteness and philanthropy, however, brought prestige. In 1875 Mair was appointed by Lieutenant-Governor Morris to membership on the Manitoba Education Board; in 1876 he was elected to the Manitoba Club; numerous letters testify to his leading position in the community. When Morris visited the area he invariably stayed at the Mair residence—although a friendship dating back to youthful days in Perth was probably as much a factor here as Mair's position in the community.

But what of literature? What of Canada First? What had become of the young poet who was to sing of his pride in the great nation-to-

[16]PWF, series 98, subject 429, Mair to Minister of Public Works, March 23, 1871. On September 11, Mair asked Langevin's deputy, T. Trudeau, to place his account "into the hands of Sir George Cartier."

[17]MP, A. W. Burrows to Mair, May 1, 1874.

be? The answers to such questions are to be inferred, it would seem, from the figure of Charles Mair, merchant; Mair the poet and Mair the patriot were, for the time at least, relegated to secondary roles. In later years he was often to quote from the Scott of whom he was so fond: "Literature is a good stick but a poor crutch"; his own comments were to be as direct in meaning and as picturesque in form. Certainly, during the eighteen-seventies, Mair often indicated his yearning to return to writing: "I have not given up all hopes of a dash with literature yet," he told Denison; "my first venture so far as unprejudiced criticism is concerned was a fair success . . . , and bye and bye I shall have leisure again."[18] In the meantime, however, even the requests of friends for occasional contributions had to be refused; "Let merchandize alone for a little every week," in vain asked W. Coldwell, one of the new owners of Schultz's old *Nor' Wester*, "while you give me a blast for the *Manitoban*."[19] Another factor, one that, Mair said, "broke my literary heart," was the loss of his manuscripts when Riel sacked Schultz's house. Mair always insisted that "the villain Donahue [*sic*] . . . [had] them,"[20] although a more probable fate, as friends who had been at the scene told him, was their perishing in the flames that destroyed a great pile of loose papers after the Ontario Rifles had taken possession of Fort Garry. In particular, whatever its fate, did Mair regret the loss of *Zardust and Selima*, the long narrative poem "founded on some incidents of the early life of Zoroaster," and on which he had worked for some five years before going to Red River. He had kept no copies and "as my memory is not retentive in the consecutive sense I could not reproduce it, nor indeed have had time to even attempt it."[21] This poem, he often asserted, would have permanently established his literary reputation.

So the demands of a growing family—by 1878 he and Eliza had five children—despite a similarly growing prosperity, and the loss of his manuscripts in the insurrection deterred Mair from re-entering Canadian letters during the 'seventies. "Sometimes I feel sad enough when I think of these things," he wrote Denison, "but I am robust enough to shake it off, and my 'works' in the shape of five children in healthy bindings take their own place."[22]

Canada First had also suffered a severe blow. In fact as an association of young Canadian patriots it had had its finest hour when the

[18]DP, 724, Feb. 20, 1878. [19]MP, Aug. 6, 1874.
[20]DP, 724, Mair to Denison, Feb. 20, 1878.
[21]*Ibid.* [22]*Ibid.*

Wolseley expedition was dispatched to Fort Garry, although its members even a year later were not aware of their little party's impending dissolution. Ironically, the end came progressively nearer in proportion to the degree of organization that marked the association's development.

The quintet that had gathered in Morgan's Ottawa quarters had never given itself a significant name; even when its membership increased, the designation "Twelve Apostles" had been merely jocular. But in the late summer of 1870, Denison has recorded,

several names were mentioned, and someone said that Edgar had made a suggestion. I walked across the hall into Edgar's office, and asked him what he had suggested. He seemed to have forgotten the exact words, but said, "Canada before all, or Canada first of all." I said, "That will do: Canada First," and went back to my room and proposed it to the others, and after some discussion it was unanimously decided that we should call ourselves the "Canada First" Party, meaning that we should put Canada first, before every other consideration.[23]

Not even then, not until, in fact, the publication in 1871 of Foster's pamphlet, "Canada First: or Our New Nationality," was the name to be given general currency.

For a short time the association carried on its work as it had done before the North-West disturbances. Morgan wrote Mair that "the 'old corner room set' will do well, you may depend on it. We are all on the warpath,"[24] although Foster implied that Morgan was really too busy collecting, clipping, and pasting materials for his various yearbooks and directories, and that since marrying, "the manufacture of babies distracts his mind."[25] As the movement grew in numbers it felt the need of more definite organization but was reluctant to present itself as a political party; therefore the North-West Emigration Aid Society was established, not only to make publicity releases and to organize meetings, but also, as the name implies, to further the cause of western settlement. The same Joseph McDougall to whom Mair had been instructed to report at St. Paul in 1868 was secretary and Mair himself was the Manitoba representative. The society's early success is reflected by the correspondence of both Mair and Denison in which they comment on the large numbers of settlers arriving and departing and on the boatloads of supplies and farm implements sailing northward on the Red River. And still fascinatingly present in

[23]*The Struggle for Imperial Unity*, pp. 49–50.
[24]MP, Aug. 18, 1874. [25]MP, June 10, 1875.

these North-West activities was John Schultz, evidently on his way once again to becoming a prominent figure in Winnipeg.

Denison continued to lecture throughout Ontario and even as far east as Halifax on "the Duty of Canadians to Canada" (a title changed in Halifax, "because of anti-Canadianism," to "the Duty of our Young Men to the State"), the theme of which was, as might be expected, the twofold necessity of a greater national spirit and of the British connection. Always sensitive to England's attitude towards Canada and Canadians, Denison at this time revealed himself as perceptive, even prophetic, when he remarked on what he considered the mother country's irritating indifference to Canada. England had reached a stage of great wealth and affluence, he said, and led by a commercial bloc, she viewed Canada only as an expense; but

> We have the gratifying reflection that the more we rise in the scale of nations the more will this class desire to keep us, until at length every effort will be made to return our affection and secure our fealty. It is our duty therefore to push our way onwards and upwards, to show England that soon the benefits of the connection in a material as well as a moral point of view will be all in her favour.[26]

At the same time, Haliburton, although disturbing Denison by his inclination towards Canadian independence, was delivering widely his "Men of the North" lecture. Whenever we lower our loved ones into the grave, said Haliburton, we trust that the soil thus consecrated by their dust "shall never be violated by a foreign flag or the foot of a foe"; let us learn, he warned, from the example of a mighty nation of the past that for long ages has slumbered on the banks of the Nile: "Accursed be he who holds not the ashes of his fathers sacred, and forgets what is due from the living to the dead."[27] It was through Haliburton that at this time Principal G. M. Grant of Queen's University became sympathetic to Canada First.

W. A. Foster's highly rhetorical "Canada First: or Our New Nationality" was published and enthusiastically received in 1871. "We may," Foster confessed,

> lay ourselves open to the charge of sentimentalism, but men die for sentiment and often sacrifice everything for an idea. There is a national heart which can be stirred to its depths; a national imagination that can be aroused to a fervent glow; and when noble deeds are to be done, or great triumphs of progress and reform to be achieved, we appeal in vain to

[26] *The Struggle for Imperial Unity*, pp. 52–53.
[27] *The Men of the North and Their Place in History*, p. 3.

reason to lead the forlorn hope or mount the imminent deadly breach, but at the first trumpet-blast, passion, enthusiasm, youth, step proudly to the front, and press forward with resistless, eager pace.[28]

In 1874 Foster's initiative and industry resulted in the *Nation*, a weekly journal "thoroughly national and independent of party and of all interests opposed to the broadest patriotism."[29] The same year, he helped to found in Toronto the National Club—"fine furniture, excellent grub, nice company, best of liquor, unexampled cooking," he described it to Mair.[30] In 1875 he delivered a long address, subsequently published, to the Canadian National Association in which he reaffirmed the Canada First platform with its planks of British connection, income franchise, the ballot, minority representation, the encouragement of immigration, and an improved militia system. Goldwin Smith, who had arrived from Oxford by way of Cornell, joined Foster in writing articles and editorials for the *Nation* and for the *Canadian Monthly*, the latter being almost an unofficial party organ for the group.

Even Mair, far removed from the centre of the cause and with less time to devote to patriotic concerns, managed to contribute a two-part article, "The New Canada," to the *Canadian Monthly*.[31] Actually, however, this essay was the slightly revised text of his presentation address at Belleville some years before and therefore involved little preparation. For the most part, also, the article is an abstract of his long descriptive letters to the *Globe* in 1868–69; not until its conclusion does it become a plea to Canadians to realize their present achievement and to visualize their future greatness. Canada stood, he insisted, "like a youth upon the threshold of life, clear-eyed, clear-headed, muscular and strong. Its course is westward. It has traditions and a history to make, a national sentiment to embody, and a national idea to carry out." One of the infallible signs of a national sentiment, Mair emphasized, was a national literature. The contemporary condition of a country's letters is the touchstone, the gauge, of its desire to rise above mere animal satisfactions; a Canadian national literature "must taste of the wood, and be the genuine product of the national imagination and invention." And what a noble heritage the Canadian can have! An atmosphere of crystal, a climate suited above all others to develop the broad shoulder, the tense muscle, and the clear brain,

[28]*Canada First: A Memorial*, p. 45.
[29]Goldwin Smith, introduction to *Canada First: A Memorial*, p. 10.
[30]MP, June 10, 1875.
[31]VIII (1875), 2–8 and 156–64.

and which will build up the most herculean and robust nation on earth. But above all, Canada is

the hope of the despairing poor of the world, a boundless ocean of land, diversified by rolling hills, by lakes and woods, or swelling into illimitable plain. The haunt of the Indian, the bison, and the antelope, waiting with majestic patience for the flocks and the fields, the schools, the churches, the Christian faith and love of freedom of the coming men.

These last sentences are particularly reflective of the emotive, visionary character of Canada First and of the sometimes contradictory attitudes that continue to puzzle anyone searching for consistency in its views. What, one would like to ask, might Mair's answer have been if he had been queried on the possibly opposing connotations of "the despairing poor of the world" and "the Christian faith"? Or how could he at one time write, "if we are to be a country it must be made so by Canadians of all races,"[32] and at another, "if others had seen eye to eye with us, the machinations of the H.B.Co. and Quebec would have been defeated and we should have had millions of our own people instead of running the risk of being submerged by foreigners"?[33] And these latter immigrants he often refers to in terms of "semi-barbarous hordes" or of "inundations of alien races with wild socialistic opinions and bizarre religions."[34]

But enough attention has been given already to the characters and personalities of Mair and his associates to indicate that their attitudes were a weak basis for transcontinental union. One can only feel that even if other factors had not arisen, the future of Canada First as it was constituted would have been limited. For notwithstanding the fervently patriotic urgings of Denison, Mair, Foster, and Haliburton, by 1875 Canada First had perished. The Toronto group had welcomed enthusiastically the coming into their midst of Goldwin Smith; his statement of their aims—"to cultivate Canadian patriotism, to raise Canada above the rank of a mere dependency, and to give her the first place in Canadian hearts"[35]—could not have been, they felt, more apt. But their confidence was greatly misplaced. In the very fact that under Smith's influence Canada First developed from a youthfully sentimental idealization of Canadian nationality to a more practical participation in public and political affairs, there was, paradoxically, a corruptive element. When the movement entered the political arena as

[32]DP, 1733, Mair to Denison, Aug. 13, 1889.
[33]*Ibid.*, 4728, Aug. 10, 1903.
[34]*Ibid.*, 4501, Good Friday, 1902.
[35]*Canada First*, p. 3.

a party, the big guns of the Liberals and Tories alike had little difficulty in finding a target.

The first real blow to the movement, however, came from within. At the first public meeting of the "Canadian National Party," the chairman, W. H. Howland, made a startling assertion. As Denison recorded, Howland

> held that there was too much toadyism to English aristocratic usages in this country. There was too much toadyism to titles. We would have no aristocracy in this country but the aristocracy of merit, no order but the order of merit, and the sooner the English Government recognized the fact that the adornment of a man in this country with the feelings they entertained was rather an insult than an honour to our people, the sooner would they appreciate our real sentiment. Many Canadians who had gone home had, he held, brought us into contempt by their toadying.[36]

Denison had made similar remarks himself and no one had doubted his loyalty. But Howland's father had been an American, and to the press, the Liberals and Tories, and the Canada First party alike, his remarks seemed a traitorous prelude to a campaign for annexation. "Our friend Howland," Denison wrote Mair, "killed Canada First . . . in one fifteen minute speech."[37]

In the wrangle that followed it became increasingly clear that there was a split in the party: its founders were in greater fear of the United States than of Britain, and the last thing they wanted was the severance of the British connection. Goldwin Smith now showed his true colours as an advocate of independence, even of continental union, and the disintegration from internal and external forces could not be stopped. Denison and Foster thought for a while that Edward Blake's joining their ranks would serve the cause, but even Blake's famous "Aurora" speech in 1874, hailed as it was by them, was attacked, again by both Liberal and Tory, as a dangerous preoccupation with independence and with its inevitable corollary, annexation. A year later, Blake, "his hot fit of insurgency having cooled off,"[38] defected to become Minister of Justice in Alexander Mackenzie's Cabinet, and Canada First came to an end. The *Nation* ceased publication and the National Club concentrated more upon Foster's "fine furniture, excellent grub" than upon providing a meeting place for young political reformers.

[36]*The Struggle for Imperial Unity*, p. 60.
[37]MP, Feb. 20, 1876.
[38]W. S. Wallace, *The Growth of Canadian National Feeling*, p. 53.

Historical perspective allows the contemporary critic to see with Stewart Wallace that Canada First never really had a chance as a political party. As long as it remained an intellectual movement it could exist, but "once it entered the political battlefield it caused the jealousy and suspicion of the two older parties, and so drew on itself a concentrated fire from two sides."[39] Even as an intellectual movement comprising five young men it had become involved in antipathies and prejudices that should have brought home forcefully the realization that its vision required realistic modification. But as the "Canadian National party" during a period of physical expansion and political confusion it became inextricably involved in misunderstandings and distrusts. The terms "patriotism" and "loyalty" were ambiguously interpreted—in some quarters, perhaps, intentionally. Thus the Toronto *Globe* in particular assailed the *Nation* and its supporters in terms of their "disloyalty" to England, their "anti-Britishism," because they dared to question in any way Canada's ties with Great Britain.

And yet, it is not quite correct to say with Professor A. R. M. Lower that for the *Nation* "reality was Ontario and within Ontario, Toronto and its neighbourhood."[40] For later years were to reveal the lack of unanimity of objectives that had actually existed, evidently unknown even to themselves, among the founding members. Denison, for example, without difficulty became an Imperial Federationist, and Haliburton more and more expressed a hope, like Goldwin Smith's, that Canada would sever completely her connection with Britain. Perhaps only Mair, as one of his patriotic odes was to reveal, had the vision that Canada First is now generally considered to have had—that of a strong nation "erect, unbound by Britain's side."

Certainly it is clear that the Mair of Manitoba in the 'seventies is different from the Mair of Ontario in the 'sixties. His decision to prosper with the West made him a westerner, and during the seven years of his stay in Portage la Prairie he began to evaluate national expansion and development from a new point of view. Most significant is the fact that by 1876 he no longer approved of a Government influenced strongly by Ontario opinion, as the Mackenzie régime from 1873 to 1878 undoubtedly was, and despite his own prospering, "the sullen discontent that broods over this province" appeared ominous to him. "I fear Canada raised up a grit Frankenstein in this man Mackenzie and his strange following of Canada First, reds, radicals and annexationists," he wrote; "At all events *we* have

[39] *Ibid.*
[40] *Canada, Nation and Neighbour,* p. 128.

exchanged whips for scorpions and bread for stones."[41] The "new Canada," he felt, was being divided by "a provincialism more cramped and narrow than that of '37 until the very name of Ontario stinks throughout the North-West, and its scattered natives are fain to hide their shame under the generic term of 'Upper Canadian.' "[42]

When Denison reminded Mair that they both had voted to turn out Sir John A. Macdonald and Sir George Cartier, hoping they would obtain a "Protestant" government "or at least one that would not be a tool of the R.C. priesthood,"[43] Mair insisted that Ultramontanism was "a great bug-bear" from which there was very little to fear. But he had lived, he said, to see the germ of a real national party strangled "in the embraces of a Goldwin Smith and a policy of antagonism to the North-West espoused by an Edward Blake," to see the hopes of Canada First wrecked by "audacious theorists" and " 'young Canada' looked upon as synonymous with disloyalty." The only recourse was what he had always advocated:

> Development should be the keynote for half a century to come. Our very existence depends upon it, yet we see instead of this the most rudimentary interests of this great country neglected and her people insulted. . . . A Fabian policy may suit a time of war, but the Cunctator is surely out of place in an era like this. Whilst our neighbours are building up their western interest with unparalleled rapidity, our philosophical rulers are keeping our West a sealed book.[44]

To Denison's dry remark that Mair's insistence upon the return of a Tory government revealed "a complete *bouleversement*," Mair replied that he had merely undergone a change of opinion—"the simple product of observation and experience, a thing of slow growth." But it is hardly likely that Denison, as a member of the old "Corner Room" set, would see the greater irony in Mair's declaration that a greater Canada would be the product of time "and not the sudden discovery of . . . visionaries who at a moment's notice, like the German philosopher, can evolve constitutions out of the depths of their own consciousness."[45] Such an attitude was not, as it first may appear, a contradiction of Mair's interpretation of Mackenzie's policies as "Fabian." But it appears strangely incongruous in a man who had himself not long before been a visionary among other visionaries. And once again one is led to conclude that in Charles Mair's case these

[41]DP, 380, Mair to Denison, Jan. 28, 1876.
[42]*Ibid.*, 392, March 16, 1876.
[43]MP, Feb. 20, 1876.
[44]DP, 390, March 16, 1876.
[45]*Ibid.*, 394.

shifts in assessment, evaluation, and opinion reflect an emotional rather than an intellectual personality, a rigid discipline in both home and school in matters ethical, political, and cultural, and an inability to reserve judgment, even action, at times of crisis, whether major or minor. In 1876, Mair was not yet forty; he still had to undergo another fifty years "of observation and experience, a thing of slow growth." Much of it was to be difficult, even grievous, for him.

VII. Prince Albert Crossroads of Commerce

TO THE WEST of Portage la Prairie the great plains seem unlimited even by the horizon, and the Canadian from the East, especially if he has travelled by train across the Precambrian Shield of northwest Ontario with its rock and forest, its lakes and swamps, feels that he has crossed a barrier into a new land. And, of course, in a sense he has. Even before he has reached Winnipeg or Portage, sixty miles further on, he has seen the woods disappear, the uneven landscape flatten to a monotony, and the welter of fallen trees, streams, and granite cliffs become, with little or no modulation, a broad expanse of mildly undulating grass-land here and there dotted with bluffs of poplar or willow and cut across by coulees and slow-moving creeks. If not a new land, this is certainly a different land.

And to Charles Mair in the eighteen-seventies it was more than merely new or different; it was almost the Promised Land, the dream land—he had called it both—where Canada's future lay. This was the West that he had said within a century would have over thirty millions of prosperous Canadians, the envy of the entire world; it was the West that men for centuries had been yearning to find. The disillusionment Mair began to feel after living in Portage for a few years was not due to a reappraisal of this land, but rather to what he once again considered short-sightedness at Ottawa. He himself had done his utmost to save the country, to settle it. And according to the available evidence he had flourished accordingly: "We are well," he wrote

Denison, "and thanks to . . . hard work under God's goodness, prosperous and free from care."[1] But development was not proceeding quickly enough; the long-promised railway was nowhere in sight, and although settlers were arriving, their number was insignificant compared to what had been expected.

And as far as Mair was concerned, not nearly enough were going to Portage, the outpost through which his envisioned millions were to pass. Most were going to Winnipeg and either staying there or fanning out below and beyond Portage: those who stayed, indeed, were to help John Schultz become a millionaire. But Mair had chosen Portage, and for obvious reasons. He was undoubtedly still sensitive about his past experiences in Red River and, moreover, Portage was the intensely loyal community of British and Canadians who with him as a leader had organized and manned the attempt to restore the flag at Garry. And as his letters to the *Globe* in 1869–70 had emphasized, Portage was the beginning of "the path of empire and the garden of the world." A village like Winnipeg, he admitted, was a village with a future,

> yet this was by no means assured. There were misgivings and grave uncertainties about it which lasted for years. . . . In fact, it was a little weather-boarded Tambov in the wilderness, much of the lumber used being of black poplar, green sawn, which never ceased shrinking. Indeed we used to say at the Portage that, given time enough, it would shrink out of sight.[2]

But Winnipeg was a "noisy little place" whereas Portage was one of "customary quiet and orderly existence." And the North American West grew by noisy little places, not by quiet, orderly ones.

In 1877, therefore, Mair once again headed northwest, this time going beyond the boundaries of the new province until he had reached the North Saskatchewan River; and on the banks of that great river, thirty miles west of the point where it is met by the south branch, he settled in Prince Albert Mission. The trip itself was in the western pioneering tradition and even the fragmentary relation of it that Mair's papers have left deserves recording. The greatest danger lay, evidently, in the unpredictable character of the Indians, many of whom both in the Portage district and westward were remnants of Sioux and Dakotas involved in the Minnesota massacre of 1862, although, Mair was quick to emphasize, "the brutal outrages of American frontiers-

[1]DP, 380, Jan. 28, 1876.
[2]MP, Mair to E. H. Macklin, Nov. 25, 1922.

men . . . really gave rise to it."[3] By 1877, also, these Indians had been joined by refugees of Sitting Bull's band, the annihilators of Custer's troops at Little Big Horn the year before; somewhere in Canada now, probably, is the watch that Mair bought from one of these Sioux and that had belonged to a Lieutenant Crittenden of the Kentucky Rifles, killed with Custer.[4] Mair had made fur-trading trips up the Saskatchewan twice before, in 1874 and 1876, and had evidently gained no assurance for his family's safety other than that "sometimes the Indians were friendly, sometimes the reverse."[5] Travellers and settlers waited, therefore, until a party was raised and, amid the screech of Red River carts, all started together. "At the time we left Portage there was a treck of half-breeds from High Bluff and Poplar Point going to settle in the Saskatchewan country. So [we] joined in the train, which consisted of about 25 . . . carts, numerous horses and dogs, and headed by ourselves in a democrat covered over in the true pioneer style." At night when camp was made, "the carts formed a big circle with shafts to the centre, the tents were pitched inside and each family had its own little part of the circle."[6]

Just as he had chosen Portage la Prairie in 1870, Mair decided to settle in Prince Albert for reasons that are particularly characteristic. Like the Manitoba village, Prince Albert was predominantly British, having been founded only eleven years before by the Reverend James Nesbit, a Presbyterian minister who, "true to that unyielding spirit of loyalty to the British crown which is characteristic of all Scotchmen in the Northwest, and out of respect for the memory of the late Prince consort, . . . called the mission 'Prince Albert.'"[7] Since that time many of the village's settlers had been Mair's friends in Red River—the Drevers, the MacBeths, the McKays, the Sutherlands, the Halcros (one of whom was David, the English half-breed guide of the escape to St. Paul in 1870). There are to be considered, also, some of Mair's own statements in his newspaper articles of eight years before. In the *Globe* of May 28, 1869, he had written:

The South Saskatchewan country, though doubtless a fair one, is not *the* country. It is the North Saskatchewan, which divides the rich prairie from

[3]*Ibid.*

[4]Mair sent the watch to be identified by its makers in London, England, and was informed it had been bought while Crittenden was on his wedding trip in London in 1875.

[5]MP, Mrs. E. J. Cann to Elizabeth Bailey Price, *ca.* 1926 (draft notes).

[6]*Ibid.*

[7]*McPhillips's Alphabetical and Business Directory of the District of Saskatchewan, N.W.T.* (1888), p. 31.

the equally rich timber, and through which twenty years hence we must tap the boundless and magnificent expanses of Peace River, lying beyond the so-called fertile belt, but which, according to statements made to the writer by his lordship the Bishop of St. Boniface, are superior to the fertile belt itself, both in soil and climate.

In this same article he had proposed a system of dams and canals, "a vast and comprehensive scheme" that in all probability would be accomplished within the next twenty years and that would "astonish the world." But even before this there would surely be the railway, and although the main line of the transcontinental was not to go through Prince Albert, it was to be but a few miles south and could be easily joined. And it seemed logical that this north-south route would eventually continue through Prince Albert to Hudson Bay itself, making the town a veritable crossroads not only for the commerce of Canada but, indeed, for the whole world. In 1877 all of this was an eminently practicable vision to Charles Mair when he arrived in the mission, where he "immediately built a store on river lot 68 and commenced business on eastern principles, putting counters in his store and displaying his wares to the natives."[8] Not that he himself ever stated his reasons for going westward in quite those terms. But again, as at Portage, he undoubtedly wished to flourish personally as Canada did nationally, and there is a particular significance, therefore, to the otherwise romantic assertion he once made that he was "charmed by the descriptions of the far away Saskatchewan country."[9]

Prince Albert and the events that occurred there while Charles Mair was one of its pioneering inhabitants were to constitute a shaping influence upon his life and career quite as significant as that of Lanark or of Red River. When viewed, indeed, in relation to his life as a whole, they appear as a modulation between his early and late years, between the keynotes of Lanark and Red River and those of his subsequent career. The villages on the Clyde in Ontario and the Red in Manitoba had fostered a strong personality, a young man of varied abilities and fervent aspirations. Now, another village, even farther to the west, was to provide scope for these qualities, was, indeed, to test them by providing experiences that Mair's vision of his own and his country's future had not included.

While shop-keeping and fur-trading at Portage, Mair had written very little and had published nothing. Within a few months of his arrival in Prince Albert, however, he remarked, almost incidentally,

[8] *Ibid.*, p. 33.
[9] MP, quoted by Mrs. E. J. Cann to Elizabeth Bailey Price, *ca.* 1926.

to Denison: "I dream of taking up the character of Tecumseh and making something of it. It is a noble subject."[10] Not that Mair ever believed he could be merchant and trader in the morning of any given day and poet in the afternoon, even though *Dreamland* had been written in virtually such circumstances. That work, however, had been the result of several years' intermittent labour; its unevenness, indeed, reflects the disjunct nature of its creation. And the Mair of the eighteen-fifties and 'sixties had not had a large family to draw upon his energies, inspirational and otherwise. By 1878, therefore, he had decided that if he still hoped for a position of prominence in Canadian letters he must first apply his business acumen to the pursuit of economic security, a security that would enable him to turn completely, if only for a year or so, to literary work. There is nothing particularly unusual about such an attitude, of course, but it is one that seems to have become characteristically Canadian. One is reminded, for example, of Professor E. K. Brown's relation of a conversation he had with Philip Child. The novelist had remarked that

> a writer must be the obsequious servant of his demon, must rush to write when the demon stirs, and let other things fall where they may. If you fob off the demon with an excuse, telling him to wait till you can leave the office, he will sulk, his visits will become rarer and finally he will not return at all.

And to Brown it was obvious that the weaknesses in certain types of Canadian literature—the epic, the drama—were directly related "to the need of Canadians to be something else than writers in most of their time through their best creative years."[11]

The years 1878–82, therefore, give a picture of Mair the businessman, Mair the citizen. They also give a more detailed picture of Mair the personality, the *paterfamilias*. A second daughter, Florence, had been born in 1872 and a third, Fanny George (named for her godfather and Mair's old friend, the Reverend Henry George), in 1873. In 1876 he was particularly proud to announce to Denison the birth of his first son: "the little villain bears your name";[12] and during the next two years he frequently revealed how much he cherished this child. "Have you heard of 'dream children'," he wrote, "—a supposititious *infant*ry, the gift of some wicked fairy, and which disappears after a time in thin air?" Thus, even the birth of a second son, Cecil,

[10]DP, 727, Feb. 20, 1878.
[11]*On Canadian Poetry*, p. 11.
[12]DP, 380, Jan. 28, 1876.

in 1878 could hardly temper the irony that had become pathetically explicit in such a query when Mair informed Denison:

Your poor little namesake is dead. He died of scarlet fever after a short illness of only four days. . . . Poor little fellow! He was my ideal, the light of my heart and hearth. . . . Perhaps I have been punished for my overloving him, and it may be for the best, but it is very hard to bear. . . .

Dear Denison, . . . I often pictured to myself your first meeting with him, and how delighted you would have been with him, and how delighted you would been with his beautiful eyes and frank, manly face and figure! But I trust we shall see him yet.

How futile is this heaping up of earthly goods: "We know not who shall reap them." To place him well in the world I have strained every nerve in business, and trampled every other instinct under foot. I have succeeded—and failed. . . . My ambition was to make him happy; the end of it all is the aching void in my heart and the little grave in the wilderness.[13]

After a judicious discount for Victorian sentimentality and for Mair's tendency to strike a conventional pose, the sense of loss is no less heartfelt.

The year 1878, indeed, was one of more than usual grief. To the death of a son were added the trials of nursing his other children through a diphtheria epidemic that swept the West, not to mention those of embarking upon the new life in Prince Albert. One other occurrence of the year has both tragic and comic elements. In January Mair's acquaintance and character-reference when he left Ottawa in 1868, the Reverend Aeneas Macdonell Dawson, had written to Henry J. Morgan to express his sorrow that "our friend Mair is no more," and to hope that the memory of "undoubtedly one of our best poets" could be perpetuated in a memorial volume of his best verses.[14] And the obituary he enclosed was certainly that of Charles Mair, author of *Dreamland*. Commented Morgan to the still much alive poet: "It is not often one has an opportunity of reading one's own obituary. Very few have had that experience, but Brougham."[15] The dead poet ("he wrote some very pretty verses") was actually Mair's brother Holmes, who had settled in Westbourne, Manitoba, and had become the victim of a weak constitution and diphtheria at the age of forty-nine. He had lived but a short time in the West he had helped to advertise in 1868 when he gave "Letters from Red River" to the Perth *Courier* and the Toronto *Globe*.

But Mair would remember the year for another, more gratifying

[13]DP, 768, Nov. 19, 1878.
[14]MP, Jan. 20, 1878.
[15]MP, Jan. 25, 1878.

reason: "In 1878 the Mackenzie administration came to an end in a universal shout of 'Thank God!' and the country sprang to its feet under Sir John Macdonald's National Policy."[16] And under that policy of western settlement, protective tariffs, and the transcontinental railway, both Mair and Prince Albert flourished. The railway was still far to the east, but it was definitely coming, and with it would be thousands of settlers anxious to buy land and goods. Almost immediately, depression in the West was replaced by boundless optimism and the more tangible signs of prosperity. Within a few short years the Prince Albert *Times* of November 1, 1882, could quote approvingly a letter that a recent visitor, Senator James Turner of Hamilton, Ontario, had seen fit to write to the Montreal *Gazette* and in which he had extolled Prince Albert's "splendid geographical position," its "extensive and imposing appearance," and the fact that "building seems to be limited only by the lumber supply"—and even that would be doubled soon when the third new steam saw mill came into operation. Certainly the town was "the most populous and prosperous in the Saskatchewan valley." That Turner could conclude by commenting on the considerable amount of real-estate changing hands "at enhanced values" and also on the fact that other "fortunate proprietors seem to prefer holding to await railway developments" indicates a seeming lack of attention paid to a warning implied as early as May 23, 1881, by the Saskatchewan *Herald* of Battleford: "The numerous changes of route in the railway that have from time to time been made blasted many a nice scheme on the part of speculators who thought they had the inside track, and relegated to their original solitude many ambitious hamlets that aspired to become powerful centres of trade." The *Times*, indeed, while admitting, on November 16, 1882, that changes in route had placed Prince Albert "considerably north of the line of railways," noted that the town was nevertheless "of the same latitude as Dublin, Liverpool and Berlin" and "nearly five hundred miles south of Christiania, Stockholm and St. Petersburg and other European cities which are not usually regarded as being in the extreme north." Railways were to be built from the south and "the River Navigation Company will give us direct communication with the Eastern Provinces," while "the proposed Hudson's Bay route will . . . place Prince Albert as near Liverpool as Toronto and in a more advantageous position than any other town in Manitoba or the North West Territories." Besides, as everyone in Prince Albert knew, the citizens of Battleford who had settled there "with the understanding that they would be in the vicinity of the capital and

[16]MP, Mair to King Barker, Jan. 19, 1925.

on the line of railway" had never really recovered from having "their hopes blasted" when the C.P.R. route was changed and Regina was proposed as capital.[17]

Charles Mair shared fully in the Prince Albert boom. Not only shared in, but helped to create it. To him went a large amount of the credit for establishing the newspaper; then he proceeded to write much of its persuasive, almost propagandizing, copy (one can easily suspect that Senator Turner, a close friend, wrote his account of the town at Mair's request). The river navigation development, his vision of 1869, Mair constantly urged and advertised. And the Hudson Bay railway was to be virtually an obsession with him long after other westerners had dismissed it as impracticable. As a result of his energy, resourcefulness, and journalistic talents he quickly found himself in the role of leading citizen. Not only does the Anglican bishop thank him for gifts of land and "magnificent chandeliers," as in Portage la Prairie; he also discusses with him the possibility of building a college to be affiliated with the new university in Manitoba. The same bishop asks him "in confidence" on what terms "I could secure a few lots of land *for my own private* account, not for church or school or any other Diocesan purposes" (the irony is heightened here by the reverend gentleman's addressing his correspondent as "Charles Mair, Justice of the Peace").[18] As early as September 23, 1878, the Saskatchewan *Herald* records that when Prince Albert "had the pleasure of seeing the Lieutenant-Governor for the first time," he was "a guest at the house of Charles Mair, Esq." The *Times* of November 1, 1882, reports a meeting of "the principal residents" called "at the instance of C. Mair, Esq.," to discuss construction of a telegraph line to Humboldt. Even if a somewhat incongruous note is struck by the complaint of the *Herald* on March 10, 1879, that "the Indians make night hideous with their 'hi, hi, hi' when all the settlement are abed," one can easily infer that Mair might often be seen glancing approvingly at the "handsome, well-stocked, modern-fronted stores" or chatting on the main street with "well-dressed, watch-wearing, cigar-smoking men from the East."[19] As he wrote to Denison,

Prince Albert is making gigantic strides and promises to be another Winnipeg. It is much nearer Hudson's Bay and is yet nearly 600 miles

[17]*McPhillips's Directory*, p. 53. Regina became the capital of the Territories on March 27, 1883.

[18]MP, Bishop McLean to Mair, Feb. 23, 1880, Jan. 24, 1882, and Feb. 3, 1882.

[19]E. H. Oliver, "Economic Conditions in Saskatchewan, 1870–1881," *Trans. Roy. Soc. Can.*, ser. 3, XXVII (1933), p. 22.

Charles Mair at about 14 (from a daguerreotype in the Perth Museum)

The Mair home in Lanark, 1962.

The Founders of the "Canada First" Party

When Colonel George T. Denison's new book, "The Struggle for Imperial Unity," was reviewed in these columns recently it was noted that, in the opinion of the author, the growth of Imperialism in Canada began with the organization of the Canada First party by five young men in 1868. In the spring of that year, soon after Confederation, Colonel Denison spent some time in Ottawa, where he and a young Toronto lawyer, Wm. A. Foster, were introduced by a mutual friend, Dr. Henry J. Morgan, to Charles Mair, of Lanark, Ont., and Robert J. Haliburton, of Halifax, eldest son of the famous author of "Sam Slick." These five young men were congenial spirits, bubbling over with patriotism, and they became close friends. They met almost nightly at Dr. Morgan's rooms, where they discussed the future of the new Dominion. As Colonel Denison says in his book: "It ended in our making a solemn pledge to each other that we would do all we could to advance the interests of our native land; that we would put our country first, before all personal, or political, or party consideration." Some years afterwards they chose for their association the name "Canada First."

Through the courtesy of Dr. Morgan, of Ottawa, photographs of the Canada First group, at the time they initiated the movement, are reproduced on this page, and they are interesting indeed. These patriotic idealists were then young men about twenty-eight years of age, excepting Haliburton, who was four or five years older.

The founders of the Canada First Party as they appeared in May, 1868 (Toronto *Saturday Night*, April 24, 1909)

Winnipeg, 1869; John Schultz's store and dispensary have been marked by Mair with an X
(Mair Papers, Queen's University)

Charles and Eliza Mair on their wedding trip, St. Paul, Minnesota, September, 1869 (Perth Museum)

John J. Setter, Charles Mair, Dr. Joseph Lynch, and William Drever at Fort Abercrombie, Dakota, March, 1870, after their trip across the plains (Mair Papers, Queen's University)

Thomas Scott, 1869 (Mair Papers, Queen's University)

The Honourable William McDougall in 1869 (Mair Papers, Queen's University)

Clover Cottage, 1869, the home of William Drever, where Mair sought refuge after his escape from Fort Garry in January, 1870 (Mair Papers, Queen's University)

John Schultz's house and store in Winnipeg as it appeared in April, 1912; Charles Mair is standing in the doorway (Mair Papers, Queen's University)

Charles Mair and son Cecil, 1883 (Mair Papers, Queen's University)

Charles Mair, 1925 (Mair Papers, Queen's University)

north-west of it. The South Saskatchewan Valley Railway Co. delegates were here . . . and are anxious to make Prince Albert their terminus. I am the largest land owner here and am of course deeply interested as the station is to be on my property and it will be immensely valuable. I have 800 acres in one block in the heart of the town, and I see before me a vast amount of work.[20]

He did not mention that he also had a farm of "nearly 200 acres under cultivation," of which "the grain is the finest in the world"[21] and a flour mill going "in full blast,"[22] processing that grain.

Charles Mair of Prince Albert was not merely striving for an economic security that would enable him to return to letters, notwithstanding his comment to Denison: "Business, business, if I could only shake off that Old Man of the Sea for one year!"[23] Rather he was now obviously desirous of a position of affluence and influence and of the respectability he felt to be axiomatic of these virtues. The shrewdness and determination inherited from Scots pioneers, the pride and sense of his own individuality instilled by his mother and stimulated by his association with Denison and other notables, all combined with a sincere aspiration to further the "true interests" of his country. He had become the type of missionary-speculator characteristic of imperial expansion: his own particular models were the Denisons of Toronto and Schultz of Winnipeg. He had set his stakes in "the unsullied freedom of the North," far beyond Ontario where it was too late for such as he to compete with the Robinson and Denison families, in a little town on the North Saskatchewan that was still virtually unknown east of Winnipeg. And the evidence reveals that if any of the culture—commercial, literary, and social—of Toronto or Ottawa was acquired by frontier Prince Albert, Charles Mair was the pioneer mainly responsible. "You will yet see a city [here] as big as your own," he wrote Denison, "for all your 'laffin'!"[24]

And so while his advertisements announced that he was "the largest owner of Real Estate in P.A. with the exception of the H.B.Co.," Mair maintained, or at least tried to do so, a position of social and cultural eminence in the community. Besides entertaining the Lieutenant-Governor at the largest home in Prince Albert, he instigated the establishment of the Saskatchewan Club ("to make more favourable the impressions visitors to the country may receive"), of the

[20]DP, 837, Nov. 7, 1882.
[21]Oliver, "Economic Conditions in Saskatchewan, 1870–1881," p. 22.
[22]Prince Albert *Times*, Nov. 22, 1882.
[23]DP, 837, Nov. 7, 1882.
[24]DP, 1733, Aug. 13, 1889.

Young Men's Literary and Athletic Club, and, with the help of the clergy, of schools and ecclesiastical colleges. As might be expected in the case of a frontier town, however, much of the cultural fare offered was not of a particularly high level. As proudly reported by the *Times* of November 23, 1883, the "formal opening programme" of the P.A.Y.M.L.A.C. is worth at least partial quotation:

Song:— "A Flower from my angel mother's grave" very prettily sung by Miss Mackenzie.

Reading:— By Mr. Fitz-Cochrane, "Gray's elegy on [*sic*] a Country Churchyard."

Song:— By Mrs. Col. Sproat, "Jock O'Hazeldean," which was so acceptably delivered as to call for an unanimous encore, which produced that ever-popular old song "Comin' thro' the Rye", also very nicely sung.

The next number was a reading by Mr. J. O. Davis, but he was prevented by illness from appearing. . . .

Mr. Joseph Hanafin read the celebrated speech by Sergeant Buzfuz from Pickwick, in very good form.

Mrs. Brown then favoured the audience with the song "Twickenham Ferry" in such acceptable style as to demand an encore, to which she kindly responded with "Two is Company, Three is None," which was also well received. . . .

The programme was well wound up by a comic song, in character, "Patrick, Mind the Baby," by T. O. Davis, given in his best style, which brought down the house, and he was obliged to respond with "When McGinnis Gets a Job," which also took the house by storm.

On this occasion "coffee and cake were handed around to the ladies"; but it seems safe to infer that such polite refreshments were not the general rule in Prince Albert social activities. A St. Andrew's Society dinner is described by one observer as a "veritable orgy,"[25] Dr. Bain, later to become the mayor, as "having gone on another rampage,"[26] and an election celebration as turning into "a very wet night."[27] Such incidents could occur despite the fact that the Territories were theoretically limited by an extremely restrictive permit system, for there were obviously ways to circumvent the regulations. "Your permit request rather staggard [*sic*] me," wrote Lieutenant-Governor David Laird to Mair; "however, I have [sent] all except the whisky, and if this article is much required, I would prefer to give you a permit at another date, not to let so much appear at once on my books."[28] Prince Albert's thirst aroused comment even in

[25]MP, A. Sproat to Mair, Dec. 5, 1883.
[26]*Ibid.*, April 10, 1883.
[27]*Ibid.*, June 9, 1883.
[28]MP, March 29, 1879.

Ottawa. Sir John A. remarked to the local Member that he had heard the town had become "the asylum for drunkards"; but when the Prime Minister acknowledged that "whisky was the only cure for rattlesnake bites" the M.P. seized "the opportunity of remarking that Prince Albert was full of snakes and that they were particularly thick around the Club."[29] Such pleading evidently had been of little avail, however, when Mair described to Denison a dinner party that he had recently held for Lord Boyle and other visiting dignitaries from the East:

> . . . his lordship got drunk in advance and nearly upset the dinner table before being seated. In fact, but for my catching it on the opposite side in the nick of time, it would have gone. There was a clergyman on board, and consequently some suspense. The wines were borrowed for the occasion from the various "communion" stores of diverse dominations, Roman Catholic and Protestant; but as they hadn't been "consecrated" we took them down without any special qualms. The whisky was the product of one of the native stills growing numerous under the fostering influence of an injurious law passed over our heads by the enlightened people of Ontario. Its fusil properties would have brought down a pyramid, let alone poor Boyle, who in a weak moment had taken a glass or two of it before going to the dinner party. How [they] all got home again is one of those inscrutable mysteries which can only be relegated to the Limbo of Conjecture. . . .
>
> The next night we had the same lot to a whist party and supper, and with a few bottles of old rye, which fortunately had been smuggled in by an acquaintance, restored them all to their proper selves and ordinary intelligence and condition. But for this lucky accident I believe they would have all died. I didn't ask the clergyman, though. He is a newcomer, and I thought it better to spare his feelings, for knowing the sort of article with which Boyle had been innocently tampering, it struck me he would be brought up to our house on a stretcher.

Mair is obviously enjoying himself in framing this Prince Albert social note. And any suggestion of frontier crudeness that might be inferred he explains away in a self-righteous denunciation of his old home province: "Oh! ye bigots, fools and tyrants of the East, will you never learn wisdom? . . . Shame upon you all! Be decent and abolish the brutal Permit system. . . ."[30] It seems curious, however, that he never comments on the part played by John Schultz, who by this time was Senator Schultz, in the advocacy of western prohibition. Perhaps he would have justified Schultz's concern as being in

[29]MP, D. H. Macdowall to Mair, May 1, 1883.
[30]DP, 1578, Jan. 4, 1887.

the interests of the Indian; but he undoubtedly regretted its influence upon the life of the cultivated white man.

The impression given of Charles Mair in the eighteen-eighties, both by external evidence (the local newspapers in particular) and by his own correspondence, is certainly that of an important citizen, a leader in the life of his community. In McPhillips's Saskatchewan *Directory* he "needs no introduction to the people of Canada, much less to the people of Prince Albert," and his biographical sketch, longer than any other in the book (pp. 41–42), is second in place only to that of Lawrence Clarke, Chief Factor of the local Hudson's Bay Company post. But it is not surprising that such a personality should kindle resentment as well as esteem; nor that the rivalry which evolved should pit Mair against the same Lawrence Clarke, both as a prominent local citizen and as the representative of Mair's old enemy, the Hudson's Bay Company. The Saskatchewan *Herald* of January 26, 1880, began what was to become a minor literary war of the frontier by publishing a letter from "A Prince Albert Farmer," who strongly repudiated a denunciation of the Company by the Honourable C. A. Burrows (a relative of the friend who had advised Mair to obtain the Portage land desired by his company, and a recent visitor to Prince Albert) and also Burrows's encomium of Mair as the principal opposition to the Company's monopoly in both 1880 and the past. Said the "Farmer,"

> The less said about Mr. Mair's (well paid for) devotion to Canadian interests in 1869 the better. Mr. Burrows should "let sleeping dogs lie." The Half-breed population does not forget that part of this devotion consisted in publishing through Canadian newspapers Mr. Mair's conclusions that the mixed races of the country were little better than the beasts they hunted for a living.

This attack Mair answered on March 15 in a signed, five thousand word letter-article in which he restates generally his "Insurrection at Red River" contribution to the *Globe* in May, 1870, but in which he also discusses specifically the offences further committed by the "Old Lady of Lime Street" since that time. And here again the reader is impressed by Mair's comprehension of North-West history, his discerning analysis of the Company's attempts to retain the country as its own private compound. In return for a conveyance of one-twentieth of "the public domain," what, asked Mair, has the Company done?

Is it pledged to pay one-twentieth of our public outlay, one-twentieth of our Indian, military or railway expenditure? Not at all. It simply pays the uniform municipal taxes, when imposed, and its own cost of survey. Its land, vastly enhanced in value by our own people, will be sold and the proceeds remitted to England, and that will be the end of it as far as Canada is concerned. Hitherto, most large conveyances have been granted for implied or specific services to the State, and at a valuation of some sort. It was so with the Canada Company—that great "bug-bear" to the early settler in Upper Canada, and with other corporations. Yet here is the most gigantic of them all, which has been endowed inversely to its services, and as a reward, past, present and to come, of every species of resistance to progress and the public interest.

The reference by "Farmer" to his Red River letters Mair termed a "malicious," "wanton and uncalled-for" attack on one "who has not lifted his pen in public against [the] corporation since the transfer to Canada, has given him no just offence, and has as perfect a right to conduct his business in the Territories as he or any of his fellows." He had never attacked, he insisted, the character of the half-breed, but had merely commented on some amusing social antagonisms—comment that he sincerely regretted.[31] His real sin was rather in contradicting "the thickly-sown falsehoods of the Great Monopoly," in telling "the truth about the country." His letters had, in fact, brought that "adventurous band of Canadians who in '69 formed a nucleus of resistance to the machinations of the Hudson's Bay Company." Canadians in the Territories were now numbered by tens of thousands "and every day is more fully confirming the absolute truthfulness of my correspondence to the Canadian press."

All of which implies that Mair did not believe "Prince Albert Farmer" was a farmer at all. He was sure that the anonymous correspondent was not only a staunch supporter of the Hudson's Bay Company, but was also one of its employees. "Judging by internal evidence" he proposed "a well-known Hudson's Bay Company official, more deeply interested in fur than in farming" and whose "voice is Jacob's voice," but whose hand "is the hand of Esau."

Such a charge had to be answered, and when it was, by Lawrence Clarke and in the *Herald* of March 29, the quarrel had become virtually one of personal spite and muckraking. The original issue, that between the Hudson's Bay Company's "monopoly" and the rights of the individual trader, Clarke disposed of by simply denying Mair had had anything pertinent to say. But the suggestion originally made by "Farmer" that "the less said about Mr. Mair's devotion to Canadian

[31]See chap. IV, p. 71.

interests the better" he ignored in a sardonic rehearsal of his adversary's past. The tirade directed against his company, he declared, was the expression of a monomaniac on the subject, a man whose "maunderings are so confined in the mummy-clothes of his own warped imagination that to discuss them would be nauseating." Mr. Mair belonged to that great and renowned party who believed in making money at any sacrifice. "Is it not remarkable," Clarke asked, "how easily men persuade themselves that they are honest citizens, and that they are bright and shining lights, when in reality they are of the earth earthy, and like their prototype the serpent, have the same manner of raising their heads?" Clarke's onslaught gained momentum amid such a catalogue of caustic epithets on Mair's "vomiting forth his inordinate, egotistical and bitter saliva," his "usual worm-like gliding," his "sinister conscience" and his "wicked premeditations," that his target must surely have felt himself ten years in the past and under the fire once again of Begg and Hargrave. And as Mair read on, he must just as surely have felt that the unhappy events of Red River would ever haunt him. "I cannot go into Mr. Mair's ancient history; he has got the subject off by heart," Clarke grimly persisted,

> and I remember when he was starring it in Toronto as a martyr in the winter of 1869 with another dear friend, at a public meeting, after the greater lights had had their say, our dwarfed Titan got up and began by telling them that he was going to give them the history of that villainous corporation, the Hudson's Bay Company. Alas! he was told to let it alone, and he had to ramble off into a history of his personal sufferings on behalf of his country until his befogged brain got so mixed that he suddenly collapsed and sat down, much to the delight and satisfaction of his listeners.[32]

And as for Mr. Mair's views on the half-breeds, it was surely common knowledge (this must have been the most probing cut to Mair) that "he was personally chastised by a lady in Winnipeg, a native of the country, for the wicked, malicious, lying remarks he had made on the Half-breed race"—a race, Clarke added, that "could teach Mr. Charles Mair some of the first elements of morality."

But Clarke was not content merely to reopen the old wound Mair had incurred because of Red River. In his concluding paragraphs he vented his professional and personal antipathies for Charles Mair, citizen of Prince Albert. With unrelenting irony he caricatured his

[32]As reported by the Toronto *Globe* and *Leader*, Mair's speech did end abruptly.

opponent as a pompous bearer of a supposedly superior way of life, as the unappreciated missionary who self-righteously suffers the neglect of both his town and his country:

Why, the man should have been created at once an immigration agent or at least a tide waiter. And then is he not a pioneer of civilization himself [itself?]? From the far east he has been travelling west all his life, in a vain effort to find a settlement and a country to appreciate his civilizing influences.

Like Micawber, Mair had left his native land and, pitching his tent in Prince Albert, had trusted "he would there find what he had so patiently waited for but found impossible to command at home—a confiding public." And to this literary man who, like "his ancient friend when cornered in the Temple, quoted Scripture," Clarke offered a borrowed peroration; "Do not despair, Charles," he consoled,

Justified and by success made bold,
Dull fools and coxcombs sanctified by gold
May bask in fortune's partial ray,
And spread their feathers opening to the day.

To this Mair made no reply. As far as the pages of the *Herald* were concerned the logomachy ended with Clarke's letter. Nor is there any evidence in Mair's correspondence that the controversy ever even took place; and one can fairly infer that he found it quite impossible to answer Clarke without incurring the risk of increasing his own shame and embarrassment. Particularly distressing to him, also, must have been the realization that he had perhaps brought on the attack unnecessarily. Clarke had remarked convincingly that the *Herald* editor knew very well that his signature did not cover "Farmer's" communication, but, he had added, since "Mr. Mair has fathered it on me . . . I accept the onus." Thus, once again the principle of "to strike and strike hard" as interpreted and exemplified by the impetuous Mair had returned a dividend of personal humiliation. In the whole affair there are significant yet poignant echoes, of a letter signed "L.R.," of Macdougall's reprimand to a young *protégé* of "talent and genius," of a horsewhipping by an irate postmistress, and of a satirical parody of a poet called "Dot." Real qualities of intelligence, learning, and power of expression had once again been compromised by opposing characteristics of presumptuousness, vindictiveness, and offensive self-importance, and Clarke, although incensed beyond the restraint of objectivity, presents an unfortunate confirmation of the portrait implied by both the correspondence and the actions of the subject himself. Like Hargrave and Begg before him, he employed what McPhillips's *Directory* termed "natural talents far above the average" to seek revenge upon an adversary provocatively vulnerable.

The verbal encounter between Mair and Clarke was perhaps, however, something besides a sparring for personal and economic prominence by two Prince Albert citizens. It may have been an indication, even a symptom, of a state of insecurity and tension that underlay the North-West's sudden surge to prosperity on the National Policy and that, by 1881, could not be dismissed by the inhabitants themselves, no matter how much propaganda they sent east to potential investors and immigrants. Settlers did come into the area, but as in the case of Manitoba, most of them followed the actual or proposed course of the railway, far to the south of Prince Albert. The premonition of the Battleford *Herald* had not, after all, been entirely inspired by jealous rivalry; land speculator, farmer, and town shop-keeper alike began to have disturbing qualms about their future.

The problem, however, did not arise only from the re-routing of the railway. The bountiful crops that had been coincident with the land boom suddenly dwindled in two seasons of drought and frost, and the consequent depression on the land was in turn reflected by an abrupt deflation in property values. In addition, the plight of the Indians and of the *métis*, always a matter of concern since the coming of the white settler and his way of living, was reaching even ominous proportions. These people, like their respective brethren in Manitoba, felt they were entitled to scrip or land grants as compensation for the concession of their original title (the Manitoba Act had resulted in the granting of 1,400,000 acres of land and negotiable scrip) and many of the *métis* in particular were becoming increasingly restless over the policy of delay that Ottawa seemed to be exercising against them. But the question of land ownership involved more than just the Indians and *métis*. White settlers who had bought vast acreage from the native inhabitants had not received patent or title, and legally much of even the land upon which Prince Albert was erecting its businesses and homes was of dubious ownership. This factor in itself was enough to discourage economic expansion and to engender discontent.

Mair, both as a town spokesman and as a large land owner and purveyor, became one of the most concerned in this latest obstacle to western Canadian security and progress. In 1881 and 1882 he made at least four trips to Ottawa, even to the office of Sir John A. himself, to plead the rights of the Saskatchewan territory. On each occasion, he visited Denison in Toronto and reported his relative success or failure, and as his Canada First associate was later to record,[33] each succeeding visit found him more and more alarmed. Mair even headed a deputation of Prince Albert citizens to Ottawa and after a lengthy conference with Sir David Macpherson, the Minister of the Interior, he was asked to submit to the Prime Minister a written memorial of their grievances. This was done, but as the Prince Albert *Times* of January 17, 1883, ironically commented, the document undoubtedly had been "pigeon-holed in usual form but nothing as yet has come of it." Mair made a final, almost desperate effort in the spring of 1884 to make Ottawa aware of the need for immediate action in the West; said Denison: "he told me most positively that there would be a rebellion, that the officials were absolutely indifferent and unmovable." The situation had become grave, although Denison, characteristically, "could not help laughing" at the picture Mair gave him of Macpherson, "a very large, handsome, erect man of six feet four inches, getting up, leaving his room and walking away down the corridor, while Mair, a short, stout man, had almost to run alongside of him as he made his final appeal to preserve the peace and to prevent bloodshed."[34]

But Mair was not laughing; nor had he had, during the past three years, much cause even to smile. Financially, he was more than comfortable, if not wealthy; were the Prince Albert bubble to burst, he certainly would not be destitute. But an even greater anxiety than the halting of his progress to money and leisure was unnerving him. As unrest about Prince Albert grew, so did his old fear of the *métis*. Since the outbreak of 1869 his relations with the half-breeds had evidently been peaceful; reference has been made to the fact that he found them "personally attractive" and "harmless" until they became the tools of other interests such as the Hudson's Bay Company or American expansionists. Still, the former differences, almost fatal to him at Red River, could not be forgotten, particularly since his foolish altercation with Lawrence Clarke had brought them into prominence again. In and about Prince Albert and especially in the new towns of Batoche and St. Laurent to the south were *métis* familiar with the person or name of Charles Mair, the Upper Canadian who

[33] *Soldiering in Canada*, p. 263.
[34] *Ibid.*

had represented disruption of their old life in 1869 and who, by his urgent appeals for immigrants, was still, in this respect at least, their enemy. Ironically, Mair was now really on the side of the *métis*, as were the majority of the white settlers in Saskatchewan; his cause, although for a different motive, was their cause, and the petitions he carried to Ottawa, if favourably acted upon, would benefit them equally with himself. But as the mood of the *métis* became darker, and as the signs became more obvious that if rebellion flared the Indians might be aroused, Mair felt, perhaps quite justifiably, that his safety and that of his family were conjectural. His wife and he "had been Riel's prisoners, and seeing the old rebels all around us, and everything ripe for trouble and the Indians this time joining in, [we] feared for our children."[35]

As early as August, 1882, therefore, Mair took steps preparatory to the events he felt were almost inevitable. He moved his family to Windsor, Ontario, buying a large house on Victoria Street and enrolling his two eldest daughters in a conventual school ("the teachers are of the highest class in their order and interference with the religion of Protestant children is strictly prohibited").[36] Florence, the second daughter, had died at the age of ten in March of that year, but another girl, Mabel, had arrived in 1880, and Eliza took her and the only son, Cecil, to Victoria Street while Mair returned to Prince Albert, separated from his family by over two thousand miles and by a hope, increasingly desperate, that he could avert rebellion and save his property. For two years he alternated between Windsor and Prince Albert, living for about six months at a time in each, until the spring of 1884, when a letter from the West made him realize that he would probably not return as usual the following autumn. On June 2, Colonel A. Sproat, the Land Registrar of Prince Albert and a close friend of Mair, wrote him that a deputation of "Ouellette, Dumas, Dumont and Jas. Isbister" had left for Montana to interview Louis Riel "in the hopes that they would get him to come out and head them in a rising against the Queen's Authority." Since Mair had last left Prince Albert, he said, secret meetings had been held and over nine hundred men had pledged themselves to the cause. If Riel agreed to lead them, Sproat added ominously, "there will be trouble."[37] Riel did agree. By July 1 he was in St. Laurent; a week later he addressed supporters at Batoche; and on July 19 he took the leading role in a highly

[35]MP, Mair to ?, n.d. (*ca.* 1910).
[36]DP, 837 (31), Mair to Denison, Aug. 20, 1882.
[37]MP.

successful meeting at Prince Albert itself. Once again, as Mair had said in reference to Red River, "events were moving swiftly."

But this time Mair had no desire to be a participant in such events; the safety of Windsor allowed him the luxury of commenting drolly to Denison: "It would never do for me to be hobnobbing with Riel. . . . I shall steer clear of rebellion!"[38] The half-jesting tone of this remark, however, implies more than the relief Mair felt in being far from his old enemy, Louis Riel. It is also reflective of the fact that a decision had been made for him, an arbitrary settling of a question he had been asking himself since about 1881—that of his complete return to some form of literary activity. By that year he had already achieved an economic security approaching that which he felt necessary for his entire independence from business for two or three years; Principal Grant of Queen's was, in fact, "delighted to hear" that he had "wrung the means of comfort from the world," and that the proceeds of a sketch Mair had agreed to write for Grant's *Picturesque Canada* would go "to good old Queen's."[39] Two months later Grant thanked Mair for his contribution, but far more significant was his congratulating him "on having chosen a theme so worthy of your own spirit and your powers as Tecumsheh [*sic*]. . . . I know only enough of the gallant chief to stand afar off and admire."[40] So it appears that Mair's "dream of taking up the character of Tecumseh," expressed to Denison in 1878, had by about 1880 become a reality, and only the deterioration in prosperity that began shortly afterwards made him hesitate to leave business entirely. Thus once again he found himself serving two masters. While managing his large Prince Albert interests and urging the Government to recognize the increasingly serious situation in the West, he was also undertaking the creation of an epic drama. And after August, 1882, he was hampered by the added inconvenience of living in two widely separated towns, Prince Albert and Windsor. The return of Riel to the West in the spring of 1884, therefore, could be considered a mixed blessing. It virtually finished Mair's attempts to sustain his business, except by proxy, and to maintain the peace. But it also signified to him that now he would have to be satisfied with the funds he had, by no means inconsiderable, and at last devote full time to writing.

And so once again Charles Mair was playing a part, perhaps less

[38]DP, 890, June 20, 1884.

[39]MP, Grant to Mair, Aug. 18, 1881.

[40]MP, Oct. 24, 1881. Mair's sketch, however, did not appear in *Picturesque Canada*.

directly this time, in the drama that he often said he found everywhere about him, the drama of a Canadian history that seemed almost uncannily to involve him in some of its more significant episodes. In 1884 it was over a decade and a half since a small volume of poetry had led him to the West and an encounter with Louis Riel. Nevertheless, as he was about to venture a second literary work, that same Louis Riel had returned to influence his career; how much, this time, he could not yet even estimate. Half dreading, half hoping, Mair awaited news from the Saskatchewan valley and with as much concentration as possible he tried to compose the story of an Indian chief who had fought against insuperable odds to unite his people into a great nation.

VIII. Tecumseh

CHARLES MAIR had considered Tecumseh as a subject for verse-drama long before he advised Principal Grant of Queen's of his plans in 1881 or even his close friend Denison in 1878. That he had had, when he was only in his twenties, some intention of commemorating the great Shawnee chief is implied by his inclusion of "Prologue to Tecumseh" in *Dreamland*, where he speaks of "the brave of yore" whose "mem'ries haunt adown the wid'ning years, / Still teazing us from quiet into tears." Why he turned his attention to such exotic subjects as Zoroaster and Ponce de Leon's search for the Fountain of Bimini (the manuscripts of which, he insisted, were appropriated by the rebel O'Donoghue) he never explained; but they probably represented youthfully romantic aspirations he would not have acted upon at all a few years later and particularly after his interests, both political and literary, had become avidly nationalistic. Certain is it that he had lifelong interest in the Indians, an interest begun by intimate association with the Algonquins in the Ottawa Valley and continued by living and trading with the Sioux and Dakotas in the West; as his knowledge of their character and habits increased, so did his desire to interpret at least some aspect of their history.

But Tecumseh had a special fascination. Not only had he been an unusual personality, a brilliant leader of his people; he had also played an extremely important role in defending Canada against armed invasion and, indeed, in saving her from annexation by the hated Yankee. In the story of the final months of the great red man's career, then, Mair could reflect some of his own knowledge and experience; but most important, he could urge by means of literature—that touchstone or gauge, he had called it, of a nation's desire for greatness—a recognition of Canada's heroic past and of her potentiality for a magnificent future. Even a consideration of several other factors involved in Mair's creation of *Tecumseh* does not detract from the validity of Desmond Pacey's statement that it "was consciously written as a patriotic exercise."[1] There is, indeed, Mair's own declaration of purpose, which he spelled out some years later in a second edition of the work:

> . . . the author attempts to depict dramatically the time and scenes in which the great Indian so nobly played his part—at first independently, and in his own country, and afterwards in alliance and leadership with General Brock in the war of 1812. That war was the turning point of Canada's destiny. It was maintained mainly within her borders—a community of some 70,000 souls in Upper Canada, with about thrice that number in the Lower Province, being pitted against a nation of 8,000,000. . . . In the face of such emergencies, the courage and vigor of the Canadian people of both races can be truly appreciated. Enrolling during the war over 500,000 men, and repeatedly entering Canada at many points, the invaders were at last everywhere discomfited, and at its close had been driven to a man from Canadian soil.

Both Tecumseh and Brock were men of "transcendent ability" to whose genius and self-sacrifice "at the most critical period in her history is due the preservation of Canada to the Empire"; in their story was reflected "in the clearest light the spirit and springs of action which have made Canada what she is."[2]

The concern that would stimulate a writer to the undertaking of a literary work frankly intended to inspire, to inculcate, patriotic feeling is not difficult to understand if the writer is living in Canada in the eighteen-eighties, and particularly if he is Charles Mair. It is the same concern that had existed in the years immediately following Confederation and that had been directed then towards the creation of a greater national sentiment. But as Mair had discovered only too clearly, one's feelings of well-being and security, of satisfaction in living in one's country, of hope for the future, seemed directly related to economic and political factors. The depression that had so quickly followed Confederation overpowered the efforts of patriots, literary and otherwise, to make firm the bonds by which the far-spread provinces had agreed to join themselves one to the other. Even Canada

[1]*Creative Writing in Canada*, p. 35.
[2]*Tecumseh and Canadian Poems*, pp. 4–6.

First itself had disintegrated under the impact of dissension and diverse motives. And Mair, all his efforts directed towards establishing a livelihood for himself and his family, wrote nothing in this period.

The National Policy of 1878, however, brought a surge of prosperity, and once again, as if another opportunity were being given to Canadians to glimpse what was possible for them and somehow to retain that vision, a number of writers began to express themselves in terms of a national literature. The work of some of them, it is true, was not to be published until the economic and political horizon had again darkened; Charles G. D. Robert's *In Divers Tones*, for example, with its "Ode for the Canadian Confederacy," "A Collect for Dominion Day," and "Canada," appeared in 1886. The stimulation that his earlier (1880) *Orion* gave to the young Archibald Lampman has been so often commented on that only two particularly relevant sentences of Lampman's enthusiastic reception of it require repeating; "It was like a voice from some new paradise of art," he said, "calling to us to be up and doing." And to be up and doing because it was "a wonderful thing that such work could be done by a Canadian, by a young man, one of ourselves."[3] Here is the same sort of self-consciousness, of sensitive pride, that had characterized writer and critic alike when Mair had published *Dreamland* in 1868. Fortunately for their later reputations, Roberts and Lampman did not continue in this vein, even though, as Professor Malcolm Ross has noted, Roberts "had his fling at the 'Patriotic Ode,'" and Lampman "reflects the peculiar national spirit of the immediate post-Confederation period . . . , even a hint of 'Canada First.'"[4] But as Professor Ross also notes, "the air is charged"; and Mair, in 1880, riding the crest of economic security and social respectability in Prince Albert, was encouraged to attempt a work frankly and characteristically reflective of his own ardent nationalism.

He did so, however, with considerable misgivings about the reception his book, or any book by a Canadian, would encounter. The stimulation that a poet-patriot found in a young, growing nation was not necessarily felt by everyone; bitter experience had, indeed, taught him that Canadians seemed singularly indifferent to the higher vision so fervently propounded by himself and his Canada First comrades. "What is the cause of the deadly blight which seems to rest upon and rust the public mind of Canada?" he asked despairingly in the Prince Albert *Times* of November 29, 1882. Canada's only literary magazine,

[3]*Lyrics of Earth*, p. 8.
[4]*Poets of the Confederation*, pp. ix–x.

the *Canadian Monthly*, "a very model of literary cleanliness," had recently expired from lack of support. A Canadian poet publishes a volume of admitted excellence and is driven to trade for a living. A young man of keen intellect, "of the most delicate honor and a heart swelling with love of Canada" is forced to return to his legal profession because "he preaches the not altogether unpleasant or unpardonable doctrine of Canada First." And another Canadian, "of active and vigilant intellect" and "deeply versed in military history"—who had, indeed, against all comers won the large prize offered by the Grand Duke Nicholas of Russia for the best work on the history of cavalry—is wasting his talents as Police Magistrate of Toronto. Why should this be? Surely not because of "the hordes of political adventurers who alternately misgovern us," for in the United States, where such men abound, the "higher mind of America has rescued her from degradation, and has prospered in spite of her indecent public men." Is it rather because "Canadians are a nation of intellectual eunuchs" who suffocate genius rather than nurture it, who seal their eyes to the true dignity and worth in their own country, who willingly hand over their destiny to "base and reckless money-grubbers and still baser intellectual prostitutes?"

It is significant that the examples of neglected worth Mair cites are Charles Mair, W. A. Foster, and George T. Denison. They are prophets unknown in their own country, men of vision crying in the wilderness as they had done at the time of Confederation, of the Wolseley expedition, and of the disintegration of Canada First. But that they deplore with some justification is confirmed by other commentators' lamentations on the state of Canadian letters during the period. Mercer Adam, editor of the recently defunct *Canadian Monthly*, for example, saw "an ebbing out of national spirit," "a growing intellectual callousness," and "a deadening of interest in the things that make for the nation's higher life."[5] So more than a trace of bitterness is understandable in Mair's remarking to Denison: "there is but one thing I am sure of and that is that I shall lose money. Our sweet Canadian public will take care of that."[6]

But he also said he would rather be the author of "a really good Canadian poem" than anything else "under the cape of our northern skies." And to this end he certainly applied himself diligently. His deciding upon Windsor as the place in which he would write his drama was almost entirely determined by the subject he had chosen

[5]Quoted by Alfred C. Bailey, "Literature and Nationalism," p. 411.
[6]DP, 837 (76), Nov. 23, 1883.

(almost, because Eliza's wish to be near her mother, who lived in Amherstburg, was also a factor). To Denison, who wished Mair to come to live near him in Toronto, he expressed regret that he "could not drive down stakes on College St.," but the Windsor area had much to offer, and Eliza had been to him "too faithful and loving a wife as well as adviser to thwart her in any way."[7] Mair would have settled, indeed, in Amherstburg itself if he had been able to secure a suitable house, but he did what he considered next best—bought the frame house of Victorian Gothic architecture on Victoria street, one of Windsor's more important thoroughfares; and from here he roamed over the countryside to Chatham, Amherstburg, and Moraviantown, immersing himself in the atmosphere and history of places through which Tecumseh himself had travelled seventy years before.

As he stood among Indian graves, even bones, which were still to be found, Mair sensed "a mildew of age and a time-honoured rust" about the area that completely captured his imagination. From a spot where Tecumseh had encamped in 1813 he could see the field where the chief had planted his corn, and, next to it, the mounds where he had buried his dead. The Shawnee and the Wyandotte were gone, but "the dense atmosphere of savagery" lingered on. "The old trees and older ravines which once sheltered the dark legions of Pontiac are as they were ages ago," he noted. "I have examined one where one of my wife's grand-uncles, a Frenchman of the mother's side, was killed and scalped by the Ottawas, who mistook him in the dark for an enemy." And to accentuate by contrast this impression of past, primitive times was the shrill trumpeting of steamers on the Detroit and the clangor and shrieking of the Canada Southern Railway. "The river is thick with vessels ploughing up and down with files of schooners in their train whose swell and surge against the shore at every throb loosen some mouldering rib of Huron or Ottawa from its ancient resting place." He himself had been present at the disinterment of a skeleton seven feet in length and near which was a hatchet of stone, faced and "stubborned" with iron, a connecting link of the stone and iron ages on the Detroit. "Dig where you will," he told Denison, "ear-rings are found, and bits of wampum, broken utensils and weapons—relics of the busy, naked life which worshipped and trembled at the name of Ariouska, the god of nature."[8] With a near neighbour who was to become a close friend, William L. Baby, the son and nephew of two distinguished Upper-Canadian allies of

[7]DP, 837 (41), Nov. 7, 1882.
[8]DP, 837 (30), Aug. 20, 1882.

Tecumseh and Brock, he visited the Thames battleground where Tecumseh had been killed and Baby's father taken prisoner by the Americans. Here, also, he became one of the many devotees of Tecumseh lore, before and after him, who have tried fruitlessly to find the chief's last resting place, digging for bones the location of which, according to tradition, only Indians know. At Sandwich he and his new friend inspected the old Baby mansion, commandeered in 1812 as a headquarters by General Hull and his American Army of the North-West and where, Mair believed, Brock had received Hull's capitulation of Detroit: "I could almost see the shades of Brock and Tecumseh flitting through the rooms. . . . There great issues were determined, high feasts were held and winter revelries lighted up and warmed by the blaze from old-fashioned hearths. All gone—but fragrant with memories."[9]

Mair obviously enjoyed himself in these surroundings; he was to remark later that the years spent in Windsor were perhaps the happiest of his life. "I think for the retirement I dream of bye & bye," he said, "there is no other place so suitable."[10] Even Detroit, although American, was a fine city; its women *were* over-painted, but "it is easy to find fault, and my inherited hatred of the Yankees opens me to all sorts of prejudices."[11] Most of his Victoria Street neighbours, he felt, must have wondered what he did for a living; but he preferred seclusion, relaxing from his research and writing with "old Mr. Baby" and a few others by playing whist "at each other's houses alternately every Friday evening with a little supper to wind up."[12]

It was pleasant, too, to be back in "good old Ontario," near his companions of the "Corner Room" days, and to feel himself almost a part once again of their everyday activities. Denison he saw frequently; in the months to come their friendship was to be closer than ever before. Foster, whose law practice was flourishing, was evidently content "to leave the creation of a National sentiment in Canada to the next generation (which may throw off our swaddling clothes)" and looked forward to a place on the Bench. Haliburton was ostensibly in law in Ottawa, but had "become absolutely daft over dwarfs." And Morgan seemed to have lost some of his "old *verve*" by turning into "a mere collating machine"; deplored Mair to Denison, "Ye Gods!

[9]DP, 855, Feb. 21, 1884. By the 1930's this house was virtually a ruin, standing in a garden long since gone wild; but restoration work, aided by funds from Hiram Walker and Sons Ltd., has turned it into a National Historic Site and Windsor's first public historical museum.

[10]DP, 837 (28), Aug. 20, 1882.

[11]DP, 837 (76), Nov. 23, 1883.

[12]DP, 837 (96), Jan. 6, 1884.

Think of a man's intellectual energies culminating in a pair of shears and paste-pot."[13] Shortly after his arrival in Windsor, Mair had, indeed, heard from Morgan in a rather curious way. Through the auspices of Morgan, Mair had been selected as vice-consul for "the kingdom of Hawaii," Morgan himself being a full consul, and in due time

> the "consular" document came along sure enough and a long letter from the chief Cannibal, giving details of the trade with the United States . . . which he thinks with the opening of the C.P.R. may be diverted to Canada. Shakespeare knew all about it—some have greatness thrust upon them! There is something awful in the thought that the destinies of those fair islands are to a certain extent in my hands and that Cook may yet be avenged. The chief products of the Kingdom are sugar, cotton, melted lava and leprosy. There is some hope of naturalizing that vigorous South American plant, the *Pronunciamento*, in the Islands, and, if so, the last charm will be added to a residence there.

Morgan told him there was a seal of office and a flag, but "the uniform so far as I can discover, is a breech-clout." His stout Ottawa friend in uniform "would be phenomenal," Mair commented, "but being a sort of confidential adviser of the king, Morgan will probably be allowed to wear a blanket."[14]

With such diversion from his work and from the ever present anxiety about affairs in the West, Mair proceeded with *Tecumseh*. Eliza bore yet another daughter, Elizabeth, in February, 1884, "very like the dear one we lost two years ago," but his correspondence reveals that the drama became more and more his consuming interest. Even comments on the ever deteriorating situation around Prince Albert, of which he was constantly kept informed, become less frequent. And that he was meeting difficulty with his composition he gives ample evidence. He was unfamiliar with dramatic creation, and either because of this inexperience or because of his simply following the examples of a host of nineteenth-century writers from Shelley to Browning, he decided upon the "literary" or "closet" drama to tell Tecumseh's story. The long narrative poem as written by Major John Richardson on the same subject he dismissed, "for the brief and noble career of Tecumseh was essentially dramatic . . . and it is in a play only that it can be adequately represented." But he constantly expressed his feelings of inadequacy on whether or not his "situations" were "dramatic" or "effectively put together," his plot had "action enough to give life and vigour," or his characters had "individuality"

[13] *Ibid.* [14] *Ibid.*

and "convincement." His loss of manuscripts at Red River had thrown him "out of the literary groove," he felt; but if he knew only that his work was "good" he would be content, for this would assure him of posthumous fame.[15] Such self-critical insufficiency led him to depend considerably upon the opinions and advice of others; no sooner had he finished a scene, or even less, than he sent it to Principal Grant or to Denison, who then might forward it to someone else before it was returned to Mair in Windsor. When *Tecumseh* was finished, most of it had been read and criticized not only by Grant and Denison, but also by Foster, Sir Daniel Wilson, Goldwin Smith, Charles G. D. Roberts—even by Matthew Arnold.

Concerning two aspects of his drama, however, Mair had no doubts. "The element of woman is indispensable," he stated; and accordingly into his roster of historical characters—Tecumseh, Generals Brock, Hull, and Harrison, and Tecumseh's wicked brother, the Prophet—he introduced two who were quite fictitious—Iena "the wanderer," niece of Tecumseh, and Lefroy, "a young white enthusiast" and lover of Iena, who was "suggested by the career in Canada of the unhappy Lord Fitzgerald." In addition, he was determined to avoid "the namby-pamby twaddle of the ordinary novelist when putting language into the Indian's mouth." His own experience had forcefully contradicted such representation:

> I have been surrounded with Indians for fifteen years, have been present at the most momentous treaties, and have witnessed scenes of savagery and of the most touching pathos, yet I never yet heard the Indian speak but as a sensible, intelligent man, fully alive to his interests and conscious of his rights, expressing himself always in language of remarkable vigour and directness.

The Americans, he charged, had "villainously wronged" the Indian in this respect as in others, and "to the present hour" not one Yankee was "manly enough to lift a voice against it all." If his own depiction did nothing else it would rectify this "hateful injustice."[16]

The character of Tecumseh himself Mair visualized in almost sublime terms. The great chief was a pure Indian, intellectually far in advance of his people but "filled from crown to soul with love for his race." He knew not only the strength and weakness of the Indian, but also those of the Americans, and hated the latter "with a just hatred for the unparalleled wrongs they had perpetrated upon the red man, yet was too noble to take a cruel revenge." He preferred the English

[15] *Ibid.*

[16] *Ibid.*

interest "from the spirit of justice which animated the Canadian authorities" in dealing with the Indian, but wished primarily "to range his forces against the Americans." And when his schemes, the untiring labour of years, were "blown to atoms . . . by the precipitate folly and ambition" of his brother, the Prophet, he did not in despair abandon his enterprise and retire to the remote wilderness, "as many a man of inferior genius might well have done," but instead, "like the statesman he was, flung himself heart and soul into the British interest," and became at once not only the trusted friend and counsellor of Brock but also "the right arm and strength of Canada." Nothing, perhaps, Mair said, revealed Tecumseh's shrewd perceptiveness more than the elliptical contrast he made between Brock and his cowardly second-in-command, Colonel Procter; "This man," the chief is supposed to have said, pointing at Brock, "says '*Come*, boys!'—the other says '*Go*, boys.'" And nothing, Mair admitted, would provide greater difficulty in his depicting Tecumseh than the necessity of righting the misconception by the whites about the Indian character in its original and uncontaminated condition; "I must not only lift him up to a lofty level but keep him there, so that the ideal of the man *begot of his degradation by the whites*, shall not creep in." One can well appreciate Mair's remarking: "Such is my reverence for the man that I could write all my fingers stiff."[17]

Mair's literary assiduity, indeed, is confirmed by both his rate of composition and the long detailed letters about his progress that he wrote to Denison as often as three or four times a week, even, on one or two occasions, twice a day. By February, 1884, he had completed the first act and had cast in general outline the other four, although he frankly admitted to Denison that there would be much shuffling and reshuffling of lines, even of scenes, before the play was finished:

> In thinking over the future action of my characters, when away from the desk, very often an idea strikes me which I there and then clothe with verse and put down for future use. I have scores of such in my scrap book —one at random:
>
> "When copper-coloured oaks drop miserly
> Their stiff and slow-wrought coins into the earth"
> (or "slow-wrought
> summer's mintage to the earth").
>
> We have no oaks with us but I saw them in all their deep and rich autumn copper-colour here last fall and the idea occurred to me at once. Such stray lines either descriptive of natural objects or of character may

[17]DP, 837 (121–30), Feb. 1, 1884.

never be used, and must indeed be sparingly used, but the habit of noting them is a good one for it keeps one's mind busy with one's work, and I wish I had begun the practice long ago.[18]

Denison was a source of advice and inspiration such as probably no other Canadian poet has ever had. The first act he described as "the finest piece of writing ever put to paper in Canada," and a song by Iena as "a gem," although he thought Mair might consider Foster's doubt that "a song is in place in drama of so high a class as this sets out to be."[19] Foster himself wrote Mair that this first "batch of ms." promised "something of which all Canadians will be proud" and that Denison and he could hardly wait for "the next installment." Denison, he remarked, always consulted him: "His mode of taking advice is good. First he makes up his mind—then asks advice—then is of the same opinion as before. . . . Denison has it all committed to memory and if you were robbed of the ms. to-morrow he would write out the whole drama for you."[20] Foster also suggested that Mair obtain a "type-writer," who would charge him only two cents per hundred lines ("nothing like print for opening one's eyes to one's own faults and virtues")[21] and that he "forbear reading *Henry V*" while composing *Tecumseh* because of the danger of unintentional plagiarism.[22] Such practical advice Mair accepted gratefully, but it was invariably to Denison that he turned when in doubt. Where should this song be placed—in the third act or the fifth? Or what did he think of these lines on a bison herd? Or of these on a meeting of Brock and Lefroy by moonlight?

Brock How still the night!
Here Peace has let her silvery tresses down,
And falls asleep beside these lapping waves.
The hour is late so let us to repose (our beds?)
War rises early, and will up ere dawn
to fright her with his drum.
or
To-morrow War will wake her with his drum(?)
(Is "drum" the right word? I have an idea it should be "bugle.")[23]

The first criticism of Principal Grant tended to increase such doubts concerning diction. "The power of the work," said Grant, "would sometimes be the better for being restrained, . . . such expressions as

[18] *Ibid.* (122–23).
[19] MP, Jan. 14, 1884.
[20] MP, Feb. 6, 1884.
[21] MP, March 13, 1884.
[22] DP, 850, Mair to Denison, Feb. 18, 1884.
[23] DP, 837 (112), Jan. 31, 1884.

writing of the first act. I discarded a good deal of material of this kind, and I know now that I have still to use the pruning-knife in that act to make it fit for publication. In thinking over the future action of my characters, when away from the desk, very often an idea strikes me which I seize and then clothe with verse and put down for future use. It may be just a line or a couple of lines. I have scores of such in my scrap book – one at random:

When copper-coloured oaks drop miserly
Their stiff and leather-wrought coins unto the earth ([illegible])

We have no oaks with us but I saw them in all their deep and rich autumn copper-colour here last Fall and the idea occurred to me at once. Such stray lines either descriptive of natural objects or of character may never be used, and must indeed be sparingly used, but the habit of noting them is a good one for it keeps one's mind busy with one's work, and I wish I had begun the practice long ago. — However the scene by moonlight will certainly form part of the fourth act, probably much more cut down and modified than you suggest. I sent the lines in order that I might know how they affected you, and to get your opinion as to their "keeping" with the drama. Lefroy is here in place of a chorus describing the untiring efforts of Tecumseh to unite the discordant Indian races in one giant struggle for their country, and for the establishment of a frontier which should be an inviolable boundary between the red man & the white. His devotion to this object was sublime, and constitutes one of the most astounding passages of the history of this continent; for his success did not lie so much with his own nation as with nations which had been the traditional enemies of his own – many of whom were so remote that they might naturally have felt indifferent to dangers which were too remote, and therefore not appreciated. Much of this influence was due of course to his powerful oratory and to his perfect acquaintance with Indian history from the first settlements of the whites. Says one writer: "From North to south, and from east to west, he ranged the continent, – threatening, flattering, rousing to sentiment, alarming superstition, provoking curiosity. No labour fatigued, no disappointment discouraged, no danger alarmed, no emergency surprised him".

From one of Mair's letters (February 1, 1884) to George T. Denison, concerning the writing of *Tecumseh* (Public Archives of Canada).

'their damned offal cast as messes to our hounds' exciting feelings only of disgust." Iena's song—a "gem" to Denison—he disliked for similar reasons: "I could hardly forbear using my pencil as I read slowly and carefully the second time." Such offences against good taste—"form," Grant called it—must be expunged if the work were to have real literary merit.[24] And Mair conceded that there was justification for the learned Principal's opinion; his "semi-savage life and experiences in the North-West" had probably deprived him of "form," of opportunity to mingle with "literary and artistic society." But there were terms that the context of certain scenes seemed to demand unqualifiedly. What would Grant say, he asked Denison, of Tecumseh's reviling Colonel Procter with "Shitepoke! not man—go hide your coward head"? This epithet had been a favourite term of reproach to a particularly craven boy "in my urchin days" in Lanark, and although "it wouldn't suit a drawing room . . . it certainly suits Procter!"[25] Denison's comment was characteristically direct; "Don't be afraid of Grant and his 'form,'" he advised; "It is hard work pleasing preachers and is hardly worth the trouble; as long as you keep in with the Police Magistrates it is *all right*."[26]

The critical approach of Mair's old friend was generally what it had been when *Dreamland* was published. There was little question about Mair's abilities as a poet. Perhaps a slight change might be made here and there, but what really mattered was the national spirit the work reflected, the patriotic fervour it avowed. "I expect your poem to be the first great Canadian poem written by a Canadian and depicting the grandest period of our national history," he both encouraged and advised Mair:

> the capture of Detroit saved us as a people, made us what we are to-day, and years hence when we are both gone, if it pleases God to give our Native Land a position among the great nations of the earth and free from the United States—even if in connection with our mother country—the people of Canada in those days will look back to Brock and Tecumseh and the capture of Detroit as being inseparably linked with our birth as a nation.

It was, indeed, Mair's duty to give this "Canadian national tone" to his drama; "as Shakespeare breathed forth the national spirit of England in *Henry V*, . . . let yours give voice to it for Canada." His own grandfather and two grand-uncles had fought beside Brock and

[24]DP, 837 (100), quoted by Mair to Denison, Jan. 16, 1884.
[25]DP, 837 (104), Jan. 26, 1884. [26]MP, Jan. 31, 1884.

Tecumseh in the York Volunteers; as a child he himself had heard first-hand accounts of the thrilling events of 1812. So "go on with your work," he urged, "*keep at it* until you are through—send me all you like and whenever you like—you will never regret the work when you look back on it."[27]

Even his differences of opinion with Goldwin Smith did not prevent Denison from coaxing the Oxford expatriate and advocate of continental union to read Mair's manuscript. Smith's comments other than that "the Indian was a mere savage"[28] are not extant, but they were evidently complimentary enough to stimulate Mair to pay tribute to Smith, "in spite of his unbelief in our national future,"[29] and to acknowledge that he was "proud of Goldwin Smith's opinion."[30] Charles G. D. Roberts was also in Toronto at the time, engaged in his short-lived editorship of Smith's literary periodical, the *Week*, and Denison, who had Mair's manuscript in his pocket when he met Roberts,

> showed him your lines in confidence . . . and he was delighted with every line, continually breaking out in praise. . . . He said he had studied your *Dreamland and Other Poems* very closely and rated them very highly. From the lines I showed him, he said you had improved and matured.[31]

Denison thought Roberts "a very nice fellow—Canadian from his soles to the top of his hat." He was later, naturally, to approve of the ardent nationalism that caused the young poet and editor to break with Smith and the *Week* after a sojourn of only four months and to return to Fredericton in the fall of that same year.

But the most remarkable stimulus that Denison provided for Mair was the criticism of parts of *Tecumseh* that he virtually extorted from Matthew Arnold. Arnold was visiting Goldwin Smith at the Grange before returning to England from his lecture tour of the United States, and met Denison there one evening in early February, 1884. The Colonel invited the Arnolds and Smiths to lunch with him at Heydon Villa the next day, and although Arnold said "he had a rule of not reading poetry in manuscript, as he would be so bothered with it," he did not mind "doing it for a friend" like Denison;

> So after lunch to-day, I brought him quietly upstairs into my library and pulled out of my pocket a copy of the passage by Iena and asked him to

[27]*Ibid.*
[28]DP, 837 (124), quoted by Mair to Denison, Feb. 1, 1884.
[29]DP, 837 (100), Jan. 16, 1884.
[30]DP, 837 (104), Jan. 26, 1884.
[31]MP, Feb. 14, 1884.

read it. I had had my clerk copy it out very clearly and neatly (now remember this is all between you and me). He read it very slowly and critically to himself and when he had finished it he said, "Whoever wrote that can write; it is very good." I said, "You like it?" "Yes," he said again, "Whoever wrote that can write poetry." But, said he, "I only judge from these few lines; I cannot tell how the rest may be. This may be a fine passage imbedded in a mass of stuff. I could form no opinion of a drama from a few lines. Now, if I want to criticize, my objection to the passage is this. He brings in a passage which is mere ornamentation; the reference to the clouds shearing off fleeces, etc., is a very pretty idea prettily expressed but it is pure ornamentation; it does not add to the passage but weakens it, breaks in upon the flow of it. All the rest is very fine, all matter vigorously and forcibly put and very interesting. Now look here—there are one, two, three, eight lines just thrown in for ornament—they do not add force to the passage."

"Well," said I, "would you strike those lines out?" "I don't see well how he could," said he; "but he might condense the idea."

Denison again cautioned Mair about divulging this private critique, for Arnold "would not like any opinion of his to be known outside when he has only seen a scrap of your work." And certainly, he added, the nose of "the apostle of Sweetness and Light would have gone up in the air" if he "had stumbled upon 'excrement, buttocks and offal mixed up in messes for hounds.'" But Denison's "great object in having this talk with Arnold" was accomplished. "When your book is out," he told Mair, "I can send him a copy, remind him of his having read some of it, and by having interested him in it, secure his attention to it." And this, Mair's irrepressible friend was convinced, would be "of great service in London—for I know if your book is only seen it will force its way, but it is important to have it noticed."[32] After further consideration of Arnold's remarks, Denison was equally convinced that the British scholar could really find nothing wrong with the passage he had read, but had had "to show that he could make *some* criticism" and the "simile about the clouds . . . was the only one he could make."[33] The lines remained, therefore, just as Mair had originally written them, and it is doubtful that Arnold ever read them again.

But the whole incident is illustrative of the energetic concern that Denison consistently evinced for Mair's work—"another proof," said Mair, "of your manly sympathy and affection, an affection which has been part of my being for many a year."[34] And also, perhaps, of those

[32] *Ibid.*

[33] MP, Feb. 21, 1884.

[34] DP, 838, Feb. 18, 1884.

qualities Goldwin Smith had in mind when he introduced Denison to Lord Salisbury as a man "who proposes to settle all political problems by a charge of light cavalry drawn up and armed in some improved fashion."[35]

With the encouragement of Matthew Arnold to stimulate him spiritually and the active collaboration of Denison to aid him materially as well as spiritually, Mair pressed on with his work through the summer and autumn of 1884. For a while during the spring he had thought he might publish in July or August of that year, but he considered himself "so severe" towards his writing that most of it went into the wastepaper basket. Also, as he progressed, he became increasingly enamoured with the character of Brock. Much as he revered Tecumseh, he began to feel that the British hero would offer more scope than the Indian chief: the available records, too, about Brock were more plentiful. For a time, therefore, he pondered whether or not he should include scenes on the Niagara frontier and the death of Brock at Queenston. That he eventually decided against this different emphasis was due almost as much to Denison's urging him to finish the drama as to his own realizing "it would break up the unity of incident regards Tecumseh, who had no part in the operations there."[36] There was, however, despite his early unsureness concerning dramatic writing, a growing conviction that the work might actually be staged. Eliza thought so; Denison said it "would bring down the house"; and before he was finished, Mair himself conceded "it will, I think, be a good acting play . . . for it is full of striking situations—I may live to see it on the boards in Toronto yet."[37] As a result, he returned to material he had thought to be in final form, adding, deleting, and generally revising, with at least a half-resolved intention of making *Tecumseh* a vehicle for the live stage.

To such delay were added others of varying significance. Denison, for example, objected to Mair's favourable depiction of the American General Harrison, and composition halted until Mair resolutely informed his friend: "I am sorry he was not a beast but I cannot falsify history for the sake of dramatic effect. . . . He was an upright man of kind disposition and considerable ability. . . . I am sorry for all this but it can't be helped."[38] Denison spent the summer of 1884 abroad and at his summer home in Muskoka, and Mair had to get

[35]Arnold Haultain, *Goldwin Smith's Correspondence*, pp. 5–6.
[36]DP, 837 (129), Feb. 1, 1884.
[37]DP, 1214, March 21, 1885.
[38]DP, 861, March 1, 1884.

along without either his advice or criticism; but when the Colonel returned to Toronto he found that his friend had allowed his muse to be diverted into two secondary, although related, literary creations. One was a song Mair had introduced into the fourth act, "to be sung in successive stanzas by successive companies of volunteers as they march across the stage," and the other a ballad on Laura Secord, quite separate from the drama, but inspired by his researches into the War of 1812. The song, he told Denison, had "fire in it," because "I felt on fire myself whilst writing it."[39] In it, he said, he had tried to compress the patriotic emotion of the time and the tradition it rested upon. Denison, after Foster and he had made a few changes, thought the song "magnificent," a "truly national anthem," and commissioned a Mr. Gledhill to set it to music. There were difficulties here, however, first over determining the proper key, and then over costs, until Mair, rather sharply, wrote Denison that he was leaving it up to him whether or not the song should be published in advance of the drama. And, he added, "let it be on one sheet if possible, as it is proving a mighty costly affair."[40] The humorous story of the composing of the Laura Secord ballad is given in the following chapter, but it is relevant to note here that Mair, Denison, and Foster devoted considerable time and correspondence to the frontier heroine and her cow, until Denison, this time, told Mair that he really should get on with *Tecumseh* and "never mind the sideshows."[41]

There was to be one interruption, however, that neither Mair nor Denison could avoid. By March 21, 1885, Mair was able to write his friend that he had begun the fifth and final act of *Tecumseh* and that he was confident of finishing the play "by the opening up of Navigation." In the same letter he returned to a distress he had tried to keep as much as possible out of his mind during the previous year: ". . . matters instead of improving in the North-West are getting worse."[42] On March 26 he expressed "anxiety" about "rumors" reported in the newspapers, although his concern over any outbreak in Saskatchewan was mainly that it would "probably spoil this summer's immigration."[43] By the evening of the next day Mair learned with the rest of eastern Canada that on the 26th a band of Louis

[39]DP, 970, Oct. 15, 1884.

[40]DP, 1123, Jan. 2, 1885. Gledhill's original fee was fifteen dollars. Denison sent the song to his brother, Lieutenant-Colonel F. C. Denison, Commander of the Canadian *Voyageur* Contingent to the Nile, who replied (DP, 1131, Boat 439, En Route Korti, 17 January, 1885): "I got one of my men in the boat to try Mair's song. He was not a dab at it, so I cannot form a fair idea of it, but liked it very much."

[41]MP, Oct. 16, 1884. [42]DP, 1213. [43]DP, 1227.

Riel's *métis* had defeated a force of Mounted Police at Duck Lake, thirty miles south of Prince Albert. Among the dead and wounded were friends of Mair, Prince Albert volunteers accompanying the police; the town itself had been thrown into a state of fearful expectancy and was rushing preparations for a siege.

Mair's role in the North-West Rebellion of 1885 was of an entirely different character from what it had been in the insurrection of 1869–70. Then he had been closely involved, had been, in fact, at least an indirect cause of the troubles at Fort Garry. In 1885, although he had a vital interest in the occurrences and the implications of the Rebellion, and although he was even to take part in it, he regarded the whole tragic affair not as he had its origin in 1869, a struggle between Canadian national expansion and a greedy monopoly, but as the result of official bungling and blindness. As has already been noted, although Mair felt "it would never do . . . to be seen hobnobbing with Riel," his sympathies were certainly not with the "establishment." More personally, the outbreak might be a disastrous blow to his economic security as well as a further interruption, perhaps the end, of his literary career.

The last four days of March, 1885, Mair and Denison spent waiting for news and exchanging bitter correspondence about the developments in the West. *Tecumseh* was virtually forgotten. Mair repeated his charges against a dilatory Government and again emphasized the efforts he had made to prevent rebellion: "Every species of warning was given—and thrown aside." He hastened to add, however, "I would not damage the Government openly, for the railway completion is of vast importance."[44] Denison was much less reticent. After going down to the Union Station to see the first Toronto volunteers on their way west, he wrote Mair that he wished the warlike enthusiasm he saw there could have been enlisted in a better cause. When he had led his regiment to Fort Erie in 1866, he said, it was to defend Canada, and he had never begrudged "the lives or the sacrifices in so holy a cause." But the blood of the Prince Albert volunteers killed at Duck Lake "is on the Government and all they can say or do can never wash the stain away." For, while the cause of the Toronto Militia was "nominally for Canada," it was "really to defend a Government of land sharks who have villainously wronged the poor native and the actual settler."[45] How different had been the circumstances when the Wolseley expedition had set out in 1870!

[44]DP, 1237, March 28, 1885. [45]MP, March 30, 1885.

And yet, he reminded Mair, the same John A. Macdonald had been guilty of treason even then; in fact, every move the Prime Minister had made since he had received Ritchot and Scott had proved him, George Denison, right. Allowing Riel to escape—even giving him money—the Pacific Scandal, the "humbugging" of the people into a National Policy of inflated prosperity (a "second South Sea Bubble which has brought ruin to many a Canadian home"), of all these "this same arch-conspirator and trickster" had been feloniously guilty. Denison was obviously unaware of any irony when he exclaimed to Mair: "Thank God the punishment in this case has fallen mainly on those who were bribed!"[46]

Denison did not hesitate to make such charges publicly. "It is possible," he later remarked in *Soldiering in Canada*, "that I am too combative and energetic, and am perhaps constitutionally incapable of acquiring [a] spirit of obsequious servility"[47] (he could also say that since 1879 he had been "in comfortable financial circumstances" and "quite independent" of worry about his future).[48] His constant goading of political and military authorities and his independence of opinion were indeed, he implied, the reasons that his Militia regiment, the Governor-General's Body Guard, had not been called to action as soon as the others.

Despite their varying motives for either openly criticizing the Government or prudently remaining quiet, Denison and Mair once again joined with the rest of Ontario in vilifying Louis Riel. Governmental peccancy was difficult to kick satisfactorily, even if one were prepared to take the risk; but the half-breed leader once again provided a target at which almost everyone could throw his vituperation. To Mair he immediately became "that scoundrel" who was allowed "to machinate in making incendiary and revolutionary speeches,"[49] "this horrible villain" who had "our poor people of Prince Albert at his mercy," thereby proving "what a blunder was made in 1870 by not hanging him."[50] And Denison echoed by declaring "the only thing I want to see is that Riel should receive his punishment for Scott's murder in 1870—and perhaps he may get it."[51] On April 1, Denison's regiment was ordered to prepare for active service; the same day Mair arrived from Windsor, determined, he said, to go with any unit in order to help relieve his friends in Prince Albert. "It is my duty," he told Eliza; "I should never forgive myself if I

[46]MP, March 27, 1885.
[47]P. 244.
[48]*Ibid.*, p. 333.
[49]DP, 1227, March 26, 1885.
[50]DP, 1241, March 28, 1885.
[51]MP, Denison to Mair, March 30, 1885.

failed in this trying hour for Canada."[52] Because Denison's regular quartermaster was unable to accompany his regiment Mair was immediately given a temporary commission (Denison's uncle was Deputy Adjutant-General) to fill the vacancy. By April 6, the old comrades were comrades-in-arms and aboard a troop train bound for the North-West—"perhaps never to return," Mair wrote Eliza, but also "perhaps to make Riel my captive!"[53] To add to the leave-taking a dramatic note of which Mair was unaware at the time was a letter aboard another train and sent by a Mr. "James H. Hayes" of Windsor to Louis Riel, Esq., of Prince Albert:

Dear Sir:
The Mr. C. Mair of Prince Albert with whom you came in contact during the rebellion of 1869–70 and who has been residing here for the past two years left this morning for the North-West with the object of seeing you and shooting you.
Being friendly to you and your cause I take this opportunity of letting you know in advance so you may be on your guard. I mail this from Detroit, Mich., for fear the P.O. authorities here might intercept it.
Please acknowledge receipt of this. . . .[54]

But here the drama not only begins but virtually ends. In the 1885 uprising there were acts of heroism, foolhardiness, and tragedy as there had been in 1869–70, but neither Mair nor Denison was involved in any of them, was, indeed, even close to them. The chapters in Denison's *Soldiering in Canada* that are devoted to the Body Guard's part in the Rebellion make interesting reading, but nowhere will one find references to the personal experiences of the two friends that would not have been just as appropriate to a *résumé* of Militia camp activities at Niagara-on-the-Lake. General Middleton, the British officer commanding the Canadian Militia, gave the regiment the responsibility of guarding the telegraph station at Humboldt, over fifty miles south of Batoche, the headquarters of the enemy. There Denison and Mair remained for three months, comparatively comfortable in the earthworks of the "Fort Denison" that the energetic Colonel had caused to be made, but little stimulated by the fact that the reports of action had to come to them for transmission over the

[52]MP, April 2, 1885. [53]*Ibid.*

[54]MP, "Hayes" to Riel, April 1, 1885. The letter was intercepted and a copy given to Mair by Col. Irvine of the N.W.M.P. at Prince Albert. Wrote Mair: "I have been unable to discover . . . who wrote about me to Riel, but suspicion points to the French editor of a small paper here called *Le Progrès*. . . . It is evident that old rebeldom still bears me a grudge for my correspondence of '69." (DP, 1380, Mair to Denison, Windsor, Aug. 10, 1885.)

wires. Mair had envisioned "a grand march . . . through the territories,"[55] but his letters to Eliza revealed mainly the boredom that he actually experienced. Even the excitement of a trip to Prince Albert after Riel's capture on May 15 was qualified by the sores and pains he incurred from being in the saddle for many hours. "I am wearying to get back to finish *Tecumseh*,"[56] he wrote, and Foster, indeed, with whom Denison and Mair were in constant communication, admonished, "if between both of you you have not got *Tecumseh* finished it will be very discreditable to you."[57] Foster also found considerable humour in the camp experiences of his two friends. "My dear Prairie Flower," he addressed Denison, "before [Mair] left I gave him several cautions about horse-back riding [and] warned him against attempting to recite portions of *Tecumseh* to the Indians lest fuel should thereby be added to the flame of rebellion."[58]

Such facetiousness, although more apt in reference to Mair in 1885 than had been similar remarks by Foster and other Canada Firsters in 1869, was once again unreflective of the serious, even tragic, character of events in the West. For Louis Riel and his *métis*, certainly, the end of the Rebellion was to prove the end of their cause. More immediately, the mentally deranged Riel was tried at Regina for treason, found guilty, and sentenced to be hanged. But the aftermath was to be in many respects just as tragic for Canada as a whole. The insurgent *métis* leader, for all his fiery spirit, probably never imagined the legacy of division and prejudice his life and death would leave.

By the end of July, 1885, and after four months absence, Mair was back in Windsor endeavouring to regain the sense of literary continuity and intensity that had characterized the composition of *Tecumseh* just prior to his leaving for the West. Most significant of all obstacles was the tension created in him by Riel's trial and the subsequent delay in carrying out the sentence. Mair's interest in Riel was, of course, greater than that of the ordinary Canadian who had not experienced imprisonment and even threat of death at the hands of the notorious rebel chief; but until Riel was hanged in November Mair seemed to undergo a strain that only an execution could relieve. His correspondence at this time consistently reflects a seeking of justification for wishing the supreme penalty, and implies admission that although Riel was "a horrible villain" his guilt was shared by many

[55]MP, Mair to Eliza Mair, April 24, 1885.
[56]MP, May 30, 1885.
[57]MP, May 27, 1885.
[58]DP, 1345, July 1, 1885.

who were not only going scot-free but were also on the side superintending the hanging. "The opinion of the best people here is that Riel should be hanged,"[59] Mair wrote to Denison with a smugness that belied his real uncertainty; "nothing but hanging will suit the right public mind of Ontario. . . . Sir John's Government would go down like a pack of cards if Riel gets off."[60] Such was his nervousness that he could not "get down to work on *Tecumseh*—I don't believe I shall be able to do much until after . . . that hanging!"[61]

Riel was hanged on November 16 and *Tecumseh* was finished by the middle of December; although even when the work was on the press of Hunter and Rose in Toronto Mair was still forwarding changes that he wished Denison to incorporate before the final proofs were prepared. On New Year's Eve of 1885, for example, he wrote that he had "been haunted with a fear of critics' finding incongruity in making Iena purely and simply an untrained Indian girl"; therefore he was preparing some new verses more elucidative of her character.[62] To Denison an Indian maiden in an Indian play should be an Indian maiden—there was really no problem; but, he added, Mair "had better come to Toronto" to be present at the birth pangs of the play.[63] So from Denison's Heydon Villa Mair supervised the last details of publication, reporting them faithfully to Eliza in Windsor. On January 27 the work was ready for the binder and the cover had been printed ("a pine branch thrown on the centre, 'Tecumseh' in old English letters on the upper left corner, and my own name in the lower right corner"); on the 29th, Iena's song was presented "with a fine, tender pathos," by Foster at a gathering of Toronto literary notables; and on February 12 Mair forwarded to Eliza one of the first copies of *Tecumseh*. "I am conscious that it is a great work," he wrote her, "that it has a great and good aim, and I believe that it will live."[64] The years of labour were over, and "thanks to true friends" his drama was "getting out under the best auspices."[65]

Of the "great and good aim" of *Tecumseh*—to reflect and to inculcate a great national spirit—there is no doubt. But it is not a "great" work. Mair's subordination of artistic principles, both poetic and dramatic, to those of ardent nationalism and of sentimental melodrama precludes that distinction. For five acts and twenty-eight scenes, which, if acted, would require at least four hours for presentation,

[59]DP, 1380, Aug. 10, 1885.
[60]DP, 1393, Aug. 29, 1885.
[61]DP, 1401, Sept. 12, 1885.
[62]DP, 1468.
[63]MP, Jan. 2, 1886.
[64]MP, Feb. 19, 1886.
[65]MP, Jan. 30, 1886.

Tecumseh displays a pageant of stylized and highly rhetorical history. Even the most daring of drama groups would find the mass of material it attempts to unify far too unwieldy, far too incoherent in dramatic objective, to warrant its being staged. This may be emphasized despite Mair's half-hopeful rearranging of scenes and lines as he reached the end of his play and despite the fact that patriotic groups in Chatham, Ontario, and Vancouver, for example, were to bring at least parts of it to the boards in later years.

Any unity possessed by *Tecumseh* is implicit in the theme that a patriot such as Mair could be expected to stress, the historical theme of a three-sided struggle for the North American continent. In his attempts, however, to follow historical fact and to glorify, first of all Tecumseh and then Brock, Mair loses his dramatic perspective. As one of the few comparatively recent critics of *Tecumseh*, E. K. Broadus, has written: "The materials of the play—Tecumseh's efforts to federate the Indian tribes against the encroachments of the Americans, the assistance which he tendered General Brock . . . at Detroit, and his last fight at Amherstburg—do not 'compose' into a drama."[66] And the element that Mair thought "indispensable," the element "of woman," of love, only adds an incongruously sentimental emphasis to an already overladen plot. During the period depicted by the play, three heroes, Tecumseh, Brock, and Lefroy, vie for supremacy with not only invading Americans, including low Yankee ruffians, but also traitors in their own camps—Tecumseh's villainous brother the Prophet, and Brock's cowardly subordinate commander, Colonel (later General) Procter. And since the play is a tragedy, the final "curtain" falls on a scene of desolation: Tecumseh is dead, Procter has ignominiously retreated, the Americans have won the battle of Moraviantown, and Iena is carried away lifeless in the arms of the distraught Lefroy. Brock, however, has died gloriously in victory at Queenston Heights, Tecumseh has achieved immortality even in failure, and the Canadian reader is obviously expected to realize that the ultimate outcome of the war was an American defeat.

Tecumseh, even when he yields the centre of the stage to Brock, acts with consistent gallantry and integrity. He is a superb, if wooden, figure, a romantic "noble savage" who is at once as courageous as the Cid, as incorruptible as Cato, and as eloquent and statesmanlike as Disraeli. As a dramatic creation he is at times Shakespearian, at others Miltonic, and at others Restoration Heroic, but certainly always

[66]*A Book of Canadian Prose and Verse*, p. 37.

lofty. "My brother's love," he declaims to General Harrison, "is like the trader's warmth—/O'er with the purchase":

Oh, unhappy lives—
Our gifts which go for yours! Once we were strong.
Once all this mighty continent was ours,
And the Great Spirit made it for our use.
He knew no boundaries, so had we peace
In the vast shelter of His handiwork,
And, happy here, we cared not whence we came.
We brought no evils thence—no treasured hate,
No greed of gold, no quarrels over God;

. . . .

Thus flowed our lives until your people came,
Till from the East our matchless misery came!
Since then our tale is crowded with your crimes,
With broken faith, with plunder of reserves—
The sacred remnants of our wide domain—
With tamp'rings, and delirious feasts of fire,
The fruit of your thrice-cursed stills of death,
Which make our good men bad, our bad men worse,
Aye! blind them till they grope in open day,
And stumble into miserable graves.
Oh, it is piteous, for none will hear!

. . . .

But we shall yield no more! Those plains are ours
Those forests are our birth-right and our home!
Let not the Long-knife build one cabin there—
Or fire from it will spread to every roof,
To compass you, and light your souls to death!

(II, iv)

General Brock is the idealized British soldier. Bold, energetic, decisive, but sensitive to his great responsibility, he too has an almost insuperable task, as he occasionally reveals in Shakespearian soliloquy:

Now might the head of gray Experience
Shake o'er the problems that surround us here.
I am no stranger to the brunt of war,
But all the odds so lean against our side
That valour's self might tremble for the issue.
Could England stretch its full, assisting hand
Then might I smile though velvet-footed time
Struck all his claws at once into our flesh;
But England, noble England, fights for life,

Couching the knightly lance for liberty
'Gainst a new dragon that affrights the world.
And, now, how many noisome elements
Would plant their greed athwart this country's good!
How many demagogues betray its cause!
How many aliens urge it to surrender!
Our present good must match their present ill,
And, on our frontiers, boldest deeds in war
Dismay the foe, and strip the loins of faction.

(IV, i)

The most interesting character, however, is Lefroy, "a poet-artist, enamoured of Indian life, and in love with Iena." For this young English expatriate who wanders in and out of the woods searching for love and serenity has a psychological complexity quite lacking in his fellow *dramatis personae*. Fictional though he is, Lefroy is derivative both as a type and as a person, reflecting clearly the literary and historical influences to which Mair was indebted for his creation. His name suggests Chateaubriand's romantic depictions of the wanderings of Atala and René, but more probable is his literary descent from the English Romantics. For Lefroy is a Byronic figure, the melancholy poet on a quest, but in *Tecumseh* transplanted from a corrupt Europe to an about-to-be-corrupted Canadian wilderness. Like Tecumseh, he deplores the depredations of civilization upon nature, "the sordid town that here may rise," the greed and ruthlessness of the white man. But, unlike Tecumseh, he sees no solution in clearly defined boundaries for different races. For Lefroy, as a prominent Canadian critic of the time was quick to note, was depicted "with a dash of socialism of a very modern type, not unlike that of which Mr. William Morris is perhaps the most interesting contemporary professor."[67] When General Harrison prophesies to Tecumseh that "the poor of every land shall come to this, / Heart-full of sorrows and shall lay them down" he is reviled by

Lefroy (springing to his feet) The poor! What care
Your rich thieves for the poor?
Those graspers hate the poor, from whom they spring,
More deeply than they hate this injured race.
Much have they taken from it—let them now
Take this prediction, with the red man's curse!
The time will come when that dread power—the Poor—
Whom, in their greed and pride of wealth, they spurn—
Will rise on them, and tear them from their seats;

[67]W. D. LeSueur, Toronto *Week*, March 4, 1886.

Drag all their vulgar splendours down, and pluck
Their shallow women from their lawless beds,
Yea, seize their puling and unhealthy babes,
And fling them as foul pavement to the streets.
In all the dreaming of the Universe
There is no darker vision of despairs!

(II, iv)

It is a mistake, however, to infer that in such revolutionary utterance Lefroy speaks for Mair. Historically he was based upon Lord Edward Fitzgerald, the Irish patriot whose wild experiences in Canada coupled with his revolutionary activities in Paris had a highly dramatic colour for Mair, who also saw him as "one of the kindest, most generous hearts [that] ever lived," a man "of high poetic feeling close to nature, and truth as it dwells in nature." But he became "a revolutionary wreck and a mistaken visionary patriot," unhinged "by attributing to organized society evils (which must necessarily co-exist with it) as crimes deliberate."[68] According to Mair, Lord Edward, "having seen the perfection which lives in savage life," tramped through the streets of Paris "shouting '*ca era*!' with the best and worst of them," only to return home and "perish miserably for 'liberty.'" Mair admitted that although he strongly sympathized with Fitzgerald he himself was convinced that organized society rested upon "property," and so long as men were "not born equal in intelligence and greed," so long "must the trials of the world continue." Fitzgerald's sad death was, indeed, a fitting commentary "upon his dreams of human perfectibility and possibilities."

Originally, Mair intended "to kill Lefroy" in the fifth act, "to get him out of an unhappy world,"[69] but instead he introduced an even more pathetic reversal. When Lefroy goes forth to battle, Iena dresses as an Indian boy so that she can follow him in disguise. At a critical moment she springs from "behind a large sugar maple" to save her lover:

(Second Soldier aims at Lefroy. Iena with a cry, leaps from her shelter, intercepts the fire, and is shot dead.)

[68]DP, 837 (126–29), Feb. 1, 1885, and 1213, March 21, 1885. Fitzgerald (1763–98) served with the British Army in the Revolutionary War and after spending several years with the Indians was drawn to Paris by the French Revolution. In 1796 he joined the United Irishmen and attempted to secure French support for an Irish uprising, but in 1798 he was betrayed to the English and captured, although not before he had slain one of his would-be captors. He himself died of wounds sustained at his arrest.

[69]DP, 837 (128), Feb. 1, 1884.

And Lefroy is left as

> but a shell,
> A husk, an empty case, or anything
> That may be kicked about the world.
>
> (V, vi)

Into Tecumseh, Brock, and Lefroy, Mair obviously projected many of his own attitudes and ideals—humanitarian, patriotic, military, national, romantic, and poetic. By means of three such figures, indeed, he probably managed to resolve satisfactorily, for himself at least, several conflicting points of view, to express through his characters the somewhat confused arguments he may have had with himself. Thus Tecumseh is noble, natural man living in a pristine simplicity; but since what he represents has to go in the name of progress, it behooves the enlightened white man such as Brock or Militia volunteer Robinson or the United Empire Loyalist to respect him and his prehistoric tradition, to care for him and not to exploit him out of existence as the Americans were doing. Mair romantically declines, however, even to ask how this integrated Utopia can be concretely achieved. When Lefroy with republican fervour insists

> The crippled throne
> No longer shelters the uneasy king,
> And outworn sceptres and imperial crowns
> Now grow fantastic as an idiot's dream.
> These perish with the kingly pastime, war,
> And war's blind tool, the monster, Ignorance!
> Both hateful in themselves, but this the worst,
> One tyrant will remain—one impious fiend
> Whose name is Gold—our earliest, latest foe!
> Him must the earth destroy, ere man can rise,
> Rightly self made, to his high destiny,
> Purged of his grossest faults; humane and kind;
> Co-equal with his fellow, and as free . . . ,

Brock replies with authoritarian (and Shakespearian) conviction:

> Lefroy, such thoughts, let loose, would wreck the world.
> The kingly function is the soul of state,
> The crown the emblem of authority,
> And loyalty the symbol of all faith.
> Omitting these, man's government decays—
> His family falls into revolt and ruin.
>
> (IV, vii)

But Brock and Lefroy (*and* Mair) are here compelled to "drop this rootless argument." Perhaps the romantic poet of *Dreamland* was confronted by the Canada First nationalist, by the Prince Albert real-estate speculator.

Two other aspects of *Tecumseh* warrant attention. By both soliloquy and long passages of descriptive dialogue Mair provides the reader with a vivid picture of the flora and fauna of not only the Upper Canada of Brock's time but of also the still undiscovered West. Usually the setting is pastoral rather than savage, closer to the Forest of Arden than to the wilderness of the contemporaneous Deerslayer. Lefroy's speech in "Another Part of the Forest" and beginning

> This region is as lavish of its flowers
> As Heaven of its primrose blooms by night
>
> (I, ii)

praises the bounty of nature in terms reminiscent of Friar Laurence's in *Romeo and Juliet* and Banquo's in *Macbeth*. But when he describes for Brock the "unrivalled wastes" visited by Tecumseh and himself in order to enrol the western tribes, Lefroy is expansive in his vision, broad in his poetic delineation of "ocean's paraphrase":

> We left
> The silent forest, and day after day,
> Great prairies swept beyond our aching sight
> Into the measureless West; uncharted realms,
> Voiceless and calm, save when tempestuous wind
> Rolled the rank herbage into billows vast,
> And rushing tides, which never found a shore.
>
> . . . .
>
> *Brock*. What charming solitudes! And life was there!
> *Lefroy*. Yes, life was there! inexplicable life,
> Still wasted by inexorable death.
> There had the stately stag his battlefield—
> Dying for mastery among his hinds.
> There vainly sprung the affrighted antelope,
> Beset by glittering eyes and hurrying feet.
> The dancing grouse at their insensate sport,
> Heard not the stealthy footstep of the fox;
> The gopher on his little earthwork stood,
> With folded arms, unconscious of the fate
> That wheeled in narrowing circles overhead,
> And the poor mouse, on heedless nibbling bent,
> Marked not the silent coiling of the snake.

At length this fascination with North American nature, red in tooth and claw, is interrupted by the "deep and solemn sound" of the bison herd:

A growing uproar blending in our ears,
With noise tumultuous as ocean's surge,
Of bellowings, fierce breath and battle shock,
And ardor of unconquerable herds.
A multitude whose trampling shook the plains,
With discord of harsh sound and rumblings deep,
As if the swift revolving earth had struck,
And from some adamantine peak recoiled–
Jarring.

(IV, vii)

In these passages there is to be noted again the characteristically Mair combination of derivativeness and originality. Reference to only a few lines from Bryant's "The Prairies" will reveal to the reader the striking similarity of Lefroy's vista of the West and the American poet's in 1832. And yet as he proves in parts of Lefroy's descriptive passages and as he had proved in the best lines of *Dreamland*, when Mair looked at nature directly and allowed his own experience and inspiration to guide him, he wrote verse that rises at times to the level of commendable poetry. A. J. M. Smith has justifiably praised Mair's "impressionistic picture of the wilderness, vast and unplumbed, teeming with life, but empty of man," the "intensity and power" that resulted when his "imagination caught fire" and that "anticipates the more fervid spirit of the later poets." It is in verse like this, continues Smith,

> at once traditional and full of accurate observation, that Mair makes a genuine contribution to the development of Canadian literature. . . . It cannot be denied that in a few passages where he attains his fullest power there is a firmness and clarity, a hint of Virgilian rectitude, that represents a more universal and truly classical way of looking at things than is exhibited by any Canadian poet except Archibald Lampman.[70]

Professor Smith's restraint is due to his regret that so small a part of Mair's work "should have shown this solidity and directness." In other words, as in *Dreamland*, there are reflected in *Tecumseh* strengths and weaknesses, lapses in taste and "form," the unevenness and inconsistency that Mair was never able to overcome, even, in fact, to recognize more than superficially.

[70]"Nationalism and Canadian Poetry," *Northern Review*, I (Dec.–Jan., 1945–46), 39–40.

His provision of comic relief in *Tecumseh* is an additional example of lack of literary proportion. Shakespeare had his Dogberry and Verges, Snug and Bottom, Bardolph and Pistol. Mair has his Twang and Slaugh, Gerkin and Bloat, low buffoons in the form of "Yankee ruffians" who, of course, speak in prose:

Twang. . . . Our Guvner takes a crazy sight more pains than I would to sweetin thet ragin' devil Tecumseh's temper. I'd sweetin it wi' sugar o'lead if I had *my* way.

Slaugh. It's a reekin' shame—dang me ef it aint. End that two-faced, one-eyed brother o' his, the Prophet—I'll be darned ef folks don't say thet the Shakers in them 'ere parts claims him fer a disciple!

Twang. Them Shakers is a queer lot. They dance jest like wild Injuns, and thinks we orter be kind to the red rascals, end use them honestly.

Gerkin. Wall! Thet's what our Guvner ses tew. But I reckon he's shammin' a bit. Twixt you and me, he's on the make like the rest o' us. Think o' bein' kind to a red devil that would lift your har ten minutes arter! End as fer honesty—I say "set 'em up" every time, and then rob 'em. Thet's the way to clar them out o' the kentry. Whiskey's better'n gunpowder, end costs less than fightin' 'em in the long run.

. . . .

Slaugh. . . . Jest wait till the live citizens o'these United States end Territories gits a chance, end we'll show . . . what a free people, wi' our institooshuns *kin* do. . . . I'd give them Kernel Crunch's billet.

Gerkin. What was thet, General?

Slaugh. Why, they say he killed a hull family o' redskins, and stuck 'em up as scar'-crows in his wheat fields. Gentlemen, there's nothin' like original idees!

(II, ii)

Such an interlude was incorporated, of course, for more than comic effect. Its players are not just white boors; they are American boors, and are intended to express character contrast as well as dramatic contrast to the citizens of York:

Excitement and leave-taking. The volunteers break into column and sing:

O hark to the voice from the lips of the free!
O hark to the cry from the lakes to the sea!
Arm! Arm! the invader is wasting our coasts,
And tainting the air of our land with his hosts.

(IV, iii)

And to such patriotic aspects of his drama did Mair devote his most painstaking attention and the largest share of his creative talents. Nowhere in his writings and correspondence does he give evidence of believing his work might live for other than patriotic reasons. "As long as Canadians are true to their country" or "until Canada is no longer Canada" are typical conditionalities; and the verse of real literary excellence, like that of bathos and tastelessness, seems to be unappreciated for what it is. The merit of *Tecumseh*, he was always to insist, arose from its being "a labour of love and patriotism," from the "Canadian feeling . . . that is in my bones." Even the inclusion of parts of it in school texts was to be determined almost entirely, it would appear, by its contribution to the inculcation of national sentiment: ". . . all sentiments, discipline and training," he insisted, "must be contributory to the adjustment of that Imperial system to which, as a race, we as naturally belong as planets to their sun."[71]

The reception of *Tecumseh* in 1886 by press and public alike was far more enthusiastic than even that accorded *Dreamland* eighteen years before. This time, of course, there were certain aspects of publication, added "frills," that had been non-existent in 1868 and that now attracted comparatively wider notice. The growing awareness of the plight of the Indian, the part he had played in the recent Rebellion, the author's exciting involvement with the notorious Riel in 1869 and his subsequent participation in the campaign of 1885, the fact that here for the first time was a Canadian drama dealing with a Canadian subject, were undoubtedly among the varied reasons for a special response. And the public presentation of the song of the York Volunteers—"For Canada Fight"— at a concert on March 11 must have been a timely incentive to further interest.[72]

But in addition there was the significant role of the literary periodical and its experienced reviewer. Although limited in circulation and struggling against great odds, magazines and papers such as the *Week* and the *Varsity* were competently edited and, within their scope, influential in forming taste and opinion. And these periodicals along with their brethren, the daily newspapers, acclaimed *Tecumseh* almost without qualification. W. D. LeSueur of Ottawa contributed a long review to the *Week* of March 4 in which he praised the "very superior" poetical merits of the work, the whole pages of "sustained excellence, strong and graceful in expression, appropriate in imagery, and instinct with noble feeling." G. Mercer Adam's commentary in the *Varsity* was so long as to require two instalments, on February 27 and March 5, in which the former editor of the *Canadian Monthly*

[71]DP, 3057, May 18, 1896.

[72]The concert was sponsored by the Commercial Travelers' Association and drew a packed house to the Pavilion Music Hall, Toronto. Nordheimer's Music Store had a full window display devoted to "the new Canadian patriotic song."

stated that Mr. Mair had "achieved a great and complete success" and that "in the choice and handling of a grand Canadian theme" he had "amply justified the poet's function and art," indeed, had "done more for the future study and appreciation of Anglo-Canadian history than it is possible at present to realize." For, said Adam,

. . . it is important that the heroic deeds of the faithful Indian allies of Britain, in the struggle to plant and maintain the flag of the Empire on this continent, should be treasured, and a fitting memory preserved of their loyal services and staunch friendship. Nor should gratitude be lacking, particularly in the Canadian nation, which owes so much to the Indian tribes for the heritage it now peacefully enjoys, and from which it has rudely dispossessed the children of the woods, and done much to make them what they now are—a poor, emasculated, vanishing race. To perpetuate the memory of these services, and outline on the poet-painter's canvas the grand figure of an Indian ally of Britain in the early struggle on Canadian soil, with the invader of the western peninsula of this Province, is the work Mr. Mair has set himself to do; and skilfully and artistically he has accomplished his task, and indisputably put the hall mark of genius upon one more production of Canadian verse.

Throughout *Tecumseh,* continued Adam, was evidence of the author's "large knowledge of the dramatist's art," his "constructive skill, his felicity of language . . . , the fire of his genius, and the tenderness which bespeaks the poet's heart." Particularly did the *Varsity* critic enjoy the love story of Lefroy and Iena, an aspect of "heightened interest" that kept the reader "on the tenter-hooks of anxiety and suspense until the pathetic close of the drama." And surely "the beauty and melody of some of the love songs . . . are hardly surpassed by the best of England's lyric poets." But above all else was the manner in which the drama rose to its "true mission"—"to preserve the memory of an heroic period in the country's annals, and to stimulate national interest in the events and characters of the time."

Most of the daily newspapers expressed their critiques of *Tecumseh* in similar terms. Said the Toronto *Globe* on February 20: "As the play of *Henry V* was a song of triumph to the English of Shakespeare's time, so is this a song of triumph for the Canadians of to-day." The Montreal *Gazette* of March 2, highly pleased that Mr. Mair had not passed "beyond the pale of our own romantic story" in selecting a subject, was confident that "Manitoba [*sic*] may well be proud of a work that is sure of honorable recognition in the metropolis of English literature." George Stewart Jr., an increasingly prominent literary critic, wrote in the Quebec *Morning Chronicle* of February 27 that *Tecumseh* in tone and spirit was purely Canadian ("not a classical allusion appearing in the text") and by such works "the lessons of true patriotism are taught." The Hamilton *Times* succinctly noted on March 19 that "as a purely Canadian production it is something to be proud of"; the Kingston *British Whig* of March 27 that it had a claim "for all Canadian royalists—in fact, for all Canadians"; and the highly practical Orillia *Packet*, on the day before, that "its low price ought to introduce it to every family in Canada." Even the New York *Critic* was impressed from a patriotic bias. Graciously commented the April number:

Mr. Mair, as is natural and proper in a Canadian poet, is ardently loyal, and is somewhat vehemently anti-democratic; but these sentiments do not prevent him from doing full justice to the good qualities of Harrison, Cass, and other republican leaders; and as the drama finds its catastrophe in the triumph of their arms and the rather ignominious flight of the British general, American readers have certainly no reason to be out of humor with it.

In addition to this expression of tolerant fairness the *Critic* also offered some specifically literary criticism. *Tecumseh,* it said, was a drama in the Tennysonian style, not really actable. Nor could the "startling effects" with which the author was fond of concluding his scenes be altogether admired:

The first Act ends with a desperate struggle, in which Lefroy, Iena, Tecumseh, and his nefarious brother, the Prophet, are involved, in a fashion which reminds one of a celebrated scene in Sheridan's "Critic." The author, however, does not resort to the English dramatist's device of the convenient Beefeater, imperiously bidding the combatants "let fall their swords and daggers." Tecumseh, according to the stage-directions, "Grasps the Prophet's uplifted arm," exclaiming, "One blow and you are doomed!" and suddenly the curtain comes down. It is only from the subsequent scenes that the anxious reader learns, to his relief, that the fraternal strife ended without bloodshed.

But, the *Critic* continued, Mr. Mair's verse often rose "into passages of much imaginative beauty" and his characters were "well delineated and distinguished." If the style of those who spoke in metre was "somewhat too archaic for the time," and that of the low characters who spoke slang was "altogether too modern," there was nevertheless "ample Shakespearian precedent" for such liberty. Therefore, although Tecumseh could not be considered a great poem, "even for these degenerate days," it did present with lively dramatic effect a succession of interesting historical scenes that "often glowed with true poetic fire."

The diction of Mair's characters, both high and low, proved to be a contentious point even with the highly commendatory Canadian critics. LeSueur thought "some characters . . . might perhaps have been spared" without marring the verisimilitude of the drama; Gerkin, Slaugh and Company were probably represented correctly enough, but "we cannot help feeling as if there were a trace of U. E. Loyalist prejudice in this portraiture." Some of Brock's speeches, also, were "affected," and the citizens of York, meeting casually in the streets, were too Shakespearian in conversation, "particularly the one who says, speaking of the danger of navigating Lake Erie in all kinds of chance craft,

'Tis an awful hazard
Yet palpable unto the spirit's touch
As earth to finger."

G. Mercer Adams, not having read the *Critic*'s calumet-offering appraisal, believed that "our neighbours across the line won't take kindly to the rather slangy prose dialogues . . . nor will Brock's colloquy . . . to the seditious class in . . . Ontario be any more palatable." And he himself preferred "that Canadian literature should do nothing to revive the now slumbering acrimony which the separation at the Revolution brought about"; Canadian loyalty, surely, was "too lofty a virtue to give needless offence." George Stewart Jr. felt the American ruffians "cheapened the work," and an unidentified critic of the April *Canada Educational Monthly* was convinced their "very names . . . betrayed the prejudiced spirit in which the Yankee caricatures are drawn." Thus the literary critic of the New York *Sun*, proving himself far less genial than his countryman of the *Critic*, went far to justify the fears of Adam and the other apprehensive Canadians by dismissing *Tecumseh* in one sweeping statement. "To say this book is absurd," he snapped, "is to exhaust compliment."[73]

From Mair's Canadian literary contemporaries came praise and encouragement similar to that voiced by the native press. Charles Sangster, now fading physically and mentally as a civil service clerk in Ottawa, promised that as soon as his "brain got clearer" he would "dive into" *Tecumseh*. "I had got as far as the fourth Act," he wrote, "when my brain gave out, and my doctor will not let me read just

[73]Quoted in MP, Denison to Mair, March 8, 1886.

now, as I am unfit for brain work. . . . [But] you are all right now. Go ahead."[74] William Kirby, of *Golden Dog* fame, saw *Tecumseh* as a "fine composition written with a correct knowledge of history and finished with care." Particularly pleasing to him was the work's obvious intention "to make Canadians proud of their country and of the great men who have lived and died among us."[75] And Charles G. D. Roberts, now teaching at King's College in Nova Scotia, assured Mair that the promise of *Dreamland* had been fulfilled and that although he had considered his own poetry "the best yet done in Canada," *Tecumseh* was quite superior: "It is much more artistic, masterly in technique than *Saul*—as a Canadian and your friend I am simply dilated with pride . . . and shall certainly spare no effort to do something myself that shall equal it."[76] About a year later, in June, 1887, the gracious Roberts expressed his praise publicly in the Halifax monthly *Critic*—and gave, incidentally, a comment on Mair and his poetry quite rare in previous reviews:

> About a year ago there appeared in Toronto . . . a dramatic poem of much force and beauty. The author is Mr. Charles Mair, who in boyhood, published a volume of crude, but promising fragments and brief lyrics. From that time till just before the production of *Tecumseh*, he buried himself in the wilds of the North-West and was utterly removed from the sweep and stress of life in the modern world. Hence we may look upon him as now making a new beginning, and may regard his new work as a product of the new times. Viewed in this light, and as an earnest of future achievements, its defects, which are a certain provincialism of tone and lack of sympathy with modern mental attitudes, sink into unimportance, and its excellences, which are those of imagination, vigor, sincerity and freshness, become deeply significant for us who are watching for the new light within our borders. By his long security from attrition with other minds, he has preserved his individuality in all its sharpness of line and angle. He shows the influence of scarce any master saving Shakespeare, and him he has studied not unworthily. His illustrations are native and new, got at first hand, his atmosphere and coloring unmistakably Canadian; his patriotism full-blooded and fervid. His utterance is such as fits the lips of a son of this land of splendid heritage and heroic stock—it is forceful, straightforward, and virile.

Principal George Grant had suggested to Mair that some of his verse was "crude"; but to have been accused, even politely, of "provincialism" and "lack of sympathy with modern mental attitudes" must

[74]MP, Feb. 23, 1886.
[75]MP, March 4, 1886.
[76]MP, March 10, 1886.

have been most unexpectedly upsetting to an ardent Canada Firster. But Mair's conception of his poetic calling did not include consideration of "the sweep and stress of life in the modern world" or of the possible benefits from "attrition with other minds." If it had, he would probably never have written *Tecumseh*.

Pauline Johnson, perhaps the most appropriate critic of all, was certainly not concerned with such aspects. As the daughter of an Indian chief Miss Johnson was most interested in Mair's depiction of Indian character; and for it she had nothing but praise. Writing in the Toronto *World* some years later, on March 22, 1892, she was pleased that

> Mair has not fallen into that unattractive fashion of making his Indians "assent with a grunt"—or look with "eyes of dog-like fidelity" or to appear "very grand, very dignified, and not very immaculate clean." Mair avoids the usual commonplaces used in describing Indians by those who have never met or mixed with them. His drama bears upon every page evidence of long study and life with the people whom he has written of so carefully, so truthfully.

Particularly did Miss Johnson admire the portrayal of Iena ("Oh! happy inspiration vouchsafed to the author") and her greatest regret was that Mair should have the maiden die at the end of the play:

> Oh! Lefroy, where is your fellowman in fiction? Iena, where your prototype? Alas, for all the other pale-faced lovers, they are indifferent, almost brutal creations, and as for the redskin girls that love them, they are all fawn-eyed, unnatural, maidenly idiots. . . . But the inevitable doom of death could not be stayed even by Mair's sensitive Indian-loving pen.

It is little wonder that Miss Johnson could personally write to Mair, "Oh! you are half an Indian, I know—the best half of a man, anyway —his heart."[77]

In the spring of 1886 congratulatory messages came to Mair from all over Canada, even from the United States and Great Britain. John G. Bourinot, the Honorary Secretary of the Royal Society of Canada; James MacPherson Lemoine, whose works had earned him election to the Society; W. D. Lighthall, also a member and whose anthology, *Songs of the Great Dominion*, was soon to appear; J. H. Duvar, the "Bard of Hernewood"; Lord Lansdowne, the Governor-General; Lord Wolseley of Red River fame; Judge Hiram C. Biddle of Indiana; even Miss Rosa Hughes of Guernsey, the Channel Islands, a descendant of General Brock; these were only a few contributing their

[77]MP, Dec. 18, 1892.

words of esteem. Some of their letters were little more than notes of appreciation for gift copies; others were capsules of polite criticism. Judge Biddle thought that Iena's fighting as a boy was "the finest touch in the play,"[78] Wolseley that the play clearly revealed "what splendid fellows our forefathers were,"[79] Lighthall that it reflected a "spirit of duty, history and form."[80] And Samuel Woods, Principal of the Ottawa Ladies College, although objecting to certain lines and to Mair's "confusion of 'shall' and 'will'," was placing *Tecumseh* on his curriculum as a work indicative of "the literary excellence of my own, my fair, loved Canada."[81]

The personage perhaps most important of all in the excitement surrounding the publication of *Tecumseh* was George T. Denison. And as might be expected, the energetic magistrate and Militia colonel was himself largely responsible for creating that excitement. Even before *Tecumseh* was finished, Mair had described it to Denison as "*our* play—I'll be hanged if I don't think it is more yours than mine."[82] And when it was being distributed to the booksellers, as Mair had remarked to Eliza, "thanks to true friends" it was "getting out under the best auspices." He meant Denison; for his old friend of *Dreamland* days seems, as then, to have taken upon himself the responsibility for the public promotion of *Tecumseh*. Mair had returned to Windsor as soon as the first copies came from Hunter and Rose, but Denison gives, appropriately, an impression of a commander holding a literary Fort York that would gladly receive friendly overtures but from which attacks and foraging missions could be effectively made. And the communiqués he sent to Mair are a record of what was undoubtedly the most intensive selling campaign in nineteenth-century Canadian letters. "Foster and I went to see Dwight yesterday," he wrote a few days after the work appeared, "and asked him to send an Associated Press despatch by telegraph all over Canada to let the public know what a sensation *Tecumseh* has created." Other reports followed almost daily. "I made three people buy copies at Hart's this morning"; "Bain is selling plenty now; I keep sending people to him"; "I am after Ross, the Minister of Education, to use *Tecumseh* in the schools"; "Foster and I have been at work to-day to have editorials in the *Telegram* and *News* about the rapid sale of the book, complimenting the Toronto people on their taste"; "The Club has taken up *Tecumseh*

[78]MP, March 18, 1886.
[79]MP, Wolseley to Denison to Mair, April 10, 1886.
[80]MP, Oct. 27, 1888.
[81]MP, March 12, 1886.
[82]DP, 1213, March 21, 1885.

on national grounds and are shoving it all they can"; "A crowd of fellows in the Club were reading it and quoting it last night. . . . A gentleman told me that he had taken the line 'Angels are with her now for she is dead' and it putting it on the tombstone of a relative who died lately"; "It is getting to be the thing for young fellows to send to their girls with the line 'his heart is here and mine is in his breast' marked." In addition Denison organized a testimonial dinner for Mair, and insisted to all he met that they attend the concert presentation of the patriotic song. He was for over a month never without a copy of *Tecumseh* under his arm or within quick reach. A letter written to the editor of the Orillia *Packet* noted on April 2 that Mr. Mair "is being decidedly lionized in certain Toronto circles" and that "you can't go within a mile of the National Club without being enquired of by Colonel G. T. Denison if you have read *Tecumseh*, and if not, why not." Denison might well report to the author, therefore, that the booksellers had told him that "no Canadian book has sold across the counter like this has," that it "is going like blazes," and that "this edition is a goner!"

As usual the critics received Denisonian praise or invective, depending largely on the loyalty or lack of it that they disclosed in their reviews. "Mercer Adam's second notice in the *Varsity* is very good," Denison remarked, "but I went for him for saying you should have smoothed things for the Yankees. I asked him if Shakespeare worried about the feelings of the French in *Henry V*, and if a poet should be false to history to please foreigners." Denison was particularly annoyed that Goldwin Smith had seemingly stood aloof from commentary in his own *Week* and had had LeSueur of Ottawa contribute a review. And as for the latter's criticism "about the citizens of York talking in Shakespearian style, it must seem strange to him living in a lumbering village like Ottawa, but we who live in the Athens of Canada see nothing incongruous in our citizens using the very finest language." In any case Denison had spelled out an answering letter that was to appear in the *Week* over J. E. Collins' signature ("to indicate impartiality") and that would justify the characterization of Gerkin and friends.[88] "I am afraid Goldwin Smith will not like to fall in and walk at the tail end of a procession," Denison commented; "he likes to lead a procession for himself, and if he tries it with your book he will find himself down a back street alone." Smith was "disloyal," and Denison felt that he should never have

[88]Collins had recently published his *Story of Louis Riel* (see chap. IV, n. 51) and had met Mair at Denison's home.

asked him to criticize *Tecumseh.* Nor, he added, after reading the N.Y. *Sun*'s curt remark, should he have advised Mair "to tone down a line about the Yankees—d—n them anyway." But the Toronto patriot was virtually impervious to the connotations of criticism offered to *Tecumseh* on other than nationalistic grounds; "It has been criticized by one crank," he wrote Mair, "a professor of Toronto University who in dead earnest complained that it reminded him too much of Shakespeare and Milton. I feel very sorry about him."[84]

The part played by Denison in the launching (as he himself called it) of *Tecumseh* was obviously a major factor in its successful reception. For years afterwards, also, he continued to quote it and refer to it at every possible opportunity. From the other original members of Canada First, however, there is no extant commentary as there is in reference to *Dreamland.* Foster evidently aided Denison considerably; Haliburton had last been heard of from South America where he was engaged in his anthropological researches, but evidently sent no comment; and Morgan, unusually non-committal now, was within a few years to express his opinion in an unexpected way.

Mair himself was elated. "I grovel in the dust of ten thousand apologies for having doubted for an instant your opinion," he told Denison; "It is inspiring to think that Canadians are proud of a Canadian book and are buying it. It repays me for many dreary hours and gloomy forecasts."[85] Through arrangements with Chief Peter Jones of the Six Nations, there was even a possibility that *Tecumseh* would be translated into Ojibway—"certainly . . . an event in the history of the drama!"[86] But most important was that fifty copies had been sent to Chapman and Hall in London (the book bears their imprint in addition to that of Hunter and Rose), who were to await English reviews before undertaking publication themselves. Mair had purposely included copious notes on Indian lore and Canadian history for the benefit of English readers, and through D. H. Macdowall, a Prince Albert friend who was the cousin of "one Andrew Lang," critiques were to appear in the *Saturday Review* and other British periodicals. These hopes failed to materialize, however, for there was neither criticism nor publication in Britain. Mair charged later that Chapman and Hall did not even bother to distribute the copies sent to them, nor to return the money enclosed for obtaining English copyright. And Macdowall he subsequently and significantly referred to as his "quondam friend."

[84]MP, Feb. 28; March 1, 3, 4, 5, and 8, 1886.
[85]DP, 1490, March 6, 1886. [86]DP, 1441, Dec. 7, 1885.

In Canada in the spring of 1886 *Tecumseh* was widely acclaimed as the country's outstanding literary achievement and Mair as its greatest national poet. When Hunter and Rose suggested that a second printing be run off as quickly as possible he declined only when told there was a possibility of incurring financial loss; he estimated that the years of writing had cost him ten thousand dollars—the number of his apologies to Denison—and his return had been but five hundred; "so I have bled for my country," he said, "with a vengeance."[87] But such thoughts were probably farthest from his mind on Victoria Day as Mrs. John Beverley Robinson, the wife of the Lieutenant-Governor, pinned on his Rebellion medal and dubbed him "our warrior bard." Literary eminence had at last been attained. There remained the problem of resurrecting financial eminence in a post-Rebellion Prince Albert, although, as the Toronto *Truth* remarked on March 27, 1886, Mr. Mair "possesses much valuable property" and would soon be known as a wealthy as well as a talented Canadian. But it may have been one of fate's little ironies that a paper called *Truth* should make such a happy prophecy.

[87]DP, 1871, Nov. 3, 1890.

IX. Westward to a Setting Sun

DURING THE SUMMER OF 1886 Mair and his family returned to their home on the banks of the North Saskatchewan, eager to renew life in a Prince Albert they had left four years before, but not without some misgivings about what they would find there. Mair recalled that Franklin had said three removes were as bad as fire, and this was his third. Yet, although the house itself had been badly damaged by refugees who had taken possession of it during the Rebellion, he was able to record, "we are as jolly as crickets—the brass band serenaded us, . . . the children are wild with the river . . . and my dear wife is happy to get back to the North-West, and that makes me happy." They had even taken time to visit Fort Denison, already overgrown with grass, where, Mair reported, "I thought unutterable things."[1] Maude, the eldest daughter, had been left at Miss Dupont's School for Young Ladies in Toronto, and shortly after their arrival in Prince Albert the other children were enrolled at the convent ("an admirable school with English nuns"),[2] the former home of Lawrence Clarke, who, after being cleared of charges that he had helped Riel, had gone for an extended holiday in Florida.

For some time Mair gave every indication of being able not only to recover the prosperity and prominence he had enjoyed before 1882 but also to improve his financial and social position in the community. Besides the two hundred acres he had under cultivation, he had another six hundred lying right beside the town, on which he began

[1]DP, 1556, Aug. 9, 1886.
[2]DP, 1560, Oct. 26, 1886.

to raise stock. His general-merchandise store and his real-estate business continued to provide large advertisements in the *Times*, and before long these enterprises shared his time with a venture into fur-trading. Through Denison and Foster he became the Prince Albert agent for a Toronto fire and life insurance company; he even became the town postmaster, although he admitted this appointment made him really only a "bloated official." The Mair home again became a focal point of Prince Albert social life. The vision of a Toronto of the West was obviously often in his mind when Mair described to Denison the dinners and receptions he and Eliza frequently gave; "We gave an At-Home on Thursday evening last," he wrote in April, 1887, "and had eighty guests who would have done no discredit to even Toronto. I never did see as handsome a lot of ladies in one place anywhere. I danced until four o'clock in the morning." That he had somehow patched up his quarrel with Lawrence Clarke is implied in a reference to an old complaint: "I am in the throes of enforced total abstinence —no grog in the settlement. Clarke is dry, Sproat is dry, and I am dry. . . . There is much rye in Windsor and some times I wish I were there." But Fanny, the second eldest daughter, was now receiving gentlemen callers and that demanded a measure of propriety; Cecil was being prepared for Ridley or Trinity College School, and Maude was doing credit to the family at Miss Dupont's School, although "there are a lot of brewers' daughters at it whom I suppose she finds rather loud."[3]

There were other diversions from the business of becoming a western tycoon. The "lure of the woods and pineries" for Mair was still extremely strong, and in the seasons of good weather he and his family found time to board their democrat and covered wagons and to head for northern Saskatchewan. There, "in five tents, with lots of horses and a capital German servant," they enjoyed the rivers and lakes that are now part of a vast national park. On one of these trips Mair nearly lost his life in a prairie fire—"the narrowest shave of many in my experiences, even Red River"[4]—an incident that he considered describing in an article for the *Week*. And in the woods Mair probably presented a side of his character quite in contrast to that which appeared on the main street of Prince Albert, a side that his old friend of Windsor, William Baby, for example, saw:

I can imagine you now quietly settled down and pursuing the even tenor of your happy and simple life; with your cap jauntily cocked on one side,

[3]DP, 1560, Oct. 26, 1886; 1593, April 20, 1887.
[4]DP, 1751, Nov. 3, 1889.

dudeen well alight, in your blue flannel shirt sleeves, and shod in the indispensable Indian moccasins, you are ready for anything that may turn up. But above all, to meet a long absent friend, and with an iron grip from which the heart speaketh, bid him a right royal welcome. . . .[5]

It is in keeping not only with this somewhat idyllic picture of Mair but also with the pattern that he had followed since his first coming to Prince Albert in the 'seventies that he should now show at least some aspects of Mair the poet. *Tecumseh* had proved his point; given independence from financial worry a Canadian writer might make a worthwhile contribution to national literature. Thus, within a few months of his return to the West, Mair began thinking ahead to the time when he could once again "retire," perhaps permanently, and compose another drama. "I shall have much to do here for a year or two," he remarked, "but ultimately, if things turn out as I expect, I think I shall retire to the East and devote myself, like a true Scotsman, to literature and oatmeal."[6] Already he had been doing some delving into background, had even chosen a title—*The Conquest*—for a drama based on the beginnings of lasting British influence upon Canada: "*Tecumseh* is a flea-bite in comparison," he ambitiously told Denison.[7]

In the meantime, however, as he once again consolidated his financial and social position, as he once again felt comfortable in the midst of family and friends, he found time to write the verse that he contributed during the years 1885–90 to various periodicals and magazines. For the most part these isolated works bear the stamp of *Dreamland*; they are romantic to the point of sentimentalism; they are derivative and stylized; they reveal incongruous lapses in technique and taste. But they also reflect, as is to be expected, perhaps, the main influences upon Mair in these later years—his western environment, the Indian legends, and above all, the necessity of a Canadian national sentiment. "A Ballad for Brave Women," the first stages of which had diverted him from *Tecumseh*, appeared in the *Week* of June 21, 1888, and begins thus:

A story worth telling our annals afford,
'Tis the wonderful journey of Laura Secord!

and continues in this jog-trot metre of " 'Twas the Night before Christmas" to recount the now famous incident of the War of 1812. Even

[5]MP, Sept. 27, 1886.
[6]DP, 1775, Dec. 3, 1889. [7]DP, 1614, Aug. 16, 1887.

the misgivings of "a poor crippled spouse" cannot deter Mrs. Secord:

> Then a biscuit she ate, tucked her skirts well about,
> And a bucket she slung on each arm, and went out.

On approaching "the foe, full of craft and of guile," Laura employs her own cunning, and wends her way

> To the pasture's lone side, where the farthest cow lay,
> Got her up, caught a teat, and, with pail at her knees,
> Made her budge, inch by inch, till she drew by degrees
> To the edge of the forest: "I've hoaxed, on my word,
> Both you and the sentry," said Laura Secord.

After near-encounters with rattlesnakes and wolves, the brave woman warns the garrison at Beaver Dams that the Americans are preparing to attack them:

> For a moment her reason forsook her; she raved,
> She laughed, and she cried—"They are saved! they are saved!
>
> . . . .
>
> And Boerstler came up; but his movements were known,
> His force was surrounded, his scheme was o'er-thrown.
> By a woman's devotion—on stone be't engraved!—
> The foeman was beaten, and Burlington saved.

And lest the reader think that such women have "fled with the past, to be heard of no more," he is encouraged by the assurance that although "this laurelled one" sleeps forever,

> We have maidens as true, we have matrons as brave;
> And should Canada ever be forced to the test—
> To spend for our country the blood of her best—
> When her sons lift the linstock and brandish the sword
> Her daughters will think of brave Laura Secord.

This piece, as has been noted, involved Denison's talents as well as Mair's, the first comment on it being, indeed, a query by Mair to his friend on whether or not it was "imitative of anything else"; he hoped not, because he wanted the piece "to be popular at public readings."[8] Denison also had to convince Mair that the heroine's name was Laura and not Mary (Denison had known "the old lady personally") and that certain lines—"And many a man's in discernment a sinner / Who loving his wife does not know what's in her"—should be omitted.[9] When the ballad was finally finished, Mair balked at what he called

[8]DP, 981, Oct. 16, 1884. [9]MP, Oct. 16, 1884.

"easy publication" in the *World* or *Globe* "or any other foreign sheet for anything that I may write,"[10] and not until 1888 did he see it in the *Week*, evidently having allowed his scruples about Goldwin Smith's "disloyalty" to be overcome by a consideration of the prestige that Smith's paper had acquired.

In the February 1, 1889, number of the *Week* appeared another patriotic piece, but one of far more personal inspiration. In November of the previous year and after an arduous appointment as solicitor in the failure of the Central Bank, William A. Foster died at the age of forty-eight, and Mair composed a eulogy to the memory of his old friend of Canada First. Except for the few lines in which Mair allows his sincere affection to direct him—"The eager look, the lambent eye, / Still haunted by a boyish grace"—"In Memory of William A. Foster" is poetically insignificant; but it does present succinctly the ideals of the little group of the "Corner Room" and the sense of disillusionment they were later to feel. Foster is depicted as the guiding light and inspiration of the earlier days, the encourager of national integrity and pride:

. . . "Throw sickly thoughts aside—
Let's build on native fields our fame;
Nor seek to blend our patriot's pride
With alien worth or alien shame!

. . . .

"First feel throughout the throbbing land
A nation's pulse, a nation's pride—
The independent life—then stand
Erect, unbound, at Britain's side!"

At Foster's death "The veil yet hangs o'er many a brow, / The glorious dream is unfulfilled." But the future holds promise; the seed sowed by Foster shows signs of growing:

And time will realize the dream,
The light yet spread o'er land and wave;
And Honour in that hour supreme,
Will hang his wreath o'er Foster's grave.

Even this highly complimentary tribute to a Canadian patriot was not entirely acceptable in some quarters. As it appeared in the *Week*, it contained a reference to Foster's "flush of joy when o'er the wine," an allusion that Mrs. Foster considered improper. "There is *one little*

[10]DP, 989, Oct. 18, 1884.

word in *one* of *the verses*," she said, that she "would like to have *changed*. . . ."[11] In deference to the wish of his friend's widow, Mair replaced the offending phrase by "The flush of hope, the joy divine," and thus it appeared in the memorial volume of Foster's writings and in later editions of Mair's works. But Mair did at least allow himself the satisfaction of commenting to Denison that he hoped "they won't 'Methodize' poor Foster into nothing," and of drinking "*three* glasses of *whiskey* to his memory immediately after."[12]

Two poems, "The Legend of Chileeli" and "The Iroquois at the Stake,"[13] are interesting mainly for their reflection of Mair's detailed knowledge of the Indian, of the red man's history and mythology. Both, as their titles imply, are narrative, and give ample evidence that their author was more than a little influenced by Longfellow, even by Browning. "The Legend" is a romantic tale of the unrequited love of a young brave who abhors war and of the chieftain's daughter he seeks to win by going against his better nature. In "The Iroquois," Mair tries "to represent the ruling spirit, strong in death, of an Iroquois warrior . . . keenly alive to the import of white encroachment and aggression,"[14] and does, indeed, by means of Browningesque dramatic monologue and parenthetical "stage directions," manage at times to convey the sense of savage integrity and defiant pride traditionally associated with the Indian.

Another, much shorter piece, "Kanata," which Mair published in the *Dominion Illustrated* of December 29, 1888, also treats the theme of the white man's intrusion upon the Indian, but expresses in addition a note of Mair's personal bitterness for the corruption of true freedom that he feels the European has inflicted upon Canada's previously unspoiled land:

Here man's own vile and selfish schemes
Will yet enact the tyrant's part.
Alas! for equal life and laws
And Freedom 'neath the Western sun:

. . . .

Still must she fight who long hath fought;
Still must she bleed who long hath bled;
There is no consecrated spot,
No clime where she alone doth tread.

[11]MP, Margaret Foster to Mair, Dec. 19, 1889.

[12]DP, 1874, Nov. 23, 1890.

[13]Mair stated in his correspondence that both poems appeared in the *Week*, but the author found only "The Iroquois," which appeared on June 7, 1889.

[14]Notes to *Tecumseh and Canadian Poems*, p. 273.

Devise for her your "simple plan,"
Or, "perfect system," as of old;
They count not where insensate man
Spurns his own right to be controlled.

Some years later Mair was to direct his resentment more specifically; "Kanata" was written, he told John Garvin, "when our *foreign* immigrants were swarming into the country—the poem's final stanzas referring to *them* have proved to be prophetic."[15] His memory was at fault, of course, because the poem was written when few settlers of any race were coming to Canada; but both "Kanata" and the comment reflect Mair's characteristic intolerance, increasing with the years, of those who were not "the right sort."

Undoubtedly the strangest expression (Desmond Pacey calls it "inept and fantastic")[16] of the theme of the greedy white man is "The Last Bison," which appeared in the *Dominion Illustrated* on September 8, 1888, and was suggested to him, Mair said, "by a personal experience near the Elbow of the North Saskatchewan, in 1882."[17] Few men, certainly, could have a more unusual experience. He was lying on the bank of the river, Mair versifies, "Musing on change and mutability / And endless evanescence," when "a burst / of sudden roaring filled the vale with sound." There before him was a mighty bison, "the last survivor of his clan" (it was, indeed, the "burdash," or hermaphrodite bison of tremendous size), which, as the poet gazes unbelievingly, bursts into song. The song, lasting for nine Spenserian stanzas, combines praise for the Indian with lament for the departed millions of buffalo, and culminates in a prophetic vision of the passing of the white man himself from the scene:

Once more my vision sweeps the prairies wide,
But now no peopled cities greet the sight;
All perished, now, their pomp and pride:
In solitude the wild wind takes delight.
Naught but the vacant wilderness is seen,
And grassy mounds, where cities once had been.
The earth smiles as of yore, the skies are bright,
Wild cattle graze and bellow on the plain,
And savage nations roam o'er native wilds again!

[15]MP, July 8, 1918.
[16]*Creative Writing in Canada*, p. 36.
[17]Notes to *Tecumseh and Canadian Poems*, p. 271.

Then "the burden ceased," and with head bowed,

> The bison smelt, then grinned into the air.
> An awful anguish seized his giant frame,
> Cold shudderings and indrawn gaspings deep—
> The spasms of illimitable pain.
> One stride he took, and sank upon his knees,
> Glared stern defiance where I stood revealed,
> Then swayed to earth, and, with convulsive groan,
> Turned heavily upon his side, and died.

Desmond Pacey describes the burdash's language as "appropriate to an itinerant evangelist."[18] If by this he means expression that is rhetorical, overly sentimental, and coloured by biblical phrase reminiscent particularly of prophets of the Old Testament, he is correct. But such verse was evidently what Victorian Canada enjoyed, or accepted, at least, as poetry, and Mair, whose nature was given to emotional self-indulgence, to striking a pose of wounded sensibility (even on behalf of the burdash), and whose conception of the poet was based on his readings of the more romantic of "the old singers," merely synchronized his own pulse with that of the larger reading public of the country. The remarks, certainly, of the many correspondents who wrote regarding "The Last Bison" were unanimously complimentary. John Talon Lesperance of the *Dominion Illustrated*, for example, made a special point of informing Mair "how proud" he was to have published both it and "Kanata" in his paper.[19]

Romantic subjectivity, longing for the past, brooding melancholy, and a vision of perfect love, are characteristic of two shorter pieces published in the *Week*. In "Vain Regrets" (October 18, 1888), reminiscent of Longfellow's "Psalm of Life" and "The Day is Done," Mair repines

> That, sailing on the summer sea
> I dreamt not of a wintry flood,

but, finding solace in the true and lasting friendships that the past has brought, he exhorts the reader and himself:

> Then courage! to the helm, the sail,
> And let the roaring tempest frown!
> What though the billows should prevail
> What though the whelming waters drown?

[18]*Creative Writing in Canada*, p. 36.
[19]MP, Jan. 26, 1889.

In "Absence" (August 9, 1888) the note is less strident, as befitting a love lyric—in this case "inspired by the noblest of womankind, my wife."[20] With his thoughts "full of gloom," his heart "full of pain," and when tears "dull as a blind man's roll adown my cheeks like rain," Mair can find no consolation from the wonders of nature, from even his children,

> For my delight is far from me—it comes not at my call,
> The perfect womanhood, which gave a meaning to them all.
>
> . . . .
>
> Tree sighs for tree, flower sighs for flower, love binds
> them in its thrall;
> But she is far away whose love, with mine, discovered all.

All of this verse, good or bad, was significant in at least one respect —it kept Mair's name in the mind of the reading public. Editorial notices and "locals" in the periodicals and newspapers directed their readers' attentions to "another fine poem by the distinguished author of *Tecumseh*" or to the fact that "Mr. Mair, though busily engaged in the North-West fur-trade," had found time "to grace our pages with an expression of his genius." Charles G. D. Roberts, writing Mair for permission to include some of his work in an anthology, paid tribute to his reputation in yet another way: "By the way," he asked, "will you put in a spoke for me in my search for the Toronto Chair of English Literature? Your name is potent in Toronto!"[21] At this time, January, 1889, it is not surprising, therefore, that on Denison's nomination Mair was elected by a substantial majority to membership in the Royal Society of Canada.

Mair's first reply to this honour was rather ungracious, although private; "You know how little I care," he told Denison; "besides it may trammel me otherwise. Must I go down in May, for example?"[22] But modesty and inconvenience were circumvented when his paper on the American bison was read by proxy at the annual meeting in 1890[23]— and that they were has a rather curious relevance to modern Canada, certainly to modern zoology. The paper as literature is in some respects a prose rendition of "The Last Bison," but expressed with the clarity, the richness of metaphor, and the detailed knowledge that had characterized the best of Mair's *Globe* letters in '69. But as a treatise on Canadian natural history it is a plea for the preservation of a

[20]DP, 1643, Aug. 30, 1888.
[21]MP, Jan. 4, 1889. [22]DP, 1711, Feb. 19, 1889.
[23]*Trans. Roy. Soc. Can.*, VII (1890), Section II, 93–108.

vanishing species of an animal "which has been of great service on our continent, which is intimately associated with its history, and whose extinction would be a disgrace to civilized man." The result was a renewed interest in the buffalo, and within a short time the Canadian Government brought the only available herd from Montana to a sanctuary recommended by Mair, Wainwright Park, Alberta. As the present-day Canadian knows, this herd has expanded to such an extent that once again the buffalo hunt—now regulated—is an annual event in the Canadian North-West.

By 1890 Charles Mair of Prince Albert gives a public impression of the affluence and prestige that, despite his remarks to the contrary, he obviously enjoyed. To the Canadian at large he is not only a distinguished man of letters, but also a North-West pioneer of exciting background. To an old friend like Denison he is the loyal and talented spokesman of principles agreed upon at Confederation, the energetic and enterprising businessman becoming prosperous despite the lack of a progressive governmental policy. And to William Baby he is the kind, convivial ruralist, the almost Thoreau-like nature-lover "ready for anything that might turn up." A composite of these three not necessarily disparate pictures has been the one presented in later biographical sketches of Mair; but even Mair's friends, who wrote some of them, either were unaware of or, less probably, chose to omit, details that had relevance to the whole of his subsequent career. Nor does their personal correspondence give any indication of the misfortune that was about to overtake their friend of the North Saskatchewan. Baby, for example, an old man in his eighties with a propensity for very sentimental reminiscence, sees only the Mair of the whist games on Victoria Street and of the country rambles over historic western Ontario. Not only did he not see the Mair now mainly engrossed in trade and farming, in buying furs and selling land, he also did not see the old companion who, as the vision of a prosperous West began once again to fade, might be somewhat less than convivial. Lawrence Clarke had clashed with this Charles Mair nearly a decade before; for the same underlying reason as has been suggested for that dispute—the growth of feelings of economic insecurity and tension—others were to clash with him now. "Very many thanks, my dear Mair," wrote a Mr. W. D. Antrobus of Battleford,

> for the Writ of Summons you have caused to be served on me. . . . However, that is nothing, as business is business and you have a right to your

money. Still, I did not think you would have taken such an action against such an old friend. . . . In any case, I cannot, as you must be aware, put in an appearance at the time mentioned as Aerial Machines have not yet come into use. . . .[24]

For towards the end of the decade Mair began to realize that what he optimistically thought to be a period of resurgence and development was actually just the opposite. Once again his visionary conception of Canada's future did not square with contemporary facts, and he allowed himself to be deceived by confusing ideals with reality. And, perhaps, by placing unwarranted faith in promises. The hopes of the West were inextricably involved with the building of railways and with large-scale immigration. Both had been assured as forthcoming by the framers of the National Policy and the brief boom of 1879–82 had been a direct result. But the dilatoriness of the Government in turning a platform into a vigorous programme not only had stimulated the Rebellion of 1885 but had continued to exact its price in the burgeoning discontent that followed the Rebellion. The Canadian Pacific Railway had been completed a few months after Riel's defeat, but it enjoyed a twenty-year monopoly clause that prevented competing lines and consequent lower rates. And although this clause was repealed in 1888, the delay had been costly to the western development of railways running north and south and connecting the border with the central prairies and the North. Prince Albert did not even have a link with the C.P.R., far to the south. In addition to this particularly western problem was that of Macdonald's protective tariff policy, which many people insisted was restricting trade with the United States and Great Britain to a point of national economic ruin. And immigration, dependent upon transportation, a healthy economy, and an organized programme of settlement, continued to be insignificant. In the decade 1880–90 less than ten thousand settlers entered the prairies.

One solution offered to the problems confronting Canada at the time was commercial union with the United States, but such a proposal immediately aroused the old fears of annexation, particularly among ultra-loyalists like Denison. These fears increased when American authorities, even President Cleveland himself, implied that continental union was highly desirable. But to Mair in the West, the greatest danger to Canada was the "reign of monopolies" and "eastern

[24]MP, Jan. 20, 1889.

self-seeking." He confessed, he said, to "a feeling almost of hopelessness" when he thought "of the insanity which permits a stall-fed monopoly to lord it over the North-West people as if they had no rights save such as are vouchsafed to them by our friend the Hudson's Bay Co. in its new shape of the C.P.R." Thousands of Canadians, "as good as you or I," he told Denison, were muttering "annexation" because they were being forced "to look for relief anywhere rather than from their old Province."[25] As for himself, he was thinking of going to Australia—"no Yankees there to go to war with, no French and Jesuits to keep us in hot water, but a homogeneous people and a mighty country."[26]

In the light of such antipathy towards governmental policy, it may seem strange that Mair did not attempt to express his criticism and suggestions in a more formal way. He could, for example, easily have been chosen as Liberal or Independent candidate for his district in the election campaigns of 1887 and 1891—there is ample evidence for this fact among his papers—but he seems to have been determined to shun such participation. He may have feared the personal muckraking that characterized much nineteenth-century campaigning; or, more likely, he may have been maintaining faith with his old Canada First principles. "It takes a deal of common sense to keep out of politics," he remarked; "nothing short of an explosion could blow me into the political stinkpot."[27] At various times he referred to sitting in the House of Commons as "a snare" or "a dirty puddle" with which he had had to refuse, even to the point of rudeness, to have anything to do. And he had good reason, he remarked, for not bothering to write, as he had done in 1882, long memorials to the Government about the plight of western Canada.

He did take the opportunity offered by formal occasions, however, to express his opinions on the various remedies that were being prescribed for Canada's national ills; such commentary, by virtue of the importance both of the occasion and of Mair himself, invariably reached the pages of the Prince Albert *Times* or the town's new paper, the *Saskatchewan*.[28] At the banquet honouring Lieutenant-Colonel Irvine of the N.W.M.P., and as generously reported by the *Times* of January 23, 1889, he made a long reply to the toast to "The Land we

[25]DP, 1661, Nov. 6, 1888.

[26]DP, 1785, Feb. 28, 1890.

[27]DP, 1560, Oct. 26, 1886.

[28]A second newspaper might imply economic growth, but the *Saskatchewan* ceased publication in 1892.

Live in," in which he reviewed for his listeners the "three lines of argument" that were currently dividing the political mind of Canada —those of annexation, imperial union, and independent Canadian nationality. The first of these, he said, was so ridiculous as hardly to warrant comment. As one of the businessmen of the North-West no one could be more desirous than he that Canada's trade relations with the United States should be as reciprocal and as free "as a right adjustment can make them." No one could have greater admiration than he for the tremendous material progress the Americans had made. But, he said, when we consider what underlies even what is best in American life, when we think of "the frightful debasement of the marriage tie," of "the destruction of offspring in embryo," of "the inhuman treatment of the aboriginal races," of the general lawlessness, of "the growing horde of ruffianism, for which all the world is ransacked," we may well relegate the question of annexation to "the Limbo of absurdities." No argument for annexation based on self-interest, therefore, was valid. But what of the argument of fear? "We are assured," he said "that Canada would have no chance in a conflict with her mighty neighbour." Yet the War of 1812 had disproved such a contention: "In that war Canada had justice on her side. The Americans felt it, and the sense of it paralyzed their efforts. Justice and manhood go hand in hand. . . . If we are again attacked, that principle will still more conspicuously be on our side, for we shall still not be the aggressors." And Canada was at that moment "a nation of athletes, of men educated in body and mind," and these, "backed by affection for our country and faith in her future," would defend her.

The plan of imperial federation was "a very noble one," perhaps the first step "towards the realization of the positive philosopher's dream." But when one saw practical statesmen like Salisbury and Gladstone, Tupper and Blake, all doubtful about the scheme, "one feels that the difficulties in the way are grave indeed." A union of the English-speaking races was inevitable, not through a federation of dependencies, but through "a union of independent nationalities, the growth of time"; into such a union even the United States might enter "when purged of their disagreeable characteristics."

In the meantime, he continued, let all Canadians, each in his own way, contribute to their country's fame or material progress, and "to the extension of that Canadian sentiment which is already spreading from the Atlantic to the Pacific, and which will yet be carried northward to the Arctic coast." Particularly necessary, however, was that the westerner's brethren to the east rid themselves of "their narrow provincialism" and realize the potentiality of the West:

Life in the North-West has a larger faith and more liberal hand. . . . We feel that we are moving about in a wilderness which is yet to be the theatre of mighty interests. We are in the heart of one of the greatest wheat regions on the continent. We are within twenty hours run, by rail, to Churchill. We lie directly across the shortest path from ocean to ocean; and over this route, nay through this very town, may yet pass, in the not remote future, the largest portion of the commerce of the world. We feel proud of our region. We have unbounded faith in it as a future province; and this pride and this faith lead naturally to the higher ground—to the prayer which continually wells from the heart to the lips of every true Canadian—God bless our Common Country!

This theme of the urgent need for western development, particularly of railways, was repeated and emphasized by Mair on the occasion of the visit of Lieutenant-Governor Royal to Prince Albert in July of the same year. And now there was no hesitancy in conceding that a serious depression had befallen Prince Albert. The deflected course of the transcontinental railway—"too far away to carry out our products or stimulate our industries, yet near enough to destroy our markets"—had reduced the town to absolute dependence upon railway extension for its existence. It was ignorance to ask, as many easterners were doing, "What on earth took you people so far into the interior?" For every man of right feeling in the West knew that he had been brought there by that same pioneer spirit that was carrying the British flag "into every continent and waste space on earth," that "was extending our commerce into the remote wildernesses," and that had "put our language into the mouths of a hundred millions of people." But it had not been pure love of the West that had brought settlers there: "They came here through public maps, through public declarations, and through public charters," but every one of which they had lived to see "traversed and cut down." He hastened to add (perhaps in deference to the guest of honour) that the lack of enterprise was not to be blamed upon the Government but rather upon "eastern jealousy." The transcontinental railway, thought by the eastern provinces to be enough to develop the West, was really, he stated, only a connecting link running through barely four hundred miles of productive agricultural country. And the fact was staring them in the face that in the twenty years since Manitoba and the Territories had been acquired, barely 150,000 immigrants had settled there—surely not indicative of true development but of "lamentable failure." And those same eastern interests chose to distort, even to hide, significant geographical factors:

Where, Mr. Chairman, you now sit, is distant from Winnipeg nearly six hundred miles. We are in fact, in the very middle of America, and this town of Prince Albert might, without the suggestion of a joke or the least exaggeration, be called the "navel" of the Continent. Yet, though we live so far inland, we are still by way of our natural route to the Ocean, a long way nearer the true port and tide water than that city. We are 1,500 miles nearer China and Japan than Montreal, yet, by way of Churchill, we are as near Liverpool and the great centres of European trade. Let any gentleman unroll a map of Canada, and draw a line from Churchill to any point on the North-Pacific Coast, and the future will dawn upon him. He will easily perceive that it is not the St. Lawrence alone which will carry the productions of the American North-Western States and Territories, those of our own Provinces and Territories and of the Pacific slopes, but the great Bay, inserted by nature into the northern half of this Continent, to substantiate its settlement, and to redress its balance.

The East was reactionary, Mair charged, "made and moulded of things past." This was no longer the age of the corduroy road and the turnpike;

it is the age of steam, and of ideas and enterprises engendered by steam. It is an age quickened and intensified by the mysterious powers of electricity upon whose mere threshold we as yet stand. The mighty agencies which science is placing in the world's hands are tunnelling rocks and hewing down mountains. They are knitting together in the bonds of commerce, nationalities which have been separated or antagonized since the beginning of history. They are casting light into the dark places of the earth, and slowly but surely lifting mankind up from its sloth, its superstition and its ignorance, into the glorious light of the fulfilment of prophecy—the time, and the realization of the dream of Burns,

"When man to man shall brothers be
The world o'er for a' that!"[29]

This Mair who quotes Burns and who sees the achievements of science as Whitman had done, is really the Mair of old, of 1869 and

[29]Prince Albert *Saskatchewan*, July 25, 1889.

of the rhetorical prose that had extolled the West in the face of what Mair had considered then, as now, the self-seeking interests of big business. To read his urgings in the twentieth century is to incur a sense of mingled respect and pathos—respect for the perception and intensity of vision, and pathos for the fact that the vision, in its most important aspects certainly, has never even come close to realization.

But lest it be thought that Mair was a lone, foolish dreamer advocating a ridiculously impracticable scheme, it should be made clear that there were many others like him, not only in Prince Albert but in other western towns as well. "The urge to the sea," said D. B. Hanna, the first president of the Canadian National Railways, "has been a feature of western Canadian life ever since the difference of five cents a bushel of wheat has meant the difference between a Windsor chair and a Morris to a Manitoba landowner." Winnipeg businessmen too were keenly enthusiastic over the possibility of a grain route through "the Bay," and like their Prince Albert contemporaries, did not regard ice floes "the same obstacles to business as they are to those who never knew what it is to trade while the thermometer is fluttering between forty and fifty below."[80] It might also be suggested that these men have their counterparts in the mid twentieth century, modern visionaries whose schemes for transporting oil and grain through the Bay and Strait by nuclear freighter and submarine are, perhaps, not impracticable.

The insistence of Mair and his townsmen finally brought the railway from Regina in 1890 and hopes were again in the ascendant. "The railway fight is over," Mair wrote Denison, "and I have gained and beaten that hoary old sinner the Hudson's Bay Co. in the struggle for the sale of property for the station."[81] Once again he could imagine his holdings, "the largest and finest here," being bought by new settlers; but once again also, he said he was determined not to sacrifice them for present advantages. He proudly informed Denison that the railway meant a traveller now did "in thirty hours what it took fifteen days to cover when I came here," but that this was only a taste of the future; "the cry now in Prince Albert," he almost exulted. "is Hudson's Bay!"[82]

Part of this cry, indeed, was some spirited verse by Mair, "Open the Bay!", in which, reversing his procedure in respect of the bison,

[80]*Trains of Recollection*, p. 101.
[81]DP, 1785, Feb. 28, 1890.
[82]DP, 1874, Nov. 23, 1890.

he versified—for the most part clumsily—the theme he had so ardently expressed in prose, both public and private:

Open the Bay! the myriad prairies call;
Let homesteads rise and comforts multiply;
Give to the world the shortest route of all,
Let justice triumph though the heavens should fall!
This is the voice of reason—manhood's cry.

And let no one be misled by the common objections to the Hudson Bay route:

Open the Bay! Who are they that say "No"?
Who locks the portals? Nature? She resigned
Her icy reign, her stubborn frost and snow,
Her sovereign sway and sceptre, long ago,
To sturdy manhood and the master, Mind!

Not these the foe! Not Nature, who is fain
When earnest hearts an earnest end pursue;
But man's old selfishness and greed of gain:
These ancient breeders of earth's sin and pain —
These are the thieves who steal the Nation's due!

More concretely,

. . . such are they who, in their Eastern place,
Say, "It is folly and the purpose vain!"
The carrier and the shallow huckster's race—
Theirs are the hands, not Nature's, which efface,
And seal the public good for private gain.

Thus,

Open the Inlet! Let them growl and grin,
And Power still hobnob with them in their sin—
Humanity, their master is about!

Upon its appearance in the *Week* of March 28, 1890, "Open the Bay" was copied by dozens of newspapers, particularly in the West, and became the slogan of prairie towns from Winnipeg to Edmonton. The American Consul in Winnipeg, J. W. Taylor (according to Mair, "that estimable old friend of Canada and myself")[33] assured the author that "his title to rank henceforth as the Poet of the North-

[33]Prince Albert Hist. Soc. Papers, Mair to T. Campbell, July 2, 1924. Mair evidently was unaware that Taylor was a life-long advocate of American annexation, had been, indeed, one of the most active agents for the movement during the 1869 insurrection.

West [was] indisputable";[34] and Denison was just as confident that the prosperity stimulated by the poem would enable Mair "all the sooner to buy up some country town like Toronto" and live like a feudal baron.[35]

During the latter half of 1890 Mair became once more the centre of an optimistic town. A bountiful harvest increased the general enthusiasm over the prospects of a Hudson Bay railway, and he was repeatedly urged to help to sustain the momentum by lecturing in the East on the need for settlers. One such trip he did undertake, going as far as Montreal; on his return he joined Flood Davin in Regina and composed page upon page of the immigration literature sent out by the legislative assembly of the North-West Council. For six months he devoted almost full time to advertising far and wide the resources of the western territories. And his hopes were reflected in several ways. His correspondence took on a typically expansive tone; a new collection of verse was considered along with *The Conquest*; son Cecil was placed in Ridley College; and daughter Fanny was married amid "two thousand dollars worth of presents" and "a champagne supper" to young Mr. E. J. Cann—"a brilliant musician, a diligent and successful man of business, sober and upright, an Englishman by descent, but a born Canadian."[36] He could even write at the beginning of the new year that Prince Albert was "getting too civilized" for him, and that he "hated to hear the Railway whistle as the train passed through [his] property."[37] And his trip east gave him opportunity to mingle with the Gaults and Molsons of Montreal ("a glorious crowd of gentlemen") and to take part in the fever surrounding Sir John A.'s last election campaign.

But elation was short-lived. Perhaps Mair and Prince Albert believed that the old Prime Minister's victorious platform, in that election, of "a British subject I was born—a British subject I will die," translated into a vigorous policy of national autonomy, would ensure the northern railway and the immigration they so desperately required. Less than a month after the election Mair qualified his satisfaction at its outcome by a concern over the delay in authorizing the railway's construction; "It must be begun *at once*," he told Denison, "it is the *only* salvation of this country."[38] But it was not begun, nor did settlers suddenly arrive in Prince Albert, eager to make new homes on Mair's properties. At long last, after a succession of rising

[34]MP, April 15, 1890.
[35]MP, April 17, 1890.
[36]DP, 1914, Jan. 14, 1890.
[37]*Ibid.*
[38]DP, 1997, March 30, 1891.

and falling hopes, after fluctuations of prosperity and minor depressions, both Mair and the little town on the North Saskatchewan that he had helped to build were vanquished. And the degree to which they had depended upon markets and settlers is indicated by the suddenness with which distress struck the community. By midsummer, 1891, long-established families were moving out, going south to the United States, or following the C.P.R. to the west coast. Some of them sold businesses for what they could get; others closed shops to await better times; others left their share of the eighty thousand bushels of wheat no one would buy. And Mair, now over fifty years old, was stricken with a fear he had not known before, the fear of poverty.

As he sat despondently in "the largest house in Prince Albert," his imagination ("I wish the old wench, Nature, had left imagination out when I was conceived")[39] may have helped to colour his recollection of the decisions and events that had led him to this particular place at this particular time. Youthful reading of the exploits of Mackenzie, Palliser, and Hind, a university friendship with a man who was now Lieutenant-Governor of the province they had both helped to preserve for the Crown, the succession of circumstances that had led to that patriotic struggle itself—a little book of verse, a room at the Revere, the patronage of a federal minister, a last-minute change in plans sending him to the West instead of across the Atlantic—an escape over hundreds of miles of blizzard-covered prairie, a shop in Portage, a covered-wagon trek to the North Saskatchewan, the personal assurances of Sir John A. and of Joseph Pope that a railway to Prince Albert would immediately follow his return to the town in 1886[40]—all were significant. And what of the visions other than those of making a home and money? What of Canada First now? What of literature now? The Dominion, reft by racial and cultural antagonisms since the hanging of Riel and stricken by a depression for almost two decades, was less unified than at Confederation. And the state of Canadian letters well reflected the level that the national sentiment had attained. On July 1, 1891 (*there* was an ironic date, he noted), he wrote Denison:

> To Canadian literature I have given more time and labor than it deserves. Canadians are mainly barbarians and consist, ninety-nine out of one hundred, of backs and stomachs. To expect our polished boors to enjoy art in any of its developments is too much.

[39]DP, 2060, Dec. 6, 1891.
[40]So he told Denison: DP, 2151, Jan. 28, 1892.

I am done with the "Canadian public," which consists of mere cattle, or worse. It will take a hundred years to lift such swine as compose it out of the ruts and troughs and swills they delight in. It only pretends to enjoy art; because its betters really do comprehend its aims and objects it thinks it does so too; but its true and only enjoyment (the heights of Canadian ambition in fact) are guzzling and drinking and rotten politics. . . . Paugh! Dirty, dishonest Canada, what is to become of thee? . . . Good bye to it! Good bye Canadian public![41]

Such extreme bitterness had been aggravated by a particularly inopportune concentration of what would have been, even at another time, more than trying circumstances. Fanny, expecting a child, had suffered a mental breakdown. Maude, about to leave Miss Dupont's, had been stricken with scarlet fever and was now seriously ill at Denison's Heydon Villa. Sarah Anne Curzon, authoress of a recent verse-drama on Laura Secord, had written him a deeply touching plea for help in defraying her publishing expenses—a plea of "a woman of true heart," but one which he had had to refuse. Perhaps worst of all was the attack suddenly made upon him by his fellow Canada Firster, Henry J. Morgan. Morgan, joining forces with one "Historicus," through the literary page of the Toronto *Mail* on January 15, 1891, accused Mair of deliberate historical misrepresentation in his depiction of General Procter in *Tecumseh*. This "acrimonious onslaught," this "breaking lances with an old friend," seemed to Mair an almost diabolical climax to his troubles, particularly since it had come over five years after the appearance of *Tecumseh*. After some hesitation, he wrote a long, authoritative reply to the *Mail*,[42] a reply so effective that Morgan could only weakly acknowledge that there must have been two Procters. But henceforth Mair could never feel his old affection for "the fat Morgan"; his former friend's disloyalty had the finality of Foster's death, and as far as he was concerned only three of the "Corner Room" comrades remained. There is little wonder that he could ask the faithful Denison: "Alas! what sort of history will be written of the year 1891 hereafter?"[43]

Mair's depression, like that of the country itself, was to become even more acute during the next few years, and both man and country

[41]DP, 2009.

[42]May 20, 1891. Mair's long delay in replying was due to his trip east in the spring of 1891. Not until his return to Prince Albert was he able to carry out research for a reply, and at that time he had become involved in his financial problems.

[43]DP, 2044, Sept. 27, 1891.

were called upon to do their utmost in an attempt to extricate themselves from the dilemma in which fate, human hopes and passions, and the groping process of growing older had placed them. Canadian nationality was to become involved in a struggle that had roots in the execution of Riel, the struggle over the rights of the individual provinces and of minority groups. The culmination was to be even a new interpretation of the constitution itself. And Mair and his fellow westerners, more and more convinced that Ottawa was in another country, were to see their vision of prosperity, even of livelihood, continue to dim as inexorably as the setting sun.

The increasingly desperate situation of the West called for measures previously not even imagined. Pamphlets continued to pour from the territorial government at Regina, but now official advertisements were placed in the newspapers and periodicals not only of eastern Canada but of Great Britain as well. When the Chicago World's Fair opened in 1893, it displayed in profusion the resources, agricultural and mineral, of the Territories. Agencies to attract and to give information to prospective settlers were established in eastern cities and in the United States. And for his part in the campaign Mair chose the appropriate role of an invader of American soil. "There is scarcely a farm house in the older provinces," the Toronto *Mail* had said in 1887, "where there is not an empty chair for the boy in the States"; and Mair became one of the many emissaries whose aim was to convince as many as possible of these nearly one million expatriates that they should return to their native land. On Christmas Day, 1891, he wrote Denison from St. Paul, Minnesota: "I shall leave no stone unturned to this end. . . . There are tens of thousands of Canadians in Dacotah and Minnesota—a people who *can be got* to remove to the North-West." So busily engaged was he that there was no time even to revive his old associations in St. Paul—"where my wife and I met Macdougall . . . and spent our honeymoon." It was with Eliza's brother, H. W. McKenney, however, that he hung out his St. Paul sign advertising "Business Chances, Real-Estate and Loans"—although the last item must have represented a precarious promise as far as Mair was concerned; and as he commented to Denison, "A queer business, you will say, for a poet. But poets need the sinews of war as well as other people and literature will not bring them in Canada."[44]

From St. Paul Mair went to Chicago to prepare an exhibit for the Fair, and in this great midwestern city he had ample opportunity to verify his antipathetic theories on America and Americans. He

[44]DP, 2155, Feb. 18, 1892.

came away once more convinced—a conviction quite contrary to that expressed in his recent diatribe to Denison—that it was "good to be a Canadian" and that the best policy for Canada was "to cling tightly to the Empire, endeavouring at the same time to redeem ourselves from mere colonialism as our status in the eyes of Englishmen."[45] How anxious and jaded were the people on the streets, how flagrant were ruffianism and general lawlessness! At a dinner party he had heard a Boston gentleman seriously declare that the object of the United States in annexing Canada would be to confer upon it the blessings of American civilization; "This was a refreshing statement in a city where the murders average one a day, and where a whole section of the civic council is under indictment for the grossest swindling and robbery of the public funds." The framework of America was rotting, and was "tied together only by the dirty thread of self-interest"; annexation "for Canada's good" all too clearly sounded like "our old Hudson's Bay Co's dodges in times past."[46] By contrast, Canada, with all its woes, was "his dear loved land"; his stay in Chicago, paradoxically, had cheered him, had encouraged him even to make a formal proposal to the Dominion Government that he be appointed as an official immigration adviser in the western States—"because I consider it a noble work to bring back to our own country Canadians who by fraudulent misrepresentation were induced to go there before we had a North-West to offer."[47] So enthusiastic was he over his efforts during the current crisis that he told Denison that they might even bring him an appointment to the Senate.

By July, however, not having been granted as much as an acknowledgement of his submission (he always maintained his being ignored was due to his outspoken criticism of governmental policy and particularly of Edgar Dewdney, former Lieutenant-Governor of the Territories and later a member of the Department of the Interior), Mair was in Montreal and discussing with A. F. Gault, his friend and financial backer, the possibility of undertaking a fur-trading expedition to the Mackenzie. He had already turned over some of his lots to Gault; something had to be done to pay the mounting taxes on the others. He returned to Prince Albert with Maude, now recovered from her illness, and was about to bid farewell once again to Eliza and the children when he received a telegram from Edward Cann, his son-in-law, urging him to come immediately to the Okanagan Valley of British Columbia. Hesitation was quickly overcome

[45]DP, 2164, April 5, 1892.
[46]*Ibid.*
[47]DP, 2174, May 5, 1892.

by Cann's covering letter, in which were glowingly described the new prospects in the Rockies, and Mair, once again as a result of a sudden change in plan, struck out westward. His purchases in Montreal were shipped to Okanagan Mission instead of to Edmonton, while Eliza remained in Prince Albert as postmistress and the only sure source of family income.

Mair is still remembered in the Okanagan, if only by few. His daughter Maude spent her last days there in 1957 and her husband, although old and feeble, was still living in a Kelowna nursing home at the time of writing. But in 1892 the valley was to Mair as Red River had been in 1868, a new, vividly different land—even far more different from the prairies than they had been from the hills and vales of Lanark. The valleys stretched in all directions around and between two magnificent lakes, with towering mountains lifting their lofty heads wherever one looked. Their lower reaches were "swarming with grizzly bears, jumping deer and wapiti, with here and there big-horns and goats." And the climate was such as "might fetch the angels down to build their tepees." Every kind of fruit seemed to grow—"the almond tree is in full bearing, and melons, canteloupes are fed to pigs." Everything was luxuriant—wheat six feet high, oats one hundred bushels to the acre, and the valleys overrun with ponies and horses, sheep and poultry. It was, Mair told Denison, like nothing he had ever seen before.

There were some blemishes, of course, in this new Eden. A "lot of political shysters at Victoria" and prospectors who "packed in over the mountains" from Oregon and Washington years before had acquired the best land. "These people know nothing of Canada," Mair complained; "in fact they deride everything Canadian and the sooner the country is municipalized the better, so that they may be forced to sell to better men." Some of the local customs were also open to question:

> As for morality there does not appear to be any at all. Two brothers here, originally from Denmark, have quarelled over an incestuous intercourse with a half-witted sister, and the half-breeds hold that at certain stages of entertainment, or as a matter of hospitality, women—wives or sisters—are common property.

But all of this, Mair felt, gave the community "a sort of patriarchal simplicity." Tom Spence, who had declared a Republic of Manitoba in 1867 and had edited Riel's *New Nation*, was there, "the same opportunist as ever"; but so were "many nice people from England and Wales—all sorts of big-wigs, including the wife of the Archbishop of York."[48] Socially, therefore, he found the settlement far superior to Prince Albert. Life was like the climate—genial, but more predictable:

Everybody here dies a natural death, and people are buried in their back yards, or under their favourite fruit-trees. It is perfectly delightful.

There are no churches. Two weeks ago I heard the brazen twang of a Methodist at the door, and in stept a typical newcomer who . . . said he meant to hold weekly services in Kelowna. . . . A "subscription" was in his eye, which glared with religious greed. . . . Sunday came . . . but not a sinner turned out to pray. . . . But Maude reads the Bible to us, and we get along.[49]

And Mair seemed to get along for some time. He established the second general store in Kelowna and shortly afterwards a branch in Benvoulin; the Vernon *News* attested to his growing importance in the Okanagan community. Eliza and daughters Maude, Mabel, and Elizabeth arrived in 1893, and the following year Maude made a highly suitable marriage to a Mr. Herbert Crichton—"a young gentleman of the English Colony here whose father was the clergyman who accompanied the Prince of Wales on his India tour, whose uncle was the late Admiral Crichton."[50] There were some hardships, of course, aside from those involved in starting a new life. A flood in 1893 carried off or otherwise ruined many of Mair's manuscripts and papers; Cecil, whose fees at Ridley had been paid by John Schultz, was compelled—for academic or economic reasons—to leave school and to enter Molson's Bank; and although Fanny had recovered, her baby's delicate health was of constant concern. Outweighing all other problems, however, was the situation in Prince Albert. "I am getting old, and my work not done," Mair wrote Denison;

I am so immersed in business now that I cannot write a line. When I feel the craving I gaze at the solemn mountains . . . and I have my dear, noble wife to sustain me when my spirits droop. . . . I am doing well and shall soon recoup the loss I incurred and the money I sank in the cursed scene of Rebellion and Governmental villainy.[51]

The truth, however, was that Mair was whistling in the dark. As he was later to admit, "the surface breath and life of Okanagan was

[48]DP, 2200–9, Aug. 23, Oct. 6, 1892. [49]DP, 2271, Dec. 5, 1892.
[50]DP, 2429, Aug. 31, 1893. [51]DP, 2227, Jan. 9, 1893.

deceptive."[52] By the end of 1893 his correspondence betrayed the tension he once more began to feel over his economic prospects. Some letters contained almost fantastic accounts of moral disintegration in the United States, of the murders and rapes supposedly committed, of "the bloody work between the rich and the poor." Even the "shooting down so heartlessly of helpless savages" by Imperial troops in Africa reminded him of "over the border" too much.[53] And from his mountain seclusion, amid his coterie of the "old British aristocracy" and of the "right sort of people," he once again vented his bitter indictment of the C.P.R., of the Government, and of "eastern buccaneering." There was even a long letter to the Winnipeg *Weekly Free Press*, of January 25, 1893, signed "Bystander" but almost certainly, because of characteristic phraseology and the revealing of details of a highly private nature, by Mair himself, in which the writer praised Mair at the expense of the "mediocre" men in governmental service, and proposed strongly that Mair be appointed as "the next Lieutenant-Governor of the North-West Territories." By John Schultz, Lieutenant-Governor of Manitoba and about to be knighted, the cause of this near-derangement was, however, directly revealed. On May 30, 1894, Schultz wrote to Eliza:

> We were . . . much touched by your description of your forlorn and helpless condition and no effort will be spared what is possible to afford you relief and I will see what chance there is for a Government berth of any kind. They are hard to get—awfully hard—and yet after your pitiful appeal I will do my best. You had better let me know in this connection whether you would prefer something in British Columbia or back in the Territories. . . .[54]

But Schultz did not obtain a position for Mair, nor is there any indication of why he did not—unless one considers that Mair's describing Mrs. Schultz as "the damndest little hypocrite and humbug" and as "a thorough Becky Sharp"[55] is significant. The once-robust Schultz had been plagued with illness ever since his eventful escape from Riel (he had seriously injured his leg in the fall from his cell window) and his last years were spent largely in convalescence and trips to the South. And when he died in Monterey, Mexico, in 1896, a shadow of the man who had led the "Canadian" party at Red River, Schultz left his considerable fortune to Lady Schultz, but nothing to his niece or her husband. And by that time the Mairs

[52] MP, Mair to ? (a nephew of A. F. Gault), *ca.* 1910.
[53] DP, 2437, Oct. 5, and 2472, Nov. 13, 1893.
[54] MP.
[55] DP, 2831, Aug. 8, 1895.

were in desperate straits. Eliza, having returned to the Post Office in Prince Albert, was trying to sell "Holmewood," the family home; and Mair, compelled to overcome the pride and conceit largely responsible for the self-portrait of success and prestige he had previously drawn for his friend, at last pleaded with Denison to do anything he could to save him. Perhaps a position in the Parliamentary Library, or in Indian Affairs, or in Toronto itself. "I think, without vanity, Toronto might be pleased to give me a decent billet amongst her citizens," he wrote; "I want to be near you too—you are the only friend I have in the world in the sacred significance of that word."[56]

But Denison was unable to help; his outspoken criticism of both the policies and characters of those people in authority who might have found a place for Mair militated against such aid. He was positive his own advancement had been similarly hindered. At the time, also, his time and attention were almost entirely devoted to the danger, imminent to him and to other Canadians like him, of the American invasion that would surely follow the Venezuela boundary dispute. "I am looking about [for] a lot of young, active men between twenty and thirty—athletic, sporting young fellows of football and lacrosse tendencies—to have around me as officers," he wrote Mair;[57] but there is no answer to his friend's plea. During the succeeding months of 1896 Mair's plight became extreme. Laurier's election meant a new Cabinet whose members he did not know; his letters of application went unanswered. On May 28, 1896, the Vernon *News* reported that because of "business difficulties, principally connected with land speculations in the North-West," Mr. Charles Mair had left for Prince Albert and in all probability would not return to the Okanagan.

And Prince Albert seemed more destitute than before. Eliza had lost her position as postmistress because, according to Mair, his "quondam friend" Macdowall—now Member of Parliament—had resented his remarks about Macdowall's failure to get British reviews of *Tecumseh*. Land could not be sold at any price. There was seemingly little to do except to continue his arraignment of both past and present. And now Mair's bitterness was directed against even those closest to him. "If my wife had consented to go to Toronto in 1882," he lamented, "it would have been all right." But he had gone to Windsor, and had consequently "muddled away $12,000 . . . with no right associate save old Baby." He himself had been "a giant ass"

[56]DP, 2970, Jan. 4, 1896.
[57]MP, Jan. 19, 1896.

in his speculations, but had not been so until "troubles appeared on the scene here—the pure fault of the heaven-born statesman and Father of the Dominion!" What hope could there be for the future, he asked Denison, when "the book of the common Canadian youth is the Yankee Sunday newspaper," when "the electorate is everybody's vote . . . and yours and mine are of no more value than dirt?"[58] Surely there had never been a darker outlook that that exemplified in the recent by-election, when a certain T. O. Davis, "an ignorant Irishman whom no one here will receive socially," was returned as Liberal member. Mair himself had refused both to accept nomination and to support Davis: "I might do something for a gentleman, but this pill sticks in my throat."[59] There was, therefore, an irony peculiarly characteristic of so many events and situations in his life in the fact that Mair, having "sawn all the wood and drawn all the water" for many months, should be notified in 1898 that through the enthusiastic efforts of the unacceptable Irishman not only had Eliza Mair been returned as postmistress but he was to receive a governmental appointment.

The influence of Davis, the small loans of Denison and of Lady Schultz, and the meagre salary of Eliza saved Mair from direst poverty. Immediately prior to the welcome news from Ottawa he had, in his desperation, even gone to Fort Steele, British Columbia, and in the hope of profiting from the stream of prospectors moving toward the Klondike, had opened a small stationery and book shop there. The venture had failed within a few weeks (Klondike miners were unlikely prospects, surely, for the book-trade) and Mair had been compelled to draw upon Denison to cover his losses. But in July, 1898, his appointment to Clifford Sifton's Ministry of the Interior was the arm of rescue offered in the nick of time. The suicide he said he contemplated[60] would probably never have occurred; even the precious property would have been sacrificed first and some form of employment obtained. But the wounds to his pride, to his sense of self-importance and worth, were deeply felt; the minor clerkship he accepted at Winnipeg only served to increase those hurts. The salary was meagre—seven hundred dollars—yet, combined with Eliza's it would keep them both and pay the property taxes until Prince Albert came into its own. And as a member of the Immigration Service Mair felt he could help,

[58]DP, 3157, Dec. 31, 1896.
[59]DP, 3127, Dec. 1, 1896.
[60]DP, 3104, Sept. 18, 1896.

perhaps, to initiate the programme of settlement so sorely needed by both the country and himself.

Thus, at the age of sixty, when his counterparts of the modern civil service are nearing retirement, Charles Mair began a new career. Over a quarter of a century had passed since Confederation and the beginning of a struggle in which he had played such an active role—the struggle for national unity and identity. To both Mair and Canada the period had been one of hope and frustration, of success and failure, of vision and revision. Even the literary movement that he and his comrades of Canada First had urged as the life-blood of any movement toward nationalism seemed to have exhausted itself. Sangster and Lampman were dead, Roberts and Carman were in the United States, he himself had been unable to devote the time he wished to literature. Even the *Week*, perhaps the best periodical ever produced in Canada, had to cease publication in 1896. The economic and political patterns had been similarly characterized by depression and defeated aims.

But Mair's role in this allegory of national aspiration and despair was at last about to end. The new Government that had been the means of a new beginning for him came into power on the eve of a prosperity previously unparalled—the prosperity for which Mair and the country had been waiting so long. Nationhood was to come closer to realization (and was to be tested more severely) than ever before. But Canada was still young; Mair was not. His struggle was no longer to be that of attaining wealth and distinction; rather it was to be virtually for existence itself.

X. Return to Red River

THE IMPORTANCE of Clifford Sifton in the development of his country is made known at some time, surely, to almost everyone who attends a Canadian school. This man's achievements in the settling of the West were so great, indeed, that by comparison the lack of imaginative and progressive policies and the indifference and procrastination of preceding governments appear, as Charles Mair so often insisted, scandalous to the degree of criminality. During the last twenty-five years of the nineteenth century there were less than 90,000 homestead entries for Dominion lands, or about 3,600 per year. During only the first five years of the new century the figures leaped to approximately 112,000 and 22,000 respectively. All but a small fraction of these entries were made in the West. Representative censuses are as revealing. In 1881 the population of the North-West Territories was 56,446; in 1891, 66,799; in 1897, 112,906; in 1901, 158,940; and in 1906, 443,175. Perhaps even more dramatic is the fact that immigration swelled from a mere 16,835 in 1896—the year Sifton took office—to 55,747 in 1901, and to an astounding 211,653 in 1906.

There were, of course, significant circumstances surrounding this growth other than an enlightened settlement policy. The Liberal party swept into power in 1896 just as the long depression was ending, and not only Canada but the whole world stood on the threshold of a new era of prosperity. But Canada was in a particularly fortunate position. The great industrial centres of Europe were increasing their demands for foodstuffs at a period when their chief supplier, the western United States, had reached into its last good lands. In Canada, however, millions of acres of land—"the last, best West"— were still as empty as they had been when their vista had thrilled Mair in 1868. Their availability at such a crucial time could not have been more propitious if it had been planned. In addition, the development of the steamship had made ocean travel fast and safe; immigrants from Europe could come to Canada at comparatively low fares, and the grain and flour they helped to produce could make the return journey at constantly falling freight rates. The transcontinental C.P.R. was by 1915 joined by two new rail lines—an ambitious undertaking that was later to be regretted, but that in the early years of the twentieth century opened up vast areas of previously unsettled land. Technology and agricultural research offered direction and mass-production methods just as the earlier settlers were at last solving the fundamental problems of home-building and land-tilling in a rigorous environment. Marquis wheat, for example, appeared in 1908, "the very moment" at which prairie farmlands were "at last ready to go into full production."[1] Everything, indeed, seemed providentially directed towards the rich development of a long-neglected West.

Sifton's achievement, therefore, lies in the way in which he took advantage of such abundant good fortune. The new Minister of the Interior was from Ontario, but years in the West had made him, like Mair, a westerner indignantly aware of the West's problems; so it is not surprising that his policy of western development should be, in general outline, that which Mair and others had so consistently urged—not only urged but, in some particulars, had actually implemented. John W. Dafoe writes that Sifton believed "the first thing to do was to settle the empty West with producing farmers: this was also the second, third, fourth and fifth thing to do."[2] But settlement had to be made attractive, and Sifton, echoing the suggestions previously unheeded, recommended the changing of those governmental policies that had all but stopped immigration westward. As a result, the giving of land grants to railways was stopped and pressure was applied to force the railways to release lands that their tardiness in exercising right of selection had reserved to them. This action, together with the authorizing of other railways, meant the end of one of the immigration deterrents so bitterly denounced by Mair, the "stall-fed monopoly" of the C.P.R., and opened up highly desirable farmlands previously fenced off from the settler. To publicize the opportunities

[1]Creighton, *Dominion of the North*, p. 386.
[2]*Clifford Sifton in Relation to His times*, p. 131.

awaiting in the Canadian West Sifton developed on a grand scale the scheme undertaken by Mair and Flood Davin, that of advertising in British and foreign newspapers and of establishing agencies to inform prospective immigrants. Most important, in the beginning at least, were the efforts to draw settlers from the United States. And especially in this respect was Mair a forerunner of his future employer. Dafoe states that the idea "was wholly original" with Sifton: "it had not occurred to anybody else that from the United States . . . immigrants for Canada could be obtained";[3] and that part of this "original" plan was the opening of offices in the western States. The memories of his efforts in St. Paul and Chicago would have caused Mair to refute such a claim. The whole Sifton programme Mair, in fact, would have found familiar, the great difference being in the crucial factor of governmental direction and support. Shortly after Sir John A.'s death in 1891 Mair had had "a long conversation" with John Abbott, the new Premier, in which he had set forth "my scheme of immigration, the very system adopted by Mr. Sifton when he came into office." But Abbott was "evidently a cypher in his own cabinet"; he is reported by Mair to have said: "I agree with you, Mr. Mair, as to the measures which should be taken, but by God, I am powerless."[4]

And thus Charles Mair, so often a pioneer during his lifetime, was once again a formative influence upon the development of his country. But the irony that seems forever part of his career lies this time in the fact that the truly significant role he played just before and during his period with the Immigration Service has been virtually unrecognized. Even he himself seemed unaware that he was then perhaps doing more for his beloved cause of national growth and unity than he had ever done before. The country began to fill in unprecedented numbers, vast changes took place in trade and communications, in attitudes and ways of life. And the Canada Mair had known at Confederation, divided by physical spaces and provincial antagonisms, was at last, despite long-lingering differences, developing the national spirit that Canada First had so idealistically urged. But Mair saw mainly that his own position now was vastly different both from what it had been in 1868 and from what he had at that time visualized it might be in 1900. He was no longer a main protagonist engaged literally in the struggle for the West and

[3]*Ibid.*, p. 140.

[4]MP, Mair to ? (a nephew of A. F. Gault), *ca.* 1910.

supported by an influential patron in Ottawa. He was no longer the young writer whose correspondence from the Red River aroused editorial comment throughout the East. Nor was he the wealthy western citizen, living in a western Heydon Villa and recognized as Canada's greatest poet. He was merely a disillusioned man over sixty, employed in the often boring, often arduous routine of a comparatively insignificant immigration agent.

For almost twenty-five years—until he was in his eighties—Mair served his department well. He conducted settlers to their new homes in Manitoba, Saskatchewan, Alberta, and British Columbia; he escorted deputations of officials from the United States, Great Britain, and Europe who had been sent to investigate immigration possibilities in a great new country. When not travelling he prepared descriptive pamphlets, wrote articles for newspapers and magazines, and handled the foreign correspondence for the several branch offices to which he was attached over the years. After five years in Winnipeg he was placed in charge of the office at Lethbridge. Shortly afterwards he was moved south to Coutts and then west, as an inspector, to Fort Steele, British Columbia. In this latter post he retired in 1921, an old man of eighty-three.

Such a tenuous outline, however, is consistent only with the meagre recognition Mair received for the many years he devoted to the Immigration Service. Not that he gave himself altruistically and singularly among many others in a similar capacity. His very terms of joining the Service were illustrative of the attitude he largely felt for it; from the beginning his employment was a means to obtain bread and butter and, perhaps more important, to retain his Prince Albert property. But his vast experience and knowledge of the West, his almost obsessive belief in the need for settlement, and his characteristic energy and initiative made him almost ideally the type of "expert" for whom Sifton said he was looking.[5] Even the private opinions he often expressed about the "semi-barbarous hordes" and the "inundations of alien races" he managed to keep from public reflection; knowing Sifton's encouragement of Central European settlers, he undoubtedly considered silence to be a judicious expedient.

There is perhaps no more representative example of this distinction between private comment and official conduct than that offered by the case of the Doukhobors. For better or for worse the settlement in Canada of these controversial people was due to Charles Mair. When

[5]Dafoe, *Clifford Sifton*, p. 105.

Prince Hilkoff arrived in Winnipeg with several Doukhobor farmers in late 1898, he was directed by McCreary, the local Commissioner of Immigration and a man roundly disliked by Mair, to "go west" and seek suitable lands. In time the Prince returned dissatisfied and intent upon going to the United States. "This was perplexing," Mair records, "for at that time great sympathy was felt for the Doukhobors, who were looked upon as the victims of a tyrannical government." But in addition, if these immigrants from the Caucasus had gone south, "it would have seriously discredited our Immigration Service . . . , as eastern Europe was being ransacked for settlers." At length McCreary asked Mair "to have a talk with them and find out what they really required and to settle them." There was undoubtedly a quality of romance about Doukhobor history that appealed to Mair and stimulated him to extra effort on their behalf; he was immediately charmed by Hilkoff, who in turn was encouraged by Mair's promise of a land combining timber, prairie, and water. After a three-weeks' journey on which the Prince constantly recounted to his guide his experiences with Count Tolstoi and as a commander of a Cossack regiment, the Doukhobors were settled to their satisfaction in the Swan River country of north-western Saskatchewan.[6] They were "a quiet, orderly people," and would make "good settlers," Mair concluded;[7] Tolstoi himself had assured Canada that his Doukhobor friends "were not addicted to outbreaks of fanaticism" and that "there could be no doubt that they would be law-abiding."[8] When history proved both him and Tolstoi wrong, Mair never made excuses for what had really been a more than routine duty; "I am not particularly proud of my responsibility to-day," he wrote in 1920, "but it was a very important matter at the time."[9]

This apparent quiet conscientiousness, so different from the bumptious self-assurance of his youth, was to be characteristic of Mair throughout most of his career with the Immigration Service. Perhaps a feeling of resignation over past losses gradually overcame his former propensity to criticize publicly, to take issue with the *status quo*, whatever it might be. Certainly, as has been noted, he felt that his position in the public service implied restraints that he had not before been particularly obliged to recognize. He was, for example, quite resentful over Denison's relation in *Soldiering in Canada* of a humo-

[6]MP, Mair to J. B. Walker, Nov. 10, 1920.
[7]DP, 3676, Jan. 31, 1899.
[8]Dafoe, *Clifford Sifton*, p. 143, n.l.
[9]MP, Mair to Walker, Nov. 10, 1920.

rous anecdote that according to Mair would cause the Conservative press to "come down" on him "as a dypsomaniac of the first order."[10] And he was certain that he had lost a promotion because Denison had contrived to make use of lines from *Tecumseh* in one of his periodic attacks on the Government. Such concern, however, was perhaps due to Mair's characteristic sensitivity to criticism, at times paranoic, for these were references and allusions that no sane higher official would consider. Unfortunately, of course, Mair often had doubts about the sanity of his superiors.

In any case, there is little record of anything but appreciation of Mair's efforts from those officials to whom he was responsible. His first superior, McCreary, probably found it difficult to be friendly because of Mair's hardly concealed dislike for him. He had been John Schultz's store clerk at Fort Garry and Mair at first had "a sort of feeling for him on that account"; but Mair soon found him to be "a low-bred vulgarian of the commonest type, who is hated by all in the office" and whose "brutal want of feeling towards the poor people who flock here has revolted me beyond description."[11] And J. B. Walker, a later Commissioner at Winnipeg, was compelled to inform Mair that "occasional gifts and candy to children at homesteads visited" could not be considered as a legitimate item on an expense account, and that many of the suggestions Mair included in his reports, "reasonable, practicable and sensible though they be" were "in the same position as the flowers that bloom in the spring—they have nothing to do with the case assigned."[12] But as the years went by, Mair became known as a responsible and valuable, if sometimes mildly pompous, servant of Canada's Immigration Service. "I have been 'buck-boarding' for two months," he wrote Denison one New Year's Day, "and I must say that sleeping in sod huts and bachelor shacks and driving in the teeth of blizzards is both unpleasant and dangerous."[13] At another time, after an arduous canvass of forty thirty-six-acre townships, he conceded that he was getting "too old for such strenuous work." Driving for days in pouring rain was "no joke for a man of seventy-six," and only an "almost sublime constitution" kept him going.[14]

But such fortitude Mair always considered a part of what he called "manliness," that quality which distinguished "the right sort" of

[10]DP, 4134, Sept. 21, 1900. Denison retorted that the anecdote would "preserve the human side of your character—the ethereal side being well shown in your poems" (MP, Dec. 8, 1901). The incident referred to is in *Soldiering in Canada*, pp. 308–9.

[11]DP, 3752, May 16, 1899.

[12]MP, Oct. 12, 1910.

[13]DP, 5804, Jan. 1, 1911.

[14]DP, 6169, Sept. 6, 1914.

humanity from their more craven brethren and which, above all perhaps, demanded the highest respect for the domestic virtues. A Lethbridge immigration clerk has related an anecdote indicative of how Mair was sometimes harmlessly ridiculed in this respect. One morning, the clerk recalled, a young bachelor employee was absent from the office. "Where is Jack this morning?" asked Mair. "He's in jail," was the answer. "In jail! What for?" asked Mair quite credulously. "Wife beating," came the straight-faced reply. "The inhuman brute!" exclaimed the scandalized Mair; and evidently "Jack wondered why Mr. Mair deliberately passed him by the next day, instead of giving the usual cheery 'Good Morning.' "[15] It is not difficult, however, to understand another contemporary's comment that Mair was "one of the most honorable and lovable men of his day and generation, but who knew more and knew less than any man I have ever met—more about the finer, nobler things of life and less about the common, understood and necessary."[16] Such a personality could also, understandably, stimulate a dinner in his honour, replete with "Consommée à la Doukhobor" and toasts "à la santé de Grand Pa," at which homage was paid to Mair's "manners particularly affable," his "exquisite courtesy," his "constant assiduity and persevering energy *à répondre aux intarissables informations* on the resources of our Canadian West."[17] Tributes like this become frequent in subsequent years. As he travelled over the prairies and the mountains, Mair found friends more than filling the gaps, in numbers at least, left by the many old-timers every day becoming fewer; and gradually he and his work became known, in terms not of fame or official importance, but rather of quiet, kindly understanding and sincerity, throughout the major part of the West.

These years, particularly those of the first decade or so of the new century, were years not only of hardship but also of heartbreak. Mair's small initial salary did not permit Eliza to live with her husband in Winnipeg, where they had first met so many years before. Whatever money could be spared from their incomes—Eliza retained her postmistresship at Prince Albert for some time—went to pay taxes on the precious lots, and Mair, who had great affection for his wife and family, lived a frugal bachelor existence in a cheap tenement house in Winnipeg. Maude was happily married and living in

[15]Thyrza Y. Burkitt, "Charles Mair, Pioneer Poet," Lethbridge *Herald*, Jan. 6, 1953.
[16]Charles F. Moberly, Sweet Grass, Montana; quoted by Thyrza Burkitt.
[17]MP, dinner menu, Aug. 8, 1903.

Kelowna, but a leg injury improperly treated by "drunken Dr. Bain" of Prince Albert became painfully crippling as she grew older. Fanny, evidently jealous of Maude's marriage to near-nobility and of that of the younger sister Mabel to a Captain Arthur Lucas, also of distinguished parentage, began to feel contempt for Edward Cann and eventually left him. Mabel and her husband, after quarreling violently with Mair over the sale of five acres of property near Kelowna, sailed for Australia and never saw or even corresponded with Mair again. And Cecil, whose "intelligence and sturdy Canadian manliness" had often been a subject of his father's letters, had difficulty holding his position in several branches of Molson's Bank—because of, according to Mair, Denison's caricature-like picture in *Soldiering in Canada* of Mair and Sir David Macpherson, whose son was general manager of Molson's. Eventually Cecil went to the Boer War with the Canadian contingent (Denison's influence outweighed his failing the markmanship requirements) and on his return began the drifting from job to job that was to continue until he died in 1935.

But far more poignant was the anguish Mair experienced when death again deprived him of those closest to him. When transferred to Lethbridge in 1903 he was at last able to have his wife and youngest daughter Elizabeth come to live with him, but within a few months, from "this desert of dust, coal smoke and chinook wind . . . , this gas-smutted and filthy town," Elizabeth contracted, like a brother and a sister before her, typhoid fever and died shortly after her twentieth birthday. A strikingly pretty girl, "Bessie" had been very close to her parents, not having gone away to schools, employment, or marriage as had the other children, and Mair could only record his and Eliza's bereavement as "unspeakable."[18]

Two years later, when only fifty-six and despite a strong constitution invigorated by years of western pioneering, Eliza herself was stricken with a cerebral hemorrhage while visiting Maude in Victoria and died before Mair could reach her side. Devoted as he had been to his wife since the turbulent days at Red River, the distraught man felt this blow more severely than the many others that had befallen him. "For nearly forty years she has been all the world to me," he wrote Denison; "her nature was full of kindness to others—to help, to do good; and so her whole life was but a preparation for the life beyond." Particularly distressing to Mair was the realization that for the last fifteen years he and Eliza had been together for only fleeting, isolated periods; "My thoughts and feelings of late have

[18]DP, 5052, Oct. 1, 1904.

undergone great change," he wrote, "so that the things of the world seem to me now visionary and unsubstantial, and I am filled with a longing . . . to be quit of a world of misery and sorrow."[19] But he did not add, as he well might have done by then, "How much land does a man need?" Eliza may have been "all the world" to him, but the Prince Albert property had divided that world. And it was to continue to do so long after Eliza was gone.

The death of his wife stimulated Mair more than anything before to turn his thoughts to a time and place of which the memories had gradually faded during the years at Prince Albert and Windsor. The events of Red River could never be forgotten; they had been too influential upon his subsequent career. But only rarely in those years, as in the altercation with Lawrence Clarke, had Mair referred to them or even seemed to think about them. The Rebellion of 1885 had recalled them sharply, but his mind was at that time too much divided between the more distant past of the War of 1812 and the bitter present of Prince Albert and the West to allow memories of Fort Garry in 1868 to distract him for long. The loss of a wife with whom Mair had lived adventures seemingly out of a romantic novel occurred, however, when other factors were combining to impinge upon a nature already sentimentally inclined. His relative insignificance in the Immigration Service demanded comparison with the fame he had enjoyed in the days of McDougall and of the letters to the *Globe*. Living in Winnipeg brought him in contact once again with persons and places intimately connected with the most exciting days of his life. As he wandered about Fort Garry or reminisced with men now known as "old-timers," his nostalgia grew and was made more acute by the sights and sounds of the great city rising where only a mud track and a tiny settlement had been forty years before. The research he undertook for the chapters on Red River in Denison's *Soldiering in Canada* re-opened the old argument over Dennis's flight from Stone Fort[20] and involved visits to the widowed Anne Farquharson Schultz and Schultz's old partner, Dr. Bown. Even R. G. Haliburton was inspired about this time to write his version of the intrigue surrounding the despatch of the Wolseley expedition; his death in 1901 sharpened Mair's memories of momentous evenings in Ottawa and of public demonstrations in Toronto.

There were also the important questions of one's reputation and

[19]DP, 5235, Sept. 12, 1906.
[20]See chap. v, n. 44.

the justness of the cause for which one had fought. Schultz's death had stimulated a number of books and articles on the "First Riel Rebellion," most of which were unfavourable to the "Canadian Party" and to McDougall, Schultz, and Mair in particular. Two churchmen, the Reverend George Bryce[21] and the Abbé Georges Dugas,[22] were publishing their versions just as McDougall died in 1905, and to Mair their attacks were hardly short of sacrilege. "And so poor Macdougall [*sic*] is gone—the most abominably-used man in Canada," he wrote; "the actors in the drama at Red River are falling fast, and I shall soon be the sole survivor."[23] And of the utmost importance, he felt, was that he or someone as qualified should correct the false and prejudiced histories beginning to influence whole new generations of Canadians; "The true inwardness of the Rebellion and its attending circumstances have never been given,"[24] he had commented while helping Denison with *Soldiering in Canada*; and when Dugas' *Histoire véridique* appeared he was irritated enough "to yearn for the leisure" that would enable him "to present our own side of the question, which has been obscured by Pope and Pagan—by the apologists of Rome and the H.B.C."[25]

This "return to Red River" by Mair is a feature, appropriately the major one, of the quite curious pattern of his life from the turn of the century on. For as he moved into what was to be an extended old age, a combination of events and circumstances gradually shaped themselves into an analogous reflection of his earlier years, but a reflection magnified over a greater period of time and a larger dimension of space. A government appointment in 1898 had sent him to Winnipeg in the interests of western immigration just as a similar appointment had sent him there exactly thirty years before. His arrival coincided with a re-awakening of interest, not only by himself but by others as well, in the events of the former period. This interest was poignantly stimulated by the passing on of many of those who had been active fellow-participants in the drama at Fort Garry. But such coincidence would not have been unusual unless supplemented in Mair's case by other important aspects of his career at this time. For not only did he undertake now another trip to a relatively unknown part of the North-West—"a sealed book as yet to the Canadian people"—and describe it in correspondence to the Toronto *Globe*, he also published a book of

[21]Bryce wrote a series of articles for the Winnipeg *Free Press* and also *A History of Manitoba.*

[22]See chap. IV, n. 44.

[23]DP, 5148, June 2, 1905.

[24]DP, 4209, Dec. 7, 1900.

[25]DP, 5148, June 2, 1905.

verse that was a collection, as *Dreamland* had been, of work previously presented in periodicals, and that included even *Dreamland* itself.

In 1899, less than a year after he joined the Immigration Service, Mair was appointed English Secretary of the Scrip Commission that was sent into the Athabaska and Peace River districts to negotiate with the Indians and half-breeds there for the transfer of their territorial rights to the Dominion. This country of the Mackenzie basin represented, as Manitoba had done in 1868, a highly desirable acquisition. Of great size and rich in resources, it was the last remaining region to be incorporated, all the others from Lake Winnipeg to the Rocky Mountains and from the international border to the District of Athabaska having been ceded by previous treaties. In some respects, then, to Mair it constituted another frontier of the North-West, another opportunity, surely the last, to be a pioneer before civilization made its inevitable inroad. And as before, he had providentially prepared himself, by reading and research at least, for the possibility of such an expedition. For over a decade, ever since the fortunes of Prince Albert had seemed to depend upon the opening up of northern trade routes, he had studiously investigated all available material on the Mackenzie and sub-Arctic regions. Mair's authority, indeed, was recognized as early as 1888 and to the extent of his being consulted by a Senate Select Committee chaired by Senator John Schultz and appointed "to enquire as to the value of . . . the Great Makenzie [*sic*] Basin—its extent of navigable rivers, lakes and seacoast, of agricultural and pastoral land, its fisheries, forests and mines."[26] Not long afterward, and probably as a result of his own and the Committee's findings, he had himself determined to go to the Mackenzie; only Edward Cann's urgent telegram had halted his last-moment preparations in 1892. But the desire and intention remained: "[I] dream of Mackenzie River," he wrote in 1895; "I believe I shall end my days in the Arctic Circle if the Government will give me a good billet."[27] And two years later, when desperately awaiting news of a government appointment, he insisted that he would go even to the North Pole: "In fact, I should like to be planted there by 'Discovery' as a universal flag-pole, with the 'Jack' in my frozen fist."[28]

The journey, which took Mair for almost four months from his duties at Winnipeg ("a great relief from the dire position" in the

[26]MP, Senate Committee on the Mackenzie Basin (Senator J. Schultz) to Mair, April 5, 1888.

[27]DP, 2882, Sept. 23, 1895.

[28]DP, 3162, Jan. 16, 1897.

office under McCreary),[29] warrants only general commentary. His responsibility, even though carried out in the midst of still primitive vastness, was quite mundane—that of keeping records of the scrip negotiations. Mair evidently enjoyed returning to the wilds, but it is not difficult to infer that his still-adventurous spirit had hoped for something exciting to occur. When Denison rebuked him for sending his letters describing the trip to the *Globe* instead of the *Empire* (a paper his brother Fred had helped to found) Mair defended himself rather curiously by replying that he had sent his first letters, those from Red River, to the *Globe*; "I began there, and thought I would end there, though the *Globe* is now a much poorer concern than it was when edited by the stiff-necked old Britisher, Brown. . . ."[30] And a "much poorer" *Globe* published letters this time from Mair that were less vivid, less enthusiastic—and less controversial—than those of 1869–70. A furious rainstorm that brought the tent down upon him while he was writing one evening seems, in fact, to have been the only excitement Mair could connect with this later correspondence. This time there were no horse-whippings, nose-pullings, parodying novels, not to mention threats of death. In thirty years Mair had grown wiser and civilization had advanced north-westward:

> The crowd of Indians ranged before the marquee had lost all semblance of wildness of the true type. Wild men they were, in a sense, living as they did in the forest and on their great waters. But it was plain that these people had achieved, without any treaty at all, a stage of civilization distinctly in advance of many of our treaty Indians to the south after twenty-five years of education. Instead of paint and feathers, the scalp-lock, the breech-clout, and the buffalo-robe, there presented itself a body of respectable-looking men, as well dressed and evidently quite as independent in their feelings as any like number of average pioneers in the East. Indeed, I had seen there, in my youth, many a time, crowds of white settlers inferior to these in sedateness and self-possession. One was prepared, in this wild region of forest, to behold some savage types of men; indeed I craved to renew the vanished scenes of old. But, alas! one beheld instead, men with well-washed, unpainted faces, and combed and common hair; men in suits of ordinary "store clothes," and some even with "boiled" if not laundered shirts.[31]

Mair felt disappointed, almost defrauded. And yet, he said, the Indians presented "a gratifying spectacle." Through the discipline

[29]DP, 3752, May 16, 1899.
[30]DP, 3881, Nov. 29, 1899.
[31]Toronto *Globe*, Aug. 12, 1899. The other instalments appeared on July 15, 22, 29, Aug. 26, and Sept. 2, 1899.

and fairness of "our venerable Queen" and their own innate goodness, these people were plainly out of barbarism and well on the way to becoming good Canadians of the North. More so, obviously, than some other people the mention of whom he confined to the private correspondence that he wrote, as if mindful of previous embarrassment, "*in strictest confidence.*" Evidence of treason to Canada, he told Denison, was still to be found in exactly the same shape as it had been in '69: "The tri-color floated at every R.C. mission we came to in the North, the Union being only floated in our honour, and in some places a miserable patched-up travesty of it *under* a fine French flag." This hypocrisy, together with his hearing "a French Inspector of Mounted Police declare that he hoped the Boers would win," had caused him to lose all confidence in French Canadians, who, still "overborne by the giant, aggressive power of the priesthood," were surely "masked foes of British rule."[32]

The published commentaries of his trip gave not an inkling of such resentment. The Roman Catholic clergy and the French Canadians, wherever they are met, are depicted with seeming sympathy, even with high praise. But his warning to Denison reveals plainly that Mair felt the restraints that his employment placed upon him; he could not incur the risk of dismissal.

There was, however, another restraint applied more directly upon him by the Government. The *Globe* letters he had hoped to publish in book form as soon as possible after his return from the North, but Sifton, aware of the enthusiastic response similar accounts by Mair had aroused on the previous occasion, asked him to delay. Until roads could be built, markets established, and other essentials of civilized life introduced and the great prairie lands to the south more thickly settled, immigration was highly undesirable. And so, therefore, was any stimulus to it. But Mair was not unduly vexed; he no longer had the missionary zeal of the Red River days, and in any case the time he had available for literary work was being devoted to the new edition of his poetry.

When the narrative of the journey finally appeared in 1908 as *Through the Mackenzie Basin*, Mair had, in fact, endured on its behalf more than the irritation of delay. For both sentimental and financial reasons he had agreed with a retired Chief Factor of the Hudson's Bay Company, Roderick MacFarlane, to publish his work jointly in one volume with MacFarlane's *Notes on the Mammals and Birds of Northern Canada.* MacFarlane, like many another Scot, had

[32]DP, 3881, Nov. 29, 1899.

spent a lifetime in the farthest outposts of the North-West, and to Mair, who had known him for years, he represented not only the rapidly dwindling "little band of old-timers" but also the means of a circulation larger than Mair's book alone might ensure. But the collaboration was a succession of recriminations and disagreements, made even more bitter when these two strong-willed men were confronted by the equally strong-willed Dr. William Briggs of the Methodist Book and Publishing Company. Briggs agreed to bring out the book without royalties on the basis of Mair's obtaining a government order of 450 copies from Sifton. Even this, however, did not seem to influence MacFarlane away from the belief that his part was the most important. His submitted manuscript was three times the length of the original one agreed upon, MacFarlane deeming necessary the inclusion of more birds and mammals as well as a forty-page brochure on Franklin's expedition of 1820. Both Mair and Briggs found this "preposterous" and some months were wasted "in snarling."[33] MacFarlane seemed blithely indifferent to the economics of publishing, and continued to insist that the book would contain "more reading matter of the kind for *two dollars* than any Canadian or American publisher has ever before given to the public."[34] But Briggs finally rebelled when Mair himself wished to include his "Open the Bay!" verses and their supporting commentary, as well as his own portrait opposite the title-page; "We have reached," the house wrote curtly, "the limit of additional expense."[35]

Briggs was required, however, to reach an even greater limit of patience. Only the government order for paper-bound copies of Mair's section made possible at all the publication of the composite book, and he urged both authors to canvass earnestly among their friends and associates—if only to pay for the large complimentary lists both had forwarded. MacFarlane, although he described himself as of "a very meek and not over-aggressive" temperament, was upset by "the "incivility" he met while seeking customers. "I have seldom if ever worked harder," he lamented; "I'd sooner break stones for a living than become a professional book canvasser."[36] Briggs, annoyed by Mair's charges that his house was making "a great profit" from the government order, replied by recommending that Mair show an assiduity similar to MacFarlane's. And so it went on; even the spelling of "Hudson's Bay" aroused a minor storm. When the book finally

[33]DP, 5321, April 14, 1908. [34]MP, April 30, 1908.
[35]MP, E. S. Caswell to Mair, May 7, 1908.
[36]MP, June 29, July 13, 1908.

appeared, marked by typographical errors and erratum slips, sensitivities had become tender. Mair conceded only that the work might "pass muster"; Briggs replied that Mair had hurried through his proofreading; and MacFarlane wanted a larger share of the royalties that Briggs had finally consented to give. "Never," said E. S. Caswell, Briggs's editor, "do I want to have anything to do again with a book where two authors are interested, unless they are the staunchest friends and in accord about everything."[37]

But the book sold well—if such can be said of the sale of a complete edition of two thousand copies—and, according to Mair, was received "in a very gratifying way."[38] Reviewers praised Mair's vivid descriptions and his confidence in the future of this new North-West, those who were old enough noting that the author's talents and beliefs had persisted over the years. Mair's complimentary copies stimulated replies from various notables, including even the Prince of Wales, at the time aboard H.M.S. *Indomitable.* Sir Charles Tupper described the book as "an important contribution"[39] and the Duke of Argyll approved of its extolling Canadian natural resources;[40] but Lord Strathcona—Mair's "old sinner," Donald Smith—noted only that "the binding of the book [was] most artistic."[41] British commentary (the work was published in London also) was generally favourable, although not without reservations. "Some Canadian words" caused difficulty, an Edinburgh critic noted; "'Muskeg' I took to be some kind of horse."[42] And the London *Times* of October 1, 1908, aiming most of its barbs at MacFarlane, described the book in general as a "rather heterogeneous volume," and "Mammals and Birds" in particular as "certain papers on Canadian natural history exhumed from the Smithsonian Institution"—an unfair comment when it is realized that MacFarlane, during his long years in the North, had sent many hundreds of pounds of specimens to the Smithsonian.[43] But for Mair the book, despite all its deficiencies, helped to recall the public mind to his connection with the growth of Canada and, perhaps most important at the time, to direct it towards the North, upon whose development his own hopes for financial recovery were still dependent.

[37]MP, Oct. 7, 1908.
[38]DP, 5376, Nov. 1, 1908.
[39]MP, Aug. 4, 1908.
[40]MP, Aug. 12, 1908.
[41]MP, Aug. 6, 1908.
[42]MP, Wm. Mair to Mair, Sept. 18, 1908.
[43]In 1863 MacFarlane and Murdoch McLeod had gone "right to the Arctic to find how far north different birds went and collected about 1400 lbs. weight of specimens for the Smithsonian. . . ." (MP, "Murdoch McLeod").

His poetic reputation Mair tried to keep alive by the volume of collected works that he published in 1901. As far back as 1894 he had considered such a venture, hoping, by drawing attention to himself as a Canadian poet, to gain some form of relief from his dire financial straits; but no publisher, especially when the author could not share costs, would take the risk, and Mair had to wait until the turn of the century and better times before he received even qualified encouragement. During these depressing years, however, he revised most of the *Dreamland* verses and composed two or three short pieces to add to those he had published comparatively recently in periodicals. As in the past, he depended much on Denison's advice. Pauline Johnson's regrets over Iena's death in *Tecumseh* ("she gave me a broadside," he noted) stimulated a succession of letters on the advisability of "only wounding Iena." Even what verses from *Dreamland* should be included and/or changed was also made largely dependent on his old friend's opinion. "All this I command you to do," Mair warned him; "for although your military slave, I am your *uncle*, and therefore by age and authority, entitled to demand."[44] But Denison, who prided himself on his military and political consistency, was equally sure of his literary tastes. Not a line of *Tecumseh* should be changed: "Now poor Foster is dead we cannot have his advice, and what he approved you and I can endure, even if Pauline Johnson should differ from us all."[45] And the changes, if any, in *Dreamland* should be minor. "I would leave out 'Prologue to Tecumseh'—there will be enough about him—and 'August' and 'Fire-Flies'." "The North Wind's Tale" must be included: "I always liked that poem, but . . . the last half *might* be left out."[46] Mair followed most of Denison's suggestions faithfully, and as it turned out, unfortunately, because he thereby excluded the best lines of *Dreamland*.

When his manuscripts were ready he confidently forwarded them to George N. Morang, Ltd., in Toronto, directing that the work "should be printed on good paper, bound in buckram" and that the three or four portraits, including his own, "should be well processed." He assured Morang's that the volume would "go off very well in

[44]DP, July 29, 1895. Denison's second wife was Helen Mair, daughter of Mair's brother James and married to Denison in Perth in 1887. Mair himself evidently had no inkling at the time that such a marriage was being considered, and when informed, only after the event had taken place, was quite curt towards his friend. Denison's son George married his stepmother's sister Margaret, thus becoming brother-in-law to his father.

[45]MP, Aug. 22, 1895.

[46]MP, Aug. 11, 1895.

Canada"; indeed, now that Canada had "come to the front in England," it was not unlikely that "one of the literary sources of Canadian Imperial sentiment" would attract attention in the mother country as well. And, although he wished his book to be judged upon its merits —"the only criticism I value or have ever got"—both he and his daughter, Mrs. Crichton, had friends in England who would "take pains to get the work reviewed."[47] But Morang's were not impressed. While "perfectly aware of the merits" of Mair's poetry and of Mair's position "in the judgment of the discerning fraction of the book-buying public," they could not risk the almost certain loss incurred in publishing verse; "our experience in the sale of poetical works," they significantly remarked, "has been exceedingly discouraging."[48] So Mair was obliged to find consolation in learning that Morang had been born in the United States ("if I had known he was a Yankee I would not likely have asked him") and to search elsewhere for a publisher.[49] And once again Denison's aggressive confidence, both in Mair and himself, was the significant factor. Deciding that the Methodist Book Room was enterprising and had "plenty of capital," he argued with William Briggs of that house that it should undertake the work; his friend Mair was Canada's greatest national poet, he was the most widely known man in the North-West, he had already had over three hundred orders, and had only recently sent assurance that T. O. Davis would "cram the book down the unpoetical throats of both Members and Senators."[50] Whether or not Denison also offered some guarantee of costs is not recorded, but the result of the colonel-magistrate's foray, whatever the weapons, was victory. Wrote Mair: "When you make an onslaught *something* must give way";[51] in this case it was Briggs.

Tecumseh, a Drama, and Canadian Poems appeared a few days before Christmas, 1901. A trim volume bound in blue or red cloth, decorated with a gold maple leaf and Indian weapons, and dedicated "to the survivors of the Canada First Association," it was meant to represent Mair's contribution to Canadian letters over almost half a century. "There it is," Mair wrote Denison, "and good-bye for ever to the Muse!"[52] Unfortunately, it was a languid swan-song. Except for a few insignificant changes, *Tecumseh* was as it had been in 1886. The later poems were identical with the original versions published

[47]DP, 4317E, Mair to George N. Morang, Ltd., March 14, 1901 (copy sent to Denison).

[48]DP, 4360, Morang to Mair, May 10, 1901 (copy sent to Denison).

[49]DP, 4356, May 31, 1901.

[50]DP, 4424, Oct. 15, 1901.

[51]DP, 4437, Nov. 24, 1901.

[52]DP, 4445, Dec. 16, 1901.

in the *Week* and the *Dominion Illustrated*. Only in the *Dreamland* verses were there indications that Mair had "benefited by the strictures" of critics now long since gone. Much, if not all, of the former crudeness in both matter and technique was removed or considerably polished, and an attempt had obviously been made to rid the work of what Mair termed "a young poet's imperfections"—the forced archaisms, the trite epithets, and the evidences of almost snobbish affectation. But with them went also lines and verses truly indicative of poetic talent—the delicate, if Keatsian, cadences of "The Fire-Flies," the concentrated iambics of "August," and the lingering nuances of "Prologue to Tecumseh." These omissions, which Mair later regretted, were due to Denison's advice and to his own inconsistent discriminatory sense. There were others due simply to shoddy bookmaking. In many copies (perhaps all those bound in blue cloth) sixteen pages (a complete signature) and, as the index reveals, six selections, of *Dreamland* were skipped by the binder; "In Memory of McGee," one of Mair's own preferences, is represented by only a little more than its last three stanzas; the notes in the back are carelessly duplicated.[53] Even the sketch, on the title-page, of Tecumseh addressing a council is marred by a pot near him on the floor, which, as Mair was quick to note, looked "too ominously like a spitoon to suit the occasion."[54]

The lukewarm reception given the book was appropriate to these unfortunate auspices. Even Denison, who had assured Mair that he would "see that the papers reviewed it properly," does not seem to have generated any of the enthusiastic response accorded his friend's previous works. Briggs had been harassed to have the book ready for Christmas sale, but his haste resulted only in poor workmanship; and the volume was still too late. The demand, he said, for Ralph Connor's *Man from Glengarry* was so great that he felt compelled to sacrifice all other publication, especially that of a collection of verse. "The whim of the flimsy day," lamented Mair, "is the novel, no matter of what sort, and . . . poetry, with all the other pure graces and simplicities of life is put aside."[55] All he could hope for, he added, was to live in literary history, and to wait for "the better day to return." Nearly two years later he remarked, however, that he could not understand "how the book miscarried," that he still owed Briggs over fifty dollars (which he trusted Denison would

[53]This is true of at least the numerous blue copies examined by the author. The flaws do not appear in the red copies he has seen.
[54]DP, 4437, Nov. 24, 1901. [55]DP, 4454, Dec. 28, 1901.

adjust for him) and that he "greatly regretted publishing at all."[56] There had not even been acknowledgment for copies sent to "the Prince and Princess of Wales and . . . to Algernon Charles Swinburne."[57] Mair would have been even more disillusioned if he could have known then that almost a quarter of a century later, Briggs's successor, the Ryerson Press, still would have boxes full of copies of *Tecumseh and Canadian Poems* that it would gladly sell for fifteen cents each.[58]

The ill-fated collection of verse and the slightly more successful—financially at least—collaboration of travel and natural history represented Mair's last attempts to regain and maintain a reputation in Canadian letters. The former was indeed a farewell to the muse, and the latter, with its implied dependence upon a quite incongruous supporting treatise, reflects concretely the transition that Mair had been gradually making from eminence to obscurity. By 1910 he was in his seventies and had already experienced an unusually varied career; to live on was to recreate only the shadows and outlines of that career.

For just as his position in the Immigration Service, his journey to the Mackenzie Basin and his last ventures into literature were all disappointing analogues of exciting experiences of the past, so were, in general, the episodes that marked an old man's decline towards death. Only his renewed attention to Red River seemed to offer Mair some promise of "doing something for Canada" and, perhaps, in terms of literary recognition, for himself. McDougall's death in 1905 underlined the fact that soon he might be the only survivor of the days of '69 who could give "the true inwardness" of Riel's insurrection. Bryce and Dugas had stimulated old controversies, and while Mair was wrangling with MacFarlane and Briggs over *Mackenzie Basin*, the events of Red River were being re-enacted in the pages of newspapers and periodicals throughout the West. Publishers quickly appreciated how timely a book upon the subject would be, particularly in the light of the recent rapid development of the West, and were soon urging Mair to undertake such a work. E. S. Caswell, Briggs's

[56]DP, 4728, Aug. 10, 1903.

[57]DP, 4451, Dec. 23, 1901.

[58]GP, July 12, 1923. John Matthews (*Tradition in Exile*, pp. 99–101) explains the failure of the book in terms of Mair's still being sensitive to Haliburton's private criticism of thirty years before and attempting to "Canadianize" his poems. By 1901, however, says Professor Matthews, "Mair was trying to do [what] had already been done by men whose poetic ability far outstripped his own . . ., by those with less self-conscious but more authentic voices."

editor, assured him, despite recent differences, that he had the gift of writing history "so as to make it *live*" and that the book would be "a monument . . . that any man might covet."[59] Robert Glasgow believed him "to be the man above all others to write the history"; perhaps he would at least do the section on the North-West for *Canada and Its Provinces*.[60] And Henry J. Morgan, suggesting that "bye-gones be bye-gones," insisted that Mair was "the *one man*" for the work, which ought to be "the mark" of his life. Even more than Caswell, Morgan was interested in monuments and memorials: Mair's history, "if well done, ought to be the means of raising monuments to both Scott and McDougall—but particularly McDougall." He himself would gladly help to make arrangements for publication.[61]

As Mair grew older, such requests grew in number and urgency. And they came not only from publishers but from the old-timers as well, from the men who wished to stimulate fading memories of their adventures as young men in a virtually unknown West. One of them was Isaac Cowie, who was devoting his last years to an evidently hopeless attempt to gain land grants for the early pioneers of Rupert's Land, and who could remark with wry humour that "the veterans were dropping off daily, needing only six feet of ground after death, but the survivors can find use for a whole quarter-section."[62] Another was W. J. Traill, who had pressed on to British Columbia with memories of the days "when the buffalo, grasshoppers, Louis Riel and other wild animals were lords of Rupert's Land," and when a half-breed "who owned a painted cart and a canvas tent was a person of wealth, culture and social distinction." Mair and he and "the other trailblazers" were the men who had made possible the winning of the West—so that "present pioneers" could endure the hardships

> of travelling into the country in a Pullman car . . . not always kept at the proper temperature nor fully ventilated, and the meals in the diner bad. When you and I crossed the plains we had no complaints of that kind to make. A dish of tea without any trimming and a piece of pemican devoured under a cart with the sun shining down your throat or when it was so cold that you had to drink your tea boiling hot for fear it would congeal before it reached your stomach were the luxuries we enjoyed.

And these were the experiences, said Traill, that must be recorded, but that could be recorded authentically by only the pioneers themselves.[63]

59MP, June 5, 1908.
60MP, Oct. 11, 1911.
61MP, June 15, 1912.
62MP, Oct. 9, 1909.
63MP, Dec. 16, 1914.

Mair determined therefore that as one last achievement he would write the "full and accurate account of North-West affairs," if only "to set to rights the truth which has been so grossly misrepresented." Surely, he said, "I could write a better book than Bryce who, I fancy, has never been in a canoe in his life."[64] But again the inability to find time and opportunity for research and writing became a familiar obstacle. His request for transfer from the Immigration Service to the National Archives met no success; instead he was moved farther westward from Lethbridge and Coutts to Fort Steele, British Columbia. Even from this outpost he began gathering material by correspondence with fellow-survivors of Red River; his papers include several letters sent to Fort Steele by former comrades who, like himself, were trying to relive in memory the adventures of Garry, Schultz's house, and the Portage expedition. But by 1920 he could report only that he hoped to apply himself "when freed by superannuation from official hindrances" and when resolved from doubt about "another serious reason into which I cannot enter."[65]

This "serious reason" was the belief that he would have to place a large share of the blame for McDougall's ruin and for the insurrection itself upon Joseph Howe. For in 1920 and at the age of eighty-two, Mair had evidently forgotten that both he and McDougall had already publicly charged Howe with complicity in the events at Red River; so there was actually no reason, other than a realization that the charge was unfounded, for this later reticence. But evidence in Mair's papers, particularly his rephrasing of letters, indicates that he really believed he had important, previously unknown information. When McClelland and Stewart urged him to publish his "memoirs," he replied that "the reputation of a certain distinguished politician from the East would suffer severely from his treachery and double-dealing in 1869, should the evidence in my possession be made public."[66] The draft of this letter reveals that Mair substituted the phrase "from the East" for "from the Maritime Provinces," evidently fearing the latter to be too explicit. In other correspondence he explained his silence as involving "matters of a very delicate political and personal nature which have never [reached] the press."[67] And later, in Garvin's *Master-Works* edition, he refers to "the sinister visit" to Red River of an "enemy in the Cabinet," who, hastening

[64]DP, 4105, Aug. 22, 1900.
[65]MP, Mair to E. Taylor, March 26, 1920.
[66]MP, Mair to McClelland and Stewart, March 15, 1923.
[67]MP, Mair to Wm. Brady, Feb. 23, 1923.

ahead of McDougall, "refused to meet a deputation of loyalists there, consorted solely with the rebel leaders, and stated that Mr. McDougall had no authority to enter the country as Governor." As a result, Mair insisted, rebellion was encouraged and McDougall's career ruined.[68]

And yet, defective as his memory had become in respect to even his own former writings, it is just possible that Mair did uncover some new evidence of Howe's supposed treachery. In 1921, at long last retired, he was enabled to begin the promised work, and letter after letter went out from Fanny's home in Calgary, where he was living, seeking information pertinent to his memoirs. "My pen is at work," he assured Murdoch McLeod;[69] and it was from this fellow-loyalist of the Fort Garry days that Mair in 1922 gleaned some information that, he felt, justified his reticence to publish. He asked McLeod, now living in Edmonton, for any details he could recall "of the meeting at St. Charles where Mr. Howe spoke against Mr. Macdougall [*sic*]." McLeod's reply does not appear in letter form in the Mair Papers, but at the conclusion of a document referred to previously,[70] there is a paragraph entitled "Murdoch McLeod's statement re Jo Howe" that appears to answer Mair's request. As recorded by Mair the statement related that "Jo Howe came in and passed Macdougall [*sic*] and all our party and went on to Winnipeg and had a council with Gov. and Jack MacTavish [*sic*], Bannatyne and others." Then, after consulting with priests and *métis* at St. Boniface, the "big man . . . from Ottawa" was reported to have told a meeting "in the French Church at St. Charles" that McDougall would treat the *métis* "as he did their priests in the Manitoulin"[71] and advised the assembly "not to consent to his coming in."

This was undoubtedly at least part of the evidence that Mair considered to be secret and that he was reluctant to make public because it "would not be very pleasant reading for some"[72] and "might offend Howe's friends."[73] And it was upon this obstacle of doubts that

68P. lvii. Garvin repeatedly asked Mair to identify the minister before the book went to press, but Mair steadfastly refused to do so.

69MP, Sept. 20, 1922.

70"Murdoch McLeod." See also F. N. Shrive, "Charles Mair: A Document on the Red River Rebellion," *Canadian Historical Review*, XI (Sept., 1959), 218–26.

71"A baseless story, evidently originated by missionaries, was circulated to the effect that in conclusion of a treaty with the Indians of Manitoulin Island in 1858, which was opposed by the Catholic missionaries, McDougall as the Minister of Public Works had accepted responsibility for grave corruption and intimidation of the Chiefs" (W. L. Morton, *Begg's Journal*, pp. 41–42; which, in turn, refers to PAC, Macdonald Papers, 516, Macdonald to Rose, Dec. 5, 1869).

72MP, Mair to McClelland and Stewart, March 15, 1923.

73MP, Mair to R. G. MacBeth, July 24, 1923.

Mair's "true account" of the insurrection foundered—that is, if simple old age and possible realization that there was really no new material to support the side of the "loyalists" are not considered more significant factors. For he delayed too long. "It has always been a question with me whether I should repress or publish," he told William Brady of McClelland and Stewart, ". . . and it is highly probable that publication will be deferred until after my death."[74] To R. G. MacBeth he wrote: "The Memoirs are postponed, perhaps until after death. I have no desire to give pain."[75] There is in this latter letter, too, at least the shadow of a suggestion that Mair at last was less confident about his conduct at Red River, that he perhaps felt compelled to justify the actions that recent historians had deplored. "I advocated the Canadian interest fearlessly in Red River," he remarked, "for I went there for that purpose, but I lost no friend worth having thereby. I was abused, but only by a recreant Canadian and some French priests, and even Jack McTavish in his cups told me that in his opinion I was 'more sinned against than sinning.'"[76] But even though he implied as late as 1924 in a letter to Lorne Pierce[77] that only ill health and the necessity to go to Winnipeg to consult Lady Schultz and her late husband's papers, and to Ottawa to interview Mrs. McDougall, were preventing him from proceeding with the memoirs, Mair must have realized by then that his story would never be written except in the isolated notes he had collected over the years. The publishers, appreciating the uniqueness of this first-hand knowledge, continued to encourage him (Lorne Pierce even offered to provide an amanuensis to record his recollections), but all that appeared in print were some rather sensationally illustrated accounts in the Toronto *Star Weekly* and other newspapers.[78] And often, to Mair's annoyance, such articles, written by women journalists, were incorrect. Mrs. Charlotte Gordon, for example, made "a sad jumble of important incidents, and added as well some incomprehensible misstatements of her own," not only confusing the first imprisonment of the Canadians at Fort Garry with the later capture of the Portage group but also ascribing to Mair the statement "that Major Boulton

[74]MP, Feb. 23, 1923.

[75]MP, Aug. 3, 1923.

[76]The "recreant Canadian" was probably A. G. B. Bannatyne. Jack McTavish was the Hudson's Bay Company's accountant at Fort Garry.

[77]MP, June 3, 1924.

[78]One such article in the Calgary *Daily Herald* of Aug. 17, 1908, was written by Mair himself; others (Calgary *Daily Herald*, Jan. 13, 1923; Toronto *Star Weekly*, Nov. 14, 1925), were written by journalists such as Elizabeth Bailey Price.

was shot as well as poor Scott." Another interview, by Elizabeth Bailey Price, was "fragmentary and incomplete."[79]

The role, therefore, that he might have played in the renewed controversy over Riel, McDougall, even himself, Mair never allowed to evolve. Instead, he turned to warning his friends against "so-called histories of the Red River Rebellion" and to excusing his remissness in not writing by "an aversion from controversy and notoriety" or by "a temperamental *laisser faire*" that he said had plagued him all his life.[80]

So the promise implicit in the reminiscences of a man who had even been sentenced to death by Riel remained unfulfilled, and elliptic notes and jottings on scraps of paper became, like the expense accounts of an immigration agent or the disappointing collection of verse and the record of a disillusioning trip to a later North-West, merely a pathetic reflection of the exciting experiences of the past.

[79]GP, Jan. 2, 1923.
[80]*Ibid.*

XI. A New Nation and an Old Man

While Mair's reputation as a nationalist and writer declined almost to oblivion with advancing years, he nevertheless retained his concern for the welfare of Canada and for the state of Canadian letters. As a civil servant he had to temper his public statements but not the opinions and judgments he expressed in private correspondence. The letters of this later period, especially after his retirement, provide a voluminous critical commentary on a changing Canada and a changing literary scene. Only in extreme old age, alienated from contemporary life, did he retreat into his own world of romantic memories.

"We are on the eve of an immense change," he assured Denison in 1899;[1] a change, indeed, the significance of which he could hardly grasp. With the expansion of Canada and the settling of the West in the quarter-century after Confederation, had came renewed faith in long-cherished ideals of unity and strength. Narrow sectionalism seemed to be giving place to pride in national achievement and confidence in Canada's future, signs that a sense of nationality was emerging. Mair's vision, which he poetically attributed to Foster, was proving prophetic:

"First feel throughout the throbbing land
A nation's pulse, a nation's pride—
The independent life—then stand
Erect, unbound, at Britain's side!"

[1]DP, 3657, Jan. 4, 1899.

Economic prosperity and national self-confidence were leading Canada from colonial dependence toward autonomy within a new British Commonwealth of Nations.

Mair's whole-hearted approval of this evolution meant considerable debate with Denison, who had become the leading Canadian advocate of Imperial Federation. Denison, of course, was all his life obsessed with the fear of American annexation and felt that a closely knit, centralized Empire, characterized by customs union, imperial parliament, and imperial defence, was the only effective way to resolve such a fear. Joseph Chamberlain, therefore, became to him the paragon of English statesmen. Mair would agree with Denison only so far as matters of trade and defence were concerned, and then not entirely. The relinquishing by the British of naval bases at Esquimalt and Halifax in 1905 he felt to be "one more step toward Canada First—our ascent to nationhood." The next step was a "duly proportioned" Regular force of Canadian soldiers and sailors,[2] which, if necessary, could come to the mother country's aid. Mair therefore supported Laurier's Naval Service Bill of 1910, although his immediate concern in doing so reflected the old conviction he had held almost as strongly as Denison—that the Americans were constantly awaiting opportunity to encompass Canada "in the magic circle of union." It was obvious to Mair, for example, that "the Yankees [were] putting war vessels on the Great Lakes, pretending they [were] only training craft."[3] Canada, he said, should immediately acquire "three or four improved Dreadnoughts" and "etceteras of destroyers"; arsenals should be built on each of the Great Lakes; the Georgian Bay canal and the Hudson Bay railway constructed as avenues to the North; the Hudson Strait buoyed and lighted; arsenals established at Churchill and York Factory—"together with a couple of 'cruisers,' thoroughly armed, in the Bay at all times." Only thus, he insisted, could the country be defended; "The sly introduction of vessels fit for war by the Yankees into the Great Lakes I look upon as a most ominous thing. They are no friends of ours—we know that, and are wrathful over the exodus of their farmers and envious of our vast resources."[4]

The question of trade he viewed with the same animus. "If Imperial preference and the opening of the Bay come together," he told Denison in 1910, "I should write a new poem!" But reciprocity with

[2]DP, 5184, Nov. 20, 1905.
[3]DP, 5663, Nov. 12, 1909.
[4]DP, 5668, Dec. 8, 1909.

the United States could not be countenanced: "The Yankees have recklessly wasted their natural resources, and want our markets. . . . It is . . . nothing but the old Continental Union scheme over again, but more 'child-like and bland.'"[5] It was curiously appropriate, he felt, that Goldwin Smith, "our old opponent," should die at this time, thus depriving Canada of an admittedly "supereminent man of letters" but also of a man "whose perverse theory as to our future," nearly any "Canadian boy in school" could have exposed.[6]

So although he viewed with approval Laurier's successful struggle against Imperial Federation, Mair shared Denison's alarm at the Prime Minister's willingness to enter reciprocal trade agreements with the United States. To the two survivors of Canada First[7] the question was as simple as it apparently was to Laurier's opponent in the 1911 election. "We must decide," said Robert Borden in his final appeal to the voters, "whether a spirit of Canadianism or of Continentalism is to prevail on the northern half of this continent."[8] When the election, one of the most exciting in Canada's history, was over, Denison could hardly contain his joy:

> Glory Hallelujah! We have had a great fight and a glorious victory! The cause for which you and I have fought all our lives has won one more battle. The work of our old Canada First party, kept up for over forty years, has helped to put a confident spirit into the Canadian people, and we have every reason to be grateful for the result.

All along the borders of their "old native province" from Rainy River to Montreal, on the shores of the rivers and lakes "facing the States where the conspirators expected to bribe our farmers with better markets," the Government had been overwhelmingly defeated. "Should we not be proud of our people?" asked Denison; "They have given the first example of pluck and patriotic spirit in the history of the Empire"—for it took more courage "to face a great nation, set it at defiance, and give up glittering offers in time of peace" than it did "to take up arms to defend one's country in time of war." Truly, Denison lyrically concluded in tribute to Mair and himself,

> "The seed we sowed has sprung at last
> And grows and blossoms through the land!"[9]

[5]DP, 5763, Oct. 24, 1910.
[6]DP, 5702, June 13, 1910.
[7]The attitude of Morgan, who was to die soon (in 1913), is unknown.
[8]Creighton, *Dominion of the North*, p. 435.
[9]MP, Sept. 23, 1911.

Mair could only echo his friend's jubilation. The plant of national consciousness had indeed grown slowly—"not much sign of it on the surface certainly, for this glorious outburst of national sentiment" was a surprise even to themselves—but now "the dominant and deep-rooted instincts of the people" had shown their vitality:

And now, my old and dearest friend, we can shake hands over the intervening mountains and prairies and lakes, and thank God that we had something to do with the origin and progress of that national sentiment which has swept treachery and disloyalty out of power on all hands.

And in this hour of triumph it was only right that he and Denison should "not be too hard on this French Canadian," Laurier. The defeated Prime Minister had tried "to keep harmony between the French and us." And, after all, Laurier was not "a genuine statesman"; the fact that he had an appreciative literary side was proof of that; "even the mightiest genius of all time could not have taken Cecil's place in the days of Elizabeth."[10]

Borden's victory represented to Mair and Denison the crushing defeat of the annexationist designs that British North America had feared for over a century. But Denison warned his friend that even the "Yankee settlers" who were being encouraged to live in Canada must be watched, for he should not forget that the men Simcoe had similarly invited at the turn of the nineteenth century had proved "a dangerous source of weakness to us in the War of 1812" and that later their descendants had been followers of William Lyon Mackenzie, sympathizers with Commercial Union and with Reciprocity. The English settlers and the Ontario men in the North-West would have to organize and educate the children. Patriotism should be taught in the schools; "the flag should be used, and a pride in Canada and the Empire hammered into the minds of the growing generation." Only in this way, insisted Denison, could the variegated West be made to feel "as one people" with the rest of Canada, and the whole country be united against the United States.[11] When Denison was asked in 1914 to aid in celebrating one hundred years of peace with the Americans, he angrily refused:

I told them our country was invaded by theirs, and our people shot down at Navy Island, Prescott, Windsor, Point au Pelee and the Short Hills in 1837, 1838, at different points in 1866 and 1870, and that their fiscal relations had been hostile.

[10]DP, 5879, Sept. 29, 1911. [11]MP, June 6, 1912.

I told one of [them] that if they put up a monument to George Washington in Westminister Abbey that I would have to go over in order to spit on it, to show my contempt for Washington and those who truckled to him.[12]

Mair was sympathetic to such sentiments, but expressed his own less vehemently. Particularly annoying to him was the "flaunting of the Stars and Stripes" by settlers from the south on the 4th of July and their refusal to stand up "when the King and Queen are thrown upon a picture screen."[13] But his association with such people for many years now had taught him that many of them were "decent people" who would eventually make good Canadians. Like the settlers from Europe they could not be assimilated overnight, and perhaps what "we cannot do with them, we must do with their children."[14] Indeed, as Mair saw Canada gradually acquiring a national consciousness he began to realize with many others that her role in international affairs was to bring involvement with powers across the Atlantic far more aggressive in their imperialistic designs than the United States. The Americans, in fact, might eventually even be allies in the rapidly shifting balance of world affairs. "We are living in ticklish times," he wrote in 1912; "Nature herself is brooding, and . . . something portentous in the world's history is going to happen."[15] Germany and England were "bound to clinch" soon, he prophesied, "and then the whole world will be at it, including ourselves."[16]

When war erupted two years later, Mair saw it as a dreadful holocaust that if survived would forge the British Empire in lasting bonds. Unlike many others he felt it would be a long struggle and one in which everyone, not just the armed forces, would have to take part. He himself, at nearly seventy-six, telegraphed Denison that he could arrive at a moment's notice to serve with his friend in "the old regiment." Even Denison had to reply, however, that "you and I would be of little use on a campaign," and that if Mair insisted, he would have to go alone. "I am not going to do anything," he said, "unless required here in Toronto to defend it."[17] In the four years that followed, however, both men reflected the vicarious concern they felt for the struggle being desperately enacted overseas. Within a year Denison could count three killed and three wounded from his

[12]MP, Jan. 31, 1914. Ironically, in 1962 Controller Dennison (double "n") of Toronto vigorously supported plans to celebrate the 150th anniversary.

[13]DP, 5932, Aug. 30, 1912.

[14]MP, Mair to E. Buchan, July 11, 1913.

[15]DP, 5932, Aug. 30, 1912.

[16]DP, 5906, Feb. 3, 1912.

[17]MP, Aug. 15, 1914.

family, and in 1917 he lost a particularly promising son, George. "But there is one consolation," he wrote; "his death was a glorious one—'killed in action'—fighting for his King, for Canada, and the Empire. . . . He was a loyal, true Canadian."[18] Mair could not suffer a like loss—Cecil was unfit for military service—but his gloom during these years is perhaps adequately reflected by his having Denison destroy the letters he wrote to him between 1915 and 1919. Such a request was made only twice, the other instance being in reference to letters he described as having been written "in a time of intense mental anxiety" between 1894 and 1897.[19] The meagre correspondence extant, however, reveals that to Mair the war provided not only a means to a more closely knit Empire in which British peoples were fighting for a common cause, but also a magnificent confirmation of the very instincts and principles upon which that Empire stood. The same spirit that had preserved Canada from her enemies in 1869–70 "is immortalizing our brave boys to-day at the Front," he wrote in 1917, "and it will hold this free Empire together as long as manhood and liberty exist."[20] There were, he felt, even the signs of the fulfilment of a prophecy he had made years ago at the Irvine banquet in Prince Albert. America's support in the war was surely a step towards an English-speaking union, for "blood does tell in the long run," Mair concluded; "the Yankees . . . are with us."[21]

Both Mair and Denison lived far enough into the nineteen-twenties to see a Canada vastly different from that of 1868, when they had first pledged themselves to her cause. And certainly, they felt, there was reason for mutual congratulation. Canada, in accordance with the principles they themselves had formulated so many years before, had at long last grown into nationhood, even though a terrible war had evidently been the ultimate price. Canada's achievement in support of the mother country had been glorious, and now she was truly "erect, unbound, by Britain's side." Within her own far-reaching borders she was united as never before. Provincialism had dwindled until "Canadian" was no longer "a term of reproach on both coasts," and old antipathies, although by no means gone, were gradually disappearing. The French Canadian, of course, was still a problem, particularly to Denison. "I think," he said, "that the great majority

18MP, May 19, 1917.
19DP, 3186, March 13, 1897.
20MP, Mair to D. E. Forbes, March 21, 1917.
21DP, 6185, Nov. 8, 1914.

of Canadians outside of Quebec are all right"[22] and all the "British provinces" would have to "unite solidly against . . . that disloyal, unprincipled gang of profiteers."[23] Mair, however, had an attitude toward the French Canadian that was far less obsessive than Denison's because it had evolved over the years not only from a more sensitive awareness of the French Canadian's heritage but also from a close association in the West with his character and personality. Not long before Mair died he wrote what can be accepted as at least an enlightened conviction in reference to a people about whom he had had in his earlier years many convictions. Although, he said, "our own people from the British Isles . . . will help us to construct along the lines which will make for a stronger tie between all of these Dominions comprising the British Commonwealth of Nations," let Canadians not forget

that we are made up of two great races, and that the Frenchman's love for this country is not second to our own. We should make the union between us stronger than it has ever been in the past, till the tie of kinship is not less than brotherhood. They have been co-workers, co-builders with us all through the centuries, and our interests are identical. I should like to see the French language taken up in the primary grades of every school throughout the Dominion, for to understand the language of a people is to understand that people's soul. And soul must speak to soul if we would build for God and Canada.[24]

And the "Yankees" who were "with us" in the Great War were no longer to be feared as in the past. Denison, of course, could never overcome an antipathy amounting almost to hatred and extending back to U.E.L. forbears; and since he refused to concede that Americans and Canadians could be friendly, he rarely referred to their relationships in the post-war era. But Mair realized eventually that the dangers of American armed invasion were over and that Canada and the United States had outgrown their previous sabre-rattlings. If there were still need for apprehension of the United States it was in a respect apart from annexation. And here Mair expressed prophetically the concern of Canadians of yet another post-war era. "Let us not be afraid to demand our rights," he said;

let us not take second place to the United States. We have a bigger country than theirs. Our resources have hardly been touched yet—timber,

[22]MP, Aug. 12, 1917.
[23]MP, Oct. 27, 1917.
[24]MP, "A Message to the Youth of Canada," MS., *ca.* 1925.

minerals, water power. Our wheat fields feed the world. . . . But do not let us permit the exploitation of our resources by any other country than our own. They are our heritage, sacred to us by the life and death of our ancestors who just as surely as those who lie in Flanders Fields have passed us the torch that we may "carry on."[25]

So Denison and Mair, supporters respectively of an Imperial Federation and of a British Commonwealth, each saw in varying degrees his dream approach fulfilment. And that each could proclaim that his old party of Canada First had at last got into power reflects once again the rather ambiguous interpretations they and their comrades of the "Corner Room" had had of their own objectives. Denison, for example, was quick to construe even the near-attainment of any Imperial Federation objective as a victory for Canada First, evidently never realizing—or at least never admitting—that there might have been differences of opinion within the group of '68 or that qualification of attitude might have occurred since. He seemed to ignore Mair's mild dissent over matters such as a centralized parliament and centralized defence, for example, and his most characteristic comment was simply "how strangely *all* the ideas of our Canada First party are coming into effect—we must have been a far-seeing set of young cubs."[26]

Mair, however, had been disillusioned too often not to realize that a complete fulfilment of his youthful hopes for Canada was virtually impossible in any given lifetime, even in one as lengthy as his own. "I remember writing in 1869 to the Toronto *Globe*," he reminisced to Frank Yeigh in 1926, "predicting thirty millions of people within a certain period . . . , but circumstances, political and otherwise were against me. We founders of the Canada First party were mistakenly enthusiastic."[27] He had lived long enough to confirm instead a few scattered opinions he had put down in the eighteen-eighties while preparing an article, never published, on the "Corner Room."[28] He and his friends at the Revere, he wrote then, had been "conspirators" in the days of '68—"young men of high promise and delightful, prophetic dreams." But as they grew older, their fiery hopes of youth were chastened and dissipated, and they saw clearly how "heavy is the hand of custom," that "society somehow has really suited itself to laws" and that "nations have after all 'the governments they deserve.' "

[25]*Ibid.*
[26]MP, Feb. 17, 1917.
[27]MP, June 11, 1926.
[28]MP, "The Corner Room," MS., *ca.* 1882.

And, he had asked, are not most clever youths "discontents"? This anomalous world is unintelligible to them; its pain and cruelty "are too shocking to be borne," its authority and governances are "but links in a slavish chain of order":

But *Senex* breathes more thoughtful breath. The world is still unintelligible, but he has grown with it, he has become habituated to it, he has come to a sort of minor understanding with it, he is unwilling to break with it, or disturb its peace. For peace, though the aversion of youth, is the comfort and natural order of age.

For Charles Mair in his eighties, then, there was a large measure of satisfaction that he could not have experienced had he died twenty or even only ten years before. It was as if he had been granted a reprieve from death until many of the more practicable, the more concrete, of his youthful proposals could evolve and materialize for the whole world to recognize, and until still others should appear on the horizon. "I am more convinced of the future greatness of our country," he wrote in 1926, "than I was in the days of my youth. . . . We have the richest heritage upon earth."[29] The British Commonwealth as it was developing in the mid twentieth century would have undoubtedly inspired his unqualified approval; and perhaps it is to emphasize unduly his sometimes quite remarkable prophetic insight to note that Mair foresaw that Commonwealth as part of a Western bloc and faced with a menace the Canadian of 1868, even of 1920, had not envisaged. How the complexities of a nuclear age would have influenced his thinking is conjectural, but in the mid 'twenties Mair was convinced that only strong government based upon principles of British tradition and justice could prolong "God's world." A dangerous "revolutionary spirit" was abroad, he warned, and forces from the East, including "the hordes of a teeming China" must be stopped before "our system of government . . . is wiped out in blood."[30]

If, however, Mair saw his country at last to have become a nation among other nations, he was compelled to feel some reservations about what he had always insisted was the real measure of such national greatness—the state of its letters. For about a decade after the turn of the century he was understandably embittered by his own experiences with *Tecumseh and Canadian Poems* and convinced that the prospect for Canadian literature was dishearteningly bleak. Poetry,

[29]MP, Mair to Yeigh, June 11, 1926.
[30]MP, Mair to Richard Secord, Jan. 9, 1924.

he remarked, was in any society for only the "select but few"; in Canada its readers seemed more select and fewer than anywhere else in the world, seemed, indeed, to be limited to the poets themselves. But such dissatisfaction as Mair expressed had a basis beyond his own personal experience. Desmond Pacey has aptly suggested that if the last three decades of the nineteenth century could be termed "the golden age" of Canadian literature, "the first two decades of the twentieth were without doubt the age of brass."[31] For Canada, indeed, the era might be regarded as a counterpart to the American "gilded age" of forty years before, even to the extent of producing its best writer, Stephen Leacock, as a satirist of his times in the manner of Mark Twain. And Mair never mentions Leacock; it is doubtful, in fact, that if he read any of the great humourist's works he appreciated their light irony and deceptive ambiguity, despite the fact that he shared many of Leacock's antipathies for the social scene around him. To Mair, the poet was the important writer, and if the "whim of the flimsy day" was one of Ralph Connor's novels so much more the pity that Canadians knew not true literary creation. Even most of the verse writers of the early twentieth century were "merely dilletantes and not poets at all." Service, MacInnes, and Drummond were "jinglers," "coarse rhymesters" or worse; "I would not name the whole crowd of them," said Mair, "in the same breath with Roberts, who will live . . . whilst the others will pass into the dust of forgotten shelves."[32]

Pauline Johnson, of course, was a poet whose name would endure. From the time of her glowing tribute to Mair's appreciation of Indian character until her death in 1913, she and Mair corresponded frequently, Miss Johnson's letters invariably beginning "My Dear 'Tecumseh' " and his containing a photograph or a memento of his travels with the Immigration Service. On one of her cross-country tours the princess-poet even wore an exquisitely made costume that Mair had sent her from Prince Albert; and he frequently insisted that if *Tecumseh* were ever brought to the boards, she alone must play Iena. Denison in cubbish jocularity even suggested to Mair that there was between him and Pauline more than just the communion of one poet for another: "I see now," he commented, "the meaning of her poem of wanting someone to lean on—she must have meant you. . . . What a wonderful thing sympathy is!"[33] But Mair disdained such frivolousness. "She is a true poet," he said, "one, too, of a race

[31]*Creative Writing in Canada*, p. 82.
[32]DP, 4424, Oct. 15, 1901.
[33]MP, May 23, 1892.

knit up in the noblest way with our history."[34] Nature, he said, "haunted her blood and brain," and her poetry breathed "that ecstatic atmosphere without which live poetry cannot exist."[35] Shortly before Miss Johnson died Mair visited her at the Bute Hospital in Vancouver, an experience "both painful and pleasant," for, he recalled, "though the end was near, her thoughts were clear, her expression sweet even to loveliness. When [I was leaving] she arose and followed me to the stair-head, and looking down, her parting was in Cree-Manjan. It was pathetic."[36] It is understandable, therefore, that Mair could not tolerate the unsavoury gossip that implicated Pauline Johnson in an unfortunate love affair with one "C. W." and in even certain "habits and inclinations attributed to her." Mair was willing to consider the possibility of an "ill-fated engagement," but in other respects there was "too much of that 'Dear me, what a pity' trashy talk amongst a certain sort."[37] Pauline Johnson, he said, was the "Canadian Sappho" and her poetry would live "even in this dark age"; and far better would it be if people interested in her were to read her work or write about her as he had done.[38] Until he learned from her sister that Miss Johnson would have wished otherwise, he even tried to engage Denison to lead a committee for the erection of a bronze statue ("with accompanying symbols") to her memory.[39] He was later satisfied to learn from Evelyn Johnson, however, that perhaps the most fitting memorial was the influence he himself had made upon Pauline's work; by his friendship and understanding, she said, he had caused "her poems . . . to take on a gentler tone regarding the Whites and the Indians."[40]

The commemorating of Canadian poets and patriots of the past seemed to Mair, in fact, to be of the utmost importance when contemporary life and literature were providing no worthy figures of their own. "Now is the time," he told Denison in 1913, "to begin a series of memorials, not to politicians, but to men and women of a nobler type . . . whose works will live when the average 'scurvy politician', of our own as well as Shakespeare's time, is forgotten." Women such as Laura Secord and Susanna Moodie, men such as

[34]DP, 5932, Aug. 30, 1912.
[35]MP, Mair to Evelyn Johnson, July 3, 1926.
[36]MP, Mair to W. D. Lighthall, May 22, 1925.
[37]DP, 6001, April 19, 1913.
[38]Mair's contribution was "Pauline Johnson: An Appreciation," *Canadian Magazine*, XLI (July, 1913), 281–83; this article was also part of the Introduction to Pauline Johnson's posthumous *The Moccasin Maker*.
[39]DP, 5991, March 28, 1913.
[40]MP, June 26, 1926.

William Kirby and Denison himself—although the redoubtable Colonel was still very much alive—should be recognized for "their great service to Canadian letters and Canadian patriotism."[41] And although he did not make explicit his own hope to be remembered as both poet and patriot, Mair more than once implied it. As the passing years drew him into old age he saw his reputation as a figure prominent in Canadian history and letters becoming increasingly dim; only the renewal of interest in Red River seemed to preserve a measure of significance to the name Charles Mair. As Walter McRaye, Pauline Johnson's business manager, had recently said to him: "How few people know of the really fine school of letters we have in Canada . . . and what a great race the old-timers were. . . . But a different race is coming in and the old hospitality, kindness, honesty is gone."[42] And the war that was then looming over the eastern horizon would surely mean a most decisive breaking of past ties and traditions.

But Mair had not reckoned with John Garvin. Until September, 1915, unless he had read the numbers of the *Public Health Journal* to which Garvin had contributed a series of articles on Canadian poets, he had probably never heard of him. Yet Garvin was to rescue Mair from the brink of literary and national oblivion; he was, perhaps, if tantalizing hope can keep a man alive, even to prolong his life.

John W. Garvin of Toronto is surely one of the more fascinating personalities in Canadian literary history. A stockbroker by profession, he had evidently decided during the early years of the war that his ability as a businessman and his enthusiasm as a student of letters could be combined to sell Canadians an awareness of their literary achievements. "My business," he once remarked, "seems akin to that of the American critic Stedman; he was a banker and broker, a dealer in securities, was he not?"[43] He admitted to having written "about 130 poems," but he had not published any, for "I have greater confidence in my philosophical theories and in my capacity as a literary critic."[44] Beginning modestly by an edition of Isabella Valancy Crawford's poems and the articles in the health journal, Garvin was to become in the nineteen-twenties a prominent literary anthologist and promoter of Canadian writing, a measure of achievement, however, that was to exact in the next decade a large price from both the man and his reputation. Garvin's "pet hobby," as he called it,

[41]DP, 6001, April 19, 1913.
[42]MP, May 23, 1913.
[43]MP, June 18, 1918.
[44]MP, Nov. 17, 1915.

was to bring him financial ruin; even worse, perhaps, it was to identify him in the minds of later rebelling poets and critics as one of F. R. Scott's "Expansive puppets" who "percolate self unction" when the "Canadian Authors Meet." For Garvin and his literary pretensions seem most at home where "The air is heavy with 'Canadian' topics," where "one is mixing with the *literati*" and the maple leaf is praised "Beneath a portrait of the Prince of Wales."[45]

In some respects, therefore, it seems natural that Garvin and Mair should establish a rapport over the miles between Toronto, Ontario, and Fort Steele, British Columbia. And on his seventy-seventh birthday, September 21, 1915, Mair received the letter from Garvin that marked the beginning of his literary resurrection:

> Too long have I neglected you, one of the very greatest of our poets. Indeed, I rank your *Tecumseh* as the greatest piece of literary work done by a Canadian. Have just finished re-reading it once again, and am profoundly impressed. Many passages would do credit to a Shakespeare. Why? Why did you not do more drama, making use of Canadian themes? It is doubtful if Canada will ever produce another dramatist equal to you. . . . Has any first-class critic done justice to your work. . . ?[46]

Perhaps Mair immediately realized that Garvin was not to be dismissed as lightly as were the newspaper feature-writers, particularly women, who had recently re-discovered him, and that the Toronto businessman-critic might do as much at least for Charles Mair, former poet, as those writers were doing for Charles Mair, former prisoner of Riel. His reply, certainly, was a considered one, relating as it did a comprehensive account of his literary career and answering fully Garvin's questions. He had discovered, he said, that no Canadian poet could live by his work unless he wrote drivel, and since he and his wife had "married from pure affection and begot a cart-load of kids," on responsible moral grounds he had never regretted his decision to place life before literature. But, slender as it was, his "tribute to Canadian verse" should endure on the basis of quality and intention —the deepening and confirming of our "Imperial sentiment and instincts, whose outcome we see today in the mighty war wherein our future is at stake as a free or conquered race." Mair also noted that his reminiscences, "which I may or may not publish before I die," ran back to a very early day in the Ottawa Valley and to the primitive days

[45]"The Canadian Authors Meet," in A. J. M. Smith, ed., *The Book of Canadian Poetry*, p. 290.
[46]MP, Sept. 14, 1915.

of the North-West where he had lived for nearly fifty years. He enclosed a recent photograph.[47]

Such encouragement was more than Garvin needed to undertake his patriotic work. Correspondence with him immediately assumed major significance in Mair's life, and a good part of the latter's spare time was undoubtedly devoted just to answering the Toronto enthusiast's letters. But what Garvin wrote could not help stimulating him. How fortunate he was, Garvin said, to have found this "great Canadian" still alive and active. "Have no fear about your place in the future in Canadian Literature," he encouraged; "no other of our poets has equalled you . . . in *constructive imagination* and in *dramatic power*"; and of this, when he had given Mair his rightful due, the whole of Canada would be aware.[48] If only Mair had written "another drama or two" to confirm his position; did not one of his children, perhaps, "have the gift of song" to add lustre to the name? But no matter, Mair's own work would be enough to assure his permanent fame.[49]

And almost overnight, it seemed to Mair, the dark literary scene brightened and offered a glow in an otherwise gloomy, war-stricken world. A few Canadians at home, after all, were reflecting Canada's literary heritage just as many abroad were reflecting her national heritage; a post-war Canada might even fulfil his vision of many years ago, for although age and distance would never allow him now to join Garvin's circle of enthusiastic *literati* in Toronto, the reports of their activities indicated a movement in Canadian letters such as he had not beheld since Confederation. "Toronto has organized a Canadian Literature Club which meets every fortnight for the study of Canadian Literature," wrote Garvin; "Canadian Dramatists is the theme tonight, and I . . . [am] to address them on *Tecumseh* and the author thereof."[50] A little later his anthology of *Canadian Poets* appeared with a generous section devoted to Mair. Then there was a lecture tour in which he proclaimed Mair as "Canada's grand old man of song" and *Tecumseh* as "the greatest drama in North American literature." There was even a newspaper controversy, organized by the energetic literary promoter, over who was the real "Father of Canadian Poetry." His anthology, Garvin felt, conclusively proved Mair's claim, and although critics such as J. D. Logan and Arthur Stringer were inclined in Roberts's favour, Albert Durrant Watson, a close friend of

[47]MP, Sept. 28, 1915.
[48]MP, Nov. 17, 1915.
[49]MP, Nov. 5, 1915.
[50]MP, Dec. 14, 1915.

Garvin, "would have a strong letter in the *Globe*" refuting their evidence.[51] And when both sides had presented their cases, Garvin was to "sum up the arguments":

> There is no doubt in my mind that you not only preceded Roberts but had a tremendous influence in shaping his verse, particularly after the publication of *Tecumseh*. His letter to you clearly proves this.
>
> In the last paragraph of p. 49 of *Canadian Poets* I speak with no uncertain sound. We cannot belittle Roberts's influence, but he himself was tremendously influenced by your *Tecumseh* and not by Wordsworth as Professor Cappon of Queen's thinks.
>
> You and Isabella Valancy Crawford have each much more poetic genius than Roberts; and had you been able to go on with your writing, you would have won world fame. You were the greatest dramatic genius of the New World. I groan in spirit when I think of the great dramas you had not time to write. But what you did will earn for you *deathless fame*.[52]

All of which was undoubtedly heart-warming to Mair; but even he must have flinched before some of Garvin's superlatives. According to Garvin "and other discriminating critics," Mair and Isabella Valancy Crawford were the "greatest" poets Canada had produced; Lloyd Roberts, son of Charles G. D., was "great," as were Albert Durrant Watson, the elder Roberts, and—particularly—Robert W. Norwood. The last-named, a minister and close friend of Garvin, had published in 1915 a sequence of highly romantic sonnets and was later to achieve affluence and prestige as rector of St. Bartholomew's in New York city. He was also to be well known in Canadian literary circles as a writer of biblical dramas after the manner of Heavysege, his *The Witch of Endor* (a rhetorical tragedy about King Saul) and *The Man of Kerioth* (Judas Iscariot) being praised by a contemporary critic as works exalting "the spirit to the Temple pinnacle where we behold Immortal Love in all its sweet beauty of humanity and in all its white radiance of redeeming light."[53] Garvin, indeed, confessed frankly to Mair that no one approached the author of *Tecumseh*, "*unless* it be the Reverend Robert W. Norwood, M.A. of the Memorial Church, London, Ontario," and that after a careful reading of Norwood's as yet unpublished "Songs of a Little Brother," he "unhesitatingly ranked him as a *great* poet."[54] Norwood had other talents as well; "Since I wrote you last," Garvin related to Mair, "we had the joy of

[51]MP, Nov. 29, 1916.
[52]MP, Dec. 12, 1916.
[53]J. D. Logan and D. G. French, *Highways of Canadian Literature*, p. 317.
[54]MP, Nov. 17, 1915.

Norwood in Toronto for three days. He is such a splendid fellow, so brilliantly versatile: read Browning's 'Calaban' [*sic*] in a masterly manner and sang comic songs incomparably. He could make a fortune on the vaudeville stage."[55] But Norwood did not dismiss Browning lightly, as he revealed when he himself wrote Mair. "Dear great poet," he began in the manner characteristic of his fellow-*littérateur*, Garvin,

> It is tragic that the greatest dramatic genius since Browning (he, in my opinion, despite prevailing criticism, is next to Shakespeare) was forced aside from a great literary career by the apathy of a Canadian public. But what, in the name of Art! was England doing that *Tecumseh* was not instantly enthroned? I shall never touch your height, but by the Grace of God, I shall stand near you in the Canadian Drama when my work is done![56]

The posturing extravagance of these men in both their verse and criticism should not have been foreign to Mair; both he and his critics had been more than tinged with it many years before. This whole literary movement of the early twentieth century had, indeed, a curiously anachronistic affinity with that of the post-Confederation period; for, as then, the poets of the later time seemed obliged, as A. J. M. Smith has noted, to gather "their singing robes about them to hymn the mysteries of Life and the grandeurs of Empire,"[57] to regard their craft as one of a very high "high seriousness." But, as Desmond Pacey remarks, with their nineteenth-century emphasis upon nature and love, they seemed unaware that a new age had come into being, and that even it was changing rapidly.[58] The poet and man of letters of the time, in fact, stood apart from the restless world around him; he was fastidious in his dress, even to celluloid collar, ribboned pince-nez, and stick-pin in his cravat; new members of the group were "new singing voices" who would surely "be heard afar"; if they were female, they were "brilliant daughters" of Toronto or Montreal; if male, they were "sons of Apollo." And if they reflected the changing currents of the world outside, they did so esoterically. Albert Durrant Watson, for example, had a Jewish medium by whom he aspired to communicate mystically with voices of the past, and was a keen follower of the adventures in spiritualism of Oliver Lodge and Conan Doyle; one of his works, *The Twentieth Plane*, Garvin described as "a remarkable book, a product of psychical research

[55]MP, Dec. 14, 1915.
[56]MP, Dec. 26, 1916.
[57]*The Book of Canadian Poetry*, p. 2. [58]*Creative Writing in Canada*, p. 84.

séances."[59] And the war Garvin seemed to view largely as an opportunity to bring out an anthology of Canadian war verse,[60] most of which expressed the bloody struggle in the patriotically romantic manner of Rupert Brooke. He had hoped that Mair would contribute to this volume a poem "of *very distinctive merit*" on "some phase of the war." Could Mair, he asked, "make Napoleon address the Kaiser, or give a soliloquy from the Kaiser in his darkest hour? But it is for the master poet to choose his own theme. I believe all lovers of Canadian verse would rejoice if you did this for me and for Canada."[61]

And so, despite his appreciation for the good intentions of these Toronto people in the name of Canadian letters (Garvin vowed he would place his *Canadian Poets* in fifty thousand homes), Mair began to feel that there was something a little strained, a little precious, about it all. If Garvin wished to restore him as he was in the eighteen-sixties and 'eighties, Mair was more than pleased, but some measure of critical restraint would surely have to be applied. As he had remarked to Denison: "I certainly could not enter upon 'up-to-date' criticism, even if I believed in its latter-day jargon, its search for the intricate phrase."[62] His friend, characteristically, reduced the problem to inconsequence; "I do not understand the drivel these people write about you," he remarked to Mair; "they think it looks wise to show their ignorance." Had he not assured Mair repeatedly that *Tecumseh* would live long after the critics and lesser versifiers? And, he added, "I don't know anything about Tanjore [*sic*] or mysticism or Sir Oliver Lodge. Like Hans Breitman, "I don't know nix about idees, no more than about St. Paul. I'm greener as the clover grass, stupid as a spoon; I'm ignoranter as der nigs, and dey takes de *Tribune*!' "[63]

But Mair became increasingly troubled over what he felt he should understand, but could not. And as if obliged to defend those principles of the poet's craft that he and "the old singers" had tried to follow, he began to write long letters of advice and commentary to younger writers and to those he considered still capable of redemption. These attempts at guidance were not always well received. When Mair suggested to Watson that his medium was "a thorough-paced liar, an imposter . . . and a fraud," the poet of the supernatural "fired up," and Mair was pleased, therefore, when Watson discovered the truth for himself and renounced Spiritualism. "We are back in the

[59]MP, March 28, 1919.
[60]*Canadian Poems of the Great War.*
[61]MP, June 18, 1918.
[62]DP, 6001, April 19, 1913.
[63]MP, Jan. 1, 1917.

Dark Ages," he remarked, "illuminated, God wot, by pseudo-science. But I am glad Watson is emancipated. . . . I like his poetry despite its mysticism; it is a curiosity."[64] Norwood, he advised, should "devote his genius to less ethereal subjects"[65] and Garvin might try "to avoid extravagant writing and fulsome praise."[66] Both men expressed their gratitude for such advice from a master-poet (although neither was to reflect its influence in his later writings) and Mair probably felt relieved at retaining their friendship as well as his own integrity.

To younger aspirants to a career in literature, however, Mair was most liberal with his advice. To all of them he repeated what appeared to be his favourite quotation from Scott—"Writing is a good stick but a bad crutch"—and also his own dictum that poets were the better for taking part in practical affairs. To Lionel Stevenson, in 1920 a young student at the University of British Columbia but later a noted critic and teacher, he also warned against "high flown" writing, especially that "punctuated with slang" and "highly seasoned with sensationalism." And obviously with his own case in mind, he assured Stevenson that the true poet hoped only to write "at least one *first-class* production by which, and by which alone, some very celebrated authors live." Perhaps most important, he added, was the poet's "duty to keep native literature free from blame, not as fanatical patriots, but as wise writers who have Canada's honour and repute at heart."[67] To Thomas Gelley, son of an old friend in the Immigration Service and just beginning his long career as teacher and administrator at the Royal Military College, he reflected his particular concern with the "cults of mysticism and superstition." That writer was wisest, he insisted, who held to firm ground and, like Shakespeare, used the supernatural sparingly and as good dramatic material; "This is a doctrine that differs very widely from that of one or more talented Canadian poets I know of, who, losing themselves in the bogs of mysticism, waste their genius in the propagation of illusions." And again it was important that the young writer should respect Canada's literary tradition, should keep it "pure and wholesome." Everywhere commercialization was making serious inroads "upon the literary calling"—the jumbling of prose and poetry with advertisements in "our illustrated family journals," for example—and the final outcome could only be the cheapening of the writer's craft. For the truly great poets

[64]MP, Mair to R. G. MacBeth, July 24, 1923.
[65]MP, Mair to Garvin, May 29, 1919.
[66]MP, Mair to L. Pierce, June 3, 1924. [67]MP, Oct. 9, 1920.

had but a single purpose: "to plead for Nature, to love her, and interpret her, and thereby elevate the thoughts of man and woman . . . is their prime function, if not their final cause."[68]

That the state of Canada's letters in the post-war era was approaching complete degeneracy was due, Mair believed, to the apparent disdain of her poets for such a literary creed. Only Roberts and Carman seemed to hold to it; the rest were mere "vocabulary jugglers." What passed for poetry, he told his old friend, E. S. Caswell, was "a squeeze of words, meaningless and fantastic as if harassed by the St. Vitus dance."[69] The so-called "New Poets," still mainly restricted to the United States and England, belonged to the "ancient family of Fudge—clever phrasemakers and mental gymnasts"; he had tried in vain to understand them. "It may be my fault—I have boggled over Browning," he confessed; "but as I have no difficulty in understanding Shakespeare and his kind I fail to account for this lack of apprehension."[70] Surely, he maintained, such verse was not written in any ordinary poetical mood; its writers seemed intent only upon "overturning language, simile and everything else in its rapid sweep."[71] And unfortunately the influence was tainting even good poets. He was disappointed to note, he told Garvin's wife, Katherine Hale, "the poetry of speed" even in her own new collection, *Morning in the West*:

> The quick eye *glances* at nature; keen *en passant* observations are characteristic of the poetical motorist, not the rambler on foot. Something is gained by this, something Kaleidoscopic, as if nature and life were viewed as through a swiftly turned optical instrument. On the other hand something is lost. But I am not going into metaphysics.

Was it right, he asked Mrs. Garvin, that the old literary culture should be displaced by this "futurist" verse? Canadian writers might "nibble at it" to be in fashion, but was it wise "to turn down the old and tried, the true, the beautiful, the good," for something that was a mere vogue in England and the United States? How, he asked, quoting a few lines from Edith Sitwell—"a wild and extravagant Futurist"—could one be inspired by such perversion of thought and language?[72]

And yet Mair could understand what was stimulating the writing of the "new poetry." "It is due possibly," he suggested perceptively,

[68]Mair to T. Gelley, Nov. 20, 1920; lent to the author by Mr. Gelley, Kingston, Ontario.

[69]MP, Oct. 5, 1923.

[70]MP, Mair to Garvin, May 29, 1919.

[71]GP, Mair to Katherine Hale, Nov. 8, 1923.

[72]*Ibid.*

"to the curious, restless and doubt-ridden new life that has dawned upon us, its craving for novelty, the grotesque in art and its feverish greed of gain compared with our old leisurely methods of the past."[73] What he could not understand was that the reflection of such life was the province of the poet as much as was the flora and fauna of "nature." And the remarks of A. J. M. Smith previously quoted in reference to *Dreamland*[74] again become relevant. It will be recalled that Smith refers to James Cappon's observing that Canadian poets "have devoted themselves too much to an almost abstract form of nature poetry which has too little savour of the national life and the national sentiment about it and is more dependent on literary tradition than they seem to be aware of"; Smith himself points out that the claim of a poet "to be truly national, adequately sustained in the field of scenery and climate, must . . . be denied to a body of work which ignored on principle the coarse bustle of humanity in the hurly-burly business of the developing nation."[75] These remarks were made, of course, in reference to the poets of the so-called "Golden Age" of Canadian letters, but as has been noted, these are precisely the poets who were still being revered in the nineteen-twenties. The true poet was the poet who wrote of nature and in keeping with the tried-and-true rules of literary tradition. His domain was the heart and, of course, if he was gifted, the soul, but it was certainly not T. S. Eliot's "cerebral cortex." And he was still striving to be "national," even though an awful war had caused nationalism and other previously cherished concepts to be questioned, if not refuted altogether. Any concession to a changing world and its literary reflection had perhaps advanced him to an equivalent of Yeats's early "Celtic Twilight"—"bogs of mysticism" to Mair—but if he wrote in the manner of T. S. Eliot, Ezra Pound, or of Edith Sitwell, he was to be dismissed as a "Futurist," and compelled to await another decade for recognition. To Mair, in fact, there was cause for satisfaction in the fact that Canadian poetry under the leadership of Roberts and Carman might maintain its integrity, despite the influences from abroad, and eventually prove to the literary world at large that "modernism" had been merely a fad.

Charles Mair in the 'twenties was not only a poet of another era; he was also a very old man. In 1922, the year of the appearance of Eliot's *The Waste Land*, of Joyce's *Ulysses*, and of the reading of *Facade* by Edith Sitwell, he was eighty-four and becoming more and

[73]*Ibid.*
[74]Chap. III, p. 41.
[75]*The Book of Canadian Poetry*, p. 23.

more alienated from the life he saw around him. His research for the proposed Red River book and the indulgences of Garvin offered some solace, but they also served to sharpen the differences between the treasured past and the superficial present, and his comments on life and literature became increasingly bitter. "The world is in such a horrible mess," he wrote C. N. Bell, a Winnipeg old-timer, "that there is not much temptation to remain in it." He had been reading Schopenhauer and had concluded "there is a world of common sense in it"; perhaps only as long as a man "could 'keep chow in,' as the old half-breeds used to say," could he hold on.[76] He had planned to visit once again some of the "delightful haunts of forty years ago"—Sandwich, Windsor, Amherstburg—but he realized that they had been "swallowed up in the fateful new . . . , smudged and buried in the smoke of factories."[77] And the passion for motoring was bringing yet another menace. "The old quiet life has disappeared," he commented to the daughter of Sir Sam Steele,

> and its place taken by myriads of tourists careening through the country at top speed. . . . For my part, I wish the inventor of internal combustion had been grilled in his own machine. For, my dear Flora, it is this machine, with all its conveniences, which is ruining our old life and hastening our decay. I must . . . confess that my youth and its kind loved swift travel too, behind the horse, but we loved him, and he was no Frankenstein like his displanter.[78]

Canada had achieved a prosperous nationhood, and for this he felt truly gratified; but to live on into a period of undoubtedly even greater political and economic stature he no longer desired. He was growing weary.

One further adventure, however, remained for him. His delvings into Mair genealogy had some years before initiated correspondence with a branch of the family that had emigrated to New Zealand at the same time his grandfather had gone to Lanark. In February, 1922, Mair boarded ship at Vancouver with his daughter Maude and made the long voyage to these doubly distant relatives. He intended to stay in New Zealand for two months, hoping to effect a cure for the bronchial asthma that he had "contracted in a blizzard many years before and neglected,"[79] but rain descended steadily during the first two weeks on the islands, and Mair returned home more tired and discouraged than before, "never to leave our old Canada again."[80] His

[76]MP, Jan. 24, 1923.
[77]GP, April 2, 1923.
[78]MP, July 28, 1924.
[79]MP, Mair to C. N. Bell, Jan. 24, 1923.
[80]DP, 6434, April 18, 1922.

relatives, however, he had found "extremely congenial"—a comment rather amusingly supported by a reference of one of them to the possibility of a general strike in New Zealand. "What a state of unrest the whole world is in," lamented Mrs. Ethel Harrington; even Fiji was having trouble with its Indians, reportedly "horrid people" overrunning "that beautiful island"; New Zealand had despatched an armed force, "but I think it is only to frighten them and perhaps as an object-lesson to our own labour people."[81] It would appear, therefore, that Mairs at opposite ends of the earth viewed the new age's restlessness with like concern. Ethel Mair Harrington's comments are, in addition, curiously reminiscent of those made by her cousin half a century before in respect to a magnificent West, the *métis*, and the necessity of sending an armed expedition. Time had shifted the problem to the Fiji Islands and added the complications of general strikes and "our own labour people."

This longest of all his trips westward, this time even beyond the shores of Canada, marked the beginning of the closing chapter of Charles Mair's life, a chapter of five years that in many respects must have seemed to him the longest of all. Its theme was well foreshadowed by the reception-committee from the Canadian Authors' Association—formed only a few months before—that met the R.M.S. *Niagara* at the Vancouver dock, by the testimonial dinner tendered to him that same evening, by the portrait taken of him seated before Pauline Johnson's memorial fountain in Stanley Park, by the flurry of articles in western newspapers. And, perhaps, by the never fulfilled promise of Association members to perform *Tecumseh* on a Vancouver stage. In the next few years to Mair's fame as an old-timer of Red River was added the lustre of his eminence as a Confederation poet, and through the auspices of Garvin, the C.A.A., and journalists, he became the "Bard of a Dominion's Cradle" as well as the "Defier of Riel's Hordes," and the topic of papers and lectures in literary clubs across Canada. In 1924, Lorne Pierce, the bright young editor of Ryerson Press and now a frequent correspondent of Mair, was influential in even having Mair awarded—in absentia—an honorary LL.D. degree by Queen's University.

Such homage Mair found gratifying, even when he felt compelled to inform Garvin that he was not "one of Canada's greatest men" and that he was "neither an angel nor an evangel" but really "a very unpretending old fellow . . . vain enough to think he *has* written something that will live."[82] But the honorary degree he considered a

[81]MP, Feb. 18, 1920. [82]GP, Oct. 25, 1925.

recognition too long delayed and in any case unsuitable to a poet. "Now that the C.A.A. is successfully formed," he wrote Lorne Pierce, "it might . . . restore the ancient laurel and devise some appropriate method of conferring it upon Canadian poets."[83] The number to be so honoured, he felt, certainly could not be great; "I should as soon think of an immortal land-speculator as of an immortal poet now-a-days," he remarked to R. G. MacBeth; "cliques and boomers and boasters . . . are all at work booming and boosting this book or that . . . and millions of 'Futurists' all writing new-fangled verse for bare life and death."[84] Even Carman and Roberts seemed to have betrayed their precious heritage. MacBeth reported that at a recent lecture in Vancouver Roberts had said nothing worthwhile—"just a few stories about 'Bliss' and himself and a few stale jokes";[85] and W. D. Lighthall similarly lamented that the Roberts "of his first patriotic songs [had] died early," for "he seemed a dapper sybarite and no more."[86] Did these Maritimers not realize, Mair asked Lighthall, that the "Republic of Letters" was universal, and not confined to New Brunswick and Nova Scotia? And what of Roberts's abandonment of poetry "for imaginary zoology"? In any case, "two cousins treking about from platform to platform and proclaiming each other the greatest living lyrists is a novel but not inspiring sight."[87]

But perhaps one of the most disturbing manifestations to Mair of what he called the "literary hysteria" of the 'twenties was the activity of lady *litterateurs*. As has been noted in reference to the renewal of interest in Red River, he viewed distaff keenness to return him to public view with some misgiving. "The feminine pen is very clever," he remarked, "and ever on the search for interviews, which one consents to rather than like Antony say 'No' to woman."[88] In addition, so many of them were "scribbling wishy-washy trash"; hundreds of them, it seemed, were writing novels, and organizing little cults in which they met "to praise each other over unlimited tea and cake, and to run each other down behind their backs."[89] But he admitted to MacBeth that he enjoyed the visits of these lady-writers even if he could not later approve of what they wrote. "I am deeply sensible of their kindness," he remarked; "it is very cheering to an old fellow like myself."[90]

For one of these "feminine pens," a poetess whom he liked personally and whose work he admired, he composed a little skit in which

[83]MP, June 3, 1924.
[84]MP, Feb. 7, 1924.
[85]MP, May 14, 1925.
[86]MP, April 30, 1925.
[87]MP, May 22, 1925.
[88]MP, Mair to C. N. Bell, Jan. 24, 1923.
[89]DP, 6446, Jan. 17, 1924.
[90]MP, March 19, 1923.

he satirized both himself and the cults, but in which he also reflected almost poignantly an old man's perplexity for the era and its letters. "My dear and honoured Katherine Hale," he wrote,

. . . it is your sex that has been trotting out this old nag of late, much against his will. But when literary women put on their binoculars and discover an antique, however secluded, nothing will do but they must drag him into the limelight and exhibit him at so much a head.

I can imagine an eloquent woman, an advanced Futurist of the Prohibition Sect, but not one of its viragos, addressing a coterie of the elect as follows:

President and Ladies: I have the curious privilege, may I say pleasure, of presenting to you today an old poet supposed to be dead long ago, but who, decrepit, bald and toothless, as you see, is still alive. Some prohibitionist friends and myself, when searching with our lanterns for a sober man . . . stumbled on him unawares in his tent, and, taken by surprise, and being too old and too weak to kick, he surrendered at discretion. When questioned he confessed that he had done much evil in his time by helping to delay the advent of the *vers libre* writers, "the Redeemers of Verse," and bowing himself before us, he entreated us to bear witness to his repentance and to consider his old age and be merciful. That this confession was hypocritical, begat of senile fear, there can be no doubt, so we exhibit him for what he is, an unregenerate survival of a race of writers known as the "Victorians," quite unlike ourselves, a race unfamiliar with the other world, and therefore incapable of writing supernatural verse. Their poetry, as you are aware, is now fossilized, and only occasionally exhumed by our experts for our astonishment . . . , and in this specimen you have the opportunity of looking upon a last, probably *the* last survivor of a race which has given way to Futurism and died the death. But we are not ungenerous to the Victorians, and we have ranked this specimen with the "classics," that is to say with the Shakespeares and the Miltons, who are so constantly talked about, and so seldom read.

I have to add that our venerable survival, before being relegated to the bookworms with his fellow Victorians, entreats our leave to ask a question or two for his own enlightenment.

"Could I have written," he asks, "advanced poetry like yours, what should it have been about?"

We reply, "the spiritual or inner world of course, in connection with the outer."

"But," he says, "if I knew nothing about either, what then?"

"Why then," we reply, "you should have hired a medium or got photos of Sir Conan Doyle's fairies, and poetized them."

"But I understand," he says, "that these fairies were cut out of tissue paper, and that he had been drinking and thought they were alive."

"That," we reply, "is simply impossible, for it would make out Conan Doyle to be a liar. Try again!"

"About Spiritualism," he says, "is there any charge for whisky and soda in the other world, or are they all Communists there? I have observed that in Sir Oliver Lodge's book he does not mention any charge."

Our answer is of course obvious, viz., that there are innumerable old Scotch distillers there, who by race are not likely to give away their spiritualized products for nothing, and we imagine there are many Scotsmen there who pay for their drinks, plying themselves as in the dark days before prohibition."

"Is Burns there?" he asks.

"Possibly," we reply; "but the reading of 'Tom O'Shanter' has been interdicted in the United States, and we do not write *vers libre* on John Barleycorn. And now, seeing that you would have been a very bibulous Futurist, we must close the discussion."

But Mair begs the ladies to consider Butler's lines on the convincing hypocrites who "Compound for sins they are inclined to/By damning those they had no mind to." The ladies express shock that their group could be so described and insist that the discussion, if continued, follow a different path:

"What about the Futurists, the Obscurantists?" we ask; "have you *read* any of them—Miss Edith Sitwell, for example?"

"No, how could I, benighted, out-of-date Victorian?"

"Well, we will test your intellect. Here is a recent verse from Miss Sitwell's 'Promenade Sentimentale':

I sat at my dressing-table (that chilly
Palely crinolined water-lily),
And watched my face as spined and brittle
As the tall fish tangled in a little
Dark weed that sea-captains keep
In bottles and perpetual sleep.

Do you note the descriptive power in these wonderful lines?"

"My mind must be gone," he says; "I cannot understand them at all."

"How lucky," we say, "that we have emerged from that doleful last century. Such verses as these mark a new era in poetry. How old are you?"

"Only ninety," he replies.

"Ah, that accounts for it—second childhood! Our modern poetry is not written in commonplace moods, but in glorious mental spates tearing banks and floatwood with it in a mighty jumble and rush of waters which overflow into the reader's soul."

But here a dinner bell rang and a general rush was made for the table.

This curious document, written on the backs of Christmas cards and envelopes loosely pinned together, was probably never sent, as quoted, to Katherine Hale.[91] But it remains today in Mair's papers as a record of his last venture at "creative writing" and of a very old man's alertness of mind, his awareness of contemporary trends and fads, and perhaps above all, his enduring sense of humour, even when the smiles were at his own expense. The last years of Mair's life, certainly, were not conducive to smiles; they were, in fact, pathetically consistent, in their provision of unhappiness, with most of the years before. The self-portrait of an aged man, "decrepit, bald and toothless," that he limned for Mrs. Garvin had by 1924 become valid, for by then the stocky form, ruddy complexion, ample hair, the confident stride and firm hand, had all been metamorphosed into a frail, almost gnomelike figure of a man racked by fits of coughing and incapable of walking more than short distances or of writing legible letters without amanuensis. Only the unusually brilliant blue of his eyes remained, perhaps reflecting the persisting keenness of mind and offering some confirmation that he was indeed Charles Mair. By the autumn of 1924 his daughter Fanny, with whom he had lived in Calgary since his retirement in 1921, evidently could no longer care for him properly, and he journeyed west for the last time and to a nursing home in Victoria. Maude was nearby, and so was the grave of Eliza, at whose side he had asked to be buried; here, among congenial surroundings and visited by a seemingly constant file of friends and literary devotees, he remained for about three years, the last of his life.

Publishers and others continued to press him for his memoirs, but Mair now gave them all the same, now quite definite answer: Fanny was collecting his papers and would herself probably write his story after he had died. He no longer had any interest in it; he was content to relive in private reminiscence the many events of a long life. His birthplace of Lanark, for example, he said, seemed clearer in his mind's eye than it had ever been in the intervening period since he had left it; the taws of dominie Mason, the timber runs on the Madawaska and Clyde, his mother's readings from Shakespeare, Spenser, and Scott, were, he said, all as of only yesterday. He even corresponded, either waveringly by his own hand or by that of his nurse, with the sons and daughters of Lanark villagers long since gone, inquiring about his old home and the fortunes of the little hamlet on

[91] A letter actually sent (GP, Mair to Hale, Nov. 8, 1923), includes the commentary on Edith Sitwell, but not the section on "prohibition" and "spiritualism."

the Clyde that had once been the scene of an exciting chapter in Canadian history. Part of this retreat into his far-distant past was, of course, stimulated by Garvin, who was busily engaged—had been for some years now—in preparing an "authoritative edition of the works of Charles Mair," which was to include a fairly full account of Mair's life. But much of it, like the return of interest in Red River, was due to an old man's nostalgia for his younger days and to the pride he felt in having belonged to "a race of true patriots" and of "lovers of good literature."

Strangely enough, however, another Canadian town and the part its fortunes had played in his life and career seem to have been almost forgotten in these days of reminiscence. Prince Albert, where he had lived for over fifteen years and where for many more he had so desperately tried to preserve what he believed would be his means of financial security, even of wealth, might never have existed as far as its reflection in Mair's later correspondence is concerned. The isolated references to the town on the North Saskatchewan (only four or five in perhaps eight hundred letters written during fifteen or so years) provide, however, strong indication that Mair wished to eschew discussion about his days as businessman and land-speculator. Dissension over property had sent his daughter Mabel to the other side of the earth; his attempts to maintain tax payments on the Prince Albert property had separated him from Eliza, almost to the time of her death in 1906. In 1913, at long last, a Winnipeg broker had offered Mair almost $45,000 for his sixty-eight lots, an offer, however, that he had refused because "I had not consulted the heirs, whose price was $54,400, but of whom three were for and one, my son, against."[92] And yet the son, Cecil, was to accuse his father ten years later and in most abusive terms of defrauding him of "the twelve to fourteen thousand dollars" that but for his father's "contemptible action," his "callousness" and "blackguardism," would have been his.[93] Whether Mair and not his son had been responsible for the retention of the land is probably undeterminable; certainly that land continued to cause him grief almost to the time of his death.

And Cecil, the "fine, sturdy, little fellow" who had written affectionate letters from Ridley and for whom Mair had visualized "a brilliant future," had become by 1923 a middle-aged n'er-do-well who drifted about Windsor and Detroit, sponging upon former neighbours and friends and dunning his father for clothing and room-rent. Even

[92]MP, Mair to J. E. Sinclair, Feb. 14, 1913.
[93]MP, Oct. 4, 21, Nov. 14, 1923.

some of Mair's most hallowed possessions were not beyond Cecil's demands. He had approached the Favourite Film Company of Detroit and they were willing to open negotiations for the filming of *Tecumseh*, the royalties to go to Cecil after his father's death. The watch plundered by a Sioux at Little Big Horn could easily be sold to a museum—Cecil had, in fact, discovered a relative of Lieutenant Crittenden living in Detroit and anxious to buy it. Such importunings Mair viewed as brazen sacrilege, but when added to the scurrilous accusations over the property, they must have brought him many hours of sadness.

The nursing home, too, became a lonely place for him, despite his many visitors, and after about a year there he began imploring Fanny to take him home to Calgary. "Of course, if you are overcrowded," he wrote in pathetic self-indulgence, "I could secure a couple of rooms elsewhere, convenient to a restaurant, so that I can get my bowl of soup and a bit of meat for dinner, and heat my milk myself."[94] Perhaps his daughter relented; Mair believed, certainly, that she was on her way to Victoria in May, 1926, to take him home. Before she arrived, however, her own daughter Bess, now over thirty and a deaf-mute since birth, was stricken with encephalitis and Fanny was forced to turn back. Bess died; and whether influential or not in determining Fanny's plans for her father, this further blow marked the end of Mair's pleadings to return to Calgary. Fanny undoubtedly realized there remained but little time until the end and, freed of a demanding responsibility at home, consoled the old man with more frequent visits to his bedside.

Between the sorrows arising from the virtual loss of his only son and the actual loss of his only grandchild occurred, however, the perhaps most poignant distress of all for Mair, and the one that compacted the others into a close, heart-breaking sequence. On June 8, 1925, he received the news that Denison had died two days before in Toronto.

The two old friends had long ceased to regard the death of either as unexpected. The once fiery colonel had retired as Toronto's Police Magistrate shortly before Mair had left the Immigration Service, and although he managed to complete and publish his recollections of over forty years on the Bench[95] his health had begun steadily to fail by 1922. "I see you complain of not being able to walk—same here," he remarked to Mair in 1923; "I have even cut out what little grog I used to take, and now run the water wagon."[96] In the next two years

[94]MP, Nov. 30, 1925.
[95]*Recollections of a Police Magistrate.* [96]MP, Dec. 8, 1923.

the frequent, long letters of the past dwindled to an occasional comment on the changing scene of politics or of literature, and finally to birthday or Christmas cards shakily inscribed to "my old quartermaster" or "my dear old friend." And that Denison should die peacefully and at a very old age was perhaps, after all, fitting. A militant man—the most distinguished, indeed, of the "Fighting Denisons" of Toronto—a world-renowned authority on cavalry tactics, and a leading figure in the development of his country's militia, he had brandished his sword in anger only during the Fenian skirmish of 1866; the "fort" named for him by his men in the North-West Rebellion had been fifty miles from actual fighting and was now long since overgrown with prairie grass. Denison's real battles had been on the public platform and the pages of the daily press; and on the basis of these encounters no one could ever doubt his courage and zealous concern for the welfare of his country. But such campaigns do not depend for their success upon their leaders' dying in decisive action and still shod in their cavalry boots; when they are won, if at all, they may be won by those who, like Denison, persist to the end and then just fade away.

To Mair, however, the loss of his old compatriot left an almost palpable void in his own flickering life. From the day in the spring of 1868 when they had first met in Morgan's quarters, the two men had been united, despite intervening lakes, prairies, and mountains, in an unusually close fellowship. It is unlikely, indeed, that Canada can anywhere show one firmer or longer lasting. "Where could be found," asked Helen Mair Denison, "two such men of eighty-six as yourself and my dear husband?"[97] And now Mair wished more than ever to die; he was weary, he was despondent. "The noblest of British Canadians has passed away," he wrote; "but death carries a mysterious magnetism which attracts us onward to the end. That this cannot come too soon is my own desire."[98]

Perhaps only another magnetism, not so mysterious as that of death, was now prolonging Mair's days—the desire to see once more his name on the cover of a book. As early as 1919 Garvin had promised this last tribute to "North America's greatest poet," had even, by 1922, promoted interest by two publishers, McClelland and Stewart and Ryerson, to bring out individual series of Canadian works, in each of which the volume on Mair was to be of first importance. Within a year, however, Garvin's ambitious scheme began to encounter unforeseen difficulties. McClelland and Stewart decided that the "time was

[97]MP, Aug. 29, 1925.
[98]DP, 6451, Mair to H. Denison, June 23, 1925.

not ripe" for the *Master-Works of Canadian Authors* series that Garvin personally was to edit ("buckram, $4.00; half-leather, $5.00; full leather, $8.00") and he was compelled to delay this half of his programme until he had found another publisher. In the meantime he put Mair to work writing a memoir of his career and culling his papers and manuscripts in preparation for the Ryerson *Makers of Canadian Literature* series. But problems of various kinds beset the publication of a Mair volume in this series too. Lorne Pierce returned to Garvin the manuscript, part of which Garvin had pressed Mair to finish by a deadline, and informed him that it had to be considerably revised—an insult Garvin found difficult to bear. "Dr. Pierce," he said, was "a young editor with much to learn; he invites well-known writers and critics to prepare books for him, bearing their names, and then knows no better than to send their manuscripts back. . . . I am standing firm."[99] Garvin may have remained adamant—and lost his publisher. An examination of his manuscript, which remained in Dr. Pierce's office cabinet until 1960, clearly reveals reasons for its rejection, reasons that Mair himself had pointed to when he told Pierce that he had warned Garvin to avoid "extravagant writing and fulsome praise" and that he had "rallied him lest he give way to a current fashion."[100] Perhaps more significant is the fact that Ryerson, like McClelland and Stewart, was reluctant at a time of economic recession to publish a volume that Garvin rather foolishly noised about would be superseded when his own *Master-Works* volume appeared. But whatever the reason, Mair never appeared in the *Makers of Canadian Literature* series; and perhaps his relief, under the circumstances, was well reflected by a rather cryptic remark he later made to Garvin: "I owe much to Dr. Pierce," he said, "more than I would venture to tell him, and one day we may be even."[101]

Garvin, however, was not to be discouraged from pressing on with his own *Master-Works* editions. Unable to find a publisher, he took out a Dominion charter for the "Radisson Society of Canada," drew up an impressive list of directors including Sir Gilbert Parker, Roberts, Norwood, and Hector Garneau, and then went about the task of selling $375,000 worth of shares. And thus began the final comedy of errors in the Mair–Garvin relationship. The Toronto critic's delay irritated Mair to the point that he rebuked Garvin for allowing "his project" to become so "uncertain" and "inchoate"; why not, he suggested, re-publish only "my first venture, viz. *Dreamland and Other*

[99]MP, June 9, 1924.
[100]MP, June 3, 1924.
[101]GP, Nov. 14, 1925.

Poems?" This latter comment filled Garvin with a "feeling of consternation"; would Mair not trust his "literary judgment and that of Katherine in this matter?" Then when Mair wrote almost casually that he had "revisions to make," Garvin countered desperately that "great poems are written under inspiration and in a white heat," and could "rarely be revised when the fires have died down."[102] So it was decided that only the original selections be reprinted, the adequate proof, according to Garvin, that Mair was "the real founder of Canada's distinguished nature school of verse"—for, he added, hardly cheeringly, "I am editing the whole volume as if you were no longer with us."[103] But further annoyances stalled Garvin's project. Cecil in Windsor took a number of photographs of the "house in which *Tecumseh* was written," but they turned out to be of the wrong house. Mair returned the introduction written for the volume by Norwood, "appalled by its egotism" and insisting that Norwood's comparison of the defence of Schultz's house in '69 with the battle of Thermopylae, and his diatribe against modern critics, be excluded.[104] One Saturday Garvin was greatly disturbed to open the pages of the Toronto *Star Weekly* and find a major part of his biography of Mair appearing in an article by Elizabeth Bailey Price. "If you are not up to time," reprimanded Mair, "you cannot blame others for stepping in."[105] Then E. S. Caswell planted the idea in Mair's mind that Garvin was delaying the book, "that in the event of your demise, he might get . . . the Lanigan poem and the photos and any other things of yours he now has";[106] and Mair for some weeks was reluctant to forward more material.

But the old man yearned to see the finished book. The delay "is the only complaint . . . that I have ever made about so dear and valued an old friend," he told Garvin in August of 1926; "for as I am nearing the end I am naturally desirous of seeing it. . . . When I say 'nearing the end' I really write as I feel, for I am gradually growing weaker."[107]

[102]MP, April 28, 1924.

[103]MP, Dec. 28, 1925. John Matthews (*Tradition in Exile*, pp. 101–2) quotes from letters in the Mair–Garvin correspondence to prove that Mair wished only the original *Dreamland* poems to appear in Garvin's edition. But other letters reveal that although Garvin wished to include both the 1868 and 1901 versions (to enable "students of literature to know the changes made by the author himself thirty years or more later") Mair really could not make up his mind on the point.

[104]GP, Jan. 6, 1926.

[105]GP, Dec. 22, 1925.

[106]MP, April 26, 1926. The "Lanigan poem" was Lanigan's tribute to Mair when *Dreamland* was published in 1868 (see chap. III, n. 22).

[107]GP, Aug. 23, 1926.

Garvin, now beset by a sea of troubles, undoubtedly sincerely wished to publish the volume before Mair died, if only to receive the old man's praise, and he sent letter after letter announcing the imminent appearance of the book. "Dear Master of Song," he had written in December, 1925, "the Mair volume will be out in February."[108] In March, 1926, it was promised for May ("The mills of the gods grind slowly"); in September Garvin exhorted Mair to "hold fast to life, dear friend; the Mair volume of *Master-Works* will be out in October";[109] in March of 1927 he assured Mair that it was actually in the bindery. But by now Mair was slipping away. Fanny was now composing as well as writing his letters for him—even perhaps the last note to Lady Schultz, in which he bade farewell to "one of the brave women of Red River," and begged her to share her "goodness" with "my children."[110]

On April 26, 1927, Garvin rushed to Mair the first copy of *Charles Mair's Tecumseh, Etc, Etc.*[111] "Every time I think of your getting this wonderful book," he said, "my heart glows afresh; it will bring you lasting fame and will always be your best monument."[112] A special copy, inscribed by him personally, would follow immediately, and many more were being prepared for the Canadian "Chatauqua" at Muskoka, where "Charles Mair, the Adventurer who Blazed the Trail," was to be the leading topic of discussion. A few weeks later he reported that a copy had been on the head table when Mazo de la Roche was honoured for winning the *Atlantic* fiction prize, and that lines from *Tecumseh* had been quoted after the toast to the king. If the book had appeared just a little earlier, Garvin implied, it might even have counteracted Pelham Edgar's influence in the awarding of the Lorne Pierce Medal of the Royal Society of Canada to Duncan Campbell Scott ("a personal friend" of Edgar)[113] instead of to Mair.

The so-long-awaited volume requires little additional comment. Mair was undoubtedly gratified to hold it in his hand, to turn its facsimile pages and to see nearly all of his prose and poetry so conveniently collected for posterity. In his pleasure at contemplating the story of his life from Lanark to Victoria—with illustrations—there was probably little room for disquieting doubts. And yet, ironically, Garvin's

[108]MP, Dec. 24, 1925.
[109]MP, Sept. 13, 1926.
[110]MP, n.d., marked "private," and beginning: "I am getting very weak. . . ."
[111]*Master-Works of Canadian Authors*, XIV (Toronto: The Radisson Society of Canada, 1926). Note that the date on the imprint is one year earlier than that of the actual appearance of the book.
[112]MP. [113]MP, May 12, 1927.

Master-Work might better have been left undone. As a piece of book-making *Charles Mair's Tecumseh, Etc., Etc*, from the informality of its title on the spine to the affectation of its deckle-edged Byronic leaves, is almost ludicrous. In any of its three maroon bindings it is over-lavishly decorated with gold tooling and the pretentious escutcheon of the "Radisson Society"; Garvin's name instead of Mair's boldly graces the title page; many of the photographs, printed on uncoated paper, are poorly reproduced, and some appear in places quite inappropriate to the text. It is Norwood's flamboyant introduction, however, that precludes any serious appreciation of the book. After a highly rhetorical essay on the nature of poetry, replete with references to "Life Unlimited," "the pipes of Pan," "the good, brown Mother Earth," and to the ignorance of contemporary critics, Norwood breathes deeply and states unequivocally that Mair "is not only the dean of Canadian letters; he is our most authentic poet." For, he concludes, "as we look over Canada's host of song, we discover one who, like Saul among the children of Benjamin, towers like a goodly oak above its companion cedars. Charles Mair is our greatest Canadian poet by every count."[114]

Mair had feared such an attempt at apotheosis; whether or not he recognized it before his eyes he never revealed. In one of his last letters to Garvin, written in June, he asked to be remembered "personally" to Norwood, a request Garvin was unable to fulfil for the clergyman-critic had already left "for Europe and the Orient to write the life of St. Paul."[115] The book was acclaimed by reviewers across Canada as the most significant literary work of the year; how appropriate it was, they almost in unison remarked, that such a reflection of enduring patriotism should appear at the moment Canada was celebrating her Diamond Jubilee. Perhaps only Bernard McEvoy of the Vancouver *Daily Province*, an old friend of Mair, foreshadowed later, more detached judgment when he described the parts played in the book by Garvin and Norwood as simply "a scream"; for only heaven, McEvoy implied, could protect a man from his blundering friends.[116] Garvin himself, certainly, was to pay dearly for his literary ambitions; his obsession with Mair and his career ruined him. Of the twenty-five projected *Master-Works* volumes, *Mair's Tecumseh, Etc., Etc.* was the third and last. To obtain it or either of the previous volumes on Paul Kane and G. M. Grant, the prospective buyer had to subscribe to the complete set of twenty-five at a cost of at least one hundred

[114]Pp. xxx–xxxi.
[115]MP, June 8, 1927.
[116]MP, June 14, 1927.

dollars, and the result was that virtually no sales were made; Garvin could not even underwrite the cost of the advertising and gift copies of the volumes already published. His diary of woe, in fact, continued almost to his death. He fought with Elizabeth Bailey Price over Mair's literary executorship (Mair had named both), and in 1930, when Cecil suggested to Lorne Pierce that a "cheap reprint edition" of his father's works be published, Garvin begged the Ryerson editor to wait until he had "unloaded a quantity of the . . . collected works . . . throughout the West and around Windsor."[117] The Depression provided the quietus to this last expedient, and when Garvin died in 1936 Katherine Hale was obliged to sell whatever she could to help defray her husband's debts.

Charles Mair was spared these unhappy postscripts to his return to national and literary prominence. He lingered through May and June of 1927 and on July 1 was able to rejoice, in a telegram to the Canadian Authors' Association, for having lived to see the Diamond Jubilee of Canada "so fittingly celebrated . . . and the pride that all Canadians took in it."[118] About July 4 he began to dictate a long letter to Cecil, at the close of which he said he now knew his death was only hours away. To this letter, on July 6, he signed his name for the last time and just before suffering an attack of intense pain that was to last for almost twenty-four hours. Then, on July 7, and, according to daughter Fanny, "his fine, clear intellect unclouded to the last . . . but longing inexpressively to go," he "closed his eyes and went to sleep."[119]

The funeral services were held in Christ Church Cathedral, among the pall-bearers being Donald Fraser, a boyhood friend in Lanark, and the Honourable C. A. Magrath, a nephew of Mair and later a Chairman of the Ontario Hydro Commission.[120] Burial took place, as Mair had asked, in the deep grave dug first for Eliza in Ross Bay cemetery, overlooking the Straits of Juan de Fuca. Maude and Fanny were present, but Cecil and Mabel were too far away to make the trip, even if they had wished to do so. Mabel cabled from Sydney a simple "At last poor old Pippy's troubles are over"; and Cecil, first noting that his own health was very poor, and that the Masons should pay his father's funeral expenses, asked Fanny not to send any effects because he would lose them and in any case he could not pay the freight. He

[117]MP, Lorne Pierce to Mrs. E. J. Cann, Feb. 3, 1930.

[118]MP, Mrs. E. J. Cann to Maud Thompson, July 15, 1927.

[119]MP, Mrs. E. J. Cann to ? , July 15, 1927.

[120]Magrath's first wife was Margaret Holmes Mair, daughter of Mair's brother Holmes and not of Charles Mair himself, as some commentators have stated.

added, however, that he was gratified to receive the watch presented to his father in Belleville in 1870, even though he would have preferred "the other one."[121]

Happily, there were other, more disinterested tributes to the memory of Charles Mair. Fanny recorded that the whole of Victoria seemed to be in mourning for him; and newspapers across Canada recognized his passing in leading articles and editorials. For weeks telegrams and letters arrived at the nursing home, all reflecting, whether from the Prime Minister or a grade-school child, the impression that Mair's life and work had made upon the national consciousness. Much of this fame was due, of course, to the efforts of Garvin, but references to the "sweet old face," the "able, loving and lovable man," and to his "proud Canadianism" and "kindness towards his junior colleagues in poetry" were undoubtedly stimulated by sincere affection and respect.

Thus, from the Canada whose history, both political and literary, he had helped to form, went Charles Mair, patriot and poet. If adventure, longevity, and service to one's country are regarded as the criteria of a full life, certainly he led such a life. But he died a long way from the scenes of his happiest and most exciting days; they were far behind in both time and space. And his death somehow seems to have marked, perhaps more than is the case of most men, not so much an end of a life as of a struggle to make reality and dreams come closer together. But like most men, he just as surely failed.

[121]MP, July 25, 1927.

XII. Epilogue

UNTIL JUNE 15, 1959, the village of Lanark, Ontario, was much as it had been for the almost one hundred years since Charles Mair had left it for the West. And that of course was a Lanark different from the bustling community of the eighteen-forties and 'fifties. Even by 1868 the forests that had surrounded it were gone, and the Clyde, though still flowing sturdily through its centre, no longer echoed the thumping of logs and the shouts of raftsmen. Gone, too, were stern Scots dominies, "training days," and carousings by wild Irish timber drivers; even the weekly Lanark *Observer* had, in a sense, fallen victim of the woodsman's axe. New Lanark-on-the-Clyde, Upper Canada, had become Lanark, Ontario, and like many a once-flourishing town or village in the province, had inherited its destiny of quiet ruralism and economic insignificance.

The first years of the twentieth century left a few physical changes here and there, the kind that could be noted by a village son returning for a visit or for Old Home Week celebrations. The Clyde Hotel, for example, which once stood on the corner just south of the river, and whose proprietor, Mr. Dobbie, had welcomed Mair to Lanark for the last time, was torn down and its advantageous location taken by a garage and service station. Fire destroyed the Clyde Woollen Mills, built next door to the old family home by Mair's father, and the resulting gap allowed an unobstructed view from beyond the river of the large advertisement for baking powder that later appeared at the side of the house. The latter's Georgian simplicity had already been marred by a large "ginger-bread" verandah of High Victorian style; but by

World War II a large frame store was to obscure the sign from view, and a new, more modest porch to represent yet another attempt to make the house conform to a contemporary fashion. North-westerly, towards the old cemetery, a few new frame or brick buildings gradually expanded the village's tenuously defined limits.

And by June 15, 1959, the name of Charles Mair was known in Lanark almost only because of the plaque that hung in the town hall. Some villagers may have known that in the Madawaska range to the north there is a Mair's Mountain, "above whose crags," according to an Ottawa journalist, "the eagles wheel in aerial combat" and which "stands out on the serrated horizon-line even as the man, Charley Mair, ranks high among his contemporaries of a great pioneering age."[1] And a few may even have known that on the Saskatchewan prairies there is a little village named after him—a hamlet, ironically enough, on a short feeder line running from the *south* to the trans-continental railway and connecting other little towns such as Lampman, Browning, Cowper and Wordsworth. John Herron, spry and of keen memory though approaching ninety, could remember well the man himself, could even recall with a chuckle the day in 1887 when Colonel Denison had come to Perth to marry Helen Mair without informing her uncle out west. Mrs. James McLaren had a scrap-book of clippings on Mair that she had collected over many years from the Ottawa *Journal* and the Perth *Courier*; Mrs. Mary Willis had referred her public-school pupils to Lanark's own poet; and Mrs. W. Machan, as village librarian, always kept Garvin's *Master-Works* edition readily available in the little town-hall library.

These few, when the ashes of their homes and shops had cooled and their minds were recovering from the tragedy of that day of wind and flame when Lanark was almost wiped out, may have noted that Charles Mair's old home still stood, even if the plaque, which had *almost* been affixed to it, had fallen with the ruins of the town hall. They may have noted also the irony implicit in the fact that Joseph Kinsey Howard's *Strange Empire*, so damning to Mair, was one of the books on loan from the library and therefore saved from destruction. If they did thus mark the memory of Charles Mair they were among the very few in Canada to do so. Perhaps Professors W. L. Morton and G. F. Stanley and other Riel scholars thought about Mair as they read the newspaper accounts of the fire; Miss Mary Rogers of the Perth museum may have devoted an even closer attention than usual to the collections of photographs and of Indian artifacts that his

[1]Harry Walker, Ottawa *Journal*, n.d., lent by Mrs. James McLaren, Lanark.

daughter had given to the old county-town on the Tay. And among students of Canadian letters, a handful, including Dr. Lorne Pierce and W. A. Deacon, who had known Mair personally or could recall his return to prominence in the 'twenties, may have connected the town and the poet. But there was no less disinterested recognition, in the newspapers for example, as there would surely have been thirty years before, of the claim that from Lanark had come one of Canada's staunchest patriots and her "dean of letters." What Mair had feared so much had come to pass; except in the minds of a few whose interest was scholarly or even parochial he was forgotten.

This rather depressing commentary upon the dreams and aspirations of a man who, for better or for worse, dedicated much of himself to the welfare of his country and of her literature is piquantly confirmed by a visit to contemporary Prince Albert. As the traveller enters the city after driving the seemingly endless miles from Saskatoon, he is encouraged by the many signs directing him to the local museum and by the sight of the Reverend James Nesbit's first mission house, now preserved in a "pioneer" park. Even the paucity of museum items related to Mair—a few letters and photographs—and the mis-naming ("Fairholm") of "Holmewood" on a water-colour sketch of 1930, are not at first discouraging. For to step out the door of this museum on a hill is to see Prince Albert as Mair and his fellow-townsmen, looking from the same site or from the old N.W.M.P. barracks to the west, must have envisaged it. Not as large as they had hoped, certainly, with its less than 25,000 population, but a much more impressive place than the little town of 1885 with its five hundred. There to the north is the Saskatchewan; between it and the hill lies the typical grid of a western city. Somewhere in the main business section, the visitor presumes wryly, is the expanse of land that Mair had to relinquish for taxes. Not far away, on the river bank, should be "Holmewood" itself, and close by, Bishop McLean's little St. Mary's Church.

Only when one has gone down the busy main street to the river does he realize that this is not at all the town that he has associated with Mair. Only then do previously unanswered questions gradually resolve themselves. River Street, a large part of whose adjoining property Mair owned, and intended as Prince Albert's main thoroughfare, is now hardly of third-rate importance; it even retains its name, whereas the Church Street of his time is now Central in both name and importance. The store of "C. Mair, the largest owner of Real Estate in P.A. with the exception of the H.B. Co.," is gone, replaced by only a vacant lot and an occasional truck or tractor.

But it is "Holmewood" and its fate that provide the appropriately bitter note to the fortunes of Charles Mair of Prince Albert. The site of the large, handsome home by the river is far from the centre of the city; the distance alone is indicative of the extent to which Mair miscalculated the way his town would develop. The house itself is gone. In February, 1960, the fire department in charge of proceedings, the city fathers saw fit to burn it to the ground as unworthy of repair and preservation. The evergreens that Mair planted long ago now tower over weeds, rubbish, and few charred remains, and here where "we are as jolly as crickets—the brass band serenaded us, . . . the children are wild with the river," the half-breed children who live nearby play games other than cowboys and Indians.

Even St. Mary's Church, still farther to the west and lovingly cared for by those who have known it for many years, reflects its little ironies. In the graveyard—almost in the shadow of the federal penitentiary—are the remains of many of Mair's old friends. Here are the still unmarked graves of the Duck Lake victims. There, a little to the north, is the tomb of Bishop McLean, interred behind his little church only a few short years after he had asked Mair to secure land for his "own private account." Immediately east is the most imposing stone of all, that of T. O. Davis, the "ignorant Irishman whom no one here will receive socially" but later to become Senator Davis and one of Prince Albert's most notable citizens. And near the far boundary is the weathered marker of Richard Mair, the son of Holmes who had come to live in Prince Albert with his uncle Charles and had, in the end, provided a last link between the Mairs of Prince Albert and of Lanark. For there is no trace of "the little grave in the wilderness" of George Denison Mair.

Lanark and Prince Albert, in a way, tell the story of Charles Mair's life. "Dear old Lanark, embosomed among its hills and vales" and about which Mair felt "there is a poetry . . . which is imperishable," illuminates the man and his later reputation just as does the town that was to be "the metropolis of the West." The influences by which Charles Mair was moulded in his first thirty years directed his aspirations, both literary and material, in Prince Albert. *Dreamland* reflected, as its author noted, "a young poet's imperfections"; but in the young Mair's case these imperfections were particularly relevant to an environment of backwoods Upper Canada, the indulgences of a proud mother, and a conception of the writer's craft gained from a reading of the more romantic, the more "manly" of the recognized British authors. By the time he had embarked upon *Tecumseh* Mair had become a practising patriot, and had been involved, indeed, in one of the most stirring events in Canada's political history. His nationalism, therefore, not only permeates the drama; it provides its very *raison d'être*. And like *Dreamland* before it, *Tecumseh* was received by Canadians who were searching—almost desperately, one feels at times—for some proof of a literary culture of their own. Even apart from its urgent promotion by Denison, the drama had critical acclaim stimulated more by its purpose and the fervent reflection of that purpose than by any intrinsic artistic merit. Explanation, therefore, of Mair's decline into near-oblivion need not take into account such factors as his use of a literary form—the closet drama—in which two greater contemporaries, Browning and Tennyson, had faltered, or the reaction that came about in the 'twenties and 'thirties against nineteenth-century nationalistic and "nature" poetry. As Tolstoi once said, every political moment of national life demands from literature reactions that correspond to it and advertise it, but only those works survive that stand higher than that moment; all the others are "social manure." *War and Peace* is a great literary work because it transcended the "moment" that it depicted; *Tecumseh* is not, because, although it may have reflected "the body and pressure" of the time (as Mair so often insisted), it did not rise to what would have given it permanence—the level of art, which is beyond limitations of time and national sentiment.

Even the material objectives that Mair attempted to achieve for himself represent a further pattern of the impact upon him of particular standards and precedents. His mother had prepared the way by instilling in her son a respect for his upper middle-class heritage; he later was to imply more than once that the financial and social prominence of the Mair family in Lanark and Perth was simply the continuation of this heritage across the sea. His attraction and subsequent closeness to Schultz, McDougall, Denison, even Morgan, are significantly consistent with these financial and social assumptions. But the Mairs did not own a good part of Toronto; nor did the timber trade any longer afford the promise it had in the past. So just as John Schultz chose Winnipeg, Charles Mair chose Prince Albert as his means to fortune and prominence. Like Schultz, Mair undoubtedly was urged on by a nationalistic pride and a zeal for the future greatness of his country; but among the altruistic ideals of both were inextricably entangled the factors of personal ambition and material gain. Schultz gambled on the future of Winnipeg and went on to wealth and knighthood. Mair unfortunately staked his future on Prince Albert, and plagued by complications in temperament and objective that did not hinder his Red River compatriot, he declined into virtual poverty and obscurity.

For to Mair Prince Albert was more than a future crossroads of commerce; it was to be the seat of a Canadian Abbotsford, a feudal estate on the North Saskatchewan such as his literary ideal, Scott, had built on the Tweed. Mair's career in Prince Albert presents instance upon instance of his attempts to assume the role of a sort of north-western laird, defending but also determining the rights of his people, dispensing hospitality to important visitors—surrounded by his family in a large home, or engaging in exploratory forays to points of archaeological and anthropological interest. Some of his most personal correspondence was with Adam Scott, a descendant of Scott's family, to whom he often revealed his almost worshipful respect for the great novelist and with whom, when both were very old, he exchanged sentimental last wishes. Curiously enough there is to be seen in Mair's ambivalent personality a conflict of ideals similar to that in Scott's. Like Scott, Mair was concerned with heroic ideals in an age of commercial progress, but having decided that the two were incompatible, still wanted both; his worldliness became complicated by his romanticism and *vice versa.* But unlike Scott, he was unable to resolve the conflict into either artistic or material success.

Both Canada and Charles Mair tried to fulfil a vision, and both found their progress marked by long years of discouraging failure. For the man, however, the consequences of both his own and his country's failures were insurmountable. When Canadians were at last able to "feel the throbbing land / A nation's pulse, a nation's pride," Charles Mair was old, and had long since seen his personal vision of success fade away. But in Canadian letters of his time there is no better example than Mair of the confusion between literary merit and national sentiment. Nor, perhaps, of the validity of the aphorism that in his confident youth he himself had quoted so often but never really believed until bitter experience confirmed it—that literature was a good stick, but a very bad crutch.

BIBLIOGRAPHY

A CATALOGUE of all the documents, books, and articles consulted during the preparation of this work would give no indication of their relative importance, and a selective list that includes those sources specifically referred to in the text, those that indirectly provided significant information and bases for commentary, and those that could be examined as "further reading" seems more valuable. Also, because a bibliography of Mair's writings has not been compiled previously, such a listing here is considered both appropriate and highly desirable. Some critical comment on the value of certain reference material has already been made in the Preface; brief annotations, mainly descriptive, are included below wherever they might be of general interest or of help in assessing the scope and worth of a book or article.

I. Published Writings of Charles Mair

(a) Books

Dreamland and Other Poems. Montreal: Dawson Brothers; and London: Sampson Low, Son and Marston, 1868. [All but approximately two hundred copies were destroyed by fire at the Ottawa bindery.]

Tecumseh, a Drama. Toronto: Hunter, Rose; and London: Chapman and Hall, 1886. [Despite the imprint, was not even distributed in England.]

Tecumseh, a Drama, and Canadian Poems. Toronto: Briggs, 1901.

Tecumseh, a Drama, and Canadian Poems; Dreamland and Other Poems; The American Bison; Through the Mackenzie Basin; Memoirs and Reminiscences. Introduction by Robert Norwood. Vol. XIV of *Master-Works of Canadian Authors* [edited by John W. Garvin]. Toronto: Radisson Society, 1926. [Did not actually appear until April, 1927.]

Through the Mackenzie Basin: A Narrative of the Athabasca and Peace River Treaty Expedition of 1899; also Notes on the Mammals and Birds of Northern Canada, by Roderick MacFarlane. Toronto: Briggs, 1908. [Also published without MacFarlane's "Notes" and in paper covers, but with the same imprint.]

(b) Verse contributed to periodicals

Mair kept no record of his many individual pieces published in magazines and newspapers; as he himself remarked, "I have been careless in not saving a great mass of fugitive materials scattered through the press." It has been impossible, therefore, to trace all of his published verses, particularly those of his early years, and the following list is undoubtedly incomplete to the extent of at least two or three titles.

"Absence," Toronto *Week*, Aug. 9, 1888.
"A Ballad for Brave Women," Toronto *Week*, June 21, 1888.
"The Chain," Toronto *Week*, Dec. 25, 1891.
"Fulfilment," Toronto *Week*, Nov. 14, 1890.
"To a Humming Bird," *British American Magazine*, I (Oct., 1863), 630.
"The Iroquois at the Stake," Toronto *Week*, June 7, 1889.
"Kanata," *Dominion Illustrated*, I (Dec. 29, 1888), 414.
"The Last Bison," *Dominion Illustrated*, I (Sept. 8, 1888), 155.
"In Memory of William A. Foster," Toronto *Week*, Feb. 1, 1889.
"Missipowistic," *Dominion Illustrated*, II (June 29, 1889) 414.
"Open the Bay!" Toronto *Week*, March 28, 1890.
"The Recompense," Toronto *Week*, March 28, 1890.
"The River of Pain," Toronto *Week*, May 24, 1889.
"To a Sleeping Child," *British American Magazine*, II (March, 1864), 498.
"Sonnet," Toronto *Week*, Jan. 31, 1890.
"Vain Regrets," Toronto *Week*, Oct. 18, 1888.

(c) Articles, including letter-articles contributed to periodicals and newspapers.

"The American Bison: Its Habits, Methods of Capture and Economic Use in the North-West, with Reference to Its Threatened Extinction and Possible Preservation," *Transactions of the Royal Society of Canada*, 1st ser., VII (1890), Section II, 93–108.
"Canada—Past, Present, and Future," Prince Albert *Saskatchewan*, July 25, 1889. [A speech given at the banquet honouring Lieutenant-Governor Royal.]
Correspondence from the Red River to eastern newspapers, 1868–69: Perth *Courier*, Jan. 1, 14, 1869; Montreal *Gazette*, Dec. 25, 1868; Jan. 23, Feb. 27, 1869; Toronto *Globe*, Dec. 14, 27, 1868; Jan. 4, Feb. 16, May 14, May 28, 1869.
Correspondence from the Athabasca and Peace River districts to the Toronto *Globe*, 1899 [published in 1908 in *Through the Mackenzie Basin*]: July 15, 22, 29, Aug. 12, 26, Sept. 2, 1899.
"The Five Nations and Pre-historic Montreal," Victoria *Colonist*, July 25,

1909. [A review article on W. D. Lighthall's *The Master of Life* (Toronto: Musson, 1908).]

"Frogs and Their Kin," *British American Magazine*, II (Nov., 1863), 37–45.

"Honor to Whom Honor is Due," Prince Albert *Times*, Nov. 29, 1882. [A fervent plea to Canadians to recognize their patriotic writers.]

"The Hudson's Bay Co.'s 'Prince Albert Farmer,'" Saskatchewan *Herald*, March 15, 1880. [The Mair–Clarke controversy.]

"The Land We Live In," Prince Albert *Times*, Jan. 23, 1889. [A speech given at the banquet honouring Lieutenant-Colonel Irvine of the N.W.M.P.]

"Memorial: To the Right Hon. Sir John A. Macdonald," Prince Albert *Times*, Dec. 6, 1882. [Grievances over governmental laxity in the West, co-signed by D. H. Macdowall.]

"The New Canada," *Canadian Monthly and National Review*, VIII (July and Aug., 1875), 2–8 and 156–64.

"The Ottawa Shiners," Toronto *Week*, Aug. 18, 1893.

"Pauline Johnson: An Appreciation," *Canadian Magazine*, XLI (July, 1913), 281–283. [Published also as part of the Introduction to Pauline Johnson's *The Moccasin Maker* (Toronto: Briggs, 1913).]

"A Public Injustice," Toronto *Week*, Aug. 30, 1895. [A protest against the Government's indifference to the patriotic services of William L. Baby.]

"Soldiering in Canada," Ottawa *Citizen*, Oct. 6, 1900. [A review of Denison's book, but also a further attempt to justify the conduct of the Red River "loyalists."]

"Souvenirs of the Past," Toronto *Week*, May 29, 1896. [A long, highly commendatory review of William L. Baby's book of the same title.]

"Twelve Trees," Montreal *Transcript* [?], 1864 [?]. [An autobiographical short story referred to by Morgan in *Bibliotheca Canadensis* p. 246), but not found.]

II. Documents and Manuscripts

(a) In libraries, archives, museums and historical societies

Canada, *Journals of the House of Commons*. Report of the Select Committee on the Causes of the Difficulties in the North-West Territory in 1869–70. Vol. VIII, Appendix No. 6, 1874.

—— *Sessional Papers*, 1870, V (12).

McDougall, R. L. "A Study of Canadian Periodical Literature of the Nineteenth Century." Unpublished Ph.D. thesis. University of Toronto, 1951.

Perth, Ontario, Museum. Uncatalogued documents, letters, and photographs.
Prince Albert, Saskatchewan, Historical Society. Uncatalogued documents.
Public Archives of Canada. Denison Papers.
——— Grant Papers.
——— Macdonald Papers.
——— McDougall Papers.
——— Morgan Papers.
——— Public Works Files, series 98, subject 429, correspondence, the Department of Works and C. Mair.
Queen's University Library, Kingston, Ontario. Garvin Papers.
——— Mair Papers.
——— McNichol Papers.
——— Miscellaneous correspondence, Redvers Buller to Henrietta Buller, August, 1870.

(b) In private collections

Gelley, T. (Kingston, Ontario). Correspondence from C. Mair.
Shrive, F. N. (Dundas, Ontario). "Sunshine and Storm: By a Rifleman." MS. of Lieutenant H. W. Snelling, 60th Royal Rifles, 1870.

III. Books

Baker, Ray P. *A History of English-Canadian Literature to the Confederation*. Cambridge: Harvard University Press, 1920.
Begg, Alexander. *The Creation of Manitoba; or, a History of the Red River Troubles*. Toronto: Hovey, 1871.
——— *"Dot-It-Down," A Story of Life in the North-West*. Toronto: Hunter, Rose, 1871.
——— *History of the North-West*. 3 vols. Toronto: Hunter, Rose, 1894–95.
Blake, Edward, *"A National Sentiment!" Speech of Hon. Edward Blake, M.P., at Aurora, with the Comments of Some of the Canadian Press thereon*. Ottawa: E. A. Perry, 1874.
Boulton, Charles A. *Reminiscences of the North-West Rebellions*. Toronto: Grip, 1886.
Broadus, E. K., ed., *A Book of Canadian Prose and Verse*. Toronto: Macmillan, 1924.
Brown, E. K. *On Canadian Poetry*. Toronto: Ryerson, 1943.
Bryce, George. *A History of Manitoba*. Toronto: Canadian History Co., 1906.
Butler, W. F. *The Great Lone Land*. London: Sampson Low, 1872.
Canada First: A Memorial of the Late William A. Foster, Q.C. With introduction by Goldwin Smith. Toronto: Hunter, Rose, 1890.

CAPPON, JAMES. *Roberts and the Influences of His Time.* Toronto: Briggs, 1905.

COLLINS, JOSEPH E. *The Story of Louis Riel, Rebel Chief.* Toronto: Hunter, Rose, 1885.

CREIGHTON, DONALD G. *The Commercial Empire of the St. Lawrence, 1760–1850.* Toronto: Ryerson, 1937.

——— *Dominion of the North.* Boston: Houghton Mifflin, 1944.

DAFOE, J. W. *Clifford Sifton in Relation to His Times.* Toronto: Macmillan, 1931.

DENISON, GEORGE T. *Reminiscences of the Red River Rebellion of 1869.* Toronto: privately printed, 1873.

——— *Soldiering in Canada.* 2nd ed. Toronto: Morang, 1901.

——— *The Struggle for Imperial Unity.* Toronto: Macmillan, 1909.

DEWART, EDWARD H. *Selections from Canadian Poets; with Occasional Critical and Biographical Notes, and an Introductory Essay on Canadian Poetry.* Montreal: John Lovell, 1864.

DUGAS, GEORGES. *Histoire véridique des faits qui ont préparé le mouvement des Métis à la rivière Rouge en 1869.* Montreal: Librairie Beauchemin, 1905.

EGGLESTON, WILFRID. *The Frontier and Canadian Letters.* Toronto: Ryerson, 1957.

FRASER, JOSHUA. *Shanty, Forest, and River Life in the Backwoods of Canada.* Montreal: John Lovell, 1883.

GARVIN, JOHN W., ed. *Canadian Poems of the Great War.* Toronto: McClelland, 1918.

——— *Canadian Poets.* Toronto: McClelland, 1926.

——— *Canadian Poets and Poetry.* Toronto: McClelland, 1916.

GRANT, G. M., ed. *Picturesque Canada: The Country as It Was and Is.* 2 vols. Toronto: Belden, 1882.

GUILLET, EDWIN C. *Early Life in Upper Canada.* Toronto: The Ontario Publishing Co., 1933.

HALIBURTON, ROBERT G. *The Men of the North and Their Place in History.* Montreal: John Lovell, 1869.

HANNA, D. B. *Trains of Recollection.* Toronto: Macmillan, 1924.

HARGRAVE, JOSEPH J. *Red River.* Montreal: John Lovell, 1871.

HAULTAIN, ARNOLD. *Goldwin Smith's Correspondence.* Toronto: McClelland and Goodchild, [1913].

HAYDON, ANDREW. *Pioneer Sketches in the District of Bathurst.* Toronto: Ryerson, 1925.

HIGINBOTHAM, JOHN D. *When the West Was Young.* Toronto: Ryerson, 1933.

HOWARD, JOSEPH KINSEY. *Strange Empire: A Narrative of the Northwest.* New York: Morrow, 1952.

Illustrated Atlas of the Dominion of Canada, containing Authentic and Complete Maps of all the Provinces . . . together with a General Descriptive History (Lanark County Edition). Toronto: Belden, 1881.

LAMB, ROBERT E. *Thunder in the North: Conflict over the Riel Risings, 1870–1885*. New York: Pageant, 1957.

LAMPMAN, ARCHIBALD. *Lyrics of Earth*. Toronto: Musson, 1925.

LIGHTHALL, W. D., ed. *Songs of the Great Dominion*. London: Scott, 1889.

LOGAN, J. D., and D. G. FRENCH. *Highways of Canadian Literature*. Toronto: McClelland and Stewart, 1924.

LOWER, A. R. M. *Canada, Nation and Neighbour*. Toronto: Ryerson, 1952.

---- *Canadians in the Making*. Toronto: Longmans, Green, 1958.

---- *Colony to Nation: A History of Canada*. Toronto: Longmans, Green, 1946.

MACBETH, R. G. *Policing the Plains*. London: Hodder and Stoughton, 1922.

---- *The Romance of Western Canada*. Toronto: Briggs, 1918.

MCDONALD, JOHN. *Narrative of a Voyage to Quebec and Journey from thence to New Lanark in Upper Canada*. 8th ed. Glasgow: Lang, 1826.

MCDOUGALL, R. L. *Canada's Past and Present: Our Living Tradition, Fifth Series*. Toronto: University of Toronto Press, 1965.

MCDOUGALL, WILLIAM. *The Red River Rebellion: Eight Letters to Joseph Howe*. Toronto: Hunter, Rose, 1870.

McPhillips' Alphabetical and Business Directory of the District of Saskatchewan, N.W.T. Qu'Appelle, 1888.

MATTHEWS, JOHN P. *Tradition in Exile: A Comparative Study of Social Influences on the Development of Australian and Canadian Poetry in the Nineteenth Century*. Toronto: University of Toronto Press, 1962.

MORGAN, HENRY J. *Bibliotheca Canadensis, or A Manual of Canadian Literature*. Ottawa: Desbarats, 1867.

---- *Canadian Men and Women of the Time: A Handbook of Canadian Biography*. Toronto: Briggs, 1898.

---- *The Place British Americans Have Won in History*. Ottawa: Hunter, Rose, 1866.

---- *Sketches of Celebrated Canadians and Persons Connected with Canada*. Quebec: Hunter, Rose, 1862.

---- *Types of Canadian Women*. Toronto: Briggs, 1905.

MORICE, A. G. *A Critical History of the Red River Insurrection*. Winnipeg: Canadian Publishers, 1935.

MORTON, A. S. *A History of the Canadian West to 1870–71*. Toronto: Nelson, 1939.

---- *History of Prairie Settlement*. Toronto: Macmillan, 1938.

Morton, William L. *Alexander Begg's Red River Journal.* Toronto: The Champlain Society, 1956.

Pacey, Desmond. *Creative Writing in Canada.* 1st ed. Toronto: Ryerson, 1952.

Percival, W. P., ed. *Leading Canadian Poets.* Toronto: Ryerson, 1948.

Pierce, Lorne. *An Outline of Canadian Literature.* Toronto: Ryerson, 1927.

Pope, Sir Joseph. *Correspondence of Sir John Macdonald.* Toronto: Oxford, 1921.

Ross, Malcolm, ed. *Poets of the Confederation.* Toronto: McClelland and Stewart, 1960.

Shortt, Adam, and Arthur G. Doughty, eds. *Canada and Its Provinces.* Vols. XIX and XX. Toronto: Glasgow, Brook, 1914.

Smith, A. J. M., ed. *The Book of Canadian Poetry.* 3rd. ed. Toronto: Gage, 1957.

Smith, Goldwin. *Canada and the Canadian Question.* Toronto: Hunter, Rose, 1891.

——— *The Political Destiny of Canada.* Toronto: Willing and Williamson, 1878.

Smith, W. H. *Canada: Past, Present and Future: Being a Historical, Geographical, Geological and Statistical Account of Canada West.* 2 vols. Toronto: Thomas Maclear, 1851.

Stanley, George F. *The Birth of Western Canada.* 1st ed. London: Longmans, Green, 1936.

——— Louis Riel. Toronto: Ryerson, 1963.

Wallace, Elisabeth. *Goldwin Smith: Victorian Liberal.* Toronto: University of Toronto Press, 1957.

Wallace, W. S. *The Growth of Canadian National Feeling.* Toronto: Macmillan, 1927.

IV. Periodicals

Bailey, A. G. "Literature and Nationalism after Confederation," *University of Toronto Quarterly*, XXV (July, 1956), 409–24.

Bissell, C. "Literary Taste in Central Canada during the Late Nineteenth Century," *Canadian Historical Review*, XXXI (Sept., 1950), 237–51.

Denison, George T. "Robert Grant Haliburton," *Canadian Magazine*, XVII (May, 1901), 126–30.

Fraser, A. Ermatinger. "A Poet-Pioneer of Canada," *Queen's Quarterly*, XXXV (May, 1928), 440–50.

Graham, W. R. "Liberal Nationalism in the Eighteen-Seventies," *Report of the Canadian Historical Association*, 1946, pp. 101–19.

MORGAN, H. R. "Dr. Charles Mair," *Willisons Monthly*, II (Aug., 1926), 110–11.

MOWATT, H. M. "Greater Canadian Independence," *Queen's Quarterly*, XI (July, 1903), 34–45.

OLIVER, E. H. "Economic Conditions in Saskatchewan, 1870–1881," *Transactions of the Royal Society of Canada*, 3rd ser., XXVII (1933), Section II, 15–39.

OXLEY, J. M. "A Habitan Hercules," *The Lake*, I (Sept., 1892), 88–94.

PRATT, E. J. "Canadian Poetry, Past and Present," *University of Toronto Quarterly*, VIII (Oct., 1938), 1–10.

SHRIVE, F. N. "Charles Mair: A Document on the Red River Rebellion," *Canadian Historical Review*, XL (Sept., 1959), 218–26.

—— "Poet and Politics: Charles Mair at Red River," *Canadian Literature*, no. 17 (Summer, 1963), pp. 6–21.

—— "Poets and Patriotism: Charles Mair and Tecumseh," *Canadian Literature*, no. 20 (Spring, 1964), pp. 15–26.

—— "What Happened to Pauline?" *Canadian Literature*, no. 13 (Summer, 1962), pp. 25–38.

—— and D. J. DOOLEY. "The Voice of the Burdash," *Canadian Forum*, XXXVIII (July, 1957), 80–82.

SMITH, A. J. M. "Colonialism and Nationalism in Canadian Poetry before Confederation," *Report of the Canadian Historical Association*, 1944, pp. 74–85.

—— "Nationalism and Canadian Poetry," *Northern Review*, I (Dec.-Jan., 1945–46), 33–42.

—— "'Our Poets': A Sketch of Canadian Poetry in the Nineteenth Century," *University of Toronto Quarterly*, XII (Oct., 1942), 75–94.

UNDERHILL, F. H. "Goldwin Smith," *University of Toronto Quarterly*, II (April, 1933), 285–309.

—— "Political Ideas of the Upper Canada Reformers, 1867–78," *Report of the Canadian Historical Association*, 1942, pp. 104–15.

WEAVER, EMILY. "Elizabeth Louise Mair—a Red River Pioneer," *Canadian Home Journal*, Dec., 1924, p. 12 and *passim*.

INDEX

www.ingramcontent.com/pod-product-compliance
Lightning Source LLC
Chambersburg PA
CBHW031618100726
47898CB00006B/1839